THE
NEW ATLAS
OF THE
ARAB WORLD

THE
NEW ATLAS
OF THE
ARAB WORLD

The American University in Cairo Press
Cairo   New York

COPYRIGHT AND PICTURE CREDITS

First published in 2010 by
The American University in Cairo Press
113 Sharia Kasr el Aini, Cairo, Egypt
420 Fifth Avenue, New York, NY 10018
www.aucpress.com

Dar el Kutub No. 10215/10
ISBN 978 977 416 419 4

Dar el Kutub Cataloging-in-Publication Data

The New Atlas of the Arab World /
        Cairo: The American University in Cairo Press, 2010
    p.   cm.
    ISBN 978 977 416 419 4
    1. Arab Countries—Atlas
    953.000223

Maps
Chief Cartographer: Glenn Riedel
Editor: Imgard Sigg
Digital Cartography: Kirsten Patzig, Liana Steinborn, Annette Wrobel
Data Management/DTP: Klaus Jost

Text Pages
Project Manager: Daniel Hunstein
Editors: Elisabeth Heueisen, Anna Meißner
Photographic Editor: Ursula Franz
Satellite source imagery provided by WorldSat International Inc., www.worldsat.ca

Photographs
(l=left, r=right, t=top, b=bottom)

AISA Media S.L., Photoaisa.com, Barcelona: 43 r.; akg-images, Berlin: 37/Lessing, 58 b, 62 t/Lessing, 94 t/Israelimages, 108 t/Degeorge, 110/Schilgen, 129 t/Hackenberg; bigstockphoto.com: 43 l/Mary Mulderig, 100 b/Styve Reineck, 124 t/Bretin, 127 t/Tiger3000, 135 b/Bongtribe; Christoph & Friends, Essen: 99/Sasse; Corbis GmbH, Düsseldorf: 49 b/Parrot, 74/Turnley, 75 b/Reuters, 76 b/Njuguna, 79 b/Freeman; Corbis-Bettmann, New York: 41 t, 56 b/UPI, 63 t, 98/UPI, 102/Reuters; dpa Picture-Alliance GmbH, Frankfurt: 47 t/Wennström, 57 b/Nelsone, 61 b/Khaled El-Fiqi, 94 b/Saber, 111 t/Nackstrand, 113 b/Andersen, 113 t/Mounzer; fotolia.com: 107/Rebecca Capell; Getty Images Deutschland GmbH/IFA-Bilderteam, München: 38/Kneuer, 39 b/Aberham, 41 b/Jon Arnold Images, 57 t/Fuste Raga, 65 b/Picture Finders, 69 b/Schmidt, 96 b/TPC, 105/Aberham, 108 b/Thouvenin, 121/Diaf, 131 b/Jon Arnold Images; istockphoto.com: 95/Oleg Babich, 97 b/Maher, 114 b/salem, 119/cherokeejones, 120 t/Glenn Rose, 122 t/Lingbeek, 132 b/Robert Bremec; Kessler Medien, Saarbrücken: 36 t, 39 t, 40, 50 b, 124 b, 126; Mauritius Images, Mittenwald: 32 b/Photononstop, 32 t/Obert, 33/Runkel, 35 b/De Foy, 36 b/Photononstop, 44 m/Scott, 44 b/Fuste Raga, 44 t/AGE, 47 b/Weyer, 50 t/Layer, 55/AGE, 59/Scott, 61 t/Steussloff, 62 b/Vidler, 66 t/Mayer, 67/CuboImages, 70 b/Warburton-Lee, 70 t/Warburton-Lee, 71/Warburton-Lee, 72 b/Winter, 73 b/Winter, 77/Flüeler, 79 t/Flüeler, 96 t/Obert, 100 t/Roxbury, 104 t/Hiltmann, 109/StuperStock, 114 t, 120 b/TWP, 130/Torino, 131/Fuste Raga, 132 t/Cubo-Images; mev, Augsburg: 54 b, 54 t, 76 t; Polylooks: 65 t; shutterstock.com: 34/Attila Jandi, 35 t/Attila Jandi, 48/WiTR, 51 t/WiTR, 52/Alexey Goosev, 53/LouLouPhotos, 56 t/Slavko Sereda, 58 t/André Klaassen, 60/salamanderman, 66 b/Imagine Images Alastair Pidgen, 72 t/Galyna Andrushko, 78/Luc Sesselle, 103/Styve Reineck, 115 b/ayazad, 118/Nasser Buhamad, 122 b/Paul Cowan, 123/Paul Cowan, 128 t/hainaultphoto, 129 b/Andrea Seemann, 134/Doug Stacey; Siemens Corporate Archives: 127 b; Sipa Press, Paris: 49 t/YLI, 63 b, 112/O'Donnell; TopFoto, Kent: 42/Topography, 46/Gardner, 64/Novosti, 68/Roger-Viollet, 69 t, 73 t, 75 t/UN, 101, 128 b/Charles O. Cecil, 131 t, 135 t; TopicMedia Service, Ottobrunn: 104 b/Hosking; Courtesy of the Tunisian Embassy in Cairo: 51 b.

Production:
Layout & DTP: Gerald Wetzel, www.smoop.de, Laubach
Production Manager: Marcel Hellmund

1 2 3 4 5 6 7 8   15 14 13 12 11 10

Printed in Spain

Some international borders in the Arab world are undefined or disputed: borders as represented in this Atlas are not necessarily accepted by all countries involved and do not imply any view of their legal status on the part of the American University in Cairo Press or wissenmedia GmbH.
Statistics cited in the country profiles were the latest available in March 2010.

CONTENTS

Overview map of the Arab World   6-7
Northern Africa: Mauritania, Morocco, Algeria, Tunisia,
    Libya, Egypt, Sudan, Djibouti, Somalia, Comoros   8-9
Africa: Morocco, Algeria   10-11
Africa: Tunisia, Libya   12-13
Africa: Egypt, Sinai   14-15
Africa: Mauritania, Mali   16-17
Africa: Algeria, Libya   18-19
Africa: Northern Sudan   20-21
Africa: Southern Sudan   22-23
Africa: Djibouti, Somalia, Comoros   24-25

Satellite image: Cairo   26-27
Satellite image: Sudan   28-29
Satellite image: Egypt   30-31

Mauritania
Geography, Population   32-33
History and Politics, Economy   34-35

Morocco
Geography   36-37
Population   38-39
History and Politics   40-41
Economy, Traffic and Communication   42-43

Algeria
Geography   44-45
Population   46-47
History and Politics, Economy   48-49

Tunisia
Geography, Population   50-51
History and Politics, Economy   52-53

Libya
Geography, Population   54-55
History and Politics, Economy   56-57

Egypt
Geography   58-59
Population   60-61
History and Politics   62-63
Economy, Traffic and Communication   64-65

Sudan
Geography, Population   66-67
History and Politics, Economy   68-69

Djibouti
Geography, Population,
    History and Politics, Economy   70-71

Somalia
Geography, Population   72-73
History and Politics, Economy   74-75

Comoros
Geography, Population   76-77
History and Politics, Economy   78-79

Southwest Asia: Lebanon, Palestine, Syria, Iraq, Jordan, Saudi
    Arabia, Kuwait, Bahrain, Qatar, U.A.E., Oman, Yemen   80-81
Southwest Asia: Syria, Jordan, Lebanon, Palestine,
    Saudi Arabia, Iraq   82-83
Asia: Jordan, Palestine, Saudi Arabia, Kuwait,
    Bahrain, Qatar, U.A.E.   84-85
Asia: Saudi Arabia, Yemen, Oman, U.A.E.   86-87
Asia: Saudi Arabia, Yemen, Oman, U.A.E., Bahrain, Qatar   88-89

Satellite image: Oman   90-91
Satellite image: Yemen   92-93

Palestine
Geography, Population,
    History and Politics, Economy   94-95

Lebanon
Geography, Population   96-97
History and Politics, Economy   98-99

Syria
Geography, Population   100-101
History and Politics, Economy   102-103

Jordan
Geography, Population   104-105
History and Politics, Economy   106-107

Iraq
Geography, Population   108-109
History and Politics   110-111
Economy, Traffic and Communication   112-113

Saudi Arabia
Geography, Population   114-115
History and Politics, Economy   116-117

Kuwait
Geography, Population,
    History and Politics, Economy   118-119

Bahrain
Geography, Population,
    History and Politics, Economy   120-121

Qatar
Geography, Population,
    History and Politics, Economy   122-123

United Arab Emirates
Geography, Population   124-125
History and Politics, Economy   126-127

Oman
Geography, Population   128-129
History and Politics, Economy   130-131

Yemen
Geography, Population   132-133
History and Politics, Economy   134-135

Index   136-144

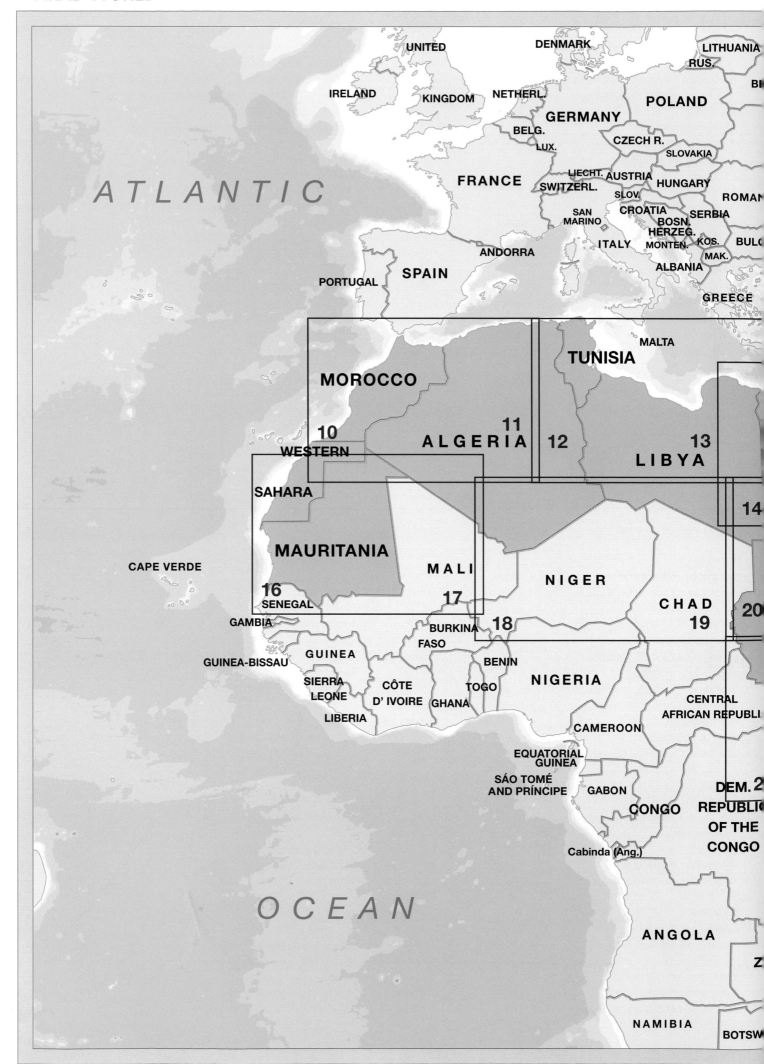

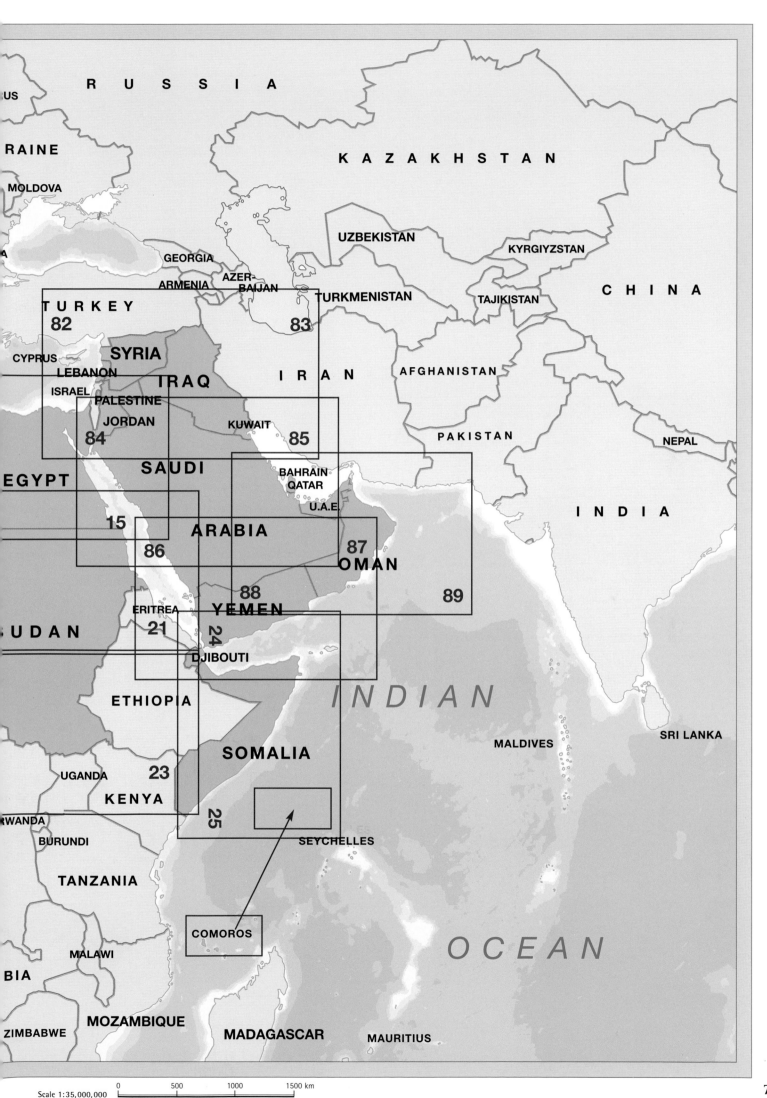

R U S S I A

US

RAINE

MOLDOVA

K A Z A K H S T A N

UZBEKISTAN

KYRGIYZSTAN

GEORGIA

ARMENIA

AZER-
BAIJAN

TURKMENISTAN

TAJIKISTAN

C H I N A

T U R K E Y
82

83

I R A N

AFGHANISTAN

CYPRUS

SYRIA

LEBANON

IRAQ

ISRAEL

PALESTINE

JORDAN

84

KUWAIT

85

PAKISTAN

NEPAL

SAUDI

EGYPT

BAHRAIN

QATAR

15

U.A.E.

I N D I A

A R A B I A

86

87

OMAN

88

89

ERITREA

YEMEN

UDAN

21

24

DJIBOUTI

I N D I A N

ETHIOPIA

SOMALIA

MALDIVES

SRI LANKA

23

UGANDA

K E N Y A

RWANDA

25

BURUNDI

SEYCHELLES

TANZANIA

COMOROS

O C E A N

MALAWI

BIA

ZIMBABWE

MOZAMBIQUE

MADAGASCAR

MAURITIUS

AFRICA

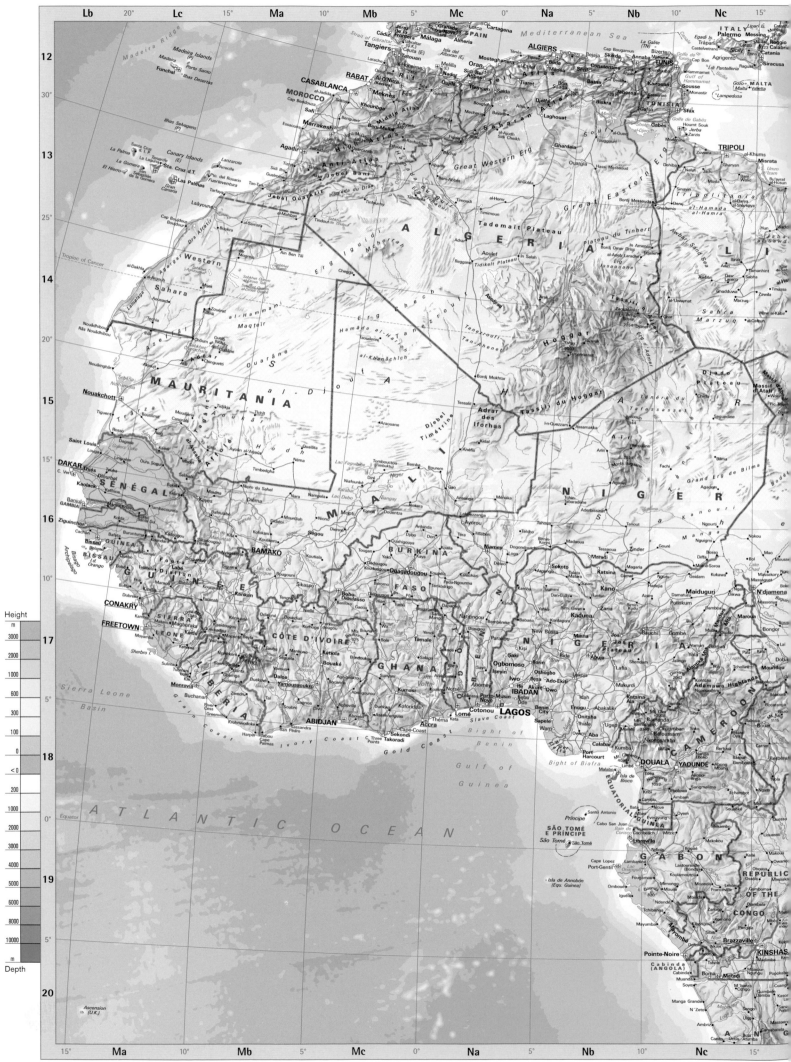

13

14

15

16

17

18

19

20

30°

25°

20°

15°

10°

5°

0°

5°

Ionian Sea

Mediterranean Sea

GREECE

ATHENS

TURKEY

CYPRUS

SYRIA

IRAQ

IRAN

BEIRUT

LEBANON

DAMASCUS

ISRAEL

AMMAN

JORDAN

BAGHDAD

KUWAIT

BAHRAIN

QATAR

DOHA

Abu Dhabi

United Arab Emirates

OMAN

Dubai

RIYADH

SAUDI ARABIA

Gulf of Sirte

Benghazi

ALEXANDRIA

CAIRO

GIZA

EGYPT

Western Desert

Libyan Desert

LIBYA

CHAD

Calanscio Sand Sea

Kufra Oasis

Red Sea

JEDDA Mecca

Medina

YEMEN

Sanaa

Gulf of Aden

SUDAN

Nubian Desert

OMDURMAN

KHARTOUM NORTH

KHARTOUM

Port Sudan

ERITREA

Asmara

DJIBOUTI Djibouti

Danakil Desert

Aden

CENTRAL AFRICAN REPUBLIC

ETHIOPIA

ADDIS ABABA

SOMALIA

MOGADISHU

DEM. REP. OF THE CONGO

UGANDA

Kampala

KENYA

NAIROBI

Lake Victoria

RWANDA

Kigali

BURUNDI

Bujumbura

TANZANIA

Dodoma

DAR ES SALAAM

Zanzibar Island

Pemba Island

Equator

SEYCHELLES

Aldabra Islands

Scale 1:20,000,000

0 100 200 300 400 500 600 km

AFRICA

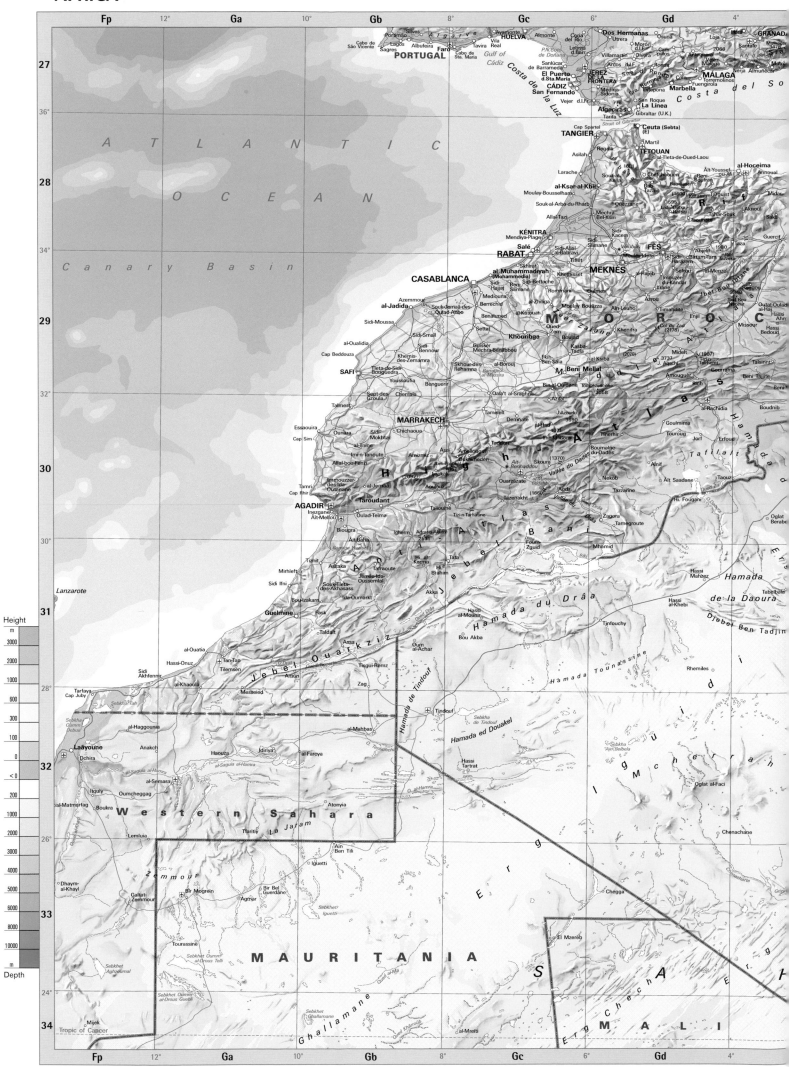

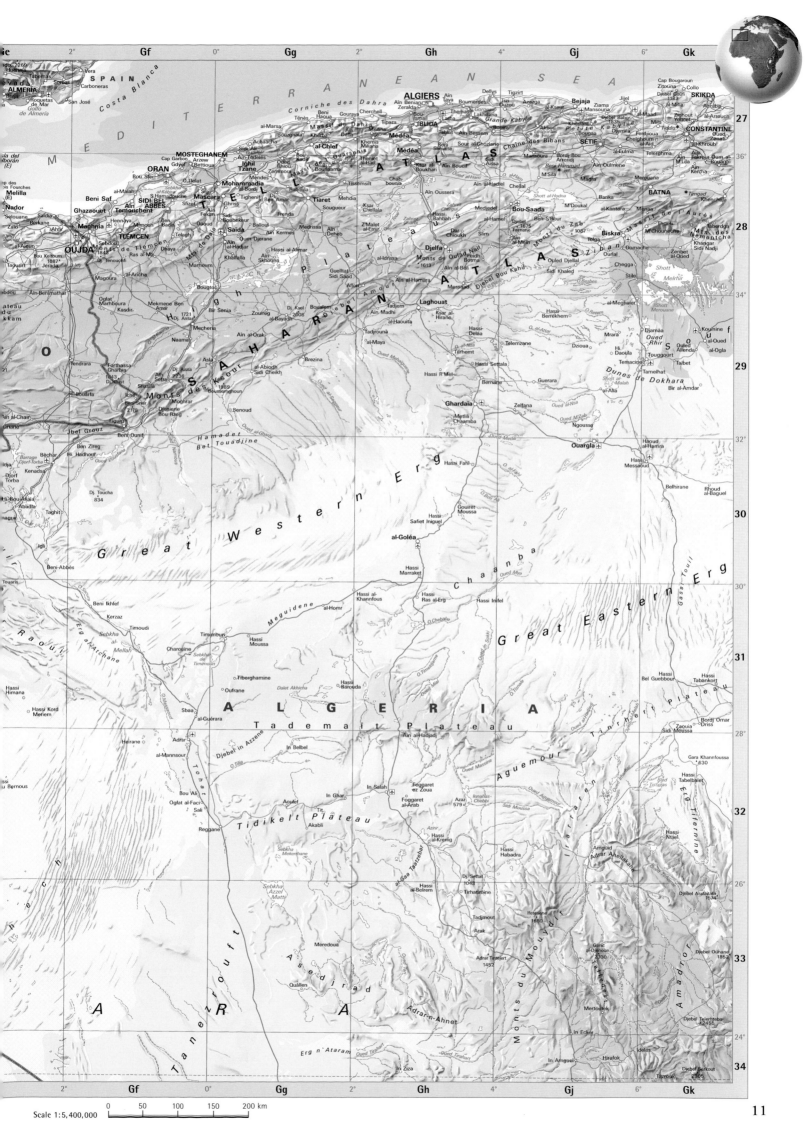

Scale 1:5,400,000

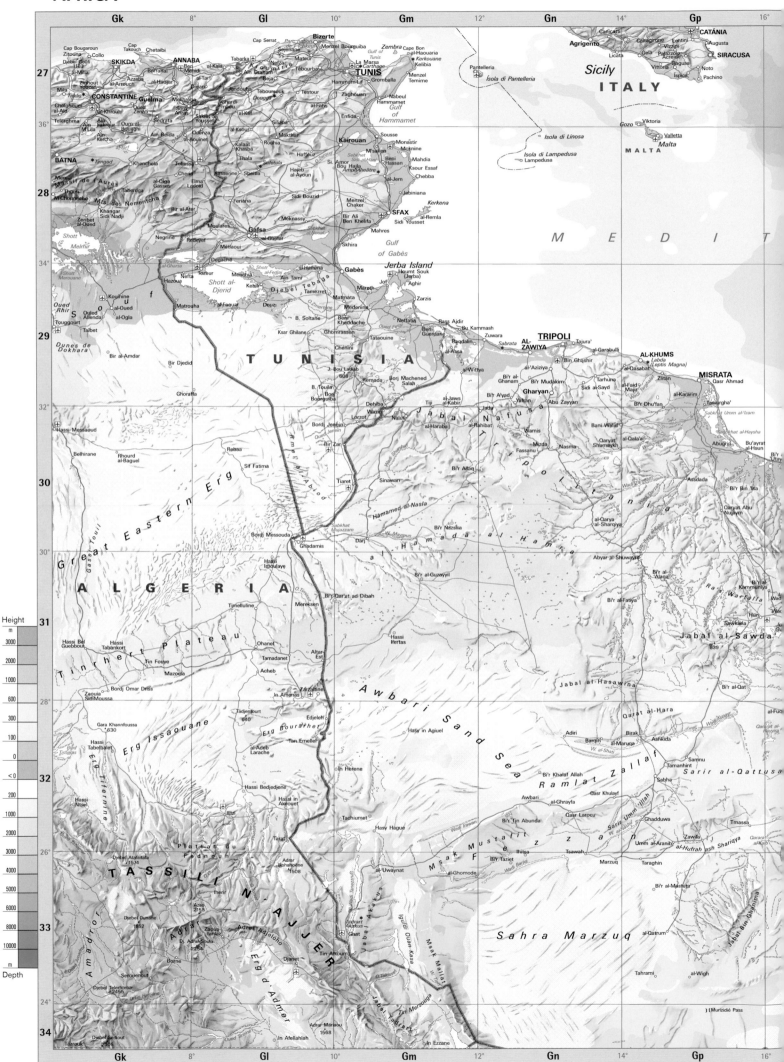

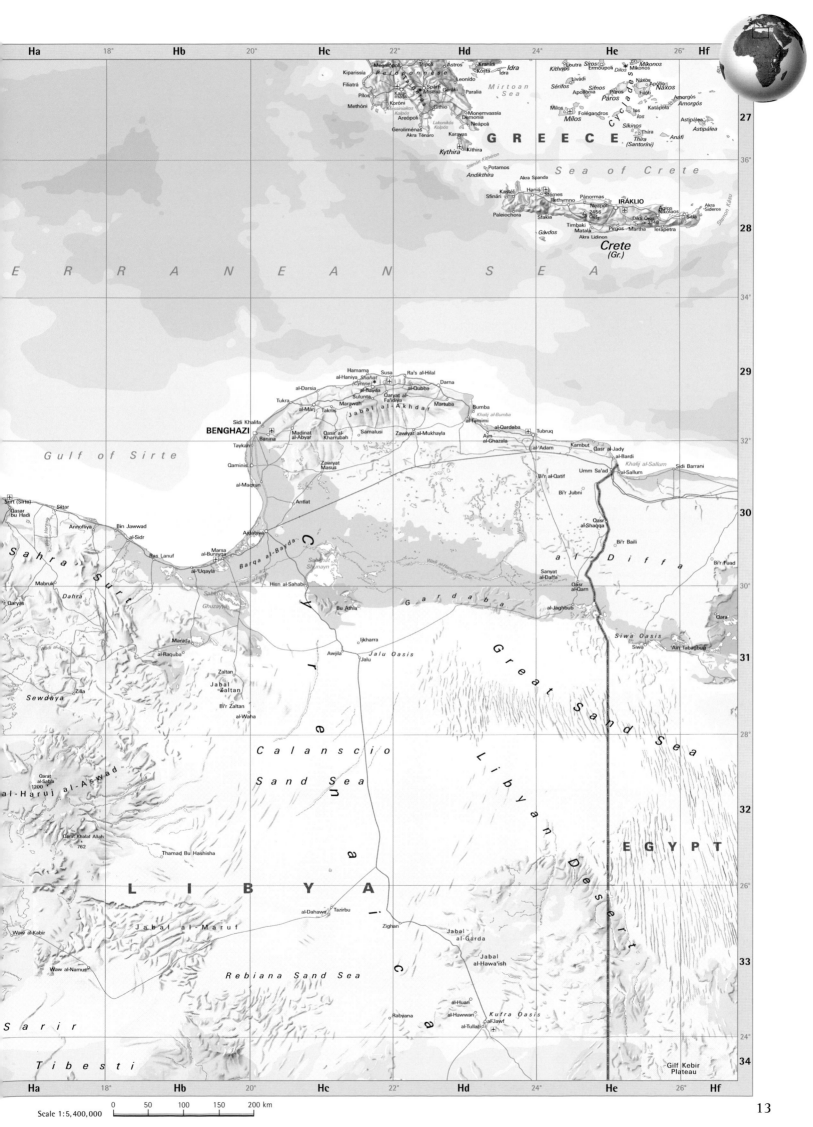

27

36°

28

G R E E C E

Mirtoan Sea

Peloponnese

Megalópoli
Tripoli
Ástros
Kranídi
Loutra
Sìros
Ermoúpoli
Míkonos
Kithnos
Kósta
Idra
Idra
Mikonos
Dilos
Filiatrá
Kalá-
máta
Sparti
Mistrás
Leonído
Serifos
Livádi
Sífnos
Apóllo-
Náxos
Pilos
Gerakí
Paralía
Apollonía
Páros
Náxos
Methóni
Koróni
Gíthio
Monemvassía
Demonía
Milos
Folégandros
Íos
Amorgós
Areópoli
Neápoli
Milos
Sikinos
Katápola
Gerolimenas
Lakonikós
Karavás
Milos
Íos
Astipálea
Akra Ténaro
Kólpos
Thira
Anáfi
Astipálea
Kythira
Kíthira
Thira
(Santoríni)

Sea of Crete

Stenón Kithérion

Potamos
Andikthíra
Akra Spanda
Kastéli
Haniá
Stérnes
Pánormas
Neapol
IRÁKLIO
Ákra
Sideros
Sfinári
Rethymno
2456
Óros
Neapol
Ágios
Nikólaos
Sitia
Paleiochora
Sfakia
Dikti Óros
2148
Stenón Kásu
Gávdos
Timbaki
Martha
Ierápetra
Matalá
Pirgos
Akra Lidinon

Crete
(Gr.)

34°

M E D I T E R R A N E A N   S E A

29

Hamama
Ra's al-Hilal
al-Haniya
Shahat
Susa
(Cyrene)
al-Darsia
al-Bayda
al-Qubba
Darna
Tukra
Sulunta
Qaryat al-
Fa'idiya
Martuba
al-Marj
Marawah
Taknis
Bumba
Sidi Khalifa
Jabal al-Akhdar
Khalij al-Bumba
al-Tamimi
BENGHAZI
Banina
Madinat
al-Abyar
Qasir al-
Kharrubah
Samalusi
Zawiyat al-Mukhayla
al-Qardaba
Tubruq
Taykan
Ayn
al-Ghazala
al-'Adam
Kambut
Qasr al-Jady
Qaminis
Zawiyat
Masus
Bi'r al-Qatif
al-Bardi
Khalij al-Sallum
Sidi Barrani
Umm Sa'ad
al-Maqrun
Bi'r Jubni
al-Sallum
Antlat
Qasr
al-Shaqqa
30°

Gulf of Sirte

32°

Surt (Sirte)
Siltar
Bi'r Baili
Qasr
bu Hadi
Bi'r Fuad
Annofliya
Bin Jawwad
al-Sidr
Sanyat
al-Daffa
a l - D i f f a
Ras Lanuf
Marsa
al-Qarn
al-Burayqa
B a r q a   a l - B a y d a
al-'Uqayla
C
Hisn al-Sahabi
y
Sabkhat
al-Jaghbub
Qara
Sahra
Mabruk
Shunayn
r
Bu Athla
G a r d a b a
Siwa Oasis
Qaryas
Dahra
Sabkhat
e
Ijkharra
Siwa
'Ain Tabagbug
Ghuzayyis
n
Awjila
Jalu Oasis
31
Marada
Jalu
al-Raquba
a
Great Sand Sea
Zaltan
i
Jabal
Zaltan
c
Libyan Desert
28°
Sewdaya
Zilla
Bi'r Zaltan
C a l a n s c i o
al-Waha
a
S a n d   S e a
Qarat
al-Sabia
1200
n
al-Haruj al-Aswad
32
Qarat Khalaf Allah
762
E G Y P T
Thamad Bu Hashisha
a
al-Dahawa
Tazirbu
L I B Y A
33
Zighan
Jabal
al-Garda
Jabal al-Maruf
Jabal
al-Hawa'ish
Waw al-Kabir
a
R e b i a n a   S a n d   S e a
i
al-Huari
c
al-Hawwari
Waw al-Namus
Kufra Oasis
Rabyana
al-Jawf
24°
S a r i r
al-Tullab
Gilf Kebir
Plateau
T i b e s t i
34

Scale 1:5,400,000
0   50   100   150   200 km

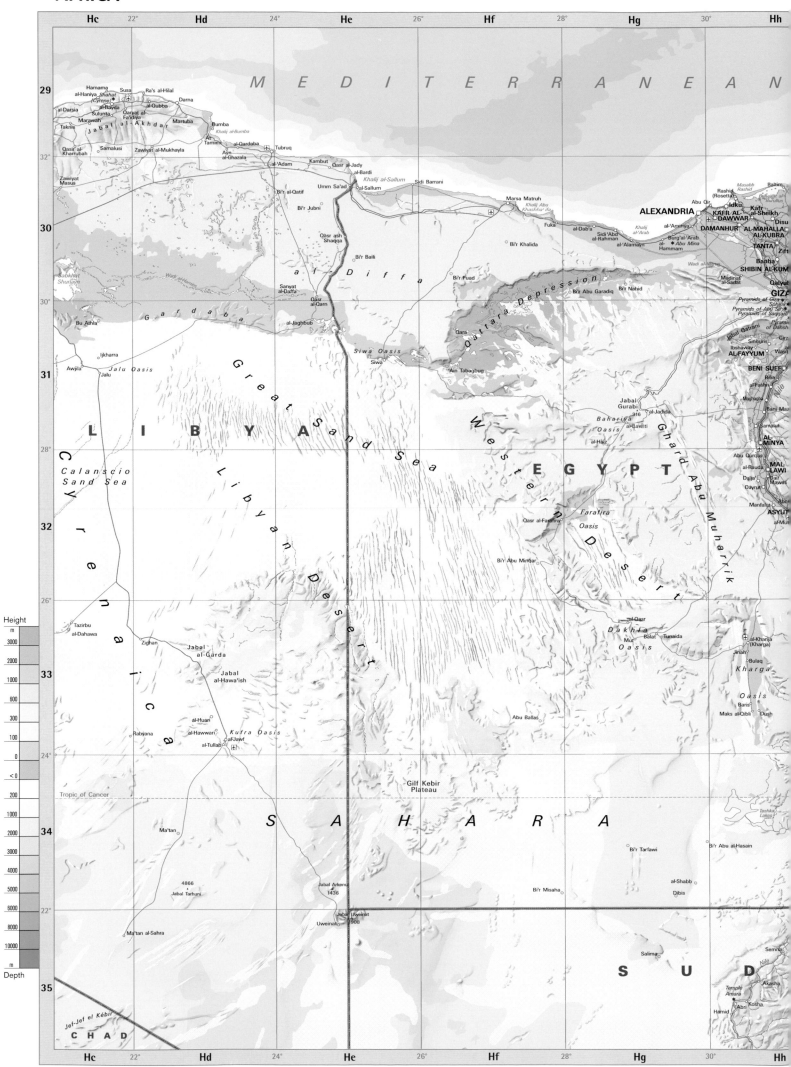

MEDITERRANEAN

Hamama
al-Haniya *Shahat* Susa Ra's al-Hilal
(Cyrene)
al-Darsia al-Bayda al-Qubba Darna
Sulunta Qaryat al-
Marawah Fa'idiya
Takniis Samalusi Martuba
Jabal al-Akhdar Bumba
Qasir al- *Khalij al-Bumba*
Zawiyat Kharrubah Zawiyat al-Mukhayla Tamimi
Masus al-Qardaba Tubruq
Ayn al-Ghazala
al-'Adam Kambut Qasr al-Jady
al-Bardi
Bi'r al-Qatif Umm Sa'ad al-Sallum *Khalij al-Sallum* Sidi Barrani
Rashid
Bi'r Jubni (Rosetta)
Marsa Matruh ALEXANDRIA Idku
Fuka *Khalij Abu* KAFR AL-
Qasr ash- *Khashha'ifa* al-Dab'a DAWWAR
Shaqqa al-'Amiriya DAMANHUR AL-MAHALLA
Sidi 'Abd al-'Arab AL-KUBRA
Bi'r Baili al-Rahman Burg'al-'Arab TANTA
Bi'r Khalida al-'Alamayn Abu Mina Banha
al-Hammam SHIBIN AL-KUM
al-Diffa Bi'r Fuad Madinat
Wadi al-Natrun al-Sadat
Sanyat *Qattara Depression* Qalyub
al-Daffa Bi'r Abu Garadiq Bi'r Nahid GIZA
Qasr Pyramids of Giza
al-Qarn Sphinx
Bu Athla Gardaba Pyramids of Abu Sir
al-Jaghbub Qara Pyramids of Saqqara
Ijkharra Jabal Qatrani of Dahsh
Awjila *Jalu Oasis* Siwa Oasis Jabal
Jalu Siwa Gurabi Simun AL-FAYYUM
Ain Tabagbug 316 al-Jadida Ibshaway
BENI SUEF
Biba
Bahariya al-Fashn
L I B Y A Oasis al-Bawiti Maghagha
Great Sand Sea al-Haiz Bani Maz
Samalut
Calanscio Western E G Y P T AL-
Sand Sea MINYA
Abu Qurqas
Libyan Desert MAL-
al-Rauda LAWI
Dalja Dair
Farafira Dayrut Mawas
Qasr al-Farafira Oasis Manfalut
ASYUT
Cyrenaica al-Mu
Bi'r Abu Minqar
Tazirbu
al-Dahawa
Zighan Dakhla al-Qasr
Jabal Oasis Balat Tunaida al-Kharija
al-Garda Mut (Kharga)
Jabal Jinah
al-Hawa'ish Bulaq Kharga
al-Huari
Rabyana al-Hawwari Abu Ballas Oasis
al-Jawl Baris
Kufra Oasis Maks al-Qibli Dush
al-Tullab

Gilf Kebir
Plateau

Tropic of Cancer

Ma'tan S A H A R A Bi'r Tarfawi Bi'r Abu al-Hasain

4866 al-Shabb
Jabal Tarhuni Jabal Arkenu Djibis
1436 Bi'r Misaha

Jabal Uweinat
Uweinat 1908

Ma'tan al-Sahra Salima S U D

Jef-Jef el Kébir
C H A D Temple
Amara

Height
m
3000
2000
1000
600
300
100
0
< 0
200
1000
2000
3000
4000
5000
6000
8000
10000
m
Depth

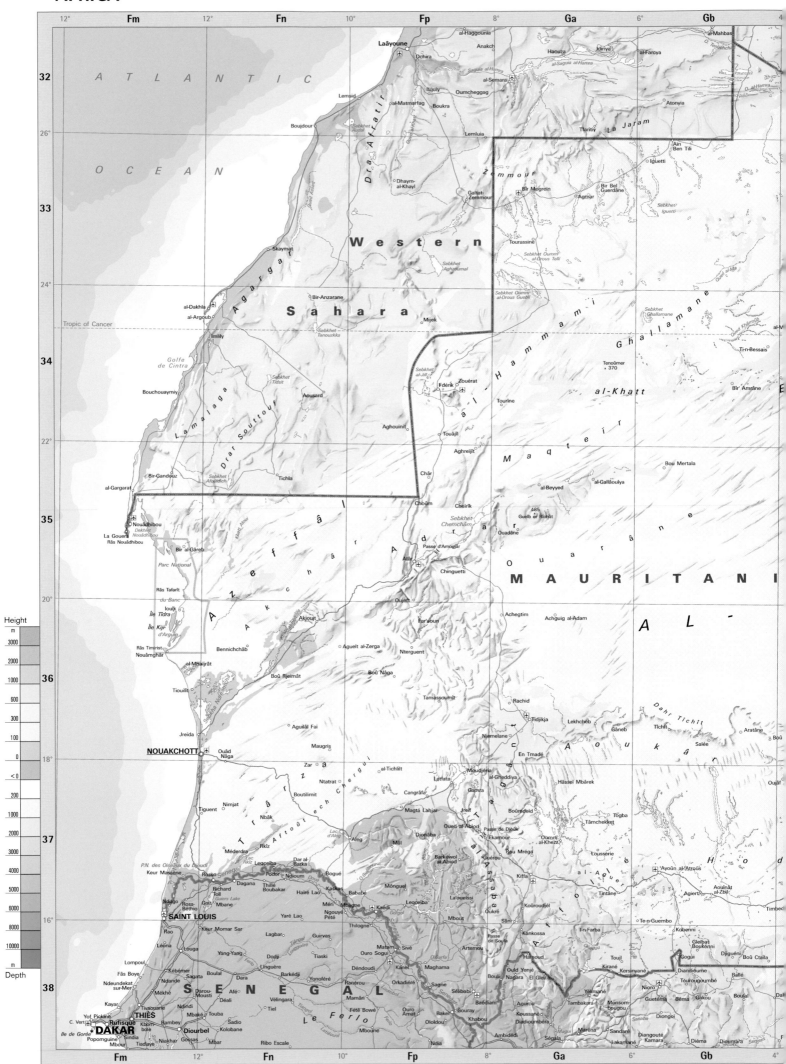

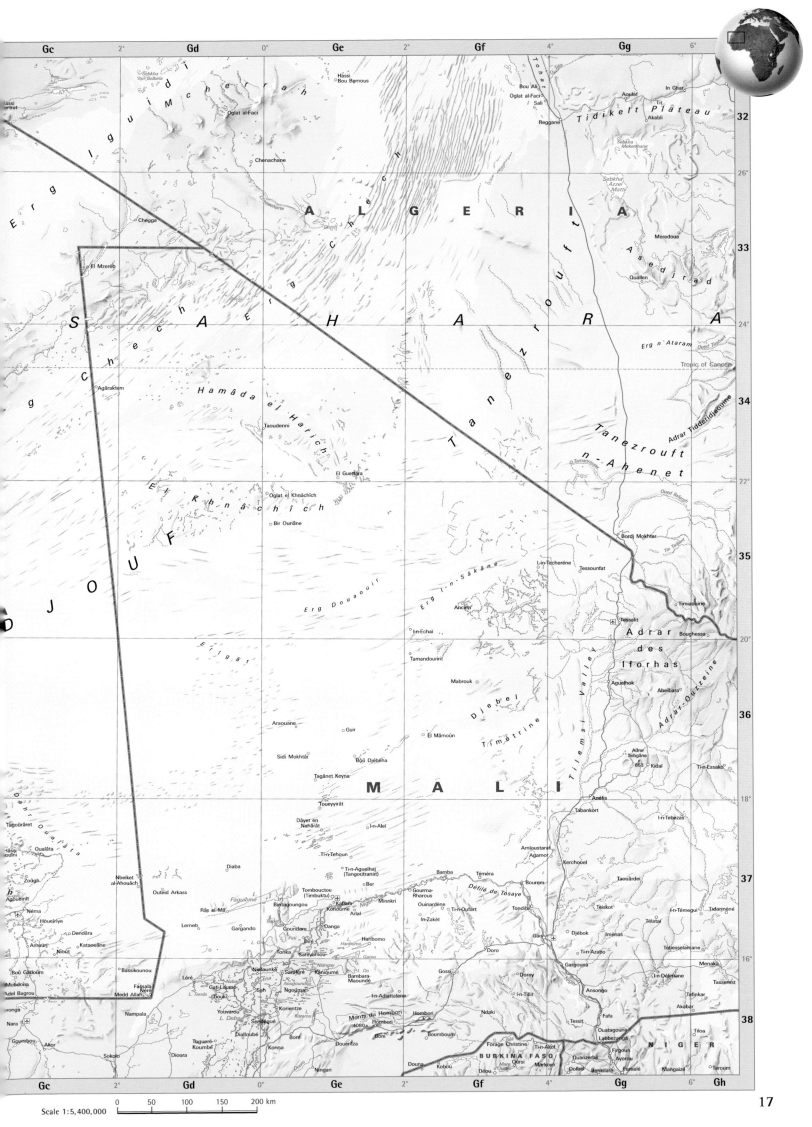

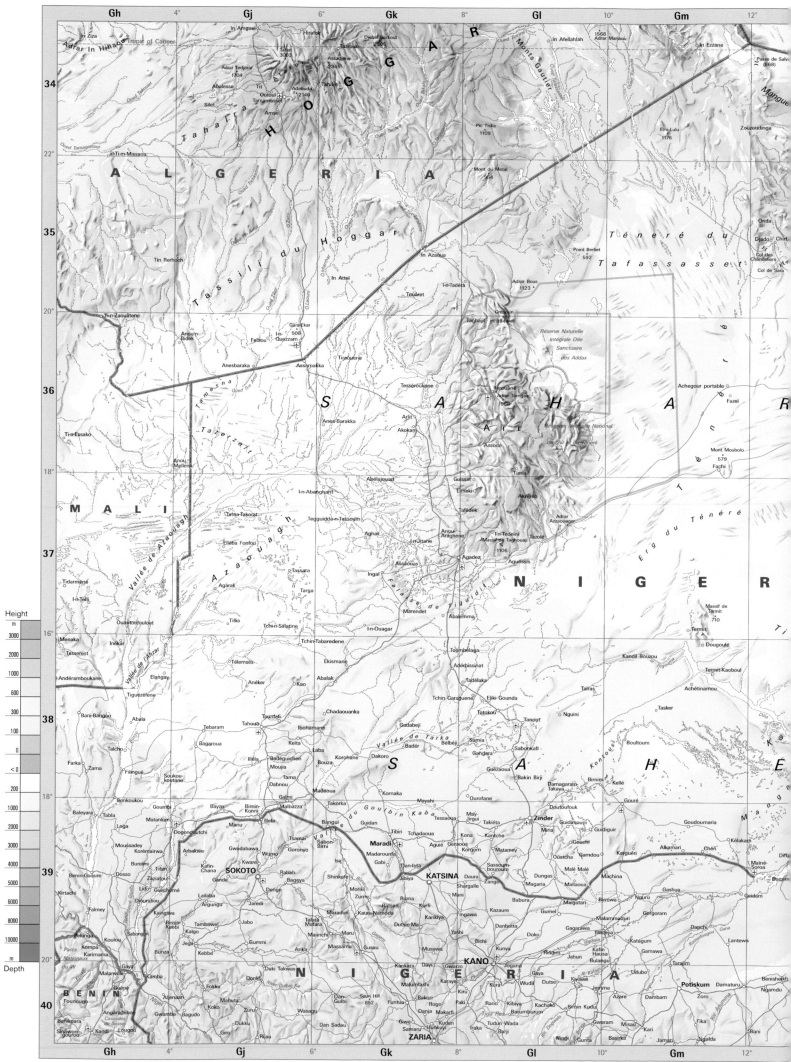

Height
m
3000
2000
1000
600
300
100
0
< 0
200
1000
2000
3000
4000
5000
6000
8000
10000
m
Depth

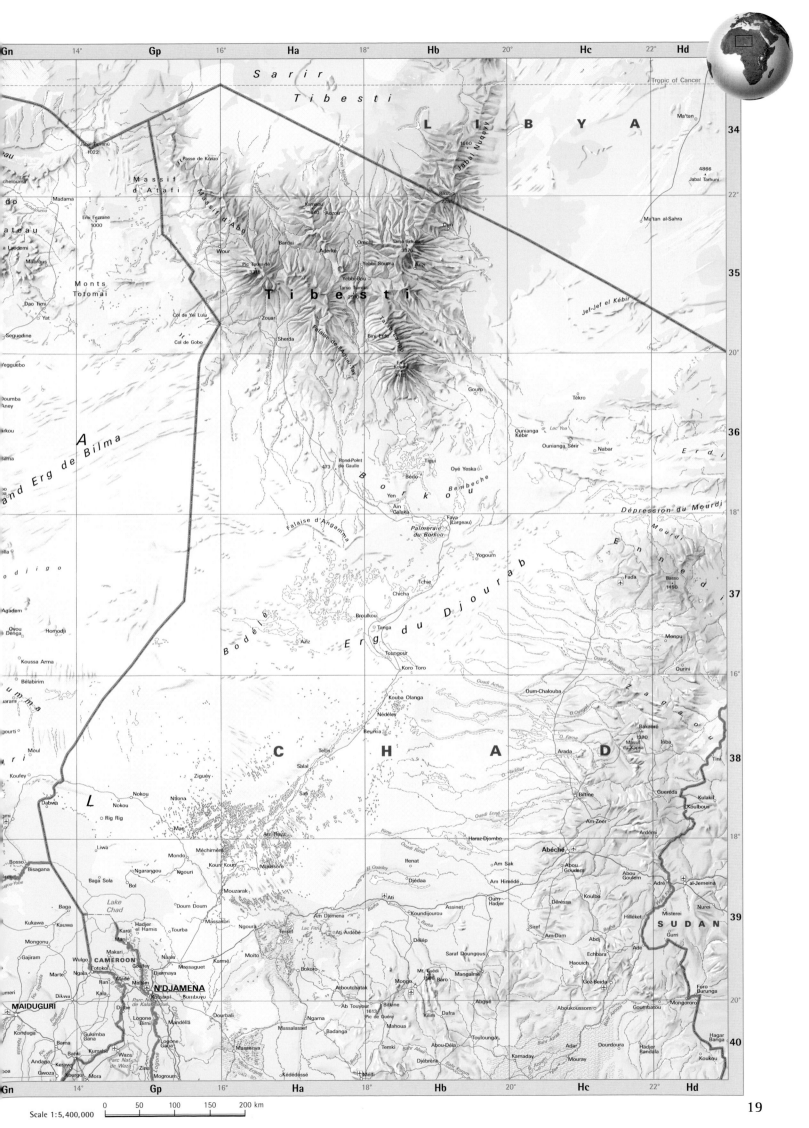

Sarir

Tibesti

Tropic of Cancer

L I B Y A

34

Ma'tan

Jabal Tummu
1022

Passe de Korizo

Massif
d'Ataïl

1660

Jabal Nuqay

22°

Madama

Massif d'Abo

Emi Fezzane
1000

Kamçou
1640 Aozou

Bikubub
2266

4866
Jabal Tarhuni

Ma'tan al-Sahra

Mabrous

Wour

Bardaï

Aderké

Orochi

Tarso Emissi
3376

Oun

Monts
Totomaï

Pic Toussidé
3315

Yebbi Souma

Aozi

35

Dao Timi
Yat

Col de Yei Lulu

Yebbi-Bou
Tarso Tieroko
2916

Seguedine

T i b e s t i

Zouar

Sherda

Bini Erde

Col de Gobo

Falaise de Maniet Tay

Tarso Uang

Jef-Jef el Kébir

Yegguebo

Emi
Koussi
3415

20°

Gouro

Doumba
Aney

Gourou

Tékro

irkou

Lac Yoa

Erdi

Grand Erg de Bilma

Rond-Point
de Gaulle
473

Tigui

Oyé Yeska

Ounianga
Kébir

Nabar

36

Bédo

Ounianga Sérir

A

B
o
r
k
o

Bembeche

u

Falaise d'Angamma

Yen

Ain
Galaka

Faya
(Largeau)

Palmeraie
du Borkou

Dépression du Mourdi

18°

o d j i g o

Yogoum

E
n
n
e
d
i

Mourdi

Fada

Basso
1450

Agadem

Tchie

37

Oyou
Denga

Homodji

Chicha

B o d é l é

Broulkou

Menou

Ourini

Koussa Arma

Aziz

Tanga

E r g   d u   D j o u r a b

Toungour

Bélabirim

Koro Toro

16°

u
m
m
a

Ouadi Achim

Oum-Chalouba

Z
a
g
a
o
u

Moul

Kouba Olanga

O. Ouaga

Koufey

Nédéley

Bakaoré
1290

Iriba

Massif
du Kapka

Dabwa

Beurkia

O. Fama

Arada

Tini

L

Tellis

C   *H*   *A*   *D*

38

Koussa

Salal

Biltine

Gueréda

Kulakit

Ntiona

Ziguéy

Haddad

Koulbous

Rig Rig

Nokou

Safi

Ouadi Enne

Am-Zoér

Ardémi

Liwa

Mao

Rima

Haraz-Djombo

Bosso

Nokou

Méchirnène

Ouadi Réné

Abéché

Adré

al-Jemeina

Bisagana

Mondo

Kour Kour

Manessoro

Ifenat

Am Sak

Abou
Goudem

Abou
Goulem

18°

ou-Yobe

Baga Sola

Ngarangou

Ngouri

Mouzarak

El Ouadey

Djédaa

Am Himédé

Oum-
Hadjer

Koulbo

Déressa

Nurei

Baga

Bol

Doum Doum

Ati

Assinet

Koundijourou

Hilléket

Misterei

Kukawa

Kauwa

*Lake
Chad*

Massakori

Batha

Koufo

Batha

Siref

Abdj

S U D A N

39

Mongonu

Hadjer
el Hamis

Tourba

Ngoura

Am Djemena

Tersel

Ati Ardébé

Délép

Am-Dam

Saraf Doungous

Gurri

Gajiram

Karal

Moïto

Saraf Doungous

Echbara

Ade

Marte

Ngala

Makari

Goulfey

Djermaya

Kamé

Massaguet

Bokoro

Mt. Guédi
1500 Biro

Mangalmé

Goz-Beida

Foro
Burunga

CAMEROON

Fotokol

Mani

Ngala

Mongororo

MAIDUGURI

Mandélia

N'Djamena

Dourbali

Bitkine

Pic de Guéra

Aboutchatak

Mongo

Abgué

Aboukoussom

Goumbatou

Hagar
Banga

20°

Kala

Djilbe

Ngama

Badanga

1613
Kilim

Dafra

Toulounga

Adar

Dourdoura

Hadjer
Bandala

Dikwa

Logone
Birni

Logone
Gana

Mahoua

Koukou

Konduga

Gulumba
Gana

Massalassef

Massenya

Temki

Abou-Déïa

Kamaday

Mouray

Bama

Banki

Kumtasé

Waza

Kédédéssé

Djébrène

Bahr Azoum

Andaga

Keraw

Zina

Mogroum

Melfi

40

Gwoza

Kourbou

Mora

Parc Nat de Waza

Scale 1:5,400,000   0   50   100   150   200 km

AFRICA

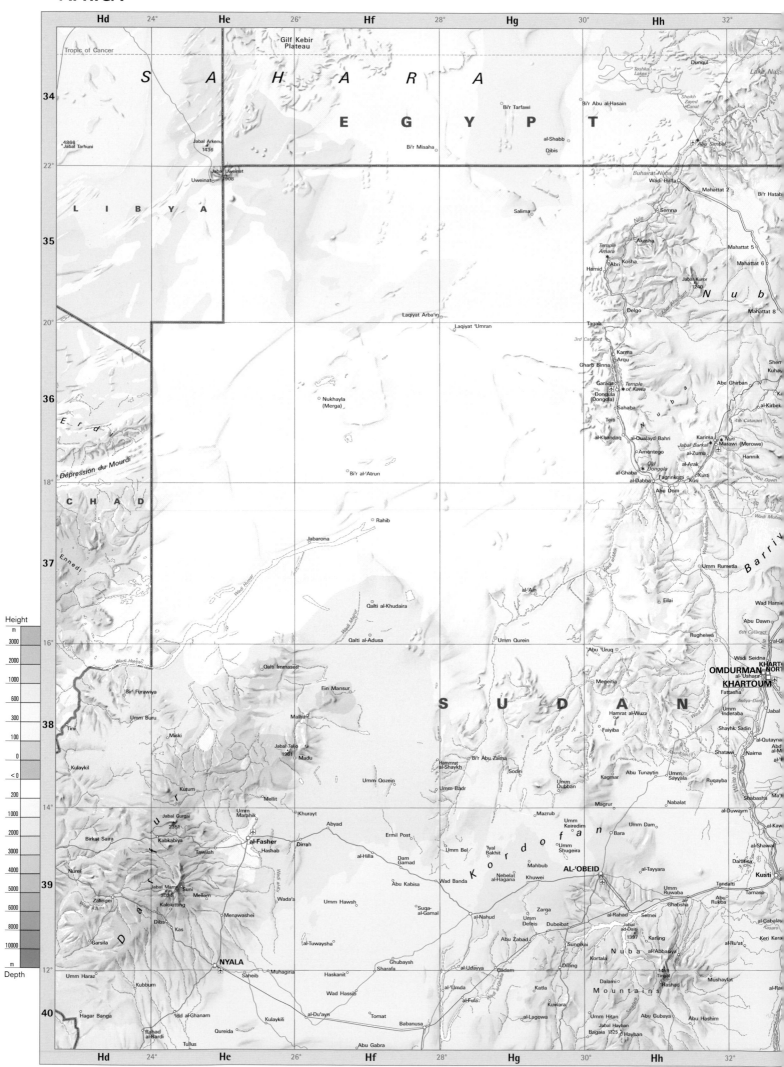

| | Hd | 24° | He | 26° | Hf | 28° | Hg | 30° | Hh | 32° |

S A H A R A

EGYPT

Gilf Kebir Plateau

Tropic of Cancer

34

Bi'r Tarfawi

Bi'r Abu al-Hasain

Dunqul

Toshka Lakes

Lake Nas

Sheikh Zayed Canal

4866 Jabal Tarhuni

Jabal Arkenu 1436

al-Shabb

Qibis

Bi'r Misaha

Abu Simbel

22°

LIBYA

Jabal Uweinat 1908

Uweinat

Buhairat Nubia

Wadi Halfa

Mahattat 2

Bi'r Hatab

Salima

35

Nile

Semna

Akasha

Temple Amara

Abri

Kosha

Mahattat 5

Mahattat 6

Hamid

Jabal Kuror 1240

N u b

Laqiyat Arba'in

Laqiyat 'Umran

Tagab

3rd Cataract

Delgo

Mahattat 8

20°

E r d

Karma

Arqu

Gharb Binna

Shem

Kuhay

Nukhayla (Merga)

Garada

Temple of Kawa

Dongula (Dongola)

Abu Ghirban

36

Depression du Mourdi

Sahaba

Teiti

a

Ka

al-Kirbek

al-Khandaq

al-Qualayd Bahri

Amentego

Karima

Nuri

Matawi (Merowe)

4th Cataract

Jabal Barkal

Bi'r al-'Atrun

al-Ghaba

Old Dongola

al-Zuma

al-Arak

Hannik

CHAD

al-Dabba

Fagrinkotti

Kurti

Küri

Abu Dom

Wadi Abu Dom

18°

Rahib

Jabarona

Wadi Howar

Wadi el-Milk

Barri

Ennedi

al-'Ain

Umm Rumetla

37

Qalti al-Khudaira

Eilai

Wad Hami

Abu Dawn

6th Cataract

Qalti al-Adusa

Umm Qurein

Rugheiwa

Val-G

16°

Abu 'Uruq

Wadi Seidna

Qalti Immaserr

KHART

Ein Mansur

Megeitia

OMDURMAN NORT

al-Ushara

KHARTOUM

Fattasha

S U D A N

Umm Inderaba

Atbiya Dam

Maliba

Hamrat al-Wuzz

Faiyiba

Umm

Jabal

38

Tini

Umm Buru

Maski

Jabal Telo 1961

Madu

Sodiri

Umm Dubban

Shatawi

Naima

Abd

al-M

Shayhk Sadin

al-Qutayna

Kulaykil

Hammrat al-Shaykh

Bi'r Abu Zaima

Umm Qozein

Umm Badr

Kagmar

Abu Tunaytin

Umm Sayyala

Ruqayba

al-Duwaym

Mellit

Kutum

Magrur

Nabalat

Shabasha

Ma'

14°

Jabal Gurgai 2351

Umm Marahik

Khurayt

Abyad

Mazrub

Umm Keiredim

Bara

Umm Dam

al-Kaw

Kabkabiya

al-Fasher

Birkat Saira

Hashab

Dirrah

Ermil Post

Umm Bel

Umm Shugeira

Umm Dam

al-Shawal

Tawilah

K o r d o f a n

Dam Gamad

al-Hilla

Darfisa

Nurel

Abu Kabisa

'Iyal Bakhit

Mahbub

AL-'OBEID

al-Tayyara

Kusti

39

Jabal Marra 3024 Suni

Mellem

Wad Banda

Nebelat al-Hagana

Khuwei

Tandalti

al-Gabala

Zalingei

Kalokitting

Wada'a

Umm Hawsh

Suga al-Gamal

Zarga

Umm Delels

Dubeibat

Umm Ruwaba

Tamaso

Abu Rukba

Dibs

Kas

al-Tuwaysha

al-Nahud

Jabal ad-Dair 1397

Keri Kera

Garsila

Menawashei

Abu Zabad

Karling

Sungikai

al-Ru'at

D

N u b a

al-Abbasiya

12°

Umm Haraz

NYALA

Saheib

Muhagiria

Ghubaysh Sharafa

Kortala

Dilling

Tinqal 1454

Kubbum

Haskanit

al-Udayya

Qadam

Dalami

Rashad

Mushaytat

M o u n t a i n s

al-Lai

40

Hagar Banga

Idd al-Ghanam

Wad Hassib

al-'Umda

al-Fula

Katla

Kuwara

Umm Hrtan

Abu Gubaya

Abu Hashim

Rahad al-Bardi

Kulaykili

al-Du'ayn

Tomat

Babanusa

al-Lagowa

Umm Hayban

Bagaia 1325

Hayban

Qureida

Tullus

Abu Gabra

| | Hd | 24° | He | 26° | Hf | 28° | Hg | 30° | Hh | 32° |

Height

m
3000
2000
1000
600
300
100
0
< 0
200
1000
2000
3000
4000
5000
6000
8000
10000
m

Depth

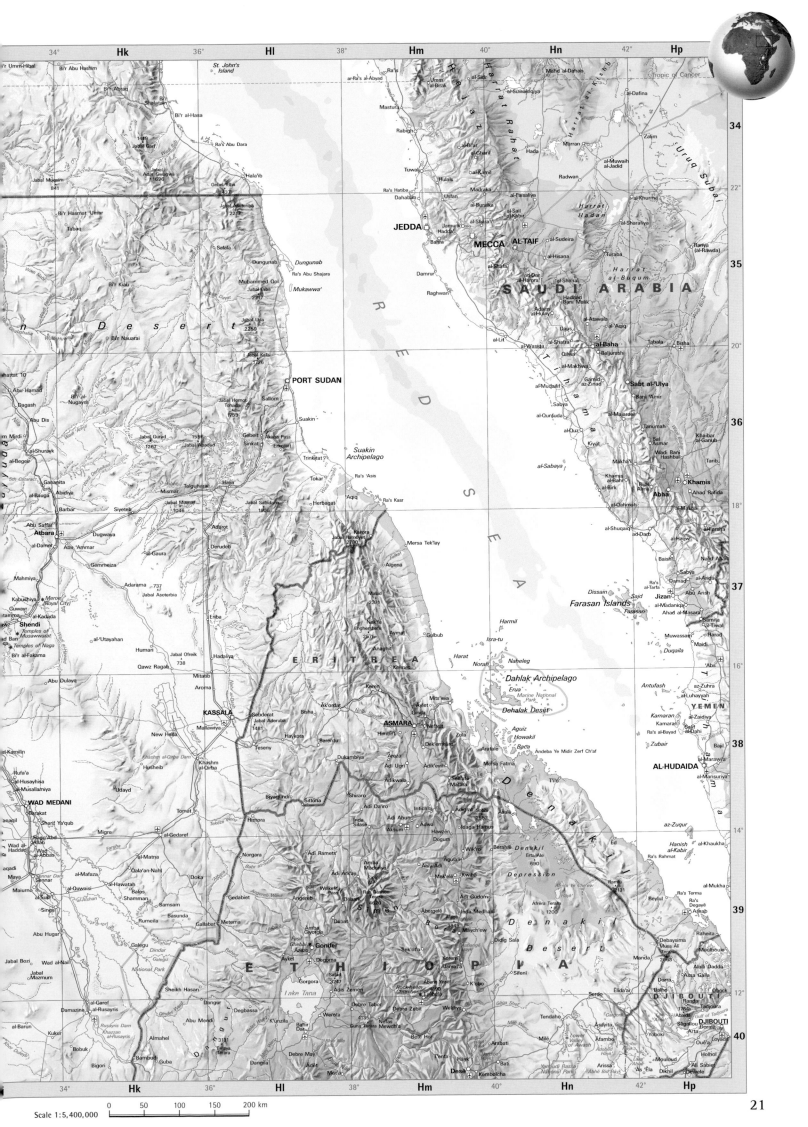

Scale 1:5,400,000

0   50   100   150   200 km

AFRICA

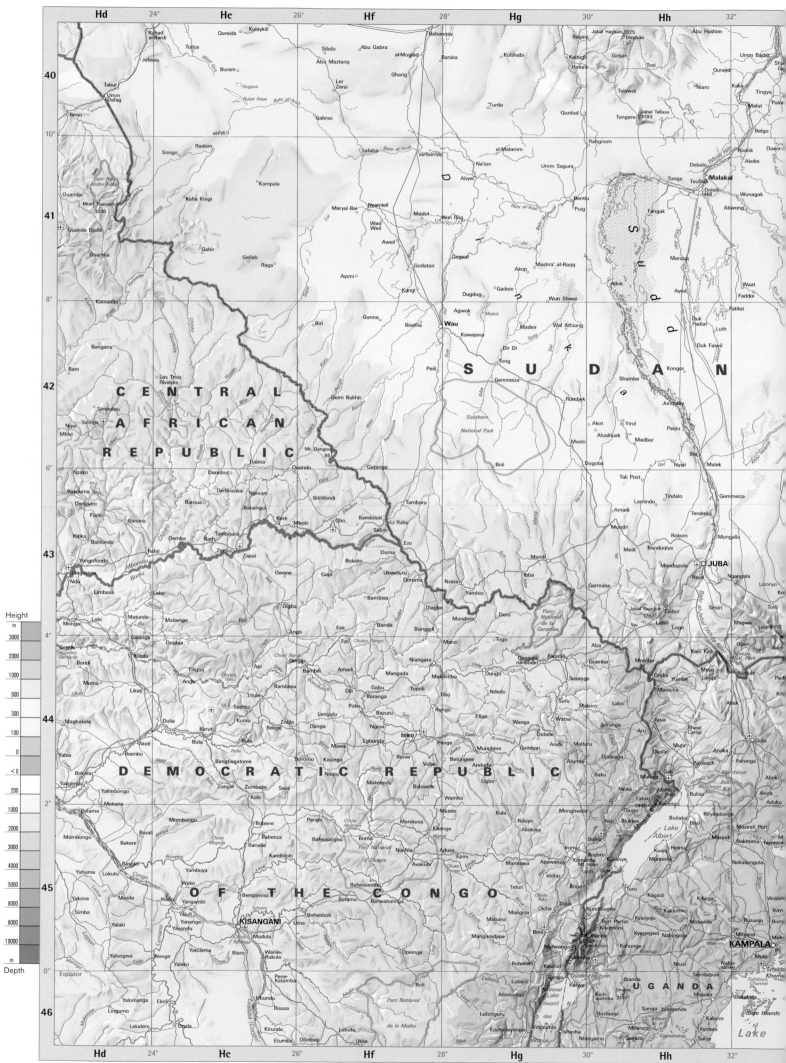

Height
m
3000
2000
1000
600
300
100
0
< 0
200
1000
2000
3000
4000
5000
6000
8000
10000
m
Depth

CENTRAL

AFRICAN

REPUBLIC

DEMOCRATIC REPUBLIC

OF THE CONGO

S U D A N

UGANDA

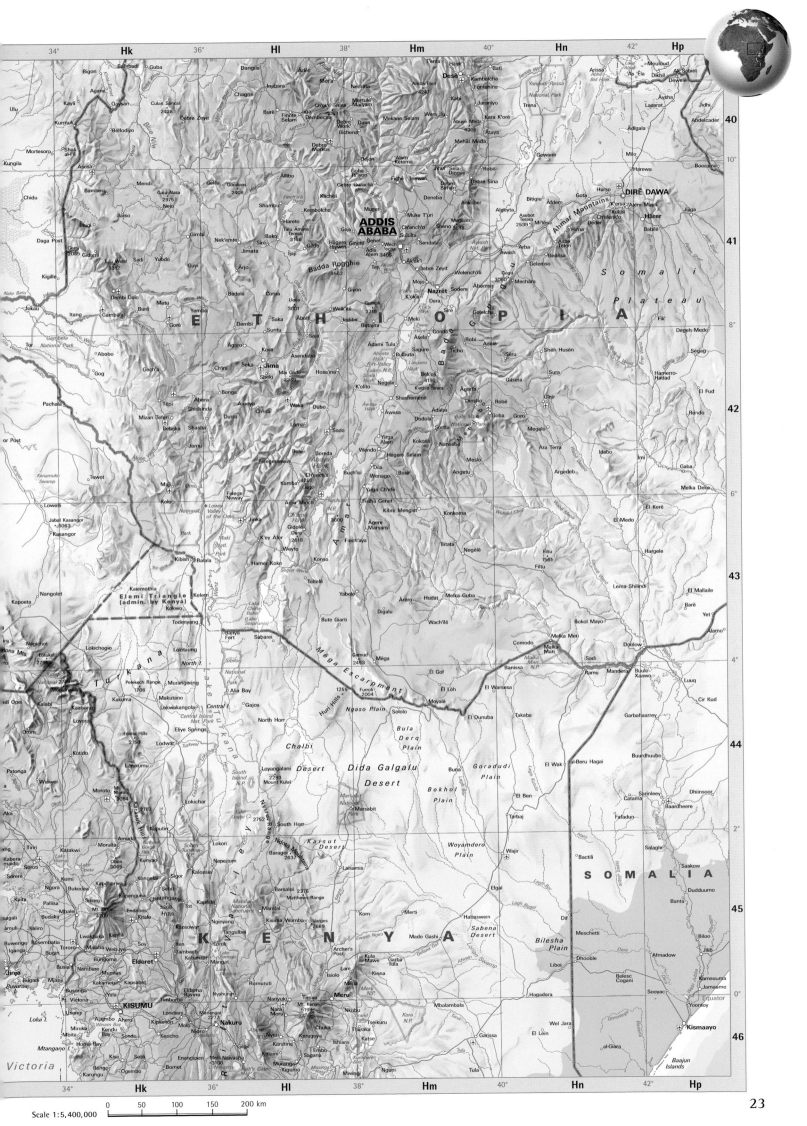

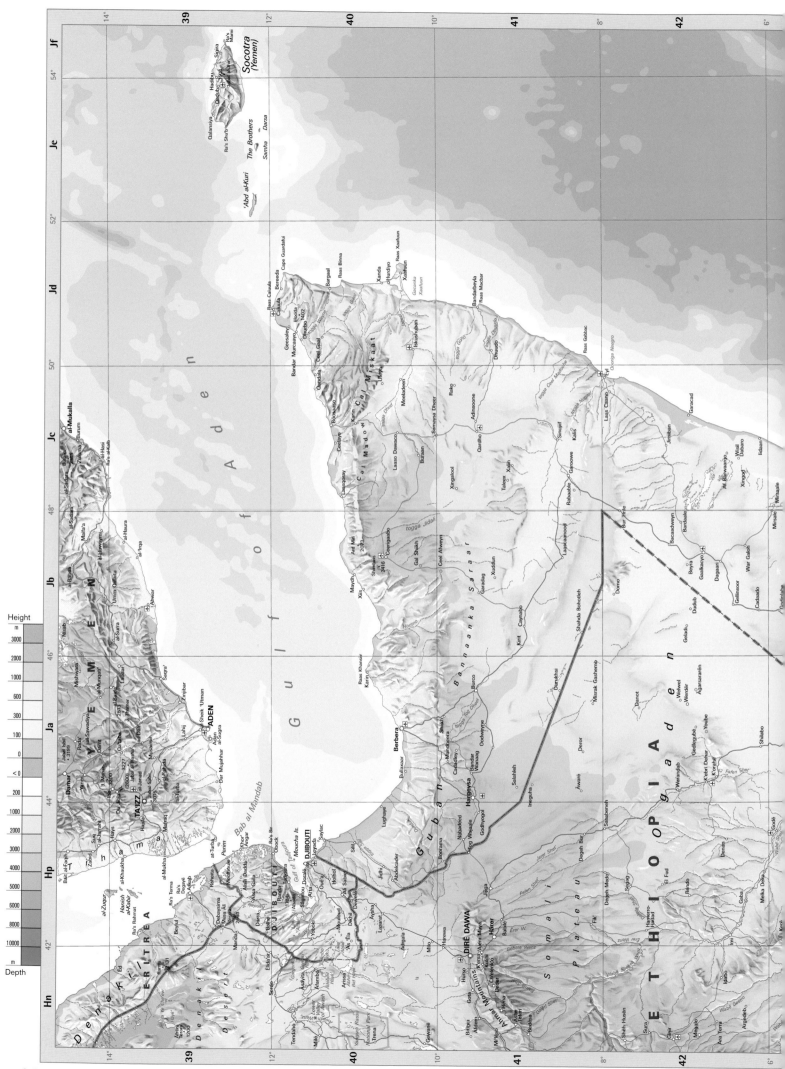

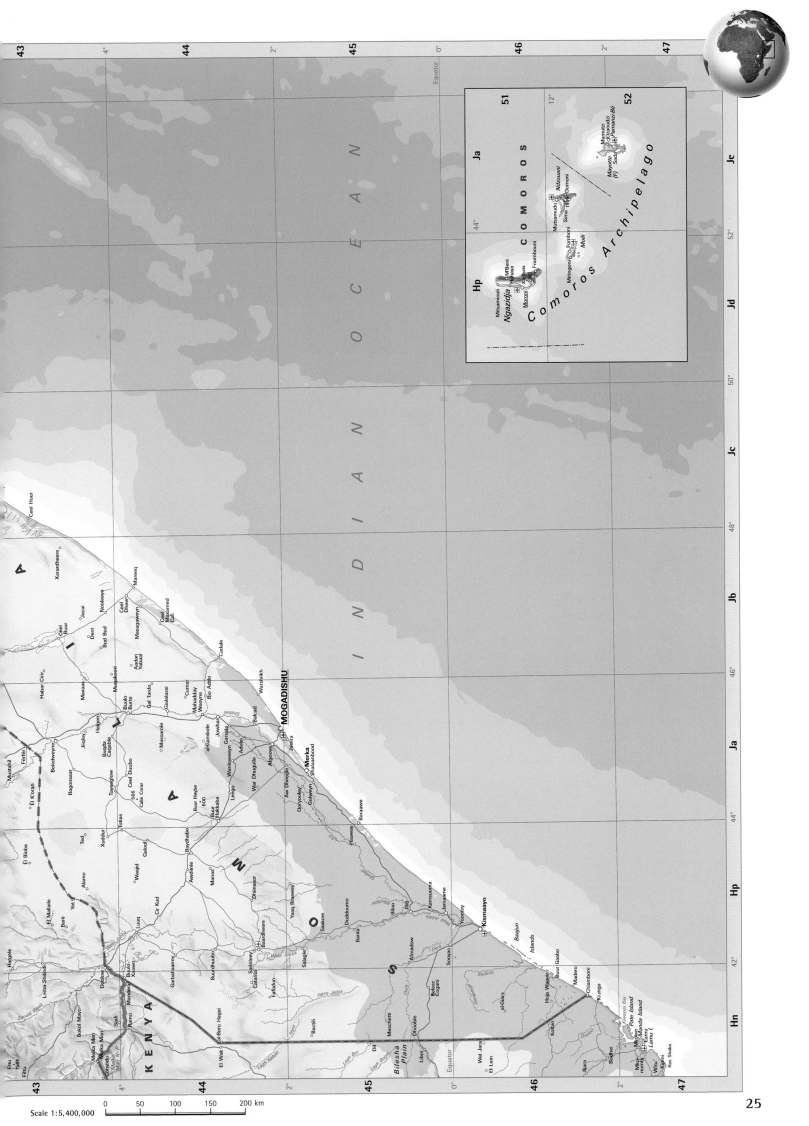

Scale 1:5,400,000

Central Cairo: *The modern suburbs west of the Nile contrast with the nineteenth-century developments on the east bank and the narrow alleys of the old Islamic city, lower right.*

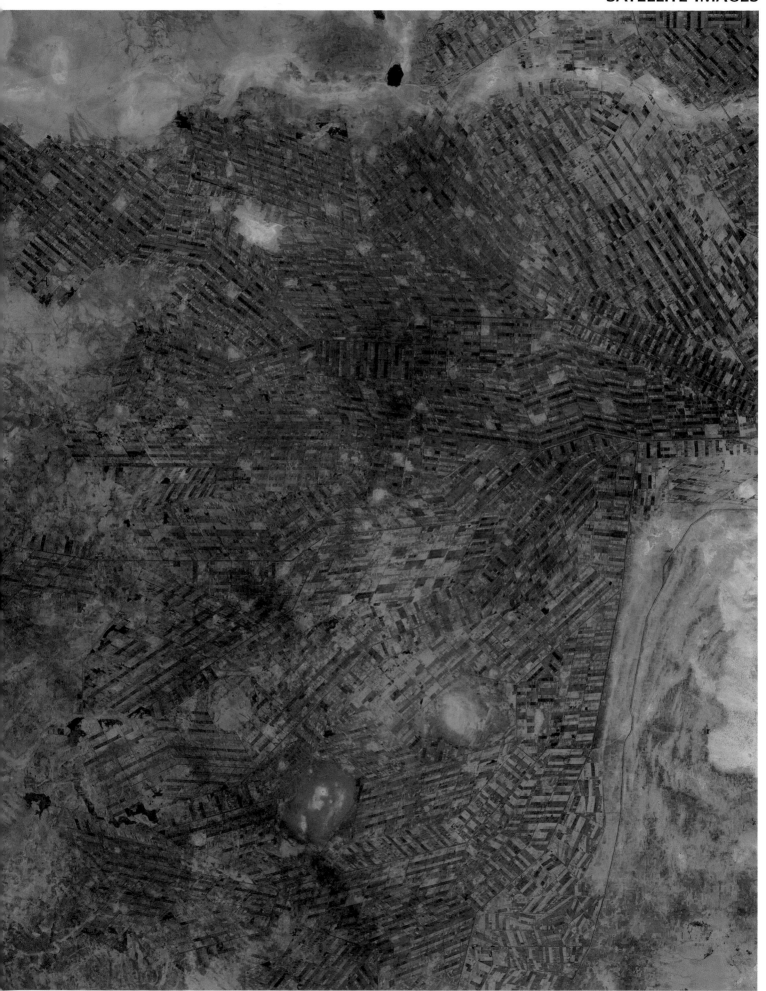

Gezira: *This landscape forms part of Gezira, meaning "island" in Arabic. It is the largest irrigated region in Africa, and spreads out between the White Nile and the Blue Nile, southeast of Khartoum.*

Sinai Peninsula and Nile Delta: *This satellite view from the north shows the Sinai Peninsula extending from the Mediterranean to the Red Sea, the Suez Canal, the Nile Delta, and the fertile green farmland close to the Nile.*

MAURITANIA

THE COUNTRY
....

Official name:
Islamic Republic of Mauritania

Geographic coordinates:
Northwestern Africa; between 14° 30' and 27° 30' north, and 4° 40' and 17° 30' west

Area:
*1,030,700 km²
(397,955 square miles)*

Capital:
Nouakchott

Climate:
*Desert climate; Nouakchott
26.5°C (79.7°F)/48 mm (1.9 in)*

Time zone:
Greenwich Mean Time +0 hours

The history of this desert nation on the eastern shores of the Atlantic Ocean is as old as trans-Sahara trade itself. Up until the 19th century, caravans traveled through the desert, stopping at oases and wandering in search of food for their animals. Today only a minority of the population lives as nomads.

Geography

Bordered by the Atlantic Ocean on its western side, Mauritania stretches out between the Western Sahara, which is still occupied by Morocco, and the Senegal River. It is bordered by Algeria to the northeast, Mali to the southeast, and Senegal to the south. Apart from a narrow coastal strip along the Atlantic and the right bank of the Senegal River, most of Mauritania consists of desert.

With the exception of a narrow strip of land in the south, the terrain is largely flat and includes the western part of the Sahara. Dominant features of the landscape are Erg Chech and al-Djouf—immense areas of dunes in the east—and the extensive sandstone plateaus of Adrar and Tagant.

Savannahs on the Senegal River

A hot, dry desert climate is characteristic of the inland and northern regions, where maximum summer temperatures can reach 50°C (112°F).

Variable air currents characterize the climate of the coastal strip: while moist air blows off the Atlantic Ocean to southern Mauritania during the summer, the dry northeast trade winds blow over the land in winter. Dry and

The Terjit oasis is situated in the Adrar region and is a popular destination for tourists

forest savannahs line the Senegal River. Summer rains, which average 300–400 mm (12–16 in), and the annual flooding of the Senegal allow baobabs, doum palms, tamarisks, and acacias to grow in the grassy savannah. This is the habitat of diverse wildlife, including elephants, warthogs, and several species of antelope.

Population

Although droughts have condemned many former nomadic cattle herders to a sedentary life on the edges of towns, a minority of Mauritania's population still lives as desert nomads. Apart from a few oases, Mauritanian territory north of the 18th parallel is virtually uninhabited. The population is concentrated in Nouakchott, the capital, and in the fertile region along the southern border.

Free and dependent peoples

About a third of the population consists of light-skinned Mauritanians, the 'white' Bidani, who constitute the country's upper, ruling class in this strict hierarchical society. Another third are Haratin. Although the dark-skinned Haratin are of black African origin, they consider themselves to be connected to the Berbers. Southern Mauritania is inhabited by peasants who belong to the Tukulor, Wolof, Soninke, Bambara, and Fulani peoples.

The contempt in which the black population is traditionally held by the Mauritanian upper class has caused repeated social tensions in the past, and has even led to persecution. Slavery was outlawed in the 1980s, but despite a law passed in 2007 which punishes slavery with prison, it has still not been truly eliminated. The state religion, Sunni Islam, is the only uniting factor between these different peoples. Mauritania is an Islamic country governed by Sharia law.

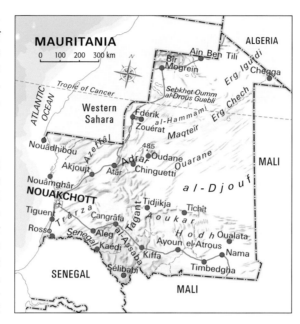

POPULATION

Number of inhabitants:
3.1 million

Population density:
3 inhabitants/km²
(8 inhabitants/square mile)

Population distribution:
41% urban
59% rural

Annual population growth:
2.5%

Life expectancy:
Women 66 years
Men 62 years

Religion:
Sunni Islam

Languages:
Arabic (official language),
French, Pulaar, Soninke,
Wolof

Literacy rate:
47%

Cattle market in Nouakchott, where Bedouins trade camels and other livestock. Camels are an integral part of Mauritania's rural subsistence economy.

HISTORY

From 7th century
Arabs settle in the country

1060–1147
The country is converted to Islam under the Almoravid dynasty of Morocco

1445
The Portuguese establish the first European base (Arguim)

16th–18th century
Arab emirate established

1903–1912
The country is conquered and occupied by France

1920
Mauritania becomes a colony within French West Africa

1960
Independence; M. Ould Daddah becomes the first president

1965
One-party system

1975–79
Occupation of the southern part of the former Spanish colony of West Sahara

1978–84
Mauritania ruled by a succession of military regimes

1989
Ethnic conflict between the Arabs and the Black Africans

1989–92
Conflict with Senegal

1991
A democratic constitution is accepted by plebiscite; Mauritania becomes an Islamic Republic (reformed in 2006)

2006
S. Ould Cheikh Abdallahi wins the first democratic presidential elections since independence

2008
Abdallahi deposed by the commander of the presidential guard, M. Ould Abdel Aziz

2009
Abdel Aziz elected president

History and Politics

Groups of Berbers have probably inhabited Mauritania since 10,000 BCE, joined by Arab cattle herders between the 7th and the 15th centuries CE. Mauritanian culture and language, Hassania, developed from the mingling of these two cultures. While northern Mauritania was virtually under Moroccan rule since the 12th century, southern Mauritania lay within the kingdom of Gana and Mali and afterwards within the Songhai Empire. Salt and the caravan trade were important sources of income for the country's nomadic people.

Colonialism and independence

From 1903 to 1910, the French, who the war-like Mauritanians resisted until 1936, occupied Mauritania. Initially part of French West Africa, Mauritania became an overseas territory in 1946, and an autonomous republic under French jurisdiction in 1958. On November 28, 1960, the country became independent, with Mokhtar Ould Daddah (1924–2003) as its first president. His term in office was marked by unrest between the Mauritanian and black African populations (1966), by the nationalization of the mining industry in 1973–74, and by Mauritania's takeover of the former Spanish Sahara.

One of the two mosques in the Mauritanian capital Nouakchott

POLITICS

Government:
Presidential republic

Head of state:
President

Legislature:
*National Assembly with
95 members and Senate with
56 elected members*

Administrative divisions:
12 regions and capital district

ECONOMY

Currency:
*1 Ouguiya (MRO)
= 5 khoums*

Gross domestic product:
$2.6 billion US

Gross per capita income:
$840 US

Overseas trade:
*Imports $1.5 billion US
Exports $1.4 billion US*

Foreign debt:
$2.4 billion US

Aid workers provide food in Nouakchott

Mokhtar Ould Daddah was overthrown by the military in 1978, and a period of political instability followed in which the constitution was abandoned. In 1979 Mauritania renounced its claim to the southern part of the Western Sahara after the local freedom movement Polisario Front led an armed resistance against Mauritania and blockaded the iron mines at Zouérat.

Colonel Maaouya Ould Sid Ahmed Taya (b. 1941) came to power in a bloodless coup in 1984 and ruled until August 2005, when he was removed by a military coup. After a period of transition presidential elections were held in 2006, and Sidi Ould Cheikh Abdallahi (b. 1938) came to power. In a military coup in August 2008 Abdallahi and the head of government, Yahya Ould Ahmed Waghf, were deposed. In 2009 Mohamed Ould Abdul Aziz was elected president.

Economy

Almost half of the population of Mauritania earns a living from agriculture. Virtually all are subsistence farmers living in the Senegal Valley in the south of the country, and small areas of the Sahel. Millet, rice, peanuts, and legumes are grown, although fields must be irrigated. Livestock farming raises sheep, goats, cattle, and camels and produces pelts, leather, and animals for export. An important part of Mauritania's exports by volume consist of fish and fish products.

A second important industry is mining, which is focused on deposits of iron ore at Zouérat, in a desert region in the north. Since 2006 Mauritania has been an oil-producing country.

*A small oasis settlement in the Sahara, where
the population often suffers from droughts*

THE COUNTRY

Official name:
Kingdom of Morocco

Geographic coordinates:
*North Africa; between 27° 40'
and 35° 56' north, and 1° and
13° 12' west*

Area:
*458,730 km2
(187,541 square miles)*

Capital:
Rabat

Climate:
*Warm Mediterranean climate the
north; steppe climate in the
south; cool climate with wet
winters in the mountains; Rabat
16.5°C (61.7°F)/728 mm (29 in);
Agadir 18.4°C (66.2°F)/195 mm
(7.7 in); Casablanca 16.8°C
(62.1°F)/463 mm (18 in);
Tangier 17°C (62.6°F)/1,176 mm
(46 in)*

Time zone:
Greenwich Mean Time +0 hours

*View of the High Atlas
mountains, with snow
on high ground.*

An Islamic general once called the conquered land in northwest Africa 'al-Maghreb al-Aqsa,' or 'the Extreme West' of the Islamic world. Perched atop the African continent, Morocco's landscape is defined by the Atlantic and Mediterranean coasts, the Atlas mountains—which according to Greek myth take their name from the Titan Atlas, on whose shoulders the whole world rested—and the beginnings of the vast Sahara. This great diversity makes Morocco one of the most popular destinations for tourists from all over the world.

Geography

Morocco is situated on the extreme northwest corner of the African continent, and is divided from the European mainland by the narrow Strait of Gibraltar. Geographically, the country is composed of the coastal plains bordering the Atlantic Ocean and the Mediterranean Sea; the Moroccan Meseta; the mountainous regions of the High, Middle, and Anti-Atlas; the eastern highland; and the desert region of the Sahara in the south and southeast.

The African Trench, which runs between the Anti-Atlas and the High Atlas and along the southeast border of the latter, marks the limit of the African continental base. It can be seen in the steep drop of the Southern Atlas mountain crests to the table and plateau lands that begin at the mountain base. These are geologically a part of the African continental base.

Coasts and the Moroccan Meseta

The northernmost part of Morocco is characterized by the jagged Rif mountains, which geologically form part of the Atlas mountains. They run parallel to the Mediterranean coast for over 400 km (248 miles), and have an average height of 1,500 m (4,920 ft). The highest mountain is Mount Tidirhine at 2,456 m (8,058 ft).

The coastal region is characterized by cork oaks, Atlas cedars, and Aleppo pines, while olives and cereals are cultivated on terraced fields. Whereas the steep Mediterranean coastline is broken up by many deep bays, the flat Atlantic coast is shaped by stretches of sandy beaches, and is rarely broken up by a bay or an inlet.

The Moroccan Meseta, a 200-km (124-mile) tableland, is bordered by the Rif mountains, the Atlas, and the Atlantic. It drops stepwise to the Atlantic coastal plain, which has quite high levels of precipitation. The 600 to 1,000 m (1,970–3,280 ft) high Meseta forms the heart-

land of Morocco, and is where the legendary royal cities of Fès, Meknès, and Marrakech were founded. Today cereals, fruit, citrus fruits, and olives are cultivated in this region.

The barren, stepped high plateau of the east Moroccan Meseta begins east of the Moulouya River and gradually gives way to the Algerian highland of the shotts (salt flats). Alfalfa grass and artemisia grasslands are typical of the eastern Meseta and the high plains in the Middle Atlas.

Atlas mountains—backbone of Morocco

Together with its subsidiary ranges, the 700-km (430-mile)-long High Atlas mountain chain forms a mountain barrier running from the southwest to the northeast of the country, parallel to the Atlantic, and continues into the Algerian Tell Atlas and Sahara Atlas. The High Atlas, in which the year-round rivers of Tensift and Sous originate, are the youngest and mightiest mountains of North Africa, with average heights of around 2,000 m (6,560 ft). Their highest mountain, Mount Toubkal (4,167 m/ 13,665 ft), is also the highest mountain in Morocco. Draining from the southeast into the Sahara, the Ziz, Todra, and Dades rivers have cut out impressive deep canyons in their course through the mountains.

In the northwest, the Middle Atlas connects with the High Atlas. In their western and middle sections they reach an average height of 1,800 to 2,000 m (5,900 to 6,560 ft): the highest point is Bou Naceur mountain (3,340 m/ 10,955 ft). The Middle Atlas is the source of the rivers Sebou, Oum er-Rbia, and Guelmine, which flow all the year round.

Another prominent range is the Anti-Atlas (up to 2,531 m/8,304 ft), which can be found in the southwest between Ouarzazate and Guelmine. With its 2,000 m (6,562 ft) high plateaus, it forms a transitional zone to the Sahara. Because it is part of the African land mass, it is older than the other mountain ranges of the Atlas, and features typical highland characteristics.

In the mountain regions, the vegetation changes according to elevation. Between 900 and 1,800 m (2,950 and 5,905 ft), false cypresses and juniper dominate. Ilex can be found in the Rif mountains up to 1,400 m (4,590 ft), in the Middle Atlas between 1,200 and 2,000 m (3,940–6,560 ft), and in the High Atlas between 1,300 and 2,800 m (4,265–9,185 ft). Beyond the deciduous tree line Moroccan fir grows along with cedar, which is particularly associated with the area around Azrou. The upper tree line of the High Atlas is marked by frankincense trees (Spanish juniper).

Many of the surfaces bared by slash-and-burn, defoliation, and pasture farming have already grown secondary vegetation (maquis), typically strawberry trees (arbutus) and juniper. Fast-growing pines and eucalyptus trees have been planted as part of a reforestation program.

The northwest edge of the Sahara

In the southeast of the Atlas Mountains, wide plateaus and plains form the transition to the Sahara. Along the Atlantic, a coastal desert runs up to the foothills of the Anti-Atlas.

Nowhere else in North Africa does such a spectacular change in landscape take place in such a short distance as in the southern tip of the Atlas mountains. Within a very short space, the high mountains, which are snow-capped in winter, give way to a semi-desert plain with scattered oases. Wide plateaus and tablelands, covered by boulders and gravel deserts, are characteristic of the Moroccan Sahara, and are displaced only by dunes up to 170 m (557 ft) high in a few areas, such as Erg Chebbi. Some of the rivers emerging from the Atlas, such as the Ziz and Draa, have cut deep canyons into the plateau landscape.

The lack of water in the Saharan part of Morocco restricts agricultural use to the oases along the foot of the mountains and the river valleys. Valley oases, in which date palms, pomegranate, and fig trees grow, can be found in the valleys of the Ziz, Dades, and Draa. Some one million date palms grow in the oasis valley of Tafilalt.

Climatic contrasts

The Atlas Mountains form a striking climatic division between wet northern Morocco and dry

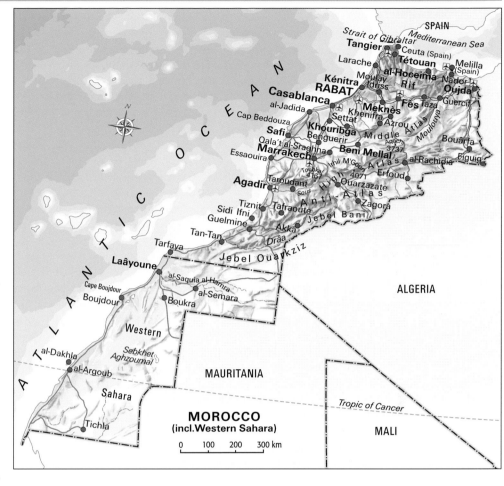

southern Morocco. A Mediterranean climate with cool, rainy winters (300–600 mm/12–24 in) and warm, dry summers prevails on the Mediterranean coast and in the northern interior of the country. The Canary Current along the Atlantic coast brings moist Atlantic air. Precipitation decreases from north to south and southeast. Abundant precipitation (600–1,200 mm/24–47 in) falls in winter on the north coast and in the mountains, and snow even falls in the high

mountains, turning the region into an exotic winter sports location. The snow, which can remain for four to five months, provides the water for the dry areas of the country in the hot summer months. The temperatures in the high mountains can drop to -20°C (-4°F).

From the north-central Meseta the rainfall decreases from 400 to 600 mm (16–24 in) to 300 to 400 mm (12–16 in) in the area around Marrakech. A dry climate with extreme temperature variations between day and night prevails in the southeast and south. Precipitation here reaches a maximum of 200 mm (8 in).

Resting point for migratory birds

The transition from Europe to Africa is also evident in the wildlife although familiar European mammals, such as red foxes, hares, and wild boar, live in Morocco. African fauna such as fennecs, gazelles, baboons, and horned vipers are also found here. Morocco is a stopping point of migratory birds heading for West Africa.

The Ait Benhaddou ksar - a typical Berber fortified adobe settlement. Ait Benhaddou was declared a UNESCO world cultural heritage site in 1987.

POPULATION

Number of inhabitants:
31.6 million

Population density:
69 inhabitants/km²
(168 inhabitants/square mile)

Population distribution:
60% urban
40% rural

Annual population growth:
1.2%

Life expectancy:
Women 73 years
Men 69 years

Religions:
Sunni Islam, Christianity, Judaism

Languages:
Arabic (official language), French, Berber languages

Literacy rate:
62%

Population

The Moroccan population has always identified itself with both the Islamic and European worlds simultaneously. Numerous cultures have left their marks on the country; in the cities, elegant, Western-style saleswomen meet veiled Arab women, and both traditional wares and modern high-tech products are offered in the historic oriental souks. Of all the Maghreb nations, Morocco is the most liberal country in terms of both its culture and religion.

The population of Morocco is primarily made up of Arabs, Berbers, and Arabized Berbers. There are, however, small minorities of Europeans (predominantly French and Spanish), Jews, and the descendants of West African slaves.

Morocco's population is relatively young and very unevenly distributed throughout the country. It is estimated that approximately 75 percent of all Moroccans live along the fertile coastal stretches of the northwest, which account for only around 10 percent of the country's total land area. About one-fifth of the population lives in the two large cities of Casablanca and Rabat alone, which are situated only about 100 km (62 miles) apart. The increasing poverty in rural areas, and the hope of work and better lives in the cities attract ever more people, especially the young, to the metropolises. There, many live in slums because of the poor living conditions and the high population growth.

The Berbers, on the other hand, live in the sparsely populated parts of the country, in particular in the mountain regions of the Atlas. The Haratins, descendants of the slaves taken out of West Africa in the 17th and 18th centuries, are concentrated in the oases scattered along the edge of the Sahara.

The Berber people

When Phoenician seafarers and traders settled the area of present-day Morocco in around 1000 BCE, they encountered the ancestors of today's Berbers, who called themselves *Imazighen* ('free, noble people'). It was then the custom for all who were not Greek or Roman to be called barbarians, or 'Berbers,' by the Romans. Arabs later restricted this title to the people living in the northwest of Africa.

Because they have no ethnic uniformity, the Berbers are merely identified as an ethnic group based on their language, which, though unified and fairly cohesive, is split into many dialects.

Among the most important Berber groups in Morocco are the Shluh and the Rif-Kabyle. The Shluh number some three million people and live primarily in the Atlas mountains and in the oases situated at the base of the mountains. The second group, the Rif-Kabyle, is settled mainly in the middle and eastern part of the Rif Mountains.

As a result of their relative geographical isolation, the Berbers have largely managed to preserve their language and culture despite centuries of Arabization and Islamization. As a minority, the Berbers, who always had their own states throughout their long history, today have

Group of Berber children

lies at around 62 percent today, though it is still considerably lower in the rural areas. Although a large number of children have a high level of schooling, there is, as with literacy levels, a big educational gap between the urban and rural populations.

Islam as the national religion

Almost the entire population is Sunni Muslim. The king, who is also the spiritual leader of his subjects, is greatly respected by the population. Along with the Muslim majority, there are also Christians, Jews, and adherents of various other sects and religions.

For the Berbers, the Islamic faith is interwoven with more strongly mystical elements. For example, Sufism, a mystical branch of Islam, is held in high esteem by the Berber people, and religious festivals and pilgrimages to the grave sites of famous Sufis are important holidays of the year.

Belief in spirits, the 'evil eye,' and black magic shape everyday religion, and amulets, fortune-telling, and magical mediums are widespread. Although these elements are sharply criticized by orthodox Sunnis and custodians of the faith, they are nevertheless tolerated.

The souk in Essaouira

Berber woman

no political influence in either Morocco or its neighboring nations. Berber women, who appear unveiled in public, have always had many economic and social rights and freedoms within their own society.

The Berbers typically live in big families in a fortified adobe settlement called a *ksar*, which can hold from between 20 to 100 families, and which often has a capacious loft storage space. The *kasbahs*, the castle-like seats of the tribal leaders, are also particularly impressive and worth seeing. Colorful woven carpets with simple geometric patterns are a characteristic feature of Berber craftwork, and can be found in Morocco's many souks. Although some income is derived from tourism, the Berbers primarily earn their living from farming and cattle-raising.

Arabs and Arabized Berbers

The history of the Arab population goes back to the descendants of the Arab conquerors who arrived in the region at the end of the 7th century CE, and who spread their Islamic beliefs throughout North Africa. Indeed, many Berbers

adopted the new religion though they continued to cultivate their own traditions and rites in the privacy of their own homelands. Along with the Arabization of the country came the adoption of rules for daily life stemming from the Qur'an, affecting aspects such as the place of a woman in society and the adoption of Arabic script.

Berbers who migrated to the cities are today considered 'Arabized.' Arabs and Arabized Berbers make up about 60 to 70 percent of the Moroccan population, and have mainly settled in the fertile coastal plains and river valleys.

On the way to a modern educational system

The official and most used language is Arabic. French is used as a second language, and is quite widespread throughout the country, although the various Berber dialects still dominate everyday life in certain areas of the Atlas mountains as well as the south.

Since gaining independence in 1956, the country has made a concerted effort to develop a modern educational system. The literacy rate

HISTORY

c. 2000 BCE
Berbers settle in North Africa

1100–146 BCE
Phoenician and Carthaginian trading posts

From 42 CE
Part of the Roman Empire

429–477
Vandals invade

533–682
Part of the Byzantine Empire

From 683
Arab-Islamic influence spreads

740–788
Berber uprisings

788
Idris I founds the Kingdom of Morocco

1061–1147
Almoravid rule

1147–1269
Almohad rule

1269–1420
Merinid rule

1465–1554
Wattasid rule

1554–1659
Sadite rule

Since 1666
Morocco ruled by the Hassanids

From 1830
France influence in North Africa grows

1843/44
Morocco defeated in war against France

1912
Divided into a French and a Spanish protectorate

1921–26
The Rif-Kabyle Revolution

1953
France sends the sultan Muhammad V into exile; the leader of the Independence Party is imprisoned. The 'National Freedom Army' is founded

1955
France reinstates the sultan

1956
Morocco becomes independent

1957
Muhammad V takes on the title of king and proclaims the kingdom

1961
After the death of Muhammad V, his son, Hassan II, becomes king

History and Politics

After a history of great change and upheaval, Morocco is today a liberal, Islamic kingdom on its way to a modern, progressive future. From early on Morocco was ruled by numerous Berber and Arab dynasties. From the 17th century its present-day rulers, the Hassanids, came to power. The country's ruler, King Muhammad VI has instituted comprehensive reforms, including changes in family law, and is pursuing closer ties to the European Union. The war against international terrorism and continuing social injustices, however, present a number of political challenges for Morocco in the 21st century.

The first Berber tribes settled in the area of present-day Morocco in around 2000 BCE. The Phoenicians followed after them, from around 1100 BCE, and established trade settlements along the coast. The region came under direct Roman rule from the 1st century as the province of Mauretania Tingitana, and the capital became Tingis, today's Tangier. In the 5th century the region came under Vandal rule, and in the 6th century it was conquered by the Byzantines.

Islamic ruling dynasties

The Arabs who invaded North Africa in the 7th century occupied a wide section of present-day Morocco by 710, and had begun the Islamization and Arabization of the population. In 789, the Arab Idris I (d. 791) founded the Idrisid dynasty and ruled the first unified country from Fès. Individual Berber tribes continually resisted the rule of the Arabs in the following centuries, but in 1061 the Almoravid dynasty took over, ruling from Marrakech until 1147. The Almohads (1147–1269) followed, and during their rule of over a hundred years, they established a kingdom extending from Libya and across Morocco to Spain. With the conquest of Marrakech, the Merinids took over from the Almohads in 1269. Following them to the throne were the Wattasids (in 1420), and the Saadians (from 1554).

Finally, the present ruling dynasty, the Arab Hassanids (also called the Alawites), came to power. They were devout Muslims, whose leader was considered to be a descendant of the Prophet.

Morocco comes between European interests

From the 15th century Morocco increasingly found itself under the gaze of European powers since the region was of great strategic importance due to its location on the Strait of Gibraltar. The Portuguese (from 1415), Spanish (Melilla in 1496, Ceuta in 1580), and later the British (in the 17th century) staked claims to the coast. In 1505 the Portuguese founded Agadir, and took over control of all Moroccan ports on the Atlantic. However, in 1684, the expulsion of the British from Tangier marked the start of the emancipation of the cities on the Atlantic and Mediterranean coasts.

Trade relationships with Europe, in particular with France, remained very lucrative. The industrialized nations of Europe were interested in the country as a source of raw materials. Accordingly, during the mid-19th century Morocco established trade agreements with a number of nations.

The Hassan Tower in Rabat is the minaret of an incomplete mosque built in the late twelfth century.

In 1844, with the flight of Berber chieftain Abd al-Kader (1808–83) from Algeria to Morocco, the country was drawn into warlike disputes with the French and later the Spanish.

Morocco remained a bone of contention until France and Spain agreed to its division at the beginning of the 20th century. A German claim led to what became known as the first Moroccan crisis. Emperor Wilhelm II (1859–1941) visited Tangier in 1905 in order to promote and safeguard German interests, and there pleaded for the sovereignty of Morocco—which, of course, was against the interests of Germany's European rivals. Nonetheless the country was placed under French and Spanish control in the Conference of Algeciras in 1906.

Another encroachment by French troops led to the second Moroccan crisis in 1911, and to the dispatch of the German warship *Panther* to the Moroccan port of Agadir. In the end, however, Germany recognized the French protectorate. At the same time as the commencement of the French protectorate in 1912, Spain received the Mediterranean coast with the Rif mountains as a colony.

Struggle for independence

During the period of the French protectorate strong protests by Berbers, especially the Rif-Kabyle, were continually made against the rule of the colonial powers of France and Spain. However attempts by the Berber leader Emir Abd al-Krim (c.1880–1963) to win autonomous government for the Rif-Kabyle by way of a revolution that began in 1921 was met by 250,000 armed French and Spanish forces. In 1926 the north of the country returned to peace, and the south followed in 1934.

In the following years an opposition movement demanding independence emerged, especially in workers' circles and among intellectuals. It had the support of Sultan Muhammad V (1909–61) and the majority of the Arab population. The French rejected the plea by the sultan for self-government, and he was forced into exile in 1953. Revolts and revolutions continued to beset the country until France finally renounced its colonial claims

The Berber leader of the Rif-Kabyle Revolution Abd el-Krim (1882-1963).

and allowed the sultan to return in 1955, leading Morocco to independence. With the proclamation of the Kingdom of Morocco on August 14, 1957, Muhammad V took on the title of king.

Under Hassan II and Muhammad VI

Hassan II (1929–99) followed his father to the throne in 1961. Although the country's first general elections were held in 1963, he dissolved parliament in 1965, and took over executive and legislative powers. Coup attempts in 1971 and 1972 failed. A poor supply of provisions and high food costs led to protests and unrest during the 1970s, and again in the 1990s.

Muhammad VI (b. 1963) succeeded his father to the throne in 1999. His intentions for reform promoted the hope of more liberal and social policies, especially with regard to women and family law. One of the biggest challenges for the king today is the Islamists, who vehemently resist plans for any kind of reform, and advocate a return to strict Islamic values. The series of terrorist bomb attacks in Casablanca in 2003 and 2007 sent a warning signal to the government.

HISTORY

1965
Hassan II dissolves parliament and suspends the constitution

1972
A military coup fails; Morocco becomes a parliamentary monarchy

1975
Spain surrenders the Western Sahara region to Morocco and Mauritania

1978
After Mauritania renounces its rights to the Western Sahara, Morocco occupies the region

1996
A bicameral parliamentary system is instituted

1999
The death of Hassan II; his son, Muhammad VI, is his successor

2004
A new family law improves the equal treatment of women

2008
The anti-terror movement against Islamic fundamentalists is extended

POLITICS

Government:
Constitutional monarchy

Head of state:
King

Legislature:
National Assembly with 325 members and a Senate with 270 members

Administrative divisions:
16 regions

The Djemaa al-Fna, Morocco's largest traditional market, located on the main square in Marrakech, is frequented by locals and tourists alike.

ECONOMY

Currency:
*1 Moroccan dirham (MHD)
= 100 santimat*

Gross domestic product:
$86.4 billion US

Gross per capita income:
$2,290 US

Overseas trade:
*Imports $39.2 billion US
Exports $20.5 billion US*

Foreign debt:
$20.4 billion US

Economy, Traffic, and Communication

The economy of Morocco is in many ways tied to that of Europe and, because of the Mediterranean Agreement, will be integrated still further into the European Economic Area (EEA) after 2012. The Moroccan government follows a policy of industrialization and diversification, with an emphasis on tourism. However, despite the structural change from an agrarian to an industrial and service-based economy, a large section of the population still lives in poverty.

The Kingdom of Morocco is regarded as one of the so-called emerging countries. Morocco receives its much-needed foreign currency mostly from Moroccans abroad, through tourism, and from the export of phosphate, fish products, and light industrial products. Among its most important economic partners are the members of the European Union (EU). Of the total working population, 40 percent work in the agrarian sector, 20 percent in industry and craftwork, and 36 percent in trade and the

The country is heavily dependent on food imports because only a fraction of the arable land, which is primarily in private ownership, is actually used for the growing of crops. Cultivation is concentrated on the coastal plains and the basins of Marrakech and Fès. The small farming enterprises use traditional methods, with little mechanization, and can scarcely produce enough for their own needs let alone a surplus. Among the main crops are wheat, barley, and other grain types, as well as potatoes, pulses, and tomatoes. Beyond that, vegetables, sugar cane, olives, dates, almonds, tobacco, wine, cotton, and citrus fruits are also cultivated, especially for export. The intention is to improve harvests by expanding the irrigated areas. In the Rif mountains there is a long tradition of illegal marijuana cultivation, which is a highly profitable business.

Cattle-rearing, which is still partly nomadic, is concentrated on the plains of the Meseta, in eastern Morocco, and within the Atlas mountains. Along with sheep, the

Phosphate-processing in Safi

service industries. Morocco's coastal regions form the industrial base and are the focus of the development efforts of the country.

Good harvests dependent on the weather

Some years, such as 2006 and 2008, have resulted in very good harvests. In years when rainfall is low, however, crops are poor. The agricultural sector is thus an unreliable economic factor. Environmentally, Morocco has many problems with which to contend: soil erosion, overfishing, as well as soil and water pollution, all have a severe impact on agricultural output.

farmers also keep goats, cattle, and chickens. Morocco's position on the Atlantic also ensures that coastal and deep-sea fishing (sardines) forms an important part of the country's economy and food production.

Because of depletion over the past century, only 10 percent of the country is still covered with forest, one-tenth of which is cork oak, another export product of the country. Morocco is today among the largest cork producers in the world. The tree population is mainly composed of cork oak, false cypress and ironwood trees, and national forestation programs have put a stop to the deforestation.

Mining and industry

Morocco is blessed with a wealth of mineral resources. Along with salt, lead, zinc, tin, antimony, uranium, oil, coal, and numerous other minerals, there are also significant phosphate deposits. The phosphate deposits in Khouribga, Youssoufia, Benguerir, and Boukra (Western Sahara) are the largest on earth. Phosphate and its processed products (phosphorus and fertilizer) are primarily exported to two main countries, the USA and France. The development and mining of the country's mineral reserves are largely supported and financed by foreign enterprises from industrialized countries.

Over one-fifth of the working population is involved in the commercial sector, the most important branches of which are the basic food and luxury foodstuff industries, the chemical industry, the phosphate- and oil-processing industries, as well as the textile, clothing, and leather goods industries. The largest industrial center is in Casablanca, but there are also important centers in Rabat, Safi, Fès, and Marrakech. Information technology companies as well as automobile manufacturers and the aviation and space industries have established bases here.

A woman selling goods in the market in Larache

A tannery in Fès using traditional methods of processing skins

Morocco is struggling to generate enough power to cover its energy consumption which is constantly growing. Morocco, which is importing almost all of its energy, plans to diversify its energy sources in order to gain more independence. Hydroelectric plants in the Atlas mountains as well as solar energy are to play a major role in the country's energy supply in the future.

Tourism

Tourism is a huge economic sector. It provides about 600,000 jobs, and is one of the biggest sources of foreign currency. About 7.4 million tourists visited Morocco in 2007, ensuring brisk sales of traditional craftwork, handwoven Berber rugs, and silver jewelry. The main focus of development lies on the Atlantic beaches and in the royal cities of Fès, Marrakech, Meknès, and Rabat.

A good transport system ready for upgrading

While the road network is the most important transportation network for personal travel, the transportation of goods by train is also especially well-developed. Three railroad tracks traverse the country. The first runs from Casablanca, through Rabat, Fès, and Meknès, and up to the Algerian border; the second from Casablanca to Tangier; and the third from Casablanca to Marrakech. In addition, two large bus corporations provide a network that almost covers the entire country. There are numerous ferries between Spain and Morocco, and with Casablanca, the most important traffic crossroads, Morocco has one of the largest trade ports in Africa. There are a dozen international airports; Casablanca is the largest.

With support from the European Union (EU), there has been substantial investment in infrastructure improvements. Over 60 percent of the roads are made up, 1000 km (625 miles) to more or less motorway standard. Attempts are being made to improve the railroad network, and to modernize the ports, airports, and telecommunication capabilities. There are even plans for a tunnel under the Strait of Gibraltar to link Morocco with Spain.

Competition in the information sector

In the big cities, large sums are being invested in the infrastructure of modern information technology. Privatization has led to competition. Apart from national radio and television (RTM) channels, there are various private stations. Daily newspapers and weekly news magazines are published in Casablanca and Rabat. The Arabic daily *Al Ahdat Maghribya* has the widest circulation. *Le Matin du Sahara* is the main French newspaper. Officially there is press freedom, but the media remain under state control and topics such as monarchy, religion and West Sahara are subject to censorship.

ALGERIA

THE COUNTRY

Official name:
*People's Democratic Republic
of Algeria*

Geographic coordinates:
*North Africa; between 19°
and 37° north, and 8° 30' west
and 12° east*

Area:
*2,381,741 km²
(919,595 square miles)*

Capital:
Algiers

Climate:
*Warm Mediterranean climate
with dry summers on the coast,
steppe climate in the Atlas, hot
desert climate south of the Atlas;
Algiers 21.6°C (71°F)/691 mm
(27 in); Tamanrasset 27.2°C
(81°F)/32 mm (1.3 in)*

Time zone:
Greenwich Mean Time +1 hour

Like a great natural barrier between the coast and the interior, the high backbone of the Atlas mountains protects the country's fertile northern region. On the northern slopes of the Tell Atlas grape vines flourish; the foothills of the Saharan Atlas peter out among the sand and rocks of the Sahara, the world's largest desert. The mountain range serves as both dividing line and transition between the Mediterranean region and the Algerian Sahara.

Geography

Algeria's territory consists of several geographical zones. The Tell Atlas and Saharan Atlas run parallel to the Mediterranean coast. In between the peaks lie wide, high plateaus. On its southern side, the Saharan Atlas drops steeply down to the Sahara Desert, which stretches out to the south. Most of the country's oases, such as Ghardaïa, Ouargla, and al-Goléa, are located in the northern Algerian Sahara. In the southeast rise the Hoggar and Tassili n'Ajjer mountains: because some rain falls here, these mountains are a less hostile environment than the surrounding bare, dusty desert.

From the Pirate Coast to the Saharan Atlas

For almost its entire length the foothills of the Tell Atlas run along the coast, right down to the sea, and the coastline is indented by many bays and inlets, which once provided shelter for buccaneers. Most of Algeria's coastal plains, such as those of Oran, Metidja (where Algiers is situated), and Annaba, are densely populated.

The Tell Atlas consists of three ranges which lie in an east-to-west chain with peaks over 2,000 m (6,562 ft) high. Between the first and second ranges lies the long valley of the Chlef, Algeria's major river. Rising south of Algiers, it flows northward then westward to empty into the Mediterranean at Mostaghanem.

*Natural sandstone
rock arch in Tassili
n'Ajjer National Park*

*The Great Eastern Erg, one of the
two large areas with sand dunes
in the Algerian Sahara*

Berber enclaves:
Greater and Lesser Kabylia

Two regions of the Tell Atlas have a special cultural and geographical significance. They are the Greater and Lesser Kabylia, which are inhabited mostly by Berbers, or Kabyle. Greater Kabylia is a fertile, densely populated region on the slopes of Djebel Djurdjura, which rises to 2,308 m (7,570 ft) southeast of the capital Algiers. Lesser Kabylia, between Sétif and Constantine, further east, is little used for agriculture, but has extensive cork oak and holm oak forests.

Salt lakes and desert mountains

To the south, the Tell Atlas descends to a high plateau dotted with *shotts*, or shallow temporary salt lakes. Here several seasonal rivers flow down from the Atlas into large, flat closed drainage basins. In summer the water evaporates, and this creates salt pans known as *shotts*. This high plateau ranges from 1,000 m (3,281 ft) in the west to 400 m (1,312 ft) in the east. Because rainfall on the plateau is markedly lower than in the coastal region, vegetation here is much sparser, and is limited to scrub and esparto grass.

The southernmost barrier between the coastal region and the Sahara is the Saharan Atlas, which runs from west to northeast, and which consists of several massifs. One is the majestic Massif de l'Aurès, which reaches 2,328 m (7,637 ft) and which is cut by deep gorges on its eastern side. The mountains are covered by high-altitude steppe, with cedar forests on the north side.

The Sahara

About three-quarters of Algeria's territory is covered by the Sahara. Beginning south of the Saharan Atlas, this great desert is punctuated by table mountains and rocky plains, high plateaus and low salt pans, oases where palm trees grow, and volcanic mountains, all of which give the desert landscape its stunning beauty.

The Great Western Erg and Great Eastern Erg, two large areas of sand dunes, conform to the classic image of a great sandy desert. Otherwise, wide areas of the Algerian Sahara consist of stony desert *(hammada)*, rocky desert *(reg)*, and dusty desert *(serir)*. The Great Eastern Erg, with pale golden sand, stretches out between the oases of El Oued and Ouargla in the north and the Tassili n'Ajjer mountains in the south. The northern part is known as the Souf, meaning 'the river' in Berber. Here, an underground river does indeed run from south to north, and is sufficiently near the surface to be tapped: the inhabitants of the Souf extract water from deep holes dug in the sand, and use it to irrigate their date palms.

Oasis on an ancient trade route

The sandy basins and the Great Western Erg and Great Eastern Erg are dotted with oases, which are strung out along dry river valleys. Tohat, between Reggane and Timimoun in western Algeria, is an oasis of legendary importance: one of the two most important caravan routes between sub-Saharan Africa and the Mediterranean passed through here. After journeying on the long, waterless route through the Tanezrouft Desert, the 'Land of Fear,' Tohat with its palm groves appeared to travelers like a promise of life, of water, even of paradise.

Bizarre desert mountains

The Hoggar and Tassili n'Ajjer mountains are two regions of magical, other-worldly beauty. Volcanic action created the blackish-red rock formations here, and erosion over millions of years gave them the bizarre forms that they have today. In the central Sahara, the Hoggar Mountains culminate in Tahat, a peak that reaches 3,003 m (9,850 ft). In the valleys rivulets merge to create small lakes *(gueltas)* around which tamarisks and palms grow, and which are also a source of water for wildlife and the herds of the Tuareg. The Tassili n'Ajjer, which are rocky, deeply cleft, and sparsely covered, are inhabited by Tuareg tribes.

Winter rain and sandstorms

Algeria's topography gives the country two distinct and sharply divided climate zones. The northern region has a Mediterranean climate, with long, hot summers and mild, wet winters. In the Tell Atlas rainfall can reach 1,000 mm (39 in). On the high plateau between the Tell Atlas and Saharan Atlas, where shotts form, the climate is drier and more continental. Rainfall here ranges from a maximum of 350 mm (14 in) to less than 100 mm (4 in) at the edge of the desert. In the desert itself, rain falls only occasionally; several years of light rainfall may be interspersed with short periods of torrential rain, when wadis are rapidly transformed into streams. Great variations between day and night temperatures are typical of a harsh desert climate. While daytime temperatures can exceed 40°C (104°F) in summer, in winter they average a constant 25°C (77°F), but can descend to below freezing at night. Snow sometimes even falls on the highest peaks of the Saharan Atlas.

Mediterranean abundance, bare desert

Oleander, pine, cork oak, holm oak, and olive trees, all of which are typical of a Mediterranean country, characterize Algeria's northern region. Wheat, figs, pomegranates, and vines are also cultivated in partially irrigated areas there.

South of the Saharan Atlas, vegetation is sparse and is confined to oases and the course of wadis, and the foothills of the mountains.

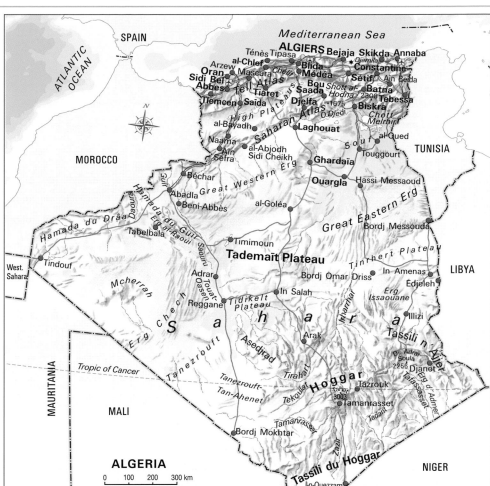

POPULATION

Number of inhabitants:
35 million

Population density:
15 inhabitants/km²
(38 inhabitants/square mile)

Population distribution:
65% urban
35% rural

Annual population growth:
1.5%

Life expectancy:
Women 75 years
Men 72 years

Religion:
Sunni Islam

Languages:
Arabic (official language),
Tamazight, French

Literacy rate:
74%

A Tuareg camel herder in the Algerian Sahara

Population

Almost 95 percent of Algerians inhabit the Mediterranean coastal region and fertile north of the country. Apart from its oases, the Sahara is uninhabited. Algeria's contrasting landscapes, its varied topography, and its unique nature are reflected in the character of its inhabitants. Algeria is, however, both a country of modern, progressive towns and cities with a Western-influenced culture, and the homeland of people who are deeply rooted in ancient customs and traditions.

Algeria has a population of about 35 million, almost 95 percent of whom live in the north of the country and occupy only one-fifth of the land area. For almost all young Algerians who come from the mountain and desert areas, the large towns and cities along the coast are a kind of 'Promised Land' that seem to offer opportunities for education and work, a better standard of living, and a modern way of life. For most of them, however, these hopes will remain unfulfilled.

Youth without hope

With its high birth rate, Algeria has long been the most heavily populated country in the Maghreb. The result of the rapid population growth is a broad-based social pyramid. Almost 30% of Algerians are under 15. This has caused a range of social problems, as the country's political and economic systems cannot accommodate the large volume of young people seeking work. Facing poverty, despair, and dim prospects, many young Algerians have found consolation, security, and hope in Islamic ideology. Conflict between the government and a growing Islamic opposition dominated Algeria's internal politics in the 1990s, and profoundly challenged the country's domestic stability.

Religious conflict

Since Algeria declared independence in 1962, Sunni Islam has been the national religion, although small Christian and Jewish minorities are also present. In the 1980s, despite cooperation between religious and political leaders, radical and militant Islamic doctrine still attracted a large following. This finally resulted in Islamic groups fighting embittered guerrilla wars against Algeria's military regime, which officially ended in 2000. The conflict between moderate and radical Muslims is still unresolved and is fuelled today by Algeria's explosive social and economic situation.

Language and culture of the Berbers

In the 7th century, when groups of Arabs began to move into North Africa, the Berbers who already lived there were driven into marginal, mostly mountainous regions. In Algeria, these regions were the desert-like Hoggar and Tassili mountains, where the Tuareg, who are descendants of the Berbers, still live, and the Greater and Lesser Kabylia, in northern Algeria. The great majority of present-day Algerians are of Arab or Arab-Berber descent: only one-sixth are of pure Berber ancestry.

architecture of their five walled cities inspired the great French architect Le Corbusier (1887–1965), and is among Algeria's greatest tourist attractions today.

The Blue Men, a proud people

Much better known than the M'zabit are the Tuareg. Historically, as camel-breeding nomads and desert warriors, the Tuareg were feared across the entire Sahara. Today, mere shadows of their glorious ancestors, they mostly lead a poor existence as goat and camel herders on the edge of the large oasis towns of Djanet and Tamanrasset. Some Tuareg men have, however, found a new way of life by working in Saharan tourism as guides and drivers.

The distinctive clothing of the Tuareg consists of an indigo tunic, which explains why they are known as the Blue Men, and a large turban with which the men cover their heads and faces: this makes them a popular subject of photographs. Tuareg women do not cover their faces in public, and have almost equal rights with men. The Tuareg are the only Berber people to have developed their own script, Tifinagh.

The old town of Algeria's capital Algiers

In Algeria, the language and culture of the Berbers have long been officially repressed. After independence the goal was to unite the country as an Arab nation, and Arabic was declared the official language. The sometimes violent protests and unrest in the Berber regions culminated in a full-scale rebellion in 2001: in 2002 President Bouteflika (b. 1937) resolved this conflict and recognized Tamazight as a national language.

Strict beliefs of the M'zabits

Algeria's Berber population includes two groups who have developed their own distinctive traditions and ways of life: These groups are the M'zabit and the Tuareg.

The M'zabit inhabit the M'zab group of oases, where the principal town is Ghardaïa. They live strictly according to Islamic law, and reject any form of entertainment and pleasure. Expelled by Sunni rulers, the M'zabit found refuge in the rugged desert plateau around Wadi M'zab. The

Tuareg nomads wearing traditional dress

HISTORY

9th century BCE
The region stands under the suzerainty of Carthage

146 BCE
Algeria becomes part of the Roman province of Africa Nova

430 CE
Country ruled by the Vandals and later by the Byzantines

681
The Arabs conquer the Byzantine provinces

1519
Algeria comes under Turkish rule

1830
France occupies Algiers

1834–47
Armed resistance by Emir Abd el-Kader is overturned by the French

1871
Suppression of the Kabyle revolt

1881
The Algerian administration is absorbed into the French one

1899–1902
After conquering large desert regions of the Sahara, France places the region under military administration as Southern Algeria

1954
Uprising of the National Liberation Front (FLN) begins

1962
Algeria obtains independence

1963
A. Ben Bella becomes president; a socialist state is created

1965
Military junta under H. Boumédienne overthrows Ben Bella

1979
B. Chadli becomes president

1980/81
The Arabization campaign leads to unrest among the Berbers

1989
Institution of a multi-party political system; founding of the Islamic Holy Front (FIS)

1991
The FIS wins the parliamentary election

1992
Chadli resigns. The results of the parliamentary elections are annulled; the Supreme National Council takes power; the FIS is banned; Islamic fundamentalists call for an armed struggle which develops into civil war

History and Politics

Algeria's fight for independence ended in 1962. In its early years, the young country embarked on an Islamic socialist experiment that brought it to bankruptcy. Following the re-establishment of the political status quo, it is hoped that the democratization process will bring greater stability despite the tense social and economic climate.

Berbers have lived in the region that is now Algeria since the 3rd millennium BCE. The scattered Phoenician trading posts along the coast later came under the domination of Carthage. After the destruction of Carthage by the Romans in 146 BCE, the coastal cities and contiguous inland areas became part of the Roman Empire. In the 7th century, the region's Arab conquerors brought the Islamic faith. After 1509 Spain established settlements along the coast until it became part of the Ottoman Empire in 1519. A combination of trading and piracy brought great wealth to the coastal towns.

Under French rule

The French conquered Algiers in 1830, and the subsequent occupation of Oran and Annaba put an end to piracy in the Mediterranean area. In 1834, the emir Abd el-Kader (1808–83) led an armed resistance against them but was ultimately unable to resist their superior strength and was forced to concede defeat in 1847.

During the following years it was above all the Berbers in Kabylia who resisted the systematic colonization of Algeria. Following the Kabylia Uprising of 1871, the French seized large areas of land, which they populated with French settlers. These settlers soon demanded that Algeria be politically united with the French motherland, while simultaneously denying the local population a share of the political power.

In 1918, after the end of World War One, demands for Algerian autonomy became increasingly clamorous, but were initially ignored by France. A number of independence movements were established. The first climax in Algeria's fight for independence came in 1954 in an uprising that began in the Aurès Mountains. At the head of this movement was the National Liberation Front (FLN).

France agrees to Algerian independence

Following the collapse of the Fourth Republic—precipitated by the French national crisis in 1958—Charles de Gaulle (1890-1970) became president of France with a mandate to find a political solution to the war with Algeria, which had been raging since 1954. After the deaths of more than one million Algerians and some 25,000 French, as well as the destruction of much of the country, de Gaulle and the FLN finally reached a peace agreement in March 1962 in Evian. On July 3, 1962, Algeria became an independent Islamic socialist state.

Algeria's first president was Ahmed Ben Bella (b. 1918). In 1965, he was overthrown by Colonel Houari Boumédienne (1927–78), who continued to govern the country under the guiding principles of Islamic socialism as his predecessor had done. However, the modernization and industrialization of the country were soon halted as its faltering oil industry could no longer finance the inflated state-run industrial sector.

A bloody road to democracy

During the early 1980s the Berbers from Greater Kabylia demanded an end to enforced Arabization and the recognition of their culture and their language. Algeria's economic situation worsened in 1988 after sudden bloody uprisings fanned the flames of Islamic fundamentalism.

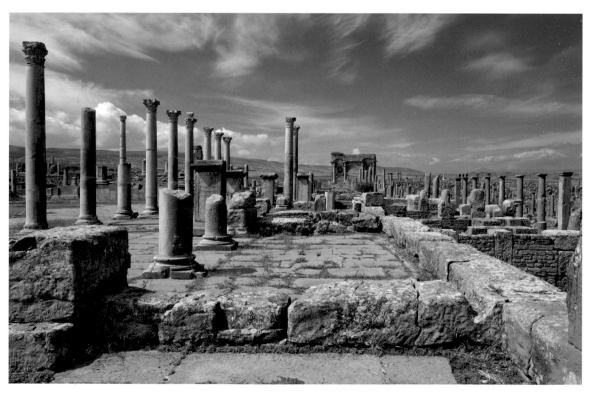

The UNESCO World Heritage Site of Timgad, an ancient Roman colonial town from the time of the emperor Trajan (around 100 CE).

People celebrate Algeria's independence from France in the streets of Algiers in 1962.

The government led by Bendjedid Chadli (b. 1929) attempted to counteract this development with political reforms and an end to the state's socialist approach.

In 1991, the first free election won by the Islamic Holy Front (FIS) was annulled and this led to the launch of an armed struggle against the government. In 1992, following Chadli's resignation, a privy council took power and a state of emergency was declared. The banned FIS went underground. In the following years, the rebellion escalated, causing the deaths of about 150,000 Algerians in the 1990s alone.

In 1997 the parliamentary elections were won by the National Democratic Rally (RND), but they were unable to end the violence. President Abdelaziz Bouteflika (b. 1937) of the FLN assumed power in 1999. His attempts to restore peace within the country were successful and he was re-elected with a large majority in 2004 and again in 2009. The motto of his second period in office was 'national reconciliation.' For his latest term Bouteflika plans large scale reforms of the judiciary system, the state-controlled economy, as well as the educational system.

Economy, Traffic, and Communication

Algeria's economy was formerly centralized, with a socialist orientation. With some difficulty it is now being transformed, with privatization heading the agenda. Privatization should make businesses more flexible, but conceals the socially dangerous potential of destroying jobs.

Date palms and bread

Algeria's cultivable land is too small to feed the country's population. Just 17 percent of Algerian territory is usable, but of this only one sixth is suitable for growing cereals and vegetables. Along the coast, olives, grain, vines, and southern Mediterranean fruits are cultivated. The date palm not only supplies the farmers with dates; its palm fronds provide shade for the fields of fruit and vegetables, without which they would be scorched by the desert sun.

Black gold

Algeria has some of the world's largest oil reserves. The center of the country's state-owned oil production is the Hassi Messaoud group of oases, east of Ouargla. From here, pipelines run through the desert to the ports of Arzew and Bejaja.

Ways through the desert

Today a large part of the Sahara is traversed by good roads, and the most important oases are connected by surfaced roads. The north of the country is served by an extensive railroad network covering 4,000 km (2,485 miles). Algeria's major ports are Algiers, Annaba, and Oran.

State controlled media

Restricted freedom of the press hinders objective reporting. Newspapers are published in Arabic and French. Daily newspapers with the widest circulation are *al-Khabar* and *al-Watan*. Television and radio broadcast in French, Arabic and the Berber language. They, like the electronic media, are subject to state control.

Tourism

With many impressive sites dating from Roman times, as well as magical oases, some idyllic coastline, and the majestic Sahara, Algeria has great potential for becoming a popular tourist destination. For many years, however, the unstable political situation has largely prevented the development of tourism. Algeria remains a destination for adventure-loving individualists and desert travelers.

HISTORY

1996
Constitutional reform

1999
A. Bouteflika is elected president (re-elected 2004 and 2009)

2003
Severe earthquake in northern Algeria

2005
The population supports the Charter for Peace and National Reconciliation advocated by President Bouteflika

POLITICS

Government:
Presidential republic

Head of state:
President

Legislature:
National Congress with 389 members elected for a 5-year term, and Senate with 144 members

Administrative divisions:
48 provinces (Wilayate)

ECONOMY

Currency:
1 Algerian dinar (DZD) = 100 centimes

Gross domestic product:
$135.29 billion US

Gross per capita income:
$3,620 US

Overseas trade:
Imports $39.5 billion US
Exports $79.3 billion US

Foreign debt:
$3.75 billion US

Oil wells near Hassi Messaoud. Natural gas and crude oil are among the most important goods exported.

TUNISIA

Despite its small size, Tunisia has as diverse a landscape as its larger neighbors in the Maghreb. From the Mediterranean coast in the north, the country stretches southward, with verdant plains and highlands, salt pans, and the dunes of the majestic Sahara. Lying where Europe and Africa meet, Tunisia has acted as a fulcrum between the two continents since antiquity. It was a center of trade for merchants from the eastern Mediterranean, as well as a granary, and a place of retirement for Roman nobles. Today, Tunisia is still the most Westernized Arab country, with many Tunisians seeing themselves as a direct link between the traditional Islamic way of life and the modern age.

Geography

Bordered by Algeria to the west and Libya to the east, Tunisia is the easternmost and smallest of the Maghrebian countries. From its northern coastal regions to the Sahara in the south Tunisia has a variety of landscapes. The Tunisian coastline is 1,300 km (808 miles) long: while in the north, it is mostly straight, further east it is bordered by lagoons. The Kroumirie, a mountainous region with forests of cork oak and holm oak, lies along the narrow coastline in the northwest. This mountainous region receives average annual rainfall of up to 1,600 mm (63 in). The foothills of the Tell Atlas rise up to the south. These impressive ridges divide the country into two regions, stretching from Kasserine, in west-central Tunisia, across the country and out onto the Cape Bon Peninsula in the east. To the north lies Tunisia's wettest region with a Mediterranean climate, where vineyards, fruit and vegetable plantations, and olive trees are grown. Cattle-breeding and agriculture are concentrated in the Mejerda Valley, through which the river Mejerda runs all year round. South of this climatic zone lies the steppe of the central Tunisian high plateau: alfalfa, a valuable source of cellulose, is the only crop here.

The east of the country: olives and palms

The Sahel, meaning the 'coast' in Arabic, is a strip of land that lies along the east coast between Hammamet and Sfax. Here, millions of olive trees grow. Tunisia is a major producer of olive oil.

South of Sfax lies a region known as Le Grand Sud (The Great South). Here, the compact olive trees of the Sahel are replaced by tall, slender date palms and the landscape becomes more desert-like: it is interrupted only by green oases, which are irrigated by water drawn from artesian wells, by natural or mechanical means. Dates are the prime agricultural produce of the south; Deglet al-Nour, the variety grown in the oases around Shott al-Djerid, is considered to be a particular delicacy. Alfalfa, pomegranates, vegetables and spices are cultivated in the shade of the palms.

The barren desert

West of the Daher mountains, the dunes of the Sahara and large salt lakes and salt pans (known as shotts) begin. Shott al-Djerid, Shott al-Fedjedj and Shott al-Gharsa lie at the bottom of a 200-km (124 mile)-wide depression. In summer, a layer of salt, produced by the evaporation of water, lines the shotts, and it is solid enough to walk on or even drive over. In autumn and winter, however, rain turns the salt crust into thick, heavy mud, which can be extremely dangerous to venture onto.

A bazaar in Sousse famous for its vast variety of spices

The castle-like kasbah in Sousse

POPULATION

Number of inhabitants:
10.3 million

Population density:
*63 inhabitants/km²
(163 inhabitants/square mile)*

Population distribution:
*65% urban
35% rural*

Annual population growth:
1.0%

Life expectancy:
*Women 78 years
Men 74 years*

Religion:
*Sunni Islam, Christianity,
Judaism*

Languages:
*Arabic (official language),
French, English*

Literacy rate:
80%

Fertile coast, arid south

While a Mediterranean climate, with typically mild, wet winters and hot, dry summers, prevails in Tunisia's coastal regions, a dry, continental desert climate is characteristic of the south. Annual rainfall ranges from 1,600 mm (63 in) in the northern highlands to 500 mm (20 in) in the south and east of the country. In the area of the shotts and the Sahara, annual rainfall is less than 200 mm (8 in).

Population

Tunisia's inhabitants consist predominantly of people of Arab or Arab-Berber descent. People of pure Berber ancestry still inhabit a few remote areas, such as Jerba Island and the Daher Mountains. Many Tunisians, especially in the south, have abandoned their traditional semi-nomadic lifestyle: most have settled in the plains regions, where they live from modest agriculture and cattle-rearing. Some former nomads still travel across the country, although now as itinerant workers and harvest workers rather than pastoralists. Tunisia's population is mostly concentrated in the north and in the eastern coastal strip: over 70 percent of the population live in these areas, where most of Tunisia's towns and cities are also located.

Cultural diversity

The overwhelming majority of the population is Muslim, but small Christian and Jewish communities practice their faith and contribute to Tunisia's rich cultural diversity. 65 % of Tunisia's population of 10.3 million live in urban areas: the capital Tunis and the main cities of Carthage, Jerba, Hammamet, Bizerte, Sousse, Sfax, and Kairouan. An open and hospitable country, Tunisia has served as

a crossroads of civilization, where Arab, Berber, African and European influences have helped shape the unique Tunisian cultural identity. Tunisia has always been an advocate of women's emancipation: immediately after independence in 1956, a Code of Personal Status was promulgated, while a set of laws enacted in 1992 established women's equality with men, reaffirming Tunisia's commitment to the promotion of women's rights.

Women participate fully in Tunisian public life

HISTORY

814 BCE
Carthage is founded by the Phoenicians

146 BCE
After the Punic Wars, Carthage is destroyed by the Romans and becomes the first African province of the Roman Empire

439–533 CE
Ruled by the Vandals

From 533
Integration into the Byzantine Empire

669–98
Arabs take control of the Byzantine province

1226
Ruled by the Hafsids

1574
Tunisia becomes an autonomous province of the Ottoman Empire

1881–1956
French protectorate

1955
Tunisia obtains internal autonomy

1956
Tunisia becomes independent

1957
H. Bourguiba becomes president

1962–69
Adoption of socialist-oriented economic policies

1977–78
Social tensions involving trades unions, general strike and unrest

1981
One-party system abandoned

1987
Z.A. Ben Ali becomes president

1994, 1999, 2004, 2009
Ben Ali is confirmed in office

2002
Terrorist attack in front of the synagogue in Jerba with 21 dead

2003
Women are allowed to serve military duty

2005
New parliamentary chamber: Chambre des Conseillers

2008
Customs Union with the EU

The amphitheater in al-Jem - remains of the Roman rule from 146 BCE to 439 CE

History and Politics

Tunisia has bowed to many rulers in the course of its history, and this may explain its distinctively liberal political stance. It is surely no coincidence that Tunisia was the first Arab country to make a radical break away from age-old traditions. Habib Bourguiba (1903– 2000), who secured independence for Tunisia, outlawed polygamy as early as the 1950s and granted women equal civil rights. He laid the basis for Tunisia's development into a modern country, in which the power and importance of religion are respected, but are not stifling or socially restricting.

Phoenician refugees from Tyre founded the city of Carthage, on the northern coast of what is now Tunisia, in 814 BCE. From the 7th century BCE the city became one of the most important centers of trade in the western Mediterranean. Carthage was the greatest rival to Greek expansion into Sicily, and later of the developing Roman Empire. From the naval battle at Himera in 480 BCE to Hannibal's march over the Alps in 218 BCE, Carthage was engaged in constant military conflict with the Greeks in Sicily and with the Romans. Only with the Roman victory over Carthage in the third Punic War (149–146 BCE) was this war brought to an end. Razed to the ground, Carthage was transformed into a province of the Roman Empire.

The eastern Maghreb: a succession of rulers

After their victory over Carthage, the Romans colonized North Africa and, with their advanced irrigation techniques, created suitable conditions for productive agriculture. As a Roman province what is now Tunisia became an important producer of grain and olive oil, and provided wild animals for the spectacles so beloved of the Romans. Rebellions and invasions by the Vandals, who also founded a kingdom here, brought the era of Roman domination to an end. From 533, Tunisia's coastal towns fell to the Byzantines, but the fundamental social and political changes were wrought by the conquest of the region by Arabs from Egypt in the mid-7th century. The new capital, Kairouan, the base from which present-day Tunisia became Islamized, developed from a military colony. From the 9th century, the Aghlabids, the first independent ruling dynasty in Tunisia, created a thriving community, promoted science and art, and conquered Sicily. The Aghlabids were superseded by the Fatimids, a dynasty of Berber descent. During the Fatimid period, which lasted from the 10th to 12th centuries, Arabic cattle-breeders settled in Tunisia and permanently Arabized the country.

Tunisia's golden age under the Hafsids

The Hafsids, who entered the political stage in 1226, were the first ruling dynasty to originate from Morocco. After a century of conflict and upheaval, the Hafsids brought Tunisia into a second golden age. They chose Tunis as their capital, and welcomed a large number of Muslims and Jews who had been expelled from Andalusia during the Reconquista of Spain. With their crafts, their literature, and their great scientific knowledge, these refugees from Andalusia enriched Tunisian culture, and also introduced more efficient agricultural methods.

On the path to independence

The Hafsid period was brought to an end by the Ottomans in 1574. Under Ottoman rule, Tunisia experienced economic and political instability, which finally led to national bankruptcy under the Hussein dynasty. During this period, Tunisia was relatively independent of its Ottoman overlords in Istanbul and established firm links with Europe. Bey Ahmad ibn Mustafa (1806–55) attempted to modernize the country without European aid, but this proved very costly, and ultimately the country became severely dependent on France, Italy and Britain for financial aid. Tunisia's independence, which had been recognized by Turkey from 1871, lasted no more than a decade.

France then forced the ruling beys (provincial governors) to sign an agreement by which Tunisia would become a French protectorate. However, in 1920 resistance to foreign rule led to the formation of the Destur Party, which became the more radical Neo Destur Party in 1934. Together with Habib Bourguiba, the party fought for the country's complete independence in 1956.

Habib Bourguiba, father of the nation
Habib Bourguiba, who became Tunisia's first prime minister in 1956, also assumed the presidency after the abdication of the beys in 1957. His greatest achievement was the revision of Tunisia's constitution, which he freed from what he saw as outdated Islamic customs and traditions. However, his rule became autocratic, and he dealt with those who opposed him by issuing harsh laws and using the services of the secret police.

Bourguiba's economic policy was that of a socialist innovator. He nationalized various industrial sectors, and placed strict controls on the tenure of land by foreigners. However, these measures soon proved unprofitable and unsuccessful. Tunisia, which had been a highly productive granary in Roman times, experienced difficult times: subsidies on basic foodstuffs were doubled, the Bread Revolts broke out in 1984, and there was widespread dissent.

Tunisia in the post-Bourguiba era
In 1975 Bourguiba had himself elected president for life. By 1987, when he was in his 80s, he had become sick and incapacitated. On November 7, 1987, then Prime Minister Zine El Abidine Ben Ali took over the presidency of the Republic, in conformity with the Tunisian Constitution, after Bourguiba had become incapable of pursuing his functions as president. General elections were held in 1989. Political life was reorganized, by prohibiting the creation of political parties on the basis of religion, race, or region, and also by promoting moderation and rejecting violence and extremism.

Economy, Traffic, and Communication
Ben Ali's main achievement was the liberalization of his predecessor's economic policies. The economy was privatized, collaboration with European partners was intensified, and investment incentives were created. Among North African countries, Tunisia is the star pupil with an exemplary economy. With almost seven million foreign visitors per year, tourism is also an important economic factor.

Solid economic foundations
Agriculture, which accounts for around 10 percent of Tunisia's gross national product, has suffered from periods of severe drought in recent years.

Oil and gas production so far make only a modest contribution to the national economy. Tunisia does, however, possess large phosphate deposits, and it is an important producer of phosphate fertilizer. Rich deposits of iron and other ores, such as lead and zinc, are located in the west of the country.

The textile and food industries (through which olive oil, preserves and sugar are produced) are concentrated in the towns along the Mediterranean coast. These, together with the crafts industry, in which handwoven rugs, traditional leather goods, and wrought-iron craftwork are produced, play a vitally important economic role for Tunisians.

Transportation and media
The traffic network is well developed. There are more than 12,000 km (7,500 miles) of all-weather roads, including some 260 km (163 miles) of highways. There is also a national railroad network. There are eight commercial ports. There are important airports at Tunis-Carthage, Enfidha, Monastir, and Jerba.

The media have gradually been liberalized. Private newspapers, radio and TV channels have been created, and the media landscape has grown more and more diverse in terms of languages and programs.

Tourism
Bathing against a backdrop of an Arab medina; going on a camel trek into the desert; investigating the traces of the past in Roman temples and villas; or haggling for souvenirs in the bustle of shady alleys in a bazaar—these are just some of the wide range of options open to visitors on vacation in Tunisia. With long sandy beaches, excellent hotels and restaurants, a pleasant climate, and a fascinating hinterland, Tunisia is an ideal tourist destination. A visit to the oases on the fringes of the shotts is another interesting option, such as the oasis town of Nefta, southwest of Gafsa, where some 350,000 date palms grow.

Tourism has been established in Tunisia for a considerable time. In the 1920s, an eccentric baron had a villa built at the old fortified town of Hammamet, set in an attractive bay on the southern tip of Cape Bon: this attracted various aristocrats and other prominent people. Today, Hammamet and Nabeul, 10 km (6 miles) further north, are two of Tunisia's most popular vacation destinations. The endless soft sand beaches here slope gently down to the sea, and both resorts have hotels built in an Oriental style, with domes and turrets.

ECONOMY

Currency:
1 Tunisian dinar (TND)
= 1,000 milimes

Gross domestic product:
$40.3 billion US

Gross per capita income:
$3,210 US

Overseas trade:
Imports $24.2 billion US
Exports $19.1 billion US

Foreign debt:
$20.8 billion US

The ancient Roman capitol is just one of several historic sights in Dougga.

LIBYA

THE COUNTRY

Official name:
*Great Socialist People's Libyan
Arab Jamahiriya*

Geographic coordinates:
*North Africa; between 20° and
33° north, and 9° and 25° east*

Area:
*1,759,540 km²
(679,362 square miles)*

Capital:
Tripoli

Climate:
*Desert climate, on the coast
warm Mediterranean climate;
Tripoli 19.4°C (67°F)/400 mm
(16 in)*

Time zone:
Greenwich Mean Time +2 hours

The geographical location of Libya makes it a connecting link, and a transitional zone, between the western Maghreb states and the Middle East countries, as well as between the Mediterranean region and the African hinterland. Desert covers 90 percent of the country's surface and is largely uninhabited except for a few, scattered oases. Agriculture is possible only in the fertile Jeffara Plain in the northwest of Tripolitania and along the narrow coastal stretches in Cyrenaica.

Geography

Apart from a narrow coastal stretch with a Mediterranean climate, the whole country has a hot, dry, subtropical climate. It consists of deserts of different types (especially sand, boulder, gravel, basalt, and clay), in which only the rare oases with their watering holes offer possibilities for habitation.

The expanse of the Libyan Sahara

The interior of Libya is defined by a cuesta landscape with wide plains and plateaus. This exhibits a diversity of form, with stone deserts *(hammada)* alternating with gravel deserts *(serir)*, and vast dune fields with peaks up to 100 m (328 ft) high. Bizarre, eroded, majestic rocks and deep canyons shape the volcanic highland landscape. While the northern Sahara, with its desert steppes, receives just 100 mm (4 in) of rain annually, significant rainfall occurs only every 20 years or so in the extremely dry south. This area is regarded as the driest of the entire Sahara Desert.

Fertile plains on the coast

Only the soils of the two narrow strips along the Mediterranean coast, in the northern part of the country, receive enough rain to suit farming purposes. Both of the big metropolises, Benghazi and Tripoli, are situated here. The coastal plain in northern Tripolitania, called the Jeffara is between 30–70 km (18–43 miles) wide. It extends from Tunisia to al-Khums and is bordered to the south by the Jabal Nafusa mountain range. With elevations between 600–1,000 m (1,968–3,280 ft), the mountain range forms a climatic divide between the coast and the dry al-Hammada al-Hamra.

*A caravan of Libyan
Tuaregs crosses a dune
field in the Sahara.*

A Mediterranean climate with warm, dry summers and mild, rainy winters prevails along the narrow coastal strip: the region receives an average annual total of between 300 and 600 mm (12–23 in) of rain, which is enough to support the cultivation of olives and cereals. Despite modern farming methods and equipment being available, traditional farming practices, such as those at the Jessour terraces, are still in widespread use.

A second, much narrower coastal plain is located in northern Cyrenaica, which is framed by the karst mountain range of Jabal al-Akhdar, the 'Green Mountains.' Both plains together make up about 5 percent of the total land area.

Artificial oases

Oases are the life-sustaining orientation points in the barren monotony of the desert. By Roman times, caravan routes were established into sub-Saharan Africa via the oases. To this day, these old routes are used by nomads, tourists, and smugglers. Along with the traditional oases such as Ghadamis (in the west) and Kufra (in the east), where artesian wells feed the palms and gardens with water, there are also artificial oases which have been created by modern irrigation techniques. Reserves of ancient water are also bored into and pumped above ground. Thus, grain grows in the middle of the Sahara.

Libyans are especially proud of the 'Great Artificial River,' a massive water pipeline going straight through the desert. Gigantic pipelines tap ancient ground water from the oases of Kufra, and transport it to the coast of the Gulf of Sirte in order to irrigate the fields and supply drinking water.

Date palms—symbol of the desert

Date palms are the ubiquitous plants of the dry regions. They provide not only fruit, but also timber and fibers for the production of ropes. Shadowed by their crowns, fodder clover, tomatoes, paprika, pomegranates, and citrus fruits can be planted.

Population

Around 94 percent of the population is of Libyan-Arab origin and Arab-Berber mixture. According to the 2006 census some 370,000 foreigners live in the country, although unofficial estimates put the figure as high as 1.5 million. Today, the various Berber tribes live pre-

dominantly in the Jabal Nafusa, as well as in the oases of Ghadamis and Awjila. Some 10,000 partly nomadic Tuareg live in the southern Fezzan and around the oases of Ghat and Ghadamis on the border with Algeria. The Libyan Tuareg community is reinforced by relatives and migrant workers from Niger. In the south, some Toubou groups also live in the border region with Chad.

Islam as the national religion

Around 97 percent of all Libyans are Muslims. Sunni Islam is the version of Islam that has become the national religion, although the Berbers in Jabal Nafusa, who still live in traditional tribal communities and adhere to their age-old ways of life, identify themselves as belonging to the Shiites.

POPULATION

Number of inhabitants:
6.5 million

Population density:
*4 inhabitants/km²
(10 inhabitants/square mile)*

Population distribution:
*78% urban
22% rural*

Annual population growth:
2.1%

Life expectancy:
*Women 80 years
Men 75 years*

Religion:
Sunni Islam

Languages:
Arabic (official language), Berber languages

Literacy rate:
87%

Date palms are perfectly adapted to the local arid desert climate

HISTORY

146 BCE
Tripoli comes under Roman influence

455–534 CE
Vandal rule in Tripoli

644–47
Arabs occupy the country

16th century
Libya is conquered by the Ottomans

1911
Italy begins the conquest of Libya

1951
Libya becomes an independent kingdom by UN resolution

1959
First discovery of oil in the Libyan desert

1969
Col. M. al-Qaddafi overthrows King Idris I

1986
The USA breaks ties with Libya

From 1992
UN economic embargo

2004
US and EU revoke sanctions

2008
Libya and the US agree on damages for the victims of the attack on a US civil aircraft over Lockerbie (Scotland) in 1988, which was attributed to Libya

History and Politics

3,000 years of history lie between the first written accounts of Libya and the present modern desert nation. However, the country has only been in the international spotlight since a young colonel, Muammar al-Qaddafi (b. 1942), deposed King Idris I (1890-1983) in 1969.

The Egyptians called the land 'Lebu', from which the modern name of Libya is derived. In about 1200 BCE Phoenician merchants established the first trading bases—Sabratha, Oea, Leptis Magna—on the coast of western Libya. Approximately 600 years later, the Greeks established their own trading posts in east Libya (Cyrene).

Libya under the Romans

After the destruction of Carthage (in modern Tunisia), western Libya initially belonged to the Kingdom of Numidia. In the second century BCE the Romans conquered the land, taking over and expanding the old Phoenician cities and Cyrene. However, the heyday for Roman Libya did not come until the second century CE, when Septimius Severus, born in Leptis Magna, became the Roman emperor and greatly developed and promoted his home region, enriching his native town with magnificent buildings. It was during his reign that the Roman provinces of North Africa were converted to Christianity. In 395 CE the Empire was divided; Tripolitania was allocated to Western Rome, while Cyrenaica became part of the Eastern Roman Empire.

Islamic dynasties

The Vandals and Byzantines followed the Romans. During the 7th century Islamic–Arab armies conquered Cyrenaica and Tripolitania. It was not until the 11th century that a far-reaching Islamization and Arabization of the Christian-Berber population took place following the influx of Arabian cattle-raisers. A succession of dynasties—Aghlabids, Fatimids, Almoravids, Hafsids, and in be-tween even the Normans—were unable to impose peace on the coastal region. Pirates operated from Libya's harbors with increasing frequency. In 1517 the Turkish Ottomans conquered Libya, and from 1711 it was a Turkish dynasty, the Karamanli, that ruled until 1835.

Libya became independent from Italy during the rule of King Idris I al-Senussi (1890-1983)

Colonial times and independence

In 1911–12 Italy began the conquest of Libya, during the Italian-Turkish War. Later, Mussolini continued the colonization process in 1922 and expanded the dominion ever farther south, bringing the Fezzan under Italian control in 1925. In 1935 the conquered regions (Tripoli, Cyrenaica, and Fezzan) were amalgamated by Italy to form the Italian colony of 'Libia'. Between 1941 and 1943 Libya became a battle ground as Rommel's Afrikacorps fought against the Allies for the coastal towns of Tripoli and Tubruq.

After the end of World War Two, Libya was placed first under a UN Mandate, then, in 1951, it was granted independence under King Idris I al-Senussi. Shortly thereafter, the first discoveries of oil were made in the Libyan desert. This once-poor country was suddenly extremely rich, which only served to increase social tensions. A junta under the young colonel Muammar al-Qaddafi overthrew the king in 1969. A year later the foreign military bases were closed down and all Italians expelled from the country.

Colonel Muammar al-Qaddafi (b. 1942) has ruled Libya since 1969 after overthrowing King Idris I.

The 'Third Way'

In 1977, on the basis of the constitution, Qaddafi declared the country a *'jamahiriya'* (in Arabic, *jamahir* means 'folk masses'), a type of basic democratic People's Republic. He formulated the ideas for this 'direct democracy' based on the Qur'an in his Green Book. Under this system, the people decide on all ongoing questions in local and regional Basic People's Congresses and delegated a representative to attend the General People's Congress, where these decisions are justified. This Congress then determines a General People's Committee, comparable to a cabinet.

Formally, the head of state is the General Secretary of the General People's Congress, although to date Qaddafi has the ultimate decision-making power in all important political and economic issues.

Skyline of Libya's capital Tripoli, which is a center for the Libyan economy

POLITICS

Government:
Islamic-Socialist People's Republic

Head of state:
General Secretary of the General People's Congress, de facto M. al-Qaddafi

Legislature:
General People's Congress

Administrative divisions:
22 districts

ECONOMY

Currency:
1 Libyan Dinar (LYD) = 1,000 dirhams

Gross domestic product:
$58.3 billion US

Gross per capita income:
$9,010 US

Overseas trade:
*Imports $25.1 billion US
Exports $60.3 billion US*

Foreign debt:
$6.2 billion US

Economy, Traffic, and Communication

At a share of only 3 percent of gross domestic product, agriculture plays a minor role in the economy. Farming that is dependent on natural rainfall is only possible along the fertile coastal plains of Tripolitania and Cyrenaica. The government is attempting to improve harvests by the use of artificial irrigation. Apart from nomadic cattle farming, coastal fishing is also quite important. Nonetheless, Libya has to import approximately three-quarters of its food requirements.

Crude oil

Over 90 percent of Libya's foreign revenues flow out of the oil wells, while recently income from natural gas has also increased. These reserves will also ensure that in the future the money flowing out of the desert does not run dry.

However, an economic structural problem is the reliance on the export of oil; hardly anything is produced internally, so that most goods and food must be brought in as expensive imports. Current Libyan economic policies focus on changing this point of emphasis.

Transportation system

Libya's transportation system is well-organized. Surfaced roads penetrate deep into the Sahara, and the coastal zone is very well-developed.

Construction has commenced on a railroad line from the Tunisian to the Egyptian border. In the long term it is also planned to add connections to the states in the south. Along the Mediterranean coast lie numerous commercial ports and oil depots. In addition to the capital Tripoli, Misrata, Benghazi, and Sabha all have international airports.

Media under strict state control

Qaddafi and his closest advisors and relatives determine public opinion. Radio, television, and all newspapers are state-controlled. People have access to the internet and international satellite television, which, however, are also censored by the state. The telephone network is fairly well developed, taking in the coastal strip and the main oases. The same applies to mobile telephones.

Tourism

Libya is an attractive destination for both cultural interest and adventure holidays. Along with its unique credentials as an ancient location, fascinating mountains, dunes, and volcanic landscapes, as well as excellent sandy beaches await the visitor. The development of tourism in Libya is hindered by the restrictions imposed by the Libyan state on the issuing of visas, which are only issued selectively.

A coppersmith at work in Tripoli

EGYPT

THE COUNTRY

Official name:
Arab Republic of Egypt

Geographic coordinates:
North Africa; between 22° and 32° north, and 25° and 36° east

Area:
*1,001,450 km²
(386,704 square miles)*

Capital:
Cairo

Climate:
*Desert and semi-desert climate;
Cairo 21.9°C (71°F)/42 mm
(2 in); Luxor 24°C (75°F)/4 mm
(16 in)*

Time zone:
Greenwich Mean Time +2 hours

From a satellite view of Egypt, the country's geographic appearance is clear—the green, fertile ribbon of the Nile runs the length of the country, distributing its lifeblood of water, while huge expanses of desert surround it on either side. For millennia the delicate equilibrium between fertile fields along the banks of the Nile and the harsh, uninhabitable desert has been the all-determining factor of Egypt's rhythm of life. The Ancient Egyptians subdivided their country into *kemet*, the fertile black earth along the banks of the Nile, and *deshret*, the surrounding red desert.

St. Catherine's Monastery at the foot of Mount Sinai was built in 557 CE by Justinian I.

Geography

Egypt stretches over two continents. Most of the country lies in Africa, but the country is also linked to Asia via the Sinai Peninsula, across the Suez Canal. The Mediterranean borders the country to the north and in the east lies the Arabian Desert, stretching to the Red Sea. To the south Egypt adjoins Sudan, and to the west lies the Libyan Desert.

Desert on all sides

Egypt is made up of 95 percent desert. In the east, the Arabian Desert follows a 2,000 m (6,562 ft) high mountain range. In an escarpment more than 1,000 m (3,281 ft) high, the mountains drop down to the Red Sea. The numerous deeply carved dry riverbeds (wadis) give the 220,000 km² (84,944 square mile) Arabian Desert its characteristic appearance.

The Libyan Desert in the west, which is part of the Sahara, exhibits an entirely different landscape. Covering an area of approximately 690,000 km² (266,415 square miles), it comprises around 65 percent of the land area of Egypt. It consists of a mostly bare limestone high plateau around 300 m (984 ft) above sea level, which towers above the lower-lying sandstone outcrops. The oases of Kharga, Dakhla, and Farafra lie in deeply carved, steep-sided valleys. In this plateau area there are several depressions, among them the Qattara Depression, which is 134 m (436 ft) below sea level.

The 60,000 km² (23,160 square mile) Sinai Peninsula is also a barren, desert landscape. In the north of the Sinai is an expansive area of dune-covered limestone and sandstone plateaus, while the crystalline rock of the Sinai Massif, with Jabal Katrina at 2,637 m (8,652 ft) forming its highest point, makes up the southern part.

The Nile—lifeblood of Egypt

The Nile Valley is approximately 1,200 km (745 miles) long and 3–5 km (2–3 miles) wide and is the longest river oasis in the world. It runs through the country from south to north, where it flows into the Mediterranean. The box-shaped river valley was eroded by the river over the millennia.

The Nile Delta extends over approximately 22,000 km2 (8,492 square miles) northward from Cairo, reaching a maximum width of 250 km (150 miles). Most arms of the Nile are channeled, and there are wide areas of dunes that separate brackish freshwater lakes from the open sea.

Like no other country in the world, Egypt is completely defined by the contrast between the desert and the fertile river valley. The Greek scholar Herodotus (c.485–25 BCE) called Egypt "a gift of the Nile." Until the building of the Aswan High Dam in the 1960s, the river always deposited fertile, black silt on its banks during its regular floods. As early as 5,000 years ago this made fruitful harvests possible for Egyptian farmers, and it was the cornerstone for one of the earliest advanced civilizations of humanity. Even in the time of the pharaohs the phases of the Nile determined the rhythm of everyday life. The seasonal pattern alternated between the flooding, usually lasting 100 days, and low water levels in the winter and summer, with their industrious harvest season. Even today, agriculture dominates the appearance of the Nile Valley. Every square meter of the valuable, fertile earth is used. Along with high-quality cotton, corn, rice, and sugar cane are grown. Cultivation of vegetables is carried out intensively in greenhouses.

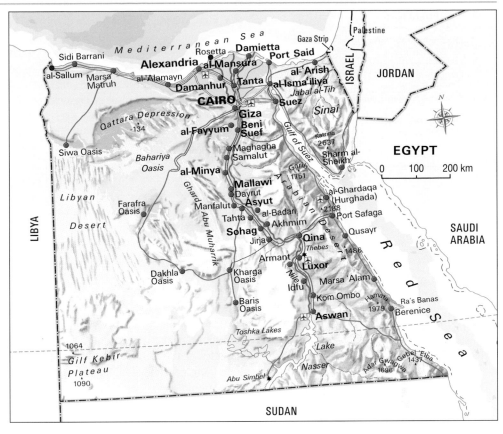

Hot days, cold nights

With the exception of the Mediterranean coast and Nile Delta, Egypt lies mainly in subtropical semi-desert and desert climatic zones. On the coast and in the delta the influence of the Mediterranean climate becomes noticeable: the winter rain brings the coastal city of Alexandria around 190 mm (7 in) of precipitation. Temperatures are generally more moderate than in the southern areas. Winter is short and comparatively mild.

The south is dry year-round. Based on the negligible air humidity, the great heat in the spring and summer is easier to tolerate. Typical for the desert climate are the extreme temperature variations between day and night. In the winter they can range between freezing point (nights) and up to 30°C (86°F) by day. In the spring, a hot desert wind, Khamsin, sometimes blows, laden with dust and sand, and can develop into severe sandstorms.

Desert and orchards, crocodiles and scarabs

The desert belt of Egypt is among the most inhospitable areas on earth; 95 percent of the land is covered with drought-resistant desert vegetation or has no plant life at all. Only in the fertile Nile Valley and Nile Delta, in the oases, and in periodically water-carrying wadis, is there any vegetation. Through the systematic cultivation of other plants, the native flora in the oases has been repressed.

The Sphinx of Giza is the oldest known monumental sculpture in the world and one of the most popular sights in Egypt.

Agriculture has been pursued in the Nile Delta for many millennia, so that here, too, the original vegetation can now scarcely be found. Papyrus marshes, widespread in the time of the pharaohs, disappeared long ago. Papyrus, the celebrated plant of Egypt, from which the ancient Egyptians made their paper, has given way to palm groves and orchards.

As a result of the changes made for food cultivation, the desert fauna has been reduced to such hardy species as the desert fox (fennec) and jackal. Among the reptiles are to be found several types of lizard, chameleons, and many types of snake, such as the horned viper. In the Nile Delta, the fauna, despite the decimation of the past 100 years, is diverse compared to the desert. Today, one finds various birds of prey, herons, and hoopoe. Hippopotamuses and lions, however, are extinct. The endangered Nile crocodile, which can be up to 3 m (10 ft) long, inhabits Lake Nasser. Small animals, such as rabbits, mice, and rats, are widespread and cause great damage to crops. Livestock and work animals include dromedaries, cattle, water buffalo, horses, and donkeys—all are part of the picture of most Egyptians' everyday life in the country. Among the best-known inhabitants of Egypt are the dung beetles. Once worshiped as the symbol of the god of the morning sun, Khepre, the beetle is known all over the world as the scarab.

POPULATION

Number of inhabitants:
76.8 million

Population density:
77 inhabitants/km²
(199 inhabitants/square mile)

Population distribution:
42% urban
58% rural

Annual population growth:
1.7%

Life expectancy:
Women 74 years
Men 69 years

Religions:
Sunni Islam, Coptic Christianity

Language:
Arabic

Literacy rate:
81%

Population

The land of Egypt traditionally acts as a link between the Orient and the Occident—this is particularly true for its capital city, Cairo. Although progress is felt everywhere, certain traditions are still widely practiced, and Islam strongly influences the life of its citizens. Because of its special environmental situation, only around 4 percent of the national area is available for residential and economic purposes; an expansion is only possible at great financial expense. The residential density of Egypt, especially in the conurbation areas, is therefore among the highest in the world.

Approximately 80 percent of the Egyptian population is made up of Fellaheen, descendants of the ancient Egyptians. The farmers living in the Nile Valley were always settled rather than nomadic, and some still live in traditional mud-brick houses. Only the Bedouins are full-blooded Arabs. Berbers live in the Siwa oasis on the northwest border with Libya.

The Coptic Christians consider themselves the direct, unmixed descendants of the ancient Egyptians. They are represented in all classes of urban society, and in the country there are also Coptic farmers. In Upper Egypt live the Nubians. Their former residential heartland was flooded to form Lake Nasser.

The official language throughout Egypt is Arabic, but English is also used primarily as the main language for business and commerce. Coptic is used as a religious language, and Nubian and Berber languages are also spoken.

Population explosion in the Nile Delta

Without the uninhabitable desert region, the ancient Egyptian civilization in the fertile Nile Valley might well never have existed. The unusually high population concentration in such a tightly limited area helped to build a cohesive and organized nation with a highly developed culture very early in its history. There is still a sharp contrast between the national area and the inhabited areas within it. Even today most of Egyptian life takes place in a relatively narrow green strip along the Nile. The population density in this area is 2,000 people per km2 (5,200 people per square mile).

The few cultivable areas were used intensively for agriculture. However, due to the ever-increasing need for new housing, more and more arable areas have had to be used for residential developments for the rapidly growing population.

Children are expected to ensure a secure existence for their parents in old age, so having a large number of children is the goal of every family. The high birth rate

Cameleer on the coast of the Red Sea

Street life in Cairo: population growth is a major issue in Egypt.

is not only based on economic necessity, however: in Egyptian culture, the idea of the blessing of children as a gift of God is very deeply rooted.

The overpopulation of Egypt has placed the country in a precarious economic and demographic position. Nearly a quarter of the population is 10 years of age or younger and one third is under 15 years of age. For a long time now, the country's agricultural production has no longer been adequate to feed the population.

Religious variety
Religion continues to play an important role in the social structure and everyday life of Egyptians. The basis for their deeply rooted religious adherence lies, among other factors, in the influence that Egypt has had on the development of the world's three most important religions: Islam, Christianity, and Judaism.

In 641 CE Egypt was conquered by the forces of the new religion of Islam, which had begun in Arabia, and became part of the Islamic world. Sunni Islam has since then been the dominant religion of the country, with approximately 90 percent of the population being adherents.

Jews and Coptic Christians (9 percent) are religious minorities in the country. Although the Copts today make up only a small proportion of the population, their traces can be found everywhere. At the Council of Chalcedon in 451 they split off from mainstream Christianity, and since then have built an independent faith community as the Coptic Orthodox Church.

Sufis, followers of a mystical dimension of Islam, celebrate the birthday of the Prophet Muhammad in the streets of Cairo.

HISTORY
....

3000 BCE
Menes unites Egypt

c.2700–2160 BCE
Old Kingdom

2040–1797 BCE
Middle Kingdom

c.1550–1075 BCE
New Kingdom; Egypt becomes a great power

332 BCE
Alexander the Great conquers Egypt

305 BCE
Ptolemy founds his dynasty

30 BCE
Egypt becomes a Roman province

395–640 CE
Egypt is part of the Byzantine Empire

c.641
Arabs conquer Egypt

969–1171
Fatimid dynasty

1171–1250
Ayyubid dynasty

1250–1517
Expansion under the Mamluks

1517
Ottomans conquer Egypt

1798
Napoleon conquers Egypt

1801
Withdrawal of the French

1805
Muhammad Ali becomes pasha of Egypt

1869
Opening of the Suez Canal

1914
Egypt becomes a British protectorate

1922
Egypt achieves official independence

1936
King Farouk I ascends the throne and Britain officially recognizes the sovereignty of Egypt; Britain's authority restricted to military control of the Suez Canal zone (Anglo-Egyptian Treaty)

1948–49
Egyptian–Israeli War

1952
Revolution by the Free Officers, led by Gamal Abdel Nasser

1953
Egypt becomes a republic

1956
Suez Crisis

History and Politics

Egypt can look back on one of the greatest and longest histories in the world. As one of the earliest civilizations, the country's countless ancient artifacts are researched throughout the world. The glorious eras of the Old, Middle, and New Kingdoms were followed by many centuries of foreign rule. Only in 1922 did Egypt become a kingdom, and later an independent republic.

As early as the 4th millennium BCE the culture on the Nile was relatively highly developed. Beginning with the rule of the first legendary pharaoh, Menes, who in 3000 BCE united Egypt, commenced the long roll call of 31 dynasties, ending with the Ptolemaic dynasty and Cleopatra's son by Julius Caesar, Ptolemy XV Caesar, in 30 BCE. From 3000 BCE the eras are divided into the Old, Middle, and New Kingdoms.

From great empire to Roman province

During the Old Kingdom period, which is also called the Age of Pyramids, the Egyptian calendar and a strongly integrated, centralized nation were created. Imhotep (around 2650 BCE), the architect of the pharaoh Djoser, who ruled in 2620–2600 BCE, built the first step pyramid in Saqqara and with it founded stone-building architecture in Egypt. In this era the legendary Khufu pyramid was also built at Giza, and Memphis became the capital city of the kingdom.

In the Middle Kingdom, the country prospered and flourished economically and culturally. The area covered by the realm at that time corresponded roughly to the same area as modern Egypt.

Finally, with the New Kingdom began the era of Egyptian supremacy in the Middle East, and it is from this period that even today many magnificent buildings commissioned by legendary rulers remain, such as the Temple of Hatshepsut (1490–68 BCE) and the buildings of Ramses II (1290–24 BCE). The New Kingdom reached its zenith during the reign of Ramses II: in his more than 60 years as pharaoh he had many monumental buildings built (among others the famous temples of Abu Simbel). Amenophis IV (c.1364–47 BCE), however, became embroiled in a conflict with the powerful priestly caste because he espoused the monotheistic cult of the Sun God. Changing his name to Akhenaten, he went down in ancient Egyptian history as the 'Heretic Pharaoh.'

The late era of ancient Egypt in the 7th to 8th centuries

The famous gold mask of Tutankhamun in the Egyptian Museum in Cairo.

BCE was a time of transition, in which the country was ruled by Nubian, and later by Persian kings. Alexander the Great (356–23 BCE) conquered Egypt in 332 BCE without a battle, and ordered the construction of the city of Alexandria, which quickly became the center of Greek world trade and a beacon of knowledge and culture. After his death, Egypt fell to one of his generals, Ptolemy I Soter (c.360–283 BCE), who founded the Ptolemaic dynasty. Cleopatra VII (69–30 BCE) was the last queen of the Ptolemies. After her death, the country was incorporated into the Roman Empire as a Roman province (30 BCE–CE 395), then, after the division of the empire into eastern and western halves, it eventually became part of the Byzantine Empire (395–640).

Islamic rulers

During the Arab conquest of the country in the years 639–42 CE the city of Fustat was founded, the nucleus of today's Old Cairo. Sultan Salah al-Din ('Saladin,' 1138–93), who was able to reconquer Syria and Jerusalem from the Crusaders, was the first ruler of the Ayyubids (1171–1250).

The year 1250 marked the beginning of Mamluk rule. In 1517 Egypt was conquered by the Ottomans and was from then on a province of their empire. In 1805 Muhammad Ali (1769–1849) proclaimed himself pasha and ejected the Turkish governor. A victory over the British in 1807 and the killing of many Mamluk leaders in 1811 consolidated his power. Today, based on his fundamental reforms of education and health, he is seen as the founder of modern Egypt.

The Step Pyramid of Saqqara, south of Cairo, was built by the architect Imhotep for the pharaoh Djoser around 2650 BCE.

Egypt under British control

Muhammad Ali's successors put the country into great debt, so even the Egyptian shares in the Suez Canal were handed over to Great Britain. After France and Great Britain seized control of Egyptian national finances in 1881, unrest and rebellion flared up, which Great Britain used as a pretext to conquer Egypt in 1882. After the country was declared an independent kingdom in 1922, British influence waned, and after 1936 the British share of the Suez Canal zone also decreased. On 23 July 1952, the Free Officers rose up against King Farouk I (1920–65) and British foreign rule, and the king was forced to abdicate.

Gamal Abdel Nasser, Egypt's president from 1954 until his death in 1970

Proclamation of the Republic and the Suez Crisis

On June 18, 1953, the Republic of Egypt was proclaimed and General Muhammad Nagib (1901–84), who was already prime minister, also took on the office of national president. He did not last long in office, however—Gamal Abdel Nasser (1918–70) overthrew him in 1954 and took power, ruling the country until 1970.

In July 1956, Nasser nationalized the Suez Canal. This led Great Britain, France, and Israel to attack Egypt with the aim of occupying the canal. The United Nations succeeded, with the help of the USA and the Soviet Union, in declaring a ceasefire and the aggressors withdrew.

The post-Nasser period

When Egypt barricaded the Gulf of Aqaba against Israeli ships in May 1967, and forced the withdrawal of the UN troops from the demilitarized zone, the so-called Six Day War began. Israeli troops invaded and occupied the Sinai Peninsula up to the banks of the Suez Canal.

After the death of Nasser, the new President Anwar Sadat (1918–81) endeavored to bring peace to the region and oriented his foreign policy more strongly toward the West.

In domestic politics he aspired to reconciliation with the religious fundamentalists, since the impoverishment of the population caused great tension and unrest. He also anchored the Islamic legal order in the country's constitution. In 1978 Sadat founded the National Democratic Party (NDP), which was established as the party of government.

The Arab–Israeli War in October 1973 brought Egypt only partial success, but allowed the reopening of the Suez Canal in 1975. The Peace Accord of Camp David accomplished the withdrawal of Israeli troops from the Sinai Peninsula (1979–82). However, there was increasing resistance and unrest against Sadat's pro-Western policies and the Peace Accord. In 1981 Sadat was assassinated by Islamic fundamentalists.

Hosni Mubarak (b. 1928) was his successor. He continued the liberalization of the economy and committed himself further to a peaceful co-existence with Israel, but also sought to join forces with Arab neighbors. After an assault on the president in 1995, the regime has made massive efforts against fundamentalist groups.

Anwar Sadat succeeded Nasser in 1970. He served as Egypt's third president until his assassination in 1981.

HISTORY

1958–61
Union with Syria to form the United Arab Republic

1960–70
Construction and opening of the Aswan High Dam

1967
Six Day War against Israel

1970
Death of G. Abdel Nasser; successor is A. Sadat

1973
October War with Israel

1975
Reopening of the Suez Canal

1979–82
Israeli withdrawal from Sinai

1981
Assassination of Sadat; H. Mubarak becomes president

2005
Mubarak begins fifth term in office, having gained almost 90% of votes in the presidential elections

The anti-terror movement against Islamic fundamentalists is extended

POLITICS

Government:
Presidential republic

Head of state:
President

Legislature:
'People's Council' with 444 elected and 10 appointed members and 'Shoura' as deliberative organ with 264 members

Administrative divisions:
29 governorates

ECONOMY

Currency:
*1 Egyptian pound (EGP)
= 100 qirsh/piastres*

Gross domestic product:
$130.5 billion US

Gross per capita income:
$1,580 US

Overseas trade:
*Imports $52.8 billion US
Exports $ 29.4 billion US*

Foreign debt:
$32.1 billion US

Economy, Traffic, and Communication

Over many centuries, Egypt was a legendarily fertile and productive country. As one of the great granaries of the ancient world it was a vital source of grain for Rome. However, the agrarian sector has increasingly lost its significance in past decades. Today, the nation attempts to confront its increasing water shortage with complex irrigation systems, although the modernization and development of the country's industrial production also presents great challenges to the economy.

any other exports to fall back on. In recent years, cultivation areas for cotton have been further decreased.

An intensive irrigation culture began with the Aswan High Dam in 1970, which holds back the Nile in the southern portion of the country and created the 500-km (311-mile)-long Lake Nasser. As a result of these ambitious measures, historic Nubia is now mostly under water. Thanks to the new water reservoirs, up to three harvests are possible every year; however, at the same time, the fertile Nile silt is kept in the lake. The dam can also hold

View of the Aswan High Dam, which was constructed between 1960 and 1970.

The former 'Granary of Egypt' can today meet only about 50 percent of the nutritional requirements of its own population. The limited cultivation areas and the general water shortage have continually diminished the productivity of the agrarian sector over the past few decades.

Cotton cultivation and irrigation systems

The country's most economically significant crop and export product is still cotton, which is also of great importance as a raw material for the Egyptian textile industry. Although the plant was not brought to the country until 1821, Egypt has been a supplier of valuable high-quality cotton since then. President Nasser encouraged the development of huge areas of cotton cultivation, but it was a measure that was scaled down by his successors in order to avoid dependence on a monoculture, putting the country at the mercy of world cotton prices without

back catastrophic floods (for example, in 1972), and can compensate for drought years in the source areas (1980s) through its reserves. However, its long-term ecological consequences are only partially predictable.

The Toshka Project

The Egyptian government began an ambitious project for expansion of the agrarian area from the current 3 percent to 20 percent of the land area with the initiation of the Toshka Project. Land in the southern Libyan desert will be made cultivable in a few years time, offering around three million people a new home as well as work. The world's largest pumping station is being installed near Abu Simbel. The pump will raise the water of Lake Aswan—an overfill basin of Lake Nasser—54 m (177 ft) to the desert plateau. A concrete canal will then transport it 200 km (124 miles) into the desert to irrigate the dry landscape.

Oil and natural gas

Oil and natural gas are Egypt's most important natural resources and they make up the major source of income for the country. Since the 1970s the production of oil has permanently changed the economic structure of the country. Through export revenues the industrial sector has been strongly developed and expanded.

The largest part of the overall production comes from the oil fields on the Gulf of Suez as well as production from the Qattara Depression. Up to 75 percent of the oil produced is refined in the country itself, but it is evident that the oil supply may dry up before long. In order to meet the increasing demand from an expanding domestic industrial sector and have surplus oil reserves available for export, oil and natural gas exploration has been intensified.

Continual drought over a period of years has also had lasting effects on the energy economy. Power, around 25 percent of which was previously obtained from hydroelectricity, must now be produced from natural gas power plants. Currently, some 80 percent of overall demand is met by these sources.

In addition, Egypt is investing in the development of solar energy and wind energy. By 2020 the government plans to replace 14 percent of the country's primary energy demands with renewable energy.

Industry

For many decades, the government has exercised strict control over the industrial economy, with restrictive and hampering measures against private enterprise. In the 1990s a slow liberalization of the economy began with the sale of national businesses.

The main problems of the industrial sector lie in inefficient work processes, outdated technology, and bureaucratic hurdles, as well as arbitrary restrictions.

The most significant industry sectors are primarily oil processing, the textile industry, automobile manufacturing, and heavy industry

A street market in Thebes. Ancient Thebes with its famous necropolis is a UNESCO world heritage site.

(steel, iron, and aluminum), as well as the armaments industry. The textile industry, which was completely nationalized, has to struggle with considerable problems, while the privatized clothing industry enjoyed a boom. About 20 percent of the labor force work in the industrial sector.

The oldest railroad in Africa

Egypt's rail network is the oldest on the African continent. The Cairo–Alexandria route was opened as early as 1856. The network covers a length of over 5,000 km (3,107 miles) and concentrates on the Nile Delta, the Mediterranean coast, and the Nile Valley.

Generally, Egypt's transportation system is well covered by an extensive sealed road network of 75,000 km (46,875 miles). Most connect the main cities in the Nile Delta, follow the Nile, and lead to the large oases of the desert, to the Suez Canal, and the Sinai Peninsula. The road network in large cities was long ago pushed to its limits: the traffic chaos of Cairo is notorious.

Ship transportation through the Suez Canal is an important economic factor. Due to their strategic geographic location, ports such as Alexandria, Port Said, and Suez are of international significance for global transportation. Ships also sail regularly along the Nile; it is of great importance not only for the transport of goods, but also for the tourism sector: a voyage on the Nile is one of the most popular aspects of any visit to Egypt.

International air traffic is channeled through Cairo, Alexandria, Hurghada, and Sharm al-

Sheikh. Port Said, Aswan, Luxor and Abu Simbel have domestic airports.

Limited freedom of the press

Since the abolition of censorship in 1974, the press has developed. It is, however, still under government control. The tightening of press laws in 1995 was seen by the opposition as limiting press freedom; since then, increasingly restrictive measures have been passed in order to eliminate criticism of the president and the government. The semi-official daily newspaper *al-Ahram* has a circulation of about 1 million copies. Founded in 1875, it is also available online and as a weekly edition in English and French. The dailies *al-Akhbar* and *al-Gumhouriya* are government-owned. Most radio and television programs are transmitted from the government's Egyptian Radio and Television Union. With the launch of the Nilesat 101 satellite in 1996, a new era of information technology was ushered in for Egypt.

Tourism

Egypt is immensely rich in cultural treasures: UNESCO has placed a number of these on its list of World Cultural Heritage Sites. Along with ancient Thebes (modern-day Luxor), with its famous necropolis, are included Islamic Cairo, Memphis and its necropolis comprising in part the pyramids and tombs of Saqqara, and the pyramids of Abu Sir and Dahshur, the Nubian monuments including Abu Simbel and Philae, the early Christian ruins of Abu Mena, and St Catherine's Monastery, as well as, of course, the pyramids of Giza.

A cargo ship passes through the Suez Canal. Average transit time is about 15 hours.

SUDAN

THE COUNTRY

·····································

Official name:
Republic of the Sudan

Geographic coordinates:
*North Africa; between 4° and 23°
north, and 22° and 38° east*

Area:
*2,505,810 km²
(967,500 square miles)*

Capital:
Khartoum

Climate:
*Desert climate in the north;
narrow strip with steppe climate
south of Khartoum; then
savannah climate; Khartoum
29°C (84.2°F)/164 mm (6.5 in);
Port Sudan 28°C (82.4°F)/
110 mm (4 in); Juba 26°C
(79°F)/982 mm (29 in)*

Time zone:
Greenwich Mean Time +3 hours

Sudan is the largest country on the African continent. It is separated from its neighbors by natural barriers, and its interior is shaped by the immense landscape of the Sudd and the fertile region along the mighty River Nile. Sudan is a country of marked geographical and cultural contrasts, however. The dry desert and semi-desert in the north form a stark contrast to the wet savannahs of the south. Meanwhile the Muslim peoples of the north see themselves as quite distinct from the Christian Africans of the south, and not only in terms of religion.

Geography

Mountains and deserts form the geographical borders of Sudan. The bordering mountains of the Red Sea lie in the northeast, giving way to the Ethiopian highland in the south. The White Nile Basin, which takes up a wide area of Sudan, is demarcated by the Imatong mountains (Kinyeti 3,187 m/10,456 ft) in the south, the North Equatorial (Asande) sill in the southwest, and the highland of Darfur with the 3,088 m (10,131 ft) Marra Massif in the west. In the northwest and north, Sudan includes part of the Libyan Desert. Wide plateaus and tablelands make the desert seem endless.

In the interior of the country, the river oasis of the Nile forms the scenic backbone of the country. In this largely flat and monotonous landscape, the Nuba mountains, which reach up to 1,459 m (4,187 ft) at Tingal, rise out of the Kordofan highlands.

The Nile: lifeline of Sudan

As the longest river on earth, the Nile flows from its source in central Africa up to the Nile Delta on the Mediterranean coast, traversing a considerable length of Sudan. To-gether with its tributaries, the river forms the flooded, marshy landscape of the Sudd ('Barrier'). It flows through extensive basin landscapes on its way north. At Khartoum, the Blue Nile, which comes from Ethiopia, unites with the White Nile, coming up from the south. In north Sudan, the Nubian Desert reaches almost up to the banks of the Nile. The fertile vegetation zone remains limited to the river oasis.

The Sudanese Nile is, of course, a very distinctive river. Five of the six Nile cataracts are situated in Sudan alone, which complicates boat travel on the river. On its course to Khartoum, the White Nile loses 60 percent of its water, especially in the Sudd, mainly through evaporation because of the increasing dryness as it flows north.

The encroaching desert

As recently as 40 years ago, extensive forests and savannahs still covered a large part of Sudan. However, the overuse of natural resources, paired with climatic variations, has brought about an unstoppable advance of full and semi-deserts, which now make up about 45 percent of the total land area.

At the beginning of the 1970s, the land was increasingly exhausted and this process was accelerated by long periods of drought (especially in 1984–85), increasing

An aerial view of Khartoum, Sudan's capital and largest city, where the White Nile and Blue Nile merge. The rivers divide the city into Khartoum, Khartoum North, and Omdurman.

Members of the Nuba people who live in the Nuba mountains in southern Sudan. Even though they are often referred to as one people they speak many different languages.

population, an increasing number of livestock, and subsequent overgrazing. Sand dunes extend ever farther because the sparse vegetation is eaten faster than it can grow back. The deserts are extending 10–15 km (6–9 miles) annually southward to the Sahel. This continuing desertification of wide areas of land to the point of full loss of fertility has led to the destruction of an estimated 65 percent of the total agricultural area in Sudan.

Climate of extremes

Sudan lies in the zone of the hot inner tropics, with its borders reaching from near the Tropic of Capricorn in the north almost to the Equator in the south. The northern half is characterized by a desert climate with extreme heat, dryness, and large daily variations. Frequently, no rain falls for several years.

In contrast, in the tropical south, the temperatures are somewhat lower, and humidity and precipitation of 500 mm (20 in) occur. The rainy period in summer varies in length, and droughts occur ever more frequently.

Outside the mountain regions and the moist south, the infamous Habub can appear at any time throughout the year. This is a sandstorm of gigantic proportions, which blocks the sun with a thick curtain of sand and blows over the country with howling winds. The Khamsin, a dry, hot, dusty and sandy desert wind is typical for the spring. It can blow for up to fifty days and removes almost every drop of water from the air and ground. The extreme climatic contrasts are also reflected in the animal and plant life. The farther south one goes in the country, the more diverse the nature becomes.

Population

The Republic of Sudan is home to more than 500 different tribes, which are classified into over 50 different ethnic groups. The northern and western peoples are predominantly Arabs (around 50 percent), Nubians, Beja, Nuba and Fur. In contrast, in the south, African peoples, among them the Azande on the border with the Congo, are predominant.

Approximately 70 percent of the Sudanese are Muslim, around five percent identify themselves as Christian, and another 25 percent are followers of traditional indigenous belief systems.

POPULATION

Number of inhabitants:
39.5 million

Population density:
*16 inhabitants/km²
(41 inhabitants/square mile)*

Population distribution:
*38% urban
62% rural*

Annual population growth:
2.2%

Life expectancy:
*Women 52 years
Men 50 years*

Religions:
*Sunni Islam, Christianity,
indigenous beliefs*

Languages:
*Arabic, English (official
languages), Nubian, Nilo-Saharan
languages*

Literacy rate:
63%

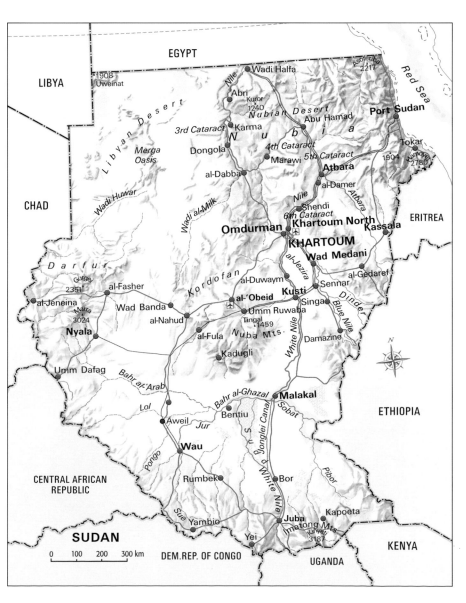

HISTORY

c.2000 BCE
The Nubian kingdom of Kerma extends across north Sudan

From 1000 BCE
The Kingdom of Kush (northeastern regions of modern Sudan) under Egyptian influence

6th–15th centuries CE
Christian kingdoms in Nubia

From 14th century
Start of Islamization

1821
Egypt gains power over Sudan

1881
Armed rebellion under Muhammad Ahmed ibn Abdallah (the Mahdi)

1884–98
Religious–autocratic Mahdist state

1899–1956
Anglo-Egyptian Condominium

1956
Sudan becomes independent

1958
After a coup, Gen. I.F. Abboud sets up a military dictatorship

1964
A people's revolution overthrows Abboud

1969
Col. Nimeiry takes over power

1972
The southern provinces receive limited autonomy

1983
Islamic law (Sharia) is instituted. A new civil war erupts in the south

1985
Nimeiry is overthrown. The multi-party system is again instituted

1989
The military again takes power, O. al-Bashir becomes president

1991
The military government proclaims a federal state

1998
Civil war causes famine; new constitution created

2003–04
Civil war between government troops and Arab militia and the freedom movement SPLA in the Darfur region

History and Politics

Although for many hundreds of years Sudan was associated with the immeasurable riches of deepest Africa, today hunger, war, and atrocities define the image of the modern republic. The economic and political systems are presently dominated by long periods of vicious armed combat. Militant Islamic fundamentalism and the highly credible reports of the rebirth of slavery make for further negative headlines.

In the shadows of the ancient Kingdom of the pharaohs, which reached up to the third Nile cataract, the Kushite Kingdom established itself in Nubia from 1000 BCE. One of its dynasties even sat on the Egyptian throne between 745 BCE and 655 BCE. Christianity reached the area of present-day Sudan in the 6th century, and several Christian-Nubian kingdoms existed until about 1500. From 1315, the northern state around Dongola and from 1504 the southern state of Alwa came under Arabian control. The people adopted Islamic beliefs. In the south of Sudan, the Kingdom of Funj survived from 1500 to 1700. In contrast, the north came under the control of the Mamluks, who ruled in Egypt. In the west, the independent sultanate of Darfur, which survived until 1874, was formed in the 17th century. This major Islamic center of Sudan was able successfully to defy Arabization, and to this day has preserved its cultural independence.

Plaything of colonial interests

From 1821, heavily supported and overseen by European technicians and officials, Egypt expanded its authority and dominion down to the Sudan in the search for gold and slaves. In 1839 the inaccessible swamps of the Sudd were opened up, and the southern area was taken by force and plundered.

In 1881, an armed rebellion rose up in the north against Egyptian rule under the Mahdi (Muhammad Ahmed ibn

Abdallah, 1844–85), who had largely taken back the country by 1883. The British used the death of General Gordon in 1885 during the Mahdi's conquest of Khartoum as an excuse to occupy Sudan. Under the leadership of General Lord Kitchener (1850–1916) the Mahdists were defeated in 1898. From 1899 to 1956, Egypt and Great Britain officially shared control of Sudan in the Anglo-Egyptian Condominium. In reality, however, Sudan was a British colony. During this time, the British tried to limit the spread of Islamic influence into the south, which they declared a 'closed district.'

From independence to civil war

Sudan became independent in 1956, and the new republic established a parliamentary system following the British model. This proved unmanageable, however; so much so that a military dictatorship took power and replaced the parliament in 1958. In 1969, General Gaafar Nimeiry (1930–2009) took control of the country after a national strike. The conflict between the Islamic north and the Christian south, which had steadily escalated into a full civil war after independence, was brought to an end only in 1972 with a negotiated peace that promised autonomy for the south of Sudan.

Economic difficulties in 1982, the institution of Islamic law (Sharia) in 1983, and the ending of autonomy in the south of Sudan through military control led to the second civil war, which was organized in the south under the leadership of the Sudanese Freedom Army (SPLA).

After the overthrow of Nimeiry in 1985, the succeeding government was also overthrown by the military. General Omar Hassan Ahmad al-Bashir (b. 1945) came to power in 1989. From the moment he took office he attempted to suppress the autonomy movements of the south with all the force at his disposal and simultaneously promoted a radical Islamic movement in Sudan.

The civil war in south Sudan was ended in January 2005 on the basis of earlier agreements. The government in Khartoum and the rebel group SPLA in south Sudan agreed that south Sudan would be granted autonomy. In 2011 a referendum will be held in which the region can decide whether it wishes to become independent.

While the tension in the south has gradually eased, from 2003 a new ethnically-motivated conflict escalated in the Darfur region. Several thousand people were killed, prompting a catastrophic wave of refugees. In the Darfur conflict, Arab mounted militia *(Janjaweed)*, supported by the central government, are fighting against black African rebel groups which belong to the Sudan Liberation Movement (SLM) and the 'Justice and Equality Movement' (JEM).

Muhammad Ahmed ibn Abdallah (1844-85), better known as the Mahdi by his followers, led a successful military campaign against British rule from 1881 to 1885.

Vendors offer groceries for sale in Khartoum's streets.

Economy, Traffic, and Communication

The economic problems are aggravated by the endless violence and civil war, which has smoldered for almost 50 years, and the recurrent periods of drought. Inherited from the British colonial period, the one-sided economy is focused on cotton and consequently dependent on world market prices. This and the absence of structural versatility and diversity in the economy are major brakes on development. Sudan is today dependent on international financial help, and its debt surpasses its export receipts several times over.

Cotton as the basis of the economy

The economy is predominately defined by agriculture. Only around 7 percent of the land is actually cultivated. Pluvial cultivation dominates in the southern savannah regions. For subsistence, the people grow sorghum, wheat, peanuts, sesame, and vegetables. Irrigated cultivation is essentially concentrated in the valley of the Nile and on the Gezira south of Khartoum.

An important agricultural export product of Sudan is cotton. Under the British cotton exports served the native textile industry, and the Gezira between the White and Blue Niles was made fertile through a gigantic irrigation system. Sudan produces 200,000 tons of valuable long-fiber cotton annually. The country is the second largest African exporter of high-quality cotton after Egypt. Other important cultivated products are sugar cane and tobacco.

Rich in mineral resources

Despite the wealth of mineral resources such as iron, copper and gold, these are not mined because of a lack of foreign currency and poor infrastructure. Since 1999

the oil deposits on the rim of the White Nile Basin have been mined. The export of raw petroleum produces over 80 percent of the country's foreign currency reserves.

Transportation and media facilities

The south has a poor transport infrastructure. Only a fraction of the roads are surfaced, and the other roads are almost impassable during the summer rains. The train network is around 4,600 km (2,875 miles) long, but only two-thirds is usable. Boat travel on the Nile between Juba and Khartoum is important, as are all-weather gravel roads. The most important sea port is Port Sudan on the Red Sea.

In the north and the south different national radio networks broadcast radio and television programs in Arabic and English. Only a small percentage of the population has access to telephones and computers.

Tourism

Today this huge country is visited by only around 65,000 foreign tourists a year. Considering the upheavals and great danger caused by continual civil war, traveling in Sudan remains, as ever, a big risk. Traveling beyond the capital Khartoum and the surrounding region is only possible to a limited extent because of the risks to personal safety and the lack of infrastructure. Despite these facts there is much to discover and enjoy there: the sights range from fascinating ruins of the ancient Nubian kingdoms to the no less impressive Nuba, Dinka, and Nuer peoples and their cultures.

Nubia, the region of north Sudan, has an ancient history even older than Egypt's.

The 10,000 km² (3,861 square mile) Dinder National Park lies on the Ethiopian border, southeast of Khartoum. It is one of the largest national parks in the world. Gazelles and lions live in the grassland and savannah landscape. Furthermore, the park is an important intermediate stop for several species of migratory birds.

Beautiful clear water, tropical fish, and stunning coral reefs are found along Sudan's Red Sea coast. Port Sudan is one of the main centers of this region, in whose vicinity the most famous Sudanese diving sites are to be found. These include Wingate Reef with the wreck site of the Italian war ship *Umbria*, sunk in 1940, the Sanganeb Reef and Shab Rumi.

HISTORY

2005
Peace agreement ends the civil war between the Islamic north and the predominantly Christian south; interim constitution and formation of a 'government of national unity' with representatives of both north and south

2007
Currency reform: the Sudanese dinar is replaced by the (new) Sudanese pound

2009
The International Criminal Court in The Hague issues an arrest warrant for President al-Bashir for war crimes and crimes against humanity during the Darfur war. African Union and Arab League denounce the court's action.

POLITICS

Government:
Presidential republic

Head of state:
President

Legislature:
Transitory parliament consisting of the National Assembly with 450 members and confederate council with 50 members; in the autonomous region of South Sudan, regional parliament with 161 members

Administrative divisions: 26 federal states, of which 10 in South Sudan; federal state of Abyei with special status

ECONOMY

Currency:
1 Sudanese pound (SDG) = 100 qirsh (piastres)

Gross domestic product:
$46.2 billion US

Gross per capita income:
$950 US

Overseas trade:
*Imports $7.7billion US
Exports $8.9 billion US*

Foreign debt:
$33.7 billion US

Transportation by bus is very popular in Sudan. Major bus stations are located in Khartoum, Kassala, Port Sudan, and al-Gedaref.

DJIBOUTI

THE COUNTRY
....

Official name:
Republic of Djibouti

Geographic coordinates:
*Northeast Africa; between 10°
55' and 12° 43' north, and 41°
48' and 43° 25' east*

Area:
*23,200 km²
(8,960 square miles)*

Capital:
Djibouti

Climate:
*Hot and dry semi-desert climate;
Djibouti 29.4°C (84.9°F)/ 97 mm
(4 in)*

Time zone:
Greenwich Mean Time +3 hours

POPULATION
....

Number of inhabitants:
848,000

Population density:
*37 inhabitants/ km²
(95 inhabitants/square mile)*

Population distribution:
*87% urban
13% rural*

Annual population growth:
1.7%

Life expectancy:
*Woman 45 years
Men 42 years*

Religions:
Sunni Islam, Christianity

Languages:
Arabic, French

Literacy rate:
68%

Djibouti is located in a strategically advantageous position, where the Indian Ocean meets the Red Sea; as a competitor to the British base Aden, this, the 'French Somali coast,' was a very important French colony. The people of Djibouti call the conflict-ridden strait of Bab al-Mandab at the Horn of Africa the 'Gateway of Tears.'

Geography

The landscape of Djibouti is dominated by deserts and semi-deserts covered with scarce vegetation, which usually consists of drought-tolerant grasses and shrubs. The coastal lowlands of the Gulf of Tadjoura, with their mangrove swamps and sandy beaches, reach deep into the heartland.

On the Red Sea are located the Afar lowlands, also known as the Denakil lowlands. The center and the south of the country are dominated by flat volcanic plateaus. Deep depressions caused by faults run parallel to the ocean and form saline lakes partly situated below sea level. The most famous of these depressions is Lake Assal, which lies at 153 m (508 ft) below sea level and is the lowest point in Africa. It is known as the most beautiful salt lake in the world. Just like the country's seawater lake, Lake Goubet, it is surrounded by extinct volcanoes and

black lava rock. Another lake, Lake Abbé on the Ethiopian border, is frequented by thousands of flamingos and pelicans.

The northern part of the country is generally mountainous, with the Musa Ali Massif rising up to a height of 2,028 m (6,653 ft).

Torrid climate

The hot climate becomes unbearable even for the inhabitants from June through August. In the summer months the average daily temperature ranges around a sweltering 40°C (104°F). Sparse rainfall with an annual average of 150 mm (6 in) occurs in the northern mountains in late summer and the end of March.

Population

Approximately 60 percent of Djibouti's population is Issa, who originate from the northern region of Somalia, while about 35 percent are Afar (Danakil). The remaining 5 percent of the population is made up of Europeans, mainly French and Arabs. The majority of Djiboutians are Muslims.

The relationship between the Afar and Issa is tense because of certain ethnic issues. The Afar have always lived in the northern and western parts of the country as well as across the Ethiopian border. The Issa, who immigrated into the south in the 10th century, formed the majority of the population.

History and Politics

The territory of Djibouti was controlled by Arabs from the 7th century, then by the Turks as part of the Ottoman Empire from the 16th century. The construction of the Suez Canal, which was opened in 1869, meant that the Gulf of Aden between the Red Sea and the Indian Ocean gained strategic significance. The overseas territory of French Somaliland was founded in 1896 by the French in order to counter the presence of the British in Aden (Yemen).

*Issa women in Djibouti's oldest town
Tadjoura perform a traditional dance.*

Lake Assal in Central Djibouti is famous for its high salt concentration. It lies 155 m (509 ft) below sea level. Salt is mined and transported on trucks and caravans to Ethiopia.

HISTORY

1896
The territory of the Afar and Issa becomes a French colony: French Somaliland

1917
Inauguration of the railway line from Djibouti to Addis Ababa

1967
The inhabitants of the Afar and Issa Territory decide to remain French; the French overseas territory is granted limited autonomy.

1977
The independent Republic of Djibouti is founded.

1991
Military conflict between government troops and rebel Afar units

1992
Introduction of a multi-party system

1993/94
Civil war between Afar and the ruling Issa

2008
Border conflict in Ras Doumeira between Eritrea and Djibouti

The railroad between Djibouti and the Ethiopian capital of Addis Ababa was established between 1897 and 1917; it helped to put the area on the map as Ethiopia's port of entry and export. The free harbor and the rail link soon formed the economic backbone of the small state.

Stability in the face of friction

Djibouti's recent history has been shaped by the rivalry between the Hamitic Issa and the Afar, and is closely linked to the frictions between Ethiopia and Somalia. Both states claim the port and the country of Djibouti. These conflicts have helped to strengthen the position of France and enabled it to keep its influence in Djibouti beyond the country's limited self-government as Afar and Issa Territory (1967) and its independence (1977). Furthermore, friction between the government and the Afar rebels led to perennial military conflicts at the beginning of the 1990s. Due to conflicts in the borderland there is also political tension with neighboring Eritrea.

Economy

Djibouti is very poor and deeply in debt. Economic aid from other countries, especially France, is crucial. The extraction of salt, fishing, and handling of Ethiopian overseas trade, as well as transportation (its rail link to Ethiopia) are some sources of income.

Salt and gypsum beds form the most important resources of the country, the biggest of their kind in the entire world. The sulfur vapor emerging from the up to 12-m (40-ft)-tall pillars of salt provides a powerful demonstration of the country's volcanic nature, while its geothermal springs are expected to free Djibouti one day from its dependence on importing its energy supplies.

Only a small percentage of the country's land is suitable for the growing of crops. Nomadic livestock herding (goats, sheep, camels, cattle, and donkeys) and fishing dominate the agricultural sector.

Industry provides jobs primarily in the building sector, food manufacture, salt extraction and energy production. Djibouti imports almost all of its food. The service industry is the most important economic sector, with the government and harbor administration as its main employers.

POLITICS

Government:
Presidential republic

Head of state:
President

Legislature:
National Assembly with 65 members, elected to 5–year terms

Administrative divisions:
5 regions and the capital

ECONOMY

Currency:
1 Djiboutian franc (DJF) = 100 centimes

Gross domestic product:
$769 million US

Gross per capita income:
$1,060 US

Overseas trade:
Imports $320 million US Exports $40 million US

Foreign debt:
$563 million US

SOMALIA

THE COUNTRY
·····································

Official name:
Republic of Somalia

Geographic coordinates:
*Northeast Africa; between 1° 40'
south and 12° north, and 41° and
51° 23' east*

Area:
*637,657 km²
(246,200 square miles)*

Capital:
Mogadishu

Climate:
*Hot and dry desert climate;
Mogadishu 30.2°C (86.4°F)/402
mm (16 in); Berbera 34.4°C
(93.9°F)/53 mm (33in)*

Time zone:
Greenwich Mean Time +3 hours

Somalia has been dominated by wars and poverty for decades. Constant conflicts between warlords and rival clans have crippled the country and led to a tripartite division within the land. Yet, despite the country's vast extent, there is a degree of cultural and linguistic cohesion and unity among its people not encountered in most other African countries.

Geography

Somalia covers a large part of the region that is known as the Horn of Africa, in the northeast of that continent. A series of mountain ranges dominates the northern part of the country. From the narrow coastal plain on the Gulf of Aden, the terrain rises up to heights of more than 2,000 m (6,562 ft). The Somali Plateau gradually descends toward the south. The coastal lowlands with their numer-

Mogadishu's old port gained importance during the Middle Ages. High walls provided protection from pirates and possible invaders.

Somali woman wearing a typical headscarf called hijab.

ous dunes bordering the Indian Ocean are much broader than the coastal region in the north. The coastline of Somalia extends for about 3,000 km (1,865 miles) in total.

Climate

Temperatures are high throughout the year; they may, for example, reach 50°C (122°F) in the coastal regions. Precipitation in this dry climate is influenced by the monsoon. From April to October the southwest monsoon may bring rain in the south, while in the north the northwest monsoon results in considerably less rain from November to March.

Population

Somalia is sparsely populated. Religion is an important unifier of the people as almost all Somalis are Muslim, most of them Sunni.

The majority is not settled: they travel the country as nomads searching for pasture for their cattle. The best grasslands are far from the coast in the center of the country; important grasslands are in the Ogaden region, most of which belongs to Ethiopia.

The traditionally difficult existence of most of the inhabitants has been intensified through decades of civil wars and seemingly endless waves of refugees from the Ogaden. A lot of people went to the north of Kenya, Yemen, Canada and the USA.

POPULATION
....

Number of inhabitants:
9 million

Population density:
14 inhabitants/km²
(37 inhabitants/square mile)

Population distribution:
36% urban
64% rural

Annual population growth:
2.9%

Life expectancy:
Women 49 years
Men 47 years

Religion:
Sunni Islam

Languages:
Somali, Arabic (official languages)

Literacy rate:
20%

Old Mosque in Mogadishu's old town. Almost all Somalis are adherents of Sunni Islam.

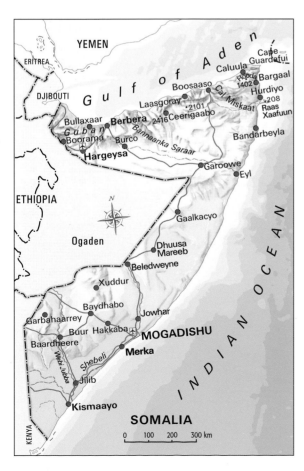

HISTORY

13th century
Kingdom of Ifat founded by immigrants from Yemen

Late 19th century
Territory divided between the colonial powers Great Britain, France and Italy

1960
British Somaliland and Italian Somaliland become independent (UN trusteeship from 1950); united to form Republic of Somalia

1969
General Muhammad Siad Barre takes power

1977–78
War against Ethiopia to take control of the Ogaden gives rise to civil war

1991
Proclamation of secessionist Republic of Somaliland in the north of the country

1991–92
Famine

1992–95
UN mission to bring peace to the country fails

1998
Proclamation of secessionist Autonomous Region of Puntland in the northeast of the country

1998–2000
Fighting between the militias of rival clans

2004
A peace treaty leads to the formation of a transitional government in exile in Nairobi

2006
The Islamist group Union of Islamic Courts (UIC) gains control of Mogadishu and large parts of central and southern Somalia; Ethiopia intervenes to support the transitional government

2007
Armed conflict between troops of Somaliland and Puntland

2009
Withdrawal of Ethiopian troops

Port workers in Mogadishu performing the midday prayer.

History and Politics

The coastal regions, which are settled by nomads, were converted to Islam by Arabs who arrived during the 7th century. In the 13th century large numbers of Yemenites came to Somalia across the Gulf of Aden. Much later, in an attempt to safeguard their shipping routes, the British occupied the city of Aden on the Yemenite side of the Gulf in 1839. The influence of European powers in the region increased after the completion of the Suez Canal in 1869. In 1887 the British government proclaimed the protectorate of British Somaliland. The French, meanwhile, took over a region that they named French Somaliland, which later became Djibouti. The Italians established Italian Somaliland near Mogadishu. There were several Somali uprisings against this foreign rule, but all were quickly and firmly defeated.

Political unrest

On July 1, 1960, the British and Italian territories were brought together to form the Republic of Somalia. In October 1969 the military under the leadership of Muhammad Siad Barre (1919–95) seized power, and brought the country under socialistic structures. The occupation of the region of Ogaden then led to a war, which was won by Ethiopia. An increasing number of refugees fleeing from the upheavals, and destruction in Ogaden, caused growing discontent and resistance against Barre's rule throughout Somalia. The opposition to his government was thus able to draw on the support of several disaffected clans. As the unrest spread and erupted into a civil war, Barre was forced to flee the capital in 1991. As the situation deteriorated, UN peacekeeping troops under the leadership of the USA were sent to stabilize the country in 1992. However, they became involved in fights between rival clans and left the country in 1994. The clan leaders met in 1997 and agreed to the establishment of an interim government. The situation remains tense, especially as the proclamation of the independent republics of Somaliland (1991) in the north and Puntland (1998) in the northeast continue to threaten national unity.

The Islamist grouping Islamic Courts Union (ICU) took control of Mogadishu and extensive regions of the interior in 2006, whereupon Ethiopia felt threatened again, declared war on the Union and forced it out of power. The transitional government was thus able to move into the liberated capital of Mogadishu. Following successful negotiations between the transitional government and moderate representatives of the Union, which had formed the Alliance for the Re-Liberation of Somalia in exile in Eritrea, the Ethiopian troops left the country once more in January 2009.

All power to the clans

Rivalry between the clans remains the main cause of instability. Their territories are not clearly defined and the structures of the extended families too diverse. There are six main clans, whose members live as nomads or farmers; settlement areas also play an important role. The majority of members of the Darod clan, for example, live as nomads in Ogaden and in the northeastern and southern regions of Somalia. Other Somalis, such as those of the clan of the Digil, live as arable farmers in the southwestern regions. The Hawiye clan has its territory around Mogadishu and in the center of the country.

POLITICS

Government:
No permanent national government

Head of state:
Interim president

Legislature:
Interim Parliament with 550 members

Administrative divisions:
18 regions

ECONOMY

1 Somali shilling (SOS) = 100 centesimi/cents

Gross domestic product:
$2.2 billion US

Gross per capita income:
$257 US

Overseas trade:
Imports $626.3 million US
Exports $249.9 million US

Foreign debt:
$4 billion US

A Somali man draws water from a well dug by UN peacekeeping forces.

Economy

Somalia is one of the poorest countries in the world and depends on extensive foreign aid. Camel breeding forms the basis of most Somalis' livelihoods. Camels supply the people with meat, milk, and skins, which are also sold to other countries, and serve as the main means of transportation. Goats, cattle and sheep are also kept. Agriculture is only really possible in the valleys of the large rivers in the south, where bananas, sugar cane, cotton, and cereals are cultivated. However, harvests are too poor to supply all the needs of the people.

Somalia's traffic infrastructure is still only poorly developed. Most roads are not surfaced. There is a surfaced road from Kismaayo in the south via Mogadishu to Hargeysa in the north. The international airport lies outside Mogadishu.

Somalia offers charming and unspoilt areas for tourists, with its sandy beaches on the southern coast and its national parks. However, traveling to Somalia is not advised due to the unstable and complex political situation and lack of security, especially in the southern regions and the center, where violent confrontations are still commonplace.

A farmer takes his sorghum crop to the market in Somalia's Bay region.

COMOROS

THE COUNTRY
··

Official name:
Union of Comoros

Geographic coordinates:
*Indian Ocean; between 11°
and 12° 30' south, and 43°
and 45° east*

Area:
1,862 km² (718 square miles)

Capital:
Moroni

Climate:
*Tropical, maritime climate;
Ngazidja 24.8°C (76.6°F)/
2639 mm (104 in)*

Arab seafarers knew the Comoros Islands as Jaza'ir al-Qamar, meaning 'Small Islands of the Moon.' Overshadowed by neighboring Mauritius and the Seychelles, whose beaches have made them renowned tourist destinations, the volcanic Comoros Islands are much less widely known. The people of the Comoros Islands can trace their roots back to the Arab, African, and Asian seafarers who settled here, and whose influence is still tangible on certain of the islands.

Geography

The group of islands that make up the Comoros is located in the Indian Ocean, about 200 km (125 miles) northwest of Madagascar's most northerly point, at the entrance to the Mozambique Channel. The archipelago consists of

Moroni's Ancienne Mosquée du Vendredi (Old Friday Mosque).

A group of guests at a traditional wedding in Mutsamudu on Ndzouani (Anjouan)

POPULATION

Number of inhabitants:
652,000

Population density:
350 inhabitants/km²
(908 inhabitants/square mile)

Population distribution:
35% urban
65% rural

Annual population growth:
2.8%

Life expectancy:
Women 65 years
Men 60 years

Religion:
Sunni Islam

Languages:
French, Arabic (official languages), Shikomoro

Literacy rate:
57%

four main islands—Ngazidja (Grande Comore), Moili (Mohéli), Ndzouani (Anjouan), and Mayotte, all of which are inhabited—and ten other islets, most of which are uninhabited. While the island of Mayotte belongs to France, the other three main islands constitute the Union of Comoros.

Volcanic islands in the Indian Ocean
All the large islands are of volcanic origin, but they were formed during different geological periods. Volcanic activity on Moili, the oldest of the Comoros Islands, ceased long ago. By a continuous process of erosion, the high mountain peaks that once covered the island have been turned into rolling hills.

In contrast, the islands of Ngazidja and Ndzouani are dominated by an imposing landscape of volcanic mountains. Kartala, a volcano that rises to 2,361 m (7,741 ft) on the island of Ngazidja, is still active; its last eruption was in April 2005. The island has many streams, which form impressive waterfalls where they plunge through narrow ravines near the coast. Parts of the islands' coasts are lined with beautiful, sandy beaches and coral reefs.

Tropical rain forests and plantations
The islands have a tropical climate. Northeasterly monsoon winds bring ample rainfall between November and April. Average annual rainfall ranges from 1,000 mm (39 in) on the coast to 4,000 mm (157 in) on the windward side of the mountains. Dry, southeasterly trade winds blow over the islands between May and October. The average year-round temperature is 20°C (68°F).

The islands support an abundant and diverse plant life. At low altitudes (up to 400 m/ 1,312 ft) the landscape is dominated by coconut palms and plantations of tropical fruits. Tropical rain forest predominates from 700 m (2,296 ft). Above 1,700 m (5,577 ft) it gives way to sparse grasslands.

Population
About 98 percent of the population of the Comoros Islands are of Indo–Melanesian, Arab, African, Madagascan, Creole, Indian, Chinese, or European descent. The same proportion is Sunni Muslim. Although Islam has a strong influence on Cormoran culture, differences between the populations of individual islands also exist. For example, most of the inhabitants of Ngazidja and Ndzouani follow Arabic Islamic traditions, whereas those of Moili follow East African customs.

Differences in wealth as social dynamite
Causes of social conflict between the inhabitants of the Comoros Islands are rooted mainly in economic and social differences. These are most marked between the islands' wealthy landowners, who are mostly of Arab-European descent, and the poor tenant farmers, the great majority of whom are black.

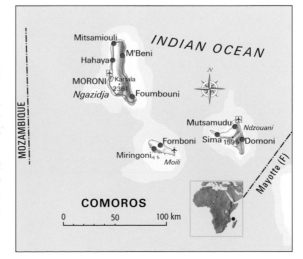

HISTORY

1841
Mayotte becomes a French protectorate

1886
France expands the protectorate to include all islands of the group

1912
French colony administrated as dependent territory of France's Madagascar colony

1961
France grants internal political autonomy

1975
Unilateral declaration of independence by the Comorian parliament; Ahmed Abdallah Abderemane is elected president

1978
Islamic Federal Republic of the Comoros is founded

1990
Said Mohamed Djohar is elected president

1996
Mohamed Taki Abdoulkarim is elected president

1997
The islands of Anjouan (Ndzouani) and Mohéli (Moili) declare their independence

1999
Military coup

2001
New Constitution; transformation into Union of Comoros

2003
Presidents of the islands Ngazidja, Ndzouani, and Moili sign a memorandum to further the national reconciliation process

2007
Island of Ndzouani occupied by government troops

History and Politics

From the 10th century until the Persians and the Arabs invaded the islands and established sultanates in the 16th century, the inhabitants of the Comoros were influenced mainly by the Swahili, who had themselves absorbed certain aspects of Arabic culture. Shortly afterwards, Europeans reached the islands, where they established trading posts.

From then until the 19th century, the islands were the object of dispute between European powers, and were also ransacked by pirates from Madagascar. It was above all France which profited; Mayotte came under French control in 1841, and in 1886 the other main islands that make up the Comoros became French colonies. By 1912, the entire archipelago was under French rule.

The path to independence

In 1961, the islands were granted internal autonomy. In a referendum held in 1974, the people of Mayotte voted in favor of the colony remaining part of France. However, the other islands voted for independence, and on July 6, 1975, they were jointly declared the Islamic Federal Republic of Comoros.

The republic's first president was Ahmed Abdallah Abderemane (1919–89). That same year he was deposed by a group of mercenaries supported by France, but he regained power in 1978. Supported by a single party, Abderemane imposed an authoritarian regime on the country, and revolts against his corrupt government were violently suppressed. Abderemane's political aim was to impose on the country a democratic socialism with an Islamic character.

Toward the end of 1989 Abderemane was assassinated. In the following years, the country's political situation was marked by power struggles, military conflicts, and revolts.

Battle for independence

The Islamic Federal Republic of the Comoros almost ceased to exist in 1997 when the islands of Moili and Ndzouani seceded from the union, although they did so without the support of the international community which was in favor of maintaining the country's integrity. Negotiations resulted in the drawing up of a unified constitution, which was ratified in 2001. According to this constitution, each island is autonomous, although they have common foreign, defense, and economic policies. A common president is elected from the population of each of the three islands in turn, but each island also elects its own president. The make-up of the General Assembly of 2004 increased the strength of opposition parties and of regional parliaments.

Economy

The Comoros Islands' main exports are vanilla, cloves, and ylang–ylang (an ingredient of perfume), which are cultivated in extensive plantations in the islands' coastal areas. Staple foods such as rice, peanut oil, and meat have to be imported.

As the revenue from export is insufficient to fund imports, the country is heavily dependent on international aid, and the Comoros is one of the poorest countries in the world. However, much hope rests on the promise of increased tourism, which went into decline as a result of the political instability.

Lemurs are endemic to Comoros and are an endangered species. They include a wide variety of species that differ greatly in size.

POLITICS

Government:
Federal republic

Head of state:
President

Legislature:
*General Assembly with 33
members*

Administrative division:
3 semi-autonomous islands

ECONOMY

Currency:
*1 Comorian franc (KMF)
= 100 centimes*

Gross domestic product:
$403 million US

Gross per capita income:
$660 US

Overseas trade:
*Imports $70.1 million US
Exports $9.1 million US*

Foreign debt:
$271 million US

Fishing boats in Moroni's port: most Comorans live on subsistence agriculture and fishing.

N'Gouni Crater on Ngazidja (Grande Comore) looms above a village situated on the coast.

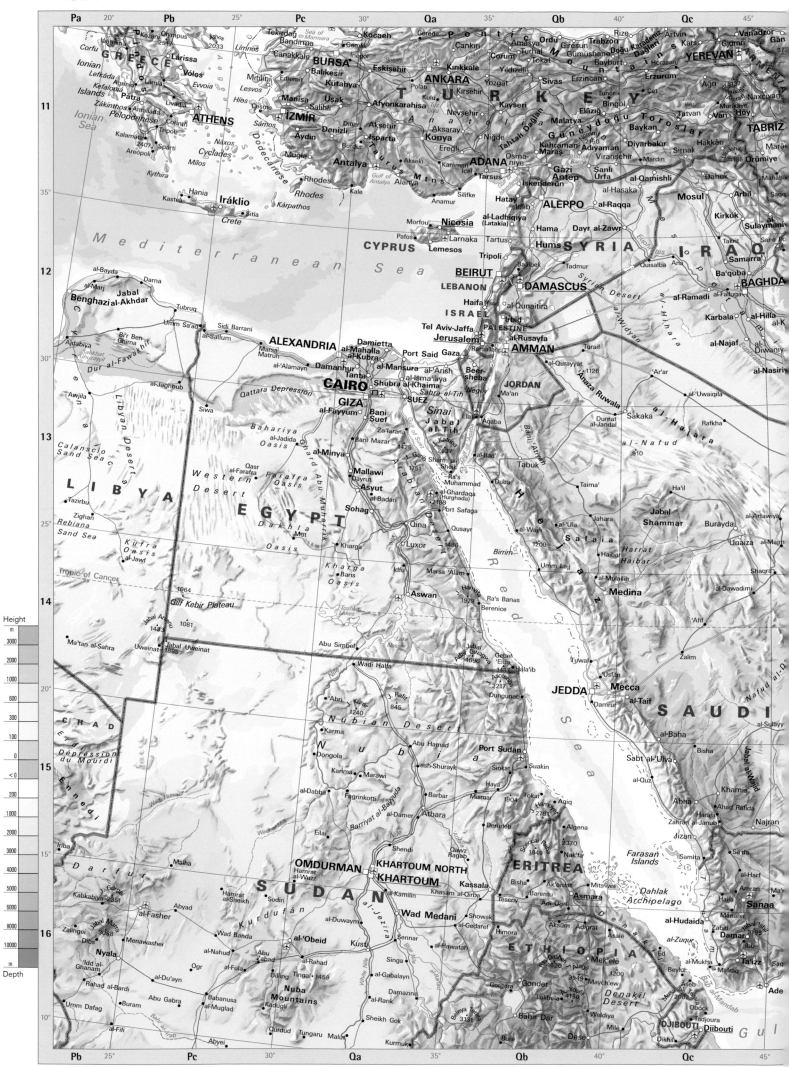

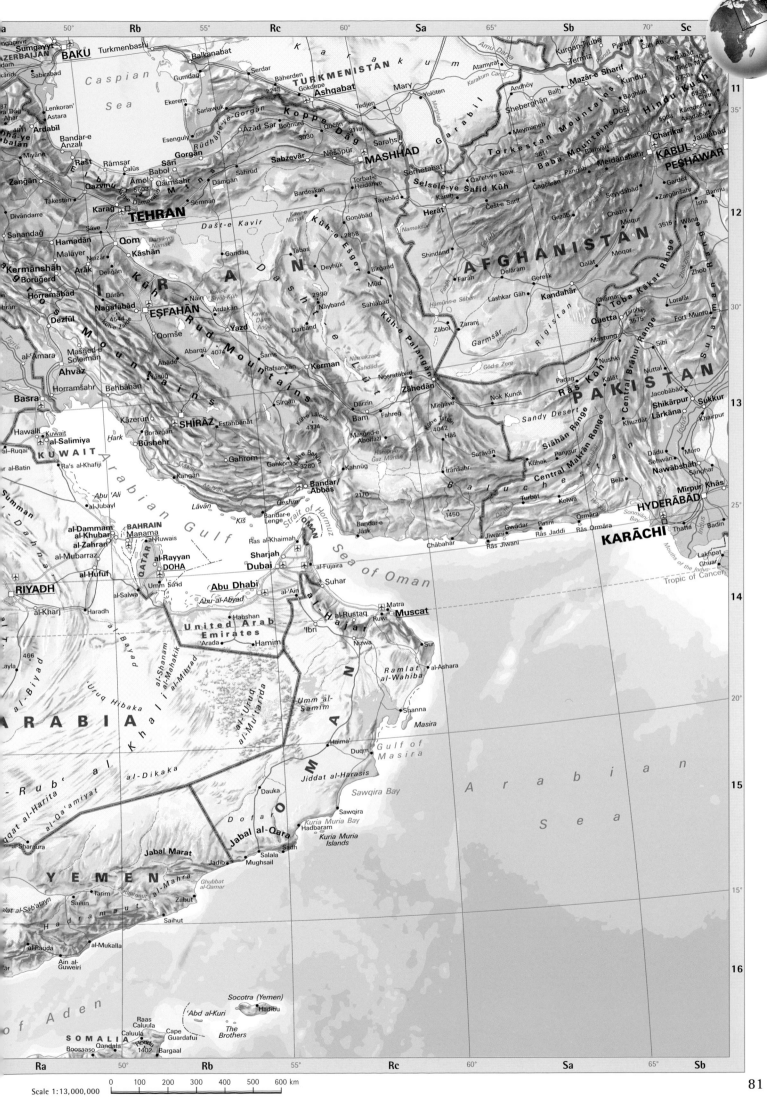

Sumgayyt
AZERBAIJAN
BAKU Turkmenbashi
Caspian Balkanabat
Sea Gumdag Serdar
Bäherden Ashgabat TURKMENISTAN Amu Dar'ya Kurgan-Tyube Pjandz
Lenkoran' Astara Esenguly Sarlawuk Gökdepe Tedjen Mary Yolöten Morghāb Atamyrat Termiz Pjandz Can. Ab
Ardabil Rüdhäpe-ye-Gorgān Koppe Dāg Garabil Sheberghān Andhöy Balh Kunduz Mazār-e Sharif Feyzabad
Rāst Rāmsar Gorgān Āzād Sar Boğnurd 3030 Quçan 3119 Sarahs Garabil Torkestan Mountains Meymaneh Dōşi Baghlän Baba Mountains Hindu Kush Chitral
Qazvin Āmol Qā'imshahr Sāri Sabzevār Nēşāpūr MASHHAD Serhetabat Selsele-ye Safid Küh Çağçarān Bāmyān Pangāb Meidānshahr KABUL PESHĀWAR
TEHRAN Semnān Shāhrūd Dāmgān Bardeskan Torbat-e Heidārīye Qal'eh-ye Now Herāt Çeśt-e Sarif Gezāb Chazni Muqur Seyydābād Zargūnshahr Gardēz
Karaj Säve Dašt-e Kavīr Kavīr Namak Gonābād Tāyebād AFGHANISTAN Helmand 3515 Isha
Hamadān Qom Darya-ye Namak Kūh-e Esger 2858 Tabas Deyhūk Bīrjand Mūd Farāh Delārām Gereśk Qalāt Moqor Zhob Wāna
Kermānshāh Arāk Kāshān Deligān Gardūq Nā'īn Kavīr-e Siyah-Kūh 2990 Nāyband Sahlābād Shindand Lashkar Gāh Kandahār Chaman Toba Kakar Range Loralāi
Borūgerd Najafābād Ardakān Darband Zābol Zaranj Garmsār Rigistan Quetta Mastung Fort Munro
Horramābād ESFAHĀN Kūh-e Zard 4544 Qomše Abarqū 4074 Yazd Kermān Namakzār-e Shāhdād Kūh-e Palangān Nosratābād Zāhedān Göd-e Zere Padag Nushki Sibi
Dezfūl Kūh-e Darre Anguū Rafsanjān Shams Kahnūg Mirjāve Nok Kundi Rās Kōh Jacobābād
al-Amara Masged-e Soleimān Qomše Sirgān Kūh-e Lālezar 4374 Barm Fahreg Kūh-e Taftān 4042 Hāš Sandy Desert Siāhān Range Khuzdar Shikārpur Lārkāna Sukkur
Ahvāz Behbahān Gahrom Kūh-e Bahūn 3280 Masged-e Abolfazl Hämün-e Gaz Mūriān Irānshahr Sarāvān Kühak Panjgur Central Makrān Range Dādu Khairpur
Basra Horramshāhr Kāzerūn SHĪRĀZ Estahbānāt Kangān Bandar/Abbās 2170 Kahnūg Turbat Kolwa Bela Sehwan Nawābshāh Sānghar
Hawalli Kuwait al-Salimiya Hark Borāzgān Būshehr Gahkom Qeshm Bandar-e Lenge Bandar-e Jāsk Chābahār Jiwani Gwādar Pasni Ormāra Mirpur Khās HYDERĀBĀD
al-Ruqai KUWAIT Ra's al-Khafiji Lāvān Kīš Strait of Hormuz Ras al-Khaimah Gwādar Rās Jaddi Rās Ormāra Sonmiāni Bay
al-Batin Abu 'Ali al-Jubayl OMAN Sea of Oman KARĀCHI
Summan Dahna al-Dammam al-Khubar BAHRAIN Manama Ruwais Sharjah Dubai al-Fujaira Ras al-Khaimah Thatta Badin
al-Zahran al-Mubarraz QATAR al-Rayyan DOHA Umm Sa'id Abu Dhabi Suhar al-'Ain al-Hajar al-Rustaq Matra Muscat Mouths of the Indus Lakhpat
al-Hufuf Umm Sa'id Abu Dhabi al-'Ain Ruwi Tropic of Cancer Ghuar
RIYADH al-Salwa Abu-al-Abyad Habshan United Arab Emirates 'Ibri Nizwa Ramlat al-Wahiba al-Ashara
al-Kharj Haradh al-Shanam al-Mahakik Arada Hamim OMAN Sur
466 al-Bayad al-Mihrad 'Uruq al-Muq'airida Umm al-Samim Shanna Masira
ARABIA Khali al-Mirad Uruq Hibaka al-Dikaka Masira
al-Biyad al-Qa'amiyat Haima' Duqm Gulf of Masira Arabian
Rub' al-Khali al-Harita Dauka Jiddat al-Harasis Sawqira Bay Sea
al-Sharaura Dofar Sawqira Kuria Muria Bay Hadbaram
Jabal al-Qara Jabal Marat Jadib Salala Sadh Kuria Muria Islands
YEMEN al-Mahra Mughsail
Plat al-Sab'atayn Saiun Tarim Zabut Ghubbat al-Qamar
Hadramaut al-Mahra Saihut
al-Rauda Ain al-Guweiri al-Mukalla Gulf of Aden Raas Caluula Cape Guardafui The Brothers Socotra (Yemen) Hadibu 'Abd al-Kuri
SOMALIA Qandala 1402 Bargaal
Boosaaso

11
35°
12
30°
13
25°
14
20°
15
15°
16

Scale 1:13,000,000
0 100 200 300 400 500 600 km

ASIA

Syria, Jordan, Lebanon, Palestine, Saudi Arabia, Iraq

84

Jordan, Palestine, Saudi Arabia, Kuwait, Bahrain, Qatar, U.A.E.

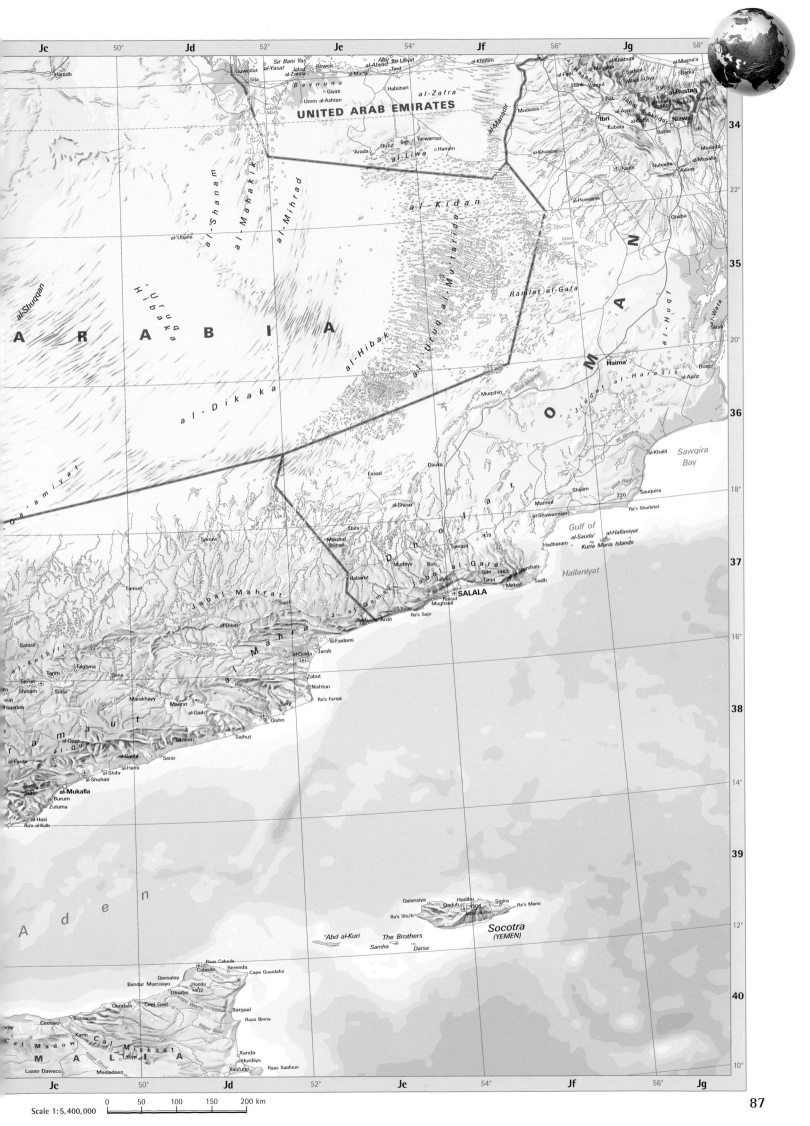

Haradh

Sir Bani Yas
al-Yasat
Guweifat
Sila
Jabal
al-Zanna
Ruweis
Abu
al-Abyad
Tarif
al-Marfa
al-Khatim

al-Hajar
al-Masalqa
Sadah
al-Masna'a
Barka

Baynuna
Giyati

Habshan

al-Zafra

al-Fath
Dank
Yanqul

Wadi Ufiya

al-Khabura

Tropic of Cancer
al-Rustaq

UNITED ARAB EMIRATES

Mudaisis

al-Manadir

Bat
al-Ayn
Jabal al-Akhdar
2980
Awabi

Nizwa
'Ibri
Kubara
al-Batil
Bahla
Izki

'Arada
Qutuf
Sah
Tarwaniya
Hamim
al-Liwa
al-Khuwayr

al-Huwaysa
Nafih
Ghaba
Mudaibi
Adam

A R A B I A

al-Shuqqan

al-'Ubaila

'Uruq
Hibaka

al-Shanam

al-Mahakik

al-Mihrad

al-Kidan

al-Hibak

al-'Uruq al-Mu'tarida

Ramlat al-Gafa

Umm
al-Samim

O M A N

al-Huqf

Jabal
Arab
al-Wata

al-Hibak

al-Dikaka

Haima'

Muqshin
Wadi Muqshin

Jiddat al-Harasis

al-Aja'iz
Duqm

al-Gamiyat

Easad

al-Shisar

Dauka
Wadi Umm al-Hait

Wadi Ghadun
Marmul

al-Shuwaimiyat

Sawqira
Bay

Sauqira
Ra's Sharbitat

Qafa

Makinat
Shihan

D h o f a r

419

Shalim
220

al-Khalil

Tamud

Jabal Mahrat

Sanaw

Habarut

Mudayy
Buri
Jabal al-Qara
Sihr 1463
Taqa
Salala
Mirbat
Jabal
Samhan

Hadbaram
al-Sauda'
al-Hallaniyat
Kuria Maria Islands

Gulf of

Jahrim

Hallaniyat
Sadh

al-Kathiri
Sarif

Jabal
Saihut

al-Dibin
al-Mahra
Ardit
Raisut
Mughsail
Ra's Sajir

Faghma
Sina

al-Faidami
Jarub

Sor'un
Shibam
Suna

Zabut
al-Gaida
Nishtun
Saqr
Ra's Fartak

inin
Hajarain
Marakhayy
Maqrat
al-Gail
Qishn

al-Ouza
Tamnun
Sarar
Saihut

al-Farda
al-Gaida
al-Hami
al-Shihr

Burum
2386
al-Mukalla
Zuluma

A d e n

Qalansiya
Hadibu
Sigira
Ra's Mami
Qadub
Hadibu
Jabal al-Jbir

Ra's Shu'b

Socotra
(YEMEN)

'Abd al-Kuri
The Brothers
Samha
Darsa

Raas Caluula
Geesaley
Caluula
Bereeda
Cape Guardafui
Bandar Murcaayo
Hooda
Dhurbo 1402
Qandala
Ceel Gaal
Bargaal
Raas Binna

ray
Ceelayo
Boosaaso
Karin
Cal Madow
Cal Miskaat
Xanda
Hurdiyo
M A L I A
Ufeyn
Raas Xaafuun

Laaso Dawaco
Meeladeen
Xaafuun

Scale 1:5,400,000
0   50   100   150   200 km

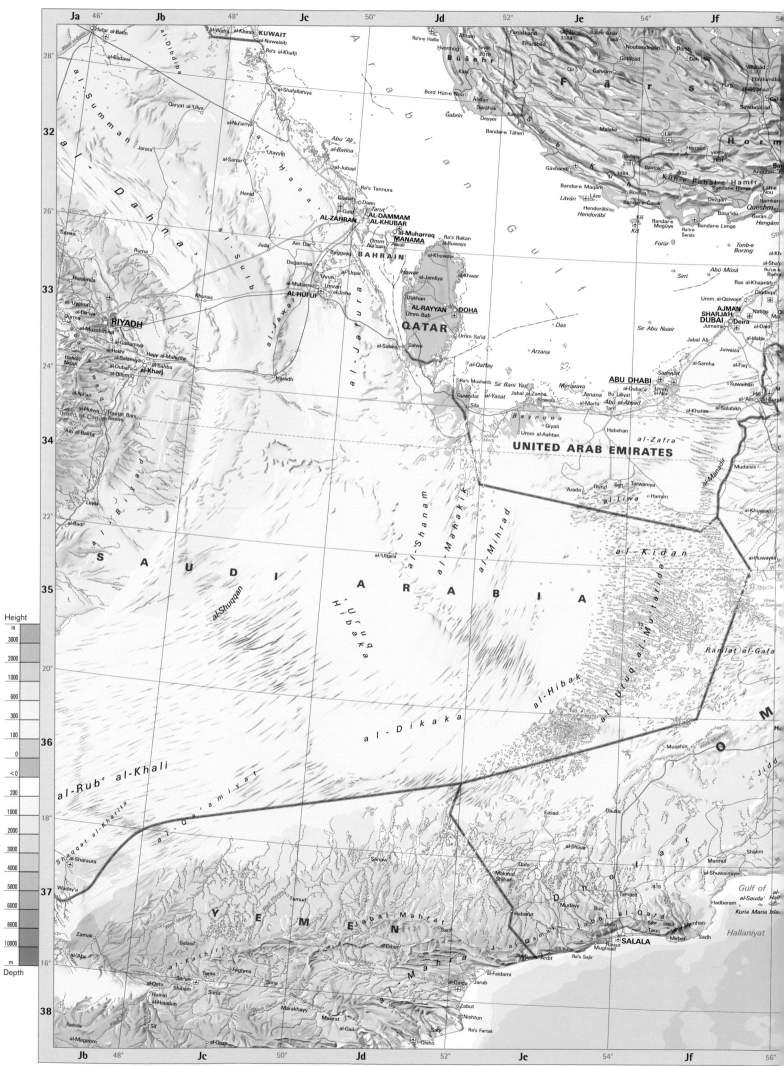

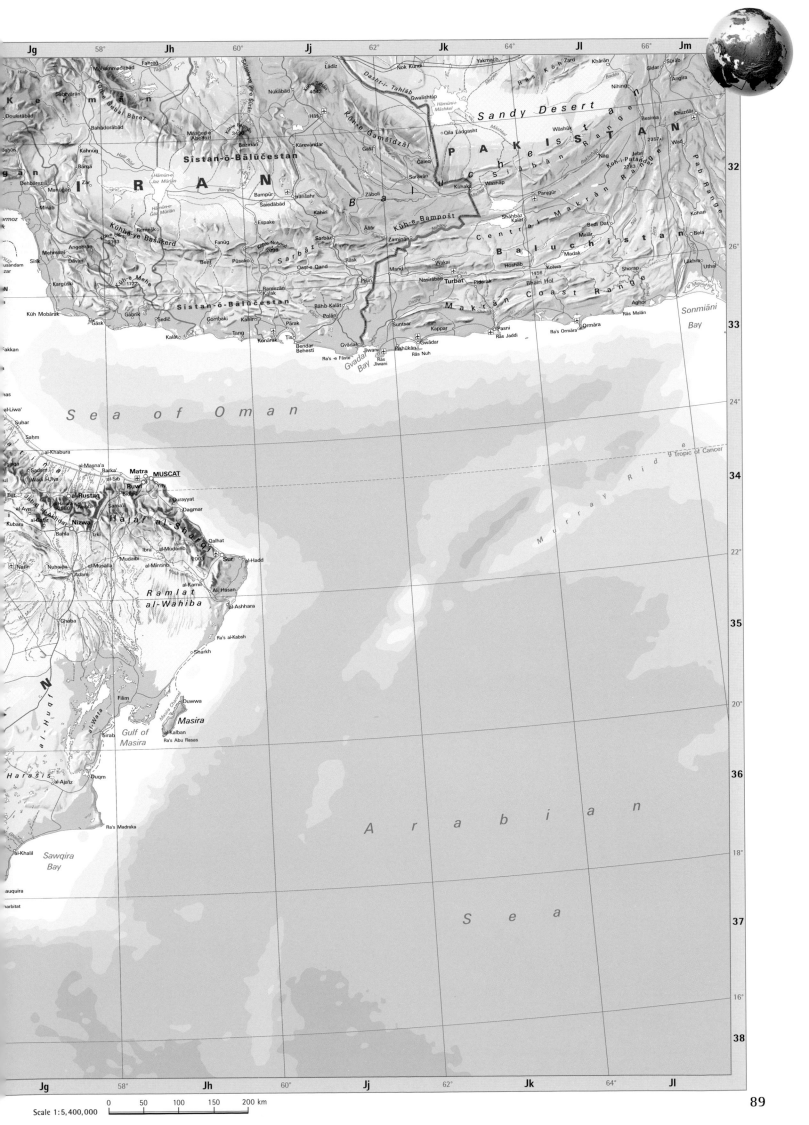

Kermān
Doulatābād
Sabzvārān
Kūh-e Gebāl Bārez
Mohammadābād
Fahreĝ
Tağābād
Salsabeye Pīre Sūrān
Fahreĝ
Lādiz
Nūkābād
Kūhe Bīrenĝa
3430
Hāš
Nok Kundi
Yakmach
Kharān
Gidar
Sūrāb
Angira
Ras Koh
Zard
Nihing
Morjen
Dasht-i-Tahlāb
Gwalishtāp
Hāmūn-i-Māshkel
Sandy Desert
PAKISTAN
Wāshūk
Besima
Washāp
Khuzdār
Wad
2357
Nag
Jebri
Koh-i-Pātandar
2283
Pab Range

Bahādorābād
Kahnūĝ
Bārna
Zar
Mahūgān
Dehbārez
Kūhha-ye Bašākerd
Kūh-e Herāz
2193
Kūh-e Mehe
1722

IRAN
Sīstān-ō-Bālūčestān
Bazmān
Kārevāndar
Gašt
Gāleĝ
Qila Lādgasht
Michael
Qila
B a l u c h i s t ā n
Siāhān Range
Central Makrān Range
Baluchistan
Kohan
Bela
Lākhra
Uthal
Aghor
Ras Malān
Sonmiāni Bay

Bampūr
Saiedābād
Espake
Kahiri
Āšār
Kūh-e Bampošt
Zāminān
Mand
Wakai
Nasirābād
Turbat
Piderak
Hoshab
1456
Bhairi Hol
Kolwa
Madak
Malar
Bedi Dat
Shorap
Shāhbāz Kalāt
Panjgūr

Mehmani
Angohrān
Bent
Fanūĝ
Pūsako
Qasr-e Qand
Rāsk
Pīšīn

Sīstān-ō-Bālūčestān
Ramezān
Kalak
Bāhū-Kalāt
Polān
Mand
Nasirābād
Makrān Coast Range
Dasht

Kūh Mobārak
Gāsk
Sediĝ
Kalāt
Tang
Gombaki
Kahiro
Pārak
Konārak
Tisō
Bandar Behesti
Gvādar
Jiwani
Pishūkān
Gwādar
Pasni
Ras Jaddi
Ra's Ormāra
Ormāra

Gvadar Bay
Ra's -e Fāste
Rās Jiwani
Rās Nuh

S e a   o f   O m a n

al-Liwa'
Suhar
Sahm
al-Khabura
al-Masna'a
Barka'
Matra
MUSCAT
Ruwi
Qurayyat

Tropic of Cancer

Murray Rid...

al-Masfalah
Sadah
Wadi Fūlya
Bat
Jabal al-Akhdar
2980
al-Ayn
Kubara
al-Gafat

al-Rustaq
Awabi
Nizwa
Izki
Bahla
Ibra
al-Mudaibi
Samā'il
Bidbid
Dagmar
Samā'il
Qalhat

Hājar al-Sharqī
2003
Sur
al-Hadd

Natih
Nuhaida
Adam
Mudaibi
al-Musalla
al-Mintirib
Ibra
al-Kamil
Ali Hasan
al-Ashhara

Ramlat al-Wahiba

Ghaba

Sharkh

N a j d

al-Hubūf
al-Waia

Filim
Duwwa
Masira
Masīra Channel
al-Kalban
Sirab
Ra's Abu Rasas

Gulf of Masira

H a r a s i s
al-Aja'iz
Duqm

Ra's Madraka

al-Khalil
Sawqira Bay

A r a b i a n

S e a

auquira

harbitat

Scale 1:5,400,000   0   50   100   150   200 km

Al-Hajar Mountain range, Oman: *Located in Oman's northeast, this mountain range stretches southeast parallel to the coast. Many rivers and creeks that supply the plains with water have their sources in these mountains.*

91

Hadramaut: *The image shows the region of Hadramaut, located on the south coast of Yemen.*
The narrow coastal plain is adjoined by the desert-like plateau of the Djol.

PALESTINE

THE COUNTRY
··
Official name:
Palestine

Geographic coordinates:
*Western Asia; between 35° 33'
north, and 35° 23' east*

Area:
6,257 km² (2,416 square miles)

Intended capital:
Jerusalem

Interim capital:
Ramallah

Climate:
*Dry Mediterranean climate;
Gaza: 25°C (77°F)/
468 mm (18.4 in)
Ramallah 22°C (72°F)/
440 mm (17.3 in)*

Time zone:
Greenwich Mean Time + 2 hours

POPULATION
··
Number of inhabitants:
4 million

Population density:
*623 inhabitants/km²
(1,614 people/square mile)*

Annual population growth:
3.5%

Life expectancy:
*Women 75 years
Men 72 years*

Religion:
Sunni Islam, Christianity

Languages:
Arabic, Hebrew, English

Literacy rate:
88.5%

After decades of violence some of the areas occupied by Israel in 1967 were placed under the administration of the Palestinian National Authority. It is the internationally recognized representative body of the Palestinian people. The international community hopes that if there is a relaxation of the tensions within the region that peace will then be possible throughout the entire Middle East.

Geography

The regions administered by the Palestinian National Authority—the West Bank (5,879 km²/ 2,269 square miles) and the Gaza Strip (378 km²/ 146 square miles)—do not form a contiguous territorial unit. Both lie in a region of semi-desert. While the West Bank consists principally of imposing mountainous landscapes with altitudes that can rise to over 1,000 meters (3,280 ft), the Gaza Strip is a narrow, flat coastal region bordering the Mediterranean Sea. The River Jordan and the Dead Sea form the natural eastern boundary between the West Bank and Jordan.

Population

Some 2.45 million people live in the West Bank, while the population of the Gaza Strip is about 1.55 million. Most of them are Arabs and profess to be Sunni Muslims. There are also Christian communities in the West Bank. In the Gaza Strip there is enormous pressure on the land; Gaza City in particular, the largest settlement in the region, is almost bursting at the seams: conflicts seem unavoidable.

Palestinian civilians run for cover during clashes between Hamas and Fatah militants in Gaza City, 13 June, 2007.

History and Politics

The conflicts between Israel and the Palestinians go back to the time of the British mandate. After the British had occupied Palestine during the First World War with Arab support in the fight against the Ottoman Empire, the British government offered the Arabs the prospect of control over the region. However, the British also promised the Jews a national territory in Palestine. These conflicting promises, however, could not be reconciled with each other. Following the end of the British mandate Ben-Gurion proclaimed the state of Israel in 1948. The conflict between the newly formed state and the Palestinians, who were supported by many Arab states, escalated into the Arab–Israeli Wars.

The peace process

After a succession of failed peace negotiations between Israel and the Palestinian Liberation Organization (PLO) under the leadership of Yasser Arafat (1929–2004), a phase of reduced tension began in 1993. With the signing of the Gaza–Jericho Agreement in 1994, Israel and the newly formed Palestinian National Authority agreed on Palestinian self-rule in areas controlled by Israel. Israel withdrew its troops from parts of the Gaza Strip and Jericho; in 1995 some 30 percent of the West Bank was returned to the Palestinians. However they were not given a single continuous territory, which continues to cause problems in the exercise of their autonomy. In the so-called Road Map for Peace the Palestinians were given the prospect of a sovereign state. After the death of Arafat in November 2004, Mahmoud Abbas (b.1935) became President of the Palestinian National Authority.

Hamas and Fatah

In the first parliamentary elections in the Palestinian areas in January 2006 the strongest faction was the radical Islamic resistance movement Hamas. Israel's refusal to negotiate with Hamas, whose power base lies primarily in the Gaza Strip, places a question mark over the continuation of the détente. Furthermore, a domestic Palestinian conflict arose between Hamas and Fatah, the largest group within the PLO and regarded as moderate but lacking in power. While Fatah aims at finding a final solution to the Middle East conflict and favors a two-state solution with Israel and a Palestinian state within the boundaries set in 1967, Hamas rejects the idea because its supporters refuse to recognize Israel as a sovereign state.

The Dome of the Rock is one of the most important and oldest Islamic buildings in the world. Located in Jerusalem, it was completed in 691CE. It is said to be built on the rock from which the Prophet Muhammad ascended to heaven.

HISTORY

16th century
Ottoman conquest

1917
Under British mandate

1947
UN Partition Plan

1948
Proclamation of the state of Israel, First Arab–Israeli War

1958
Founding of Fatah (Palestine National Liberation Movement) Founding of Palestine Liberation Organization (PLO)

1967
Arab–Israeli War (Six-Day War)

1973
Arab–Israeli War (October War)

1987
First Palestinian Intifada

1989
Nomination of PLO chairman Y. Arafat as President of the future state of Palestine

1993
Establishment of the Palestinian National Authority

1994
Signing of the Gaza-Jericho Agreement between PLO and Israel; limited self-rule of Palestinian territories

1998
Continuation of peace process after signing of Wye Agreement

2002
Israel begins construction of a security wall along the border with the West Bank

2004
Death of Arafat; M. Abbas becomes President of the Palestinian National Authority

2005
End of the occupation of the Gaza Strip by Israel

2007
Hamas takes control of the Gaza Strip

2008/09
Israeli military offensive against the Gaza Strip

Economy

There are very few opportunities for employment within the Gaza Strip; many Palestinians travel to work in Israel every day, although the latter periodically closes the border to the Gaza Strip. A lack of water and a scarcity of farmland are hindrances to a long-term development of the agricultural sector. It is not possible to secure the population basic food supplies. According to the United Nations Food and Agriculture Organization (FAO) some 80 percent of the inhabitants of the Gaza Strip live below the poverty line; in the West Bank it is about 60 percent. The economic situation there is somewhat less dire.

Tourism

The political tension in the West Bank and the Gaza Strip continues; the security situation is therefore problematic, which is why official bodies advise against traveling in these regions. The Israeli army periodically closes off certain Palestinian areas. In favorable circumstances, however, a visit to the sights in Bethlehem, Jericho, and East Jerusalem is possible with a local guide.

Jericho—the oldest inhabited city

The oasis city of Jericho lies in the Jordan Rift Valley and is the lowest-lying city on Earth at 250 meters (820 feet) below sea level. It is also said to be the oldest city complex in history. Traces of settlement near Tell al-Sultan were dated to 11,000 BCE. The city wall, built in around 7000 BCE, has been excavated and can be visited today.

POLITICS

Government:
Partial autonomy without a legally binding territory under international law

Head of state:
President

Legislature:
Legislative assembly with 132 members

Administrative divisions:
Governorates with 16 districts

ECONOMY

Currency:
1 Israeli shekel (NIS) = 100 agorot

Gross domestic product:
$4.05 billion US

Gross per capita income:
$1,109 US

Foreign trade:
*Imports $2.7 billion US
Exports $0.3 billion US*

Foreign debt:
$1.3 billion US

LEBANON

THE COUNTRY

Official name:
Republic of Lebanon

Geographic coordinates:
*Western Asia; between 33°
and 35° north, and 35° and
36° 40' east*

Area:
10,452 km² (4,036 square miles)

Capital:
Beirut

Climate:
*Mediterranean climate; Beirut
24°C (75°F)/501 mm (19.7 in)*

Time zone:
Greenwich Mean Time + 3 hours

Although it is a small country, Lebanon has a great variety of landscapes and many different population groups. For centuries its rugged mountains were a place of refuge for Muslim and Christian minorities fleeing persecution. Today, eighteen different religious sects are represented in Lebanon.

Geography

The Lebanese Republic is bordered by Syria to the north and east, and by Israel to the south. The country consists of four topographical belts that lie parallel to the Mediterranean coast and stretch across the land from west to east. These four belts consist of the coastal strip, the Lebanon Mountains, the Bekaa Valley, and the Anti-Lebanon. Almost half of Lebanon's landmass lies 900 m (2,953 ft) above sea level.

The coastal region

Lebanon's narrow, hilly coastal strip is no more than 10 km (6 miles) wide at its broadest point. This densely populated region is also the most intensively cultivated: fruit and vegetables, which are grown both for the domestic market and for export, are cultivated here with the aid of intensive irrigation.

Rocky Lebanon Mountains

Lying parallel to the coastal strip, the Lebanon Mountains are 174 km (108 miles) long and up to 25 km (15 miles) wide. They culminate in Qurnat al-Sauda, a 3,083 m (10,115 ft) high peak. Some of the rocky cliffs of the range project out into the sea, and east–west river valleys cut into the mountainsides.

On their eastern side, the Lebanon Mountains descend steeply to the Bekaa Valley. Their western side receives sufficient rainfall to be extensively cultivated; fruit and vines are the main crops here. On the elevated mountain plateaus, with intermittent karst landscape, animals graze on scrubland.

The fertile Bekaa Valley

A continuation of the Jordan Valley, the Bekaa Valley forms part of the great Syrian Valley. The Bekaa Valley is 120 km (75 miles) long and 8–15 km (5–9 miles) wide. Its fertile central region, which lies at altitudes of 800–1,200 m (2,625–3,937 ft), is Lebanon's granary and market garden. The country's largest rivers rise in the Bekaa Valley; they are the Orontes, which flows north-eastward, and the Litani, which flows southwestward across the plateau.

Barren Anti-Lebanon

On the eastern side of the Bekaa Valley rise the Anti-Lebanon Mountains, which mark the border with Syria. These mountains culminate in Mount Hermon, in the south, which reaches 2,814 m (9,232 ft). Because the Anti-Lebanon Mountains are lower than the Lebanon Mountains, they lie in its rain shadow and so receive less rainfall. This is reflected in their scrublike vegetation and sparse population. Agriculture is possible only in the oases at the foot of the mountains.

*The Jupiter temple at Baalbek
was built in the first century CE.*

Mediterranean climate

Along the coast, a distinctive Mediterranean climate prevails, with heavy rainfall in winter, and hot, humid conditions in summer. In the mountains the climate is mild in summer, while winters are characterized by heavy rainfall; snow lies on the highest mountains until May. The Bekaa Valley has a continental climate, with very wet winters and hot, dry summers. Another characteristic of the climate in Lebanon and the neighboring countries is the Khamsin, a wind that blows from the Sahara, carrying a yellowish-red sand across the country at the end of the rainy season.

Rare cedars of Lebanon

Lying in a fertile crescent, Lebanon has abundant water and picturesque landscapes, which are carpeted in flowers in springtime. Forests of pine trees make Lebanon the most thickly forested country in the Middle East. Even in ancient times, the renowned Cedars of Lebanon, which grow at altitudes of 1,800 m (5,906 ft), were extensively felled for use as timber. The small number of Lebanon cedars that remain are protected in a few nature reserves.

The lower slopes of the Lebanon Mountains are covered in Mediterranean vegetation. At increasingly higher altitudes, this is replaced by apple and walnut trees, which in turn give way to coniferous trees. At the highest altitudes there is only sparse vegetation. The humid Mediterranean climate along the coast is favorable for cultivating olives and fruit.

Population

Over the centuries Lebanon has been a transit point for many peoples, and it is home to a great population mixture today. But, in general ethnic terms, its population is very homogenous: 95 percent are of Arab descent, and the rest are Kurds and Armenians.

Although Christians were once the largest group, today the majority of the Lebanese population is Muslim, due mainly to a markedly higher birth rate. Lebanese mainly define themselves through their religion: most are Sunnis, Shiites, Druze, Maronites, or Greek Orthodox, and in law all are co-equal. It is only contact with foreigners that brings out the Lebanese sense of national identity.

Multi-faith Lebanon

From a religious perspective, Lebanon is a highly heterogeneous country: there are eighteen recognized religious groups. About 60 percent of the population is Muslim, of which at least 32 percent are Shiites and about 21 percent Sunnis. Muslim minorities include Ismailis and Alawites. The Druze, who make up about 7 percent of the Muslim population, belong to a sect that split from the Shiites in the 11th century. Because Druze renounce certain central elements of the Islamic faith, mainstream Muslims do not recognize them as belonging to any Islamic sect.

The largest group of Christians in Lebanon is that of the Maronites (25 percent), who came to Lebanon in the 7th century and who are part of the Eastern Church. Lebanese Christians also include adherents of the Greek Orthodox Church (7 percent) and the Greek Catholic Church (5 percent).

One million Lebanese abroad

Since the end of the 19th century, and especially because of the civil war of 1975–90, many Lebanese have emigrated. Today, more than one million Lebanese are resident outside the country. Because of the civil war, more than 500,000 Lebanese became refugees in their own country, 30 percent of whom still live in camps. There are also Palestinian refugees, half of whom also live in camps; although they are permitted to remain in Lebanon, they do not have Lebanese nationality.

Education policy

Religious affiliation determines education, professional development, and moral and legal codes. Education traditionally has a high status in Lebanon. In private and public schools English or French, as well as Arabic, are taught in the first grade. English is also used for teaching at the private American University of Beirut, which was established in 1866. With the University of Beirut and St. Joseph University, it is one of the best institutes of higher education in the country. However, neither private nor public schools, nor universities are free.

POPULATION

Number of inhabitants:
4.15 million

Population density:
397 people/km²
(1,028 people/square mile)

Population distribution:
88% urban
12% rural

Annual population growth:
1.15%

Life expectancy:
Women 76 years
Men 71 years

Religions:
Sunni Islam, Shia Islam, Druze, Christianity

Languages:
Arabic (official language), English, French

Literacy rate:
88%

A view over the old town of Byblos. This Phoenician city was included in the UNESCO world heritage list in 1984.

HISTORY

From 8th century BCE
Assyrians, Babylonians and Persians rule in succession over what is now Lebanon

64 BCE
The Romans conquer the region and make it part of the province of Syria.

637 CE
Conquered by the Arabs

655–977
Part of the Islamic Empire (Umayyads, Abbasids)

1098–1291
Lebanon becomes part of the Crusader states.

1516
Beginning of Ottoman rule

1920
League of Nations mandate gives France control of Syria and Lebanon, which is divided into autonomous regions

1943
Lebanon becomes independent

1975–76
Start of Civil War

1978
Israel invades southern Lebanon

1982
Israel invades Lebanon

1988
Syria occupies parts of Beirut

1990
End of the civil war

1991
Lebanon signs a 'Brotherhood, Cooperation and Coordination Treaty' with Syria

1998
E. Lahud replaces E. Hraoui, president for 9 years

2000
Israeli troops withdraw from the buffer zone on the Israeli–Lebanese border that they had occupied in 1985

2005
Withdrawal of Syrian troops from Lebanon

2006
War between the Lebanese Hizbollah and Israel

History and Politics

The Phoenicians established powerful city states along the Mediterranean coast from Africa to the Middle East. The international exchange of goods and culture, which began in ancient times, was the foundation on which Lebanon built its importance as a center of trade between the Middle East and the west in the 20th century.

From the 2nd millennium BCE the Phoenicians founded Tyre, Sidon, Byblos, and Beritos, key ports on the Lebanese coast. With precious purple dye, wood, and metals, the Phoenicians dominated Middle Eastern trade for centuries. In the 8th century BCE the Assyrians put an end to Phoenician dominance. Lebanon was incorporated into the Roman province of Syria in 64 BCE and it became one of the wealthiest regions of the Roman Empire. From 395 CE, the region formed part of the Byzantine Empire, and from the 6th century it fell within the Persian Empire. From the 7th to the 9th centuries it was incorporated into the Arab caliphate.

Lebanon in the age of the Crusaders and Ottomans

In the 12th and 13th centuries, when the Crusaders held sway in the Middle East, parts of Lebanon were Christian enclaves. In 1516, the Ottomans drew the Middle East into their vast empire, and for the next 400 years Lebanon was under Ottoman rule. The Ottomans tolerated the various religious groups into which the population of Lebanon was divided, and granted the region extensive autonomy in return for the payment of taxes.

In the 19th century, because of tension between the Druze and the Maronites, the Ottomans divided Lebanon into two administrative units. But the increasingly bitter conflict culminated in a massacre of Christians in 1860. The French then dispatched troops to Lebanon, where they succeeded in establishing an independent region for Lebanese Christians. From 1864 until World War One, the country was under the authority of a Christian governor, who was chosen with the approval of France and Britain.

The mandate and the early days of independence

In 1920, after the collapse of the Ottoman Empire, the League of Nations assigned the mandate over Lebanon and Syria to France. The territory that makes up present-day Lebanon, Syria, Israel, and Iraq was divided into small states. With a constitution that guaranteed all religious groups in Lebanon equal rights, the French split the country from Syria in 1926. Although France declared Lebanon independent in 1941, the French mandate did not end until 1943, and the last French and British troops left the country only in 1946.

An economic boom then triggered a 20-year period of prosperity for Lebanon: the country became known as the 'Switzerland of the Middle East.'

Drawn into the Middle East conflict

Because of a high birth rate, Lebanon's Muslim population increased. Compared with Christian Lebanese, who had been in the majority, this numerically important group saw itself at a disadvantage in access to education, and in terms of economic and political influence. An exacerbating factor was the influx of Palestinian refugees triggered by the first Arab–Israeli war of 1948–49. Tension between Muslims, who took a pro-Arab view, and Maronite Christians, who were pro-Western, escalated. The first bloody conflicts between Muslims and Christians in Lebanon were brought to an end in 1958 with intervention from the USA.

Lebanon's efforts to remain neutral in the Arab–Israeli conflict failed: when the Palestinians made southern Lebanon their base for carrying out attacks on Israel, and when the Lebanese army failed to defeat the Palestine Liberation Organization in 1973, Lebanon became embroiled in the Middle Eastern conflict. Israel, in turn, began to launch retaliatory attacks on southern Lebanon.

The civil war and its consequences

In 1969, having pledged to respect Lebanon's sovereignty, the Palestinians were granted permission to set up military training bases in southern Lebanon. This had disastrous consequences: Lebanon was increasingly destabilized, and escalating hostilities led to the outbreak of civil war in 1975. Initially the conflict was confined to militant Druze allied with the PLO, and to the Phalangists, the armed faction of the Maronites. Within a short time, however, the country was split into small zones where military units fought against each other in a succession of coalitions.

As the Lebanese authorities were unable to put an end to the escalating civil war, foreign powers intervened. Syria dispatched troops to Lebanon in 1976 (and withdrew them in 1980). Fearing a Palestinian-ruled Lebanon, Syria initially supported the Christians, but soon changed its allegiance.

Another Muslim military organization, Hizbollah, joined in the war in 1982 with the aim of spreading an Islamic revolution and of fighting against Israel. In 1982 Israeli troops invaded Lebanon once again and this time occupied West Beirut.

French troops parade in Beirut's inner city in 1941

After the Israelis withdrew from Lebanon in 1985, the Christian, pro-Israeli South Lebanese Army took control of the buffer zone in southern Lebanon that Israel had ceded. But they were still faced with intransigent Muslim militia, including Hizbollah.

In the 1980s, the escalating civil war led to a direct confrontation between Lebanon and Syria, whose troops then occupied ever-larger areas of Lebanon. In September 1989 the Arab League mediated a ceasefire. However, this was a shaky arrangement, and a year later Lebanon was under Syrian control once again.

End of the civil war, and a difficult new beginning

Negotiations held in Saudi Arabia in 1989 marked the beginning of a peace agreement between Syria and Lebanon by which the militia were to withdraw from Beirut and southern Lebanon, and by which the civil war could be brought to an end. By this time about 90,000 people had lost their lives in the civil conflict, and more than 800,000 Lebanese had fled to other countries around the world.

The ratified peace treaty altered the balance of parliamentary power in favor of the Muslim majority, and anchored the political and economic influence of Syria in Lebanon that still exists today.

Under Prime Minister Rafik al-Hariri the task of rebuilding safety, law and order, and infrastructure began.

Conflict with Israel and the presence of the Shiite Hizbollah in Lebanon is still the country's major unsolved domestic problem and destabilizing factor. Israeli troops withdrew from the southern Lebanese buffer zone only in May 2000: the vacuum was filled by Hizbollah and the Lebanese army.

Hariri resigned from office in October 2004 but was assassinated in February 2005, whereupon international pressure forced the Syrian troops to leave the country. Renewed hostilities between Hizbollah and Israel in July/August 2006 badly damaged the country's infrastructure. Lebanon's political situation continues to be unstable, dominated as it is by two almost equally strong power blocks—an anti-Syrian and a pro-Syrian camp, each pursuing different domestic and external political goals.

Economy, Traffic, and Communication

Reducing the national debt, renovating damaged industrial facilities, and increasing self-sufficiency in terms of food production are currently among the primary aims of the Lebanese government.

The European Commission, the executive arm of the European Union, is currently assisting Lebanon's program of reconstruction and under a trade agreement Lebanese trade products have tariff-free access to the European Single Market.

Promising agricultural and industrial sectors

The agricultural sector accounts for about 7 percent of the gross national product. Lebanon's agricultural infrastructure is good: about 16 percent of the land is currently under cultivation. Major agricultural exports include Lebanese wine, the finest of which is produced in the Bekaa Valley, and produce such as vegetables and citrus fruits, dessert apples, and grapes. Livestock farming is concentrated in the mountains and the northern Bekaa Valley.

Mineral resources play a less significant role in the Lebanese economy. Although its oil fields are small, the country derives revenue from the oil transit business. It is intended that oil refineries, which are starting to operate once again, will generate a surplus that can be turned into exports.

Food and luxury items, textiles, paper, and wood processing, in which a quarter of the economically active population is employed, are the major industrial activities. Top exports are precious stones and pearls.

Road transportation

Thanks to its favorable geographic position, Lebanon is economically important as a transit country. The backbone of Lebanon's transportation system is a newly built road network of about 7,400 km (4,598 miles). The most important routes are the two coastal roads running north and south from Beirut and the eastbound route to the Bekaa Valley. The country's railroad network, which once covered 220 km (137 miles), is to be developed so as to ease congestion on the roads. Beirut and Tripoli are the principal ports.

Mass media

After a new media law was passed in 1994, radio and television were reorganized; since then, the range of programs provided by the private broadcasting companies has widened. Many have either a religious or political bias. Most of Lebanon's forty daily newspapers are published in Arabic. Those with the highest circulation include the independent *Dar al-Hayat*, *al-Nahar*, and *al-Safir*. The leading French-language newspaper is *L'Orient-Le Jour*.

Tourism

In Lebanon it is possible to go skiing in the morning and bathe in the warm Mediterranean Sea in the afternoon. Such a choice of seemingly mutually exclusive activities is legendary and is partly what made the country one of the most attractive destinations in the Middle East before the outbreak of the civil war. Tourists are starting to return to Lebanon, and for several years now the country's tourist industry has been experiencing an upturn. Halted by the civil war, the Baalbek Festival, at which internationally renowned artists and dancers perform, resumed in 1998.

POLITICS

Government:
Parliamentary republic

Head of State:
President

Legislature:
National Assembly with 128 members (split equally between Christians and Muslims) elected for a 4-year term. The speaker of the National Assembly must be Shiite and the prime minister Sunni Muslim

Administrative divisions:
5 governorates

ECONOMY

Currency:
1 Lebanese pound (LBP) = 100 piastres

Gross domestic product:
$22.7 billion US

Gross per capita income:
$5,580 US

Overseas trade:
*Imports $9.4 billion US
Exports $2.3 billion US*

Foreign debt:
$20.4 billion US

Syrian workers on a construction site in Beirut

SYRIA

THE COUNTRY

Official name:
Arab Republic of Syria

Geographic coordinates:
*Western Asia; between 32° 20'
and 37° 20' north, and 35° 35'
and 42° 30' east*

Area:
*185,180 km²
(71,498 square miles)*

Capital:
Damascus

Climate:
*Mediterranean climate in the
west, desert climate in the east;
Damascus 17.6°C (64°F)/165 mm
(6.5 in); Aleppo 17.6°C
(64°F)/396 mm (15.6 in);
Latakia 18.7°C (65.7°F)/785 mm
(30.9 in)*

Time zone:
Greenwich Mean Time + 2 hours

Syria beguiles the traveler both with its ancient cultural monuments and its diverse landscapes that stretch from the Mediterranean coast to the Syrian Desert within the Fertile Crescent. Syrian society is characterized by a traditional Islamic way of life, although many ethnic and religious minorities also have their place here.

Geography

Steppes and deserts cover broad expanses of the country. Its largest rivers are the Euphrates and the Orontes. Topographically, Syria is divided into four major zones: the Mediterranean coast in the northwest, the coastal mountains in the west and the area that abuts Lebanon in the southwest, the Fertile Crescent in the interior, and desert and steppes in the southeast.

Syria's Mediterranean coast

In northwestern Syria a coastal strip 180 km (112 miles) long and up to 30 km (19 miles) wide lines the Mediterranean Sea. The coast here is partly sandy and partly rocky. The coastal strip is the most fertile and most densely populated part of the country, and the hills here are covered with typical Mediterranean-style terraces and are dotted with bare limestone knolls.

The Syrian mountain areas

East of the fertile lowlands lie the Alawi mountains, the northern continuation of the Lebanon Mountains. Rising to an average height of 1,000 m (3,281 ft), the Alauite Mountains culminate in Jabal Ansariya, whose peak rises to 1,562 m (5,125 ft). Farther east, the Orontes River flows through the deep Syrian Trench.

Joining the coastal mountains, which rise to 2,629 m (8,625 ft), the area along the border with Lebanon marks the eastern edge of the Syrian Trench. This mountain chain is also karstic, and receives only slight rainfall. The highest peak in the country is Mount Hermon, which reaches 2,814 m (9,232 ft). In the southwest of the country are the northern ridges of the Golan Heights.

The central Syrian Plateau and the Fertile Crescent

To the east of the Orontes Valley stretches the fertile Syrian Plateau which is traversed by rivers. With appreciable rainfall in spring and autumn, the plateau is a fertile agricultural area where grain, cotton, citrus fruits, tobacco, and vegetables are grown. Toward the east, the plateau rises to a high plain that is traversed by the Euphrates and Khabur rivers. Modern irrigation systems allow cotton to be cultivated in the valleys here.

The Fertile Crescent is a steppe-like area of fertile land that stretches from Israel to the Arabian Gulf, and where rainfall has made cultivation possible from very early times in the evolution of civilization. The western and central parts of the Fertile Crescent, which includes Jordan, Lebanon, Israel, Syria, Turkey, Iraq, and Iran, stretch from the volcanic landscape of Hawran in the southwest through Damascus, across the plains of Homs, Hamah, and Aleppo to al-Jazirah. Because of its fertile soil south of Jabal al-Druz, a mountain range just east of al-Suwaida, the Hawran region was already highly valued as the country's 'breadbasket' even in ancient times.

Desert landscapes of central and eastern Syria

A flat desert and steppe landscape dotted with *sabkhas* (salt lakes) covers the entire southeastern part of Syria,

Remains of a Roman temple in Palmyra in central Syria. Palmyra is a UNESCO world heritage site.

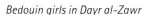
and accounts for about 58 percent of its territory. Most of this area consists of rolling steppe or rocky desert. The barrenness of the terrain here is the result of the over-exploitation of trees for timber. Only in the spring, after abundant rainfall, does a veil of greenery cover the desert steppes. The land between the Euphrates and Khabur rivers was made arable by the damming of the Euphrates.

Transition from Mediterranean to desert climate

In climatic terms, Syria is a country of contrasts. In the west, a Mediterranean climate, with wet winters, predominates; the east has an extreme continental, arid desert climate. Rainfall decreases from west to east. The areas of heaviest precipitation are the mountains in the west, where annual rainfall reaches 1,200 mm (47.2 in) and where snow often falls in winter.

The climate in the interior is generally dry. Here summers are hot and winters are cold and damp. In the northwestern highlands, most rain falls between September and May, but the pattern is very variable. In summer, there are frequent periods of drought and the Khamsin, a hot, dry wind, blows across the country from the desert. The area of lowest rainfall is, of course, the desert itself. Here, temperatures range from 50°C (122°F) in summer to below freezing (0°C/33°F) in winter. As is typical for a desert climate, variations between day and night temperatures are extreme.

Population

As a people, the Syrians are often described as being a social mosaic to a degree that is unique in the Arab world. Despite occasional tensions, the Syrians have a centuries-long tradition of social tolerance.

Tolerance in word and deed in Syrian society

At least 90 percent of Syrians are ethnic Arabs. They are the descendants of the Bedouin tribes that populated the Syrian desert steppes before the arrival of Islam, and who later became integrated with the country's Muslim conquerors when Syria became part of the Islamic Omayyad Empire.

The remaining 10 percent of Syrians belong to various minorities. Kurds, who make up 7 percent of the population, live in the northern part of the country. Armenians, who make up 2 percent, are descended from a Christian community that was established in Syria in the 5th century, and Assyrians founded their own church here in the 6th century.

The Circassians, from the Caucasus, settled here during the time of the Ottoman Empire. Turks and Turkmenis live in the western part of the country, and in modern times Palestinian refugees have also settled here.

Sunnis in the majority

About 90 percent of Syria's population is Muslim, and 10 percent Christian. Of the Muslims, an overwhelming majority is Sunni and just under 12 percent is Alawite; the Sunnis, however, do not recognize the Alawites as Muslims. Other religious minorities are the Druze in Hawran, the Yezidis in the northeast of the country, and Jews.

Although they form a minority, Christians exercise a large influence in Syrian society. This is because of their many economic and cultural ties with Europe, their cosmopolitan upbringing, and their cohesion. The Eastern Orthodox, Byzantine, Evangelical, and Catholic churches are all represented in Syria, and are split up into further subgroups.

Problems of a rapidly growing population

Within a single generation, the life expectancy of Syrians has risen remarkably from 53 years to 71 years. Because infant mortality rates have also gone down, the annual birth rate is extremely high: today, 36 percent of Syrians are under the age of 15.

For economic as well as political reasons, many well-educated Syrians work abroad. There is still a high, albeit hidden, rate of unemployment in Syria. In order to earn a basic living, many economically active people hold more than one job at a time.

POPULATION

Number of inhabitants:
20.5 million

Population density:
111 inhabitants/km²
(287 inhabitants/square mile)

Population distribution:
51% urban
49% rural

Annual population growth:
2.2%

Life expectancy:
Women 72 years
Men 69 years

Religions:
Sunni Islam, Alawi Islam, Christianity

Language:
Arabic

Literacy rate:
80%

Bedouin girls in Dayr al-Zawr

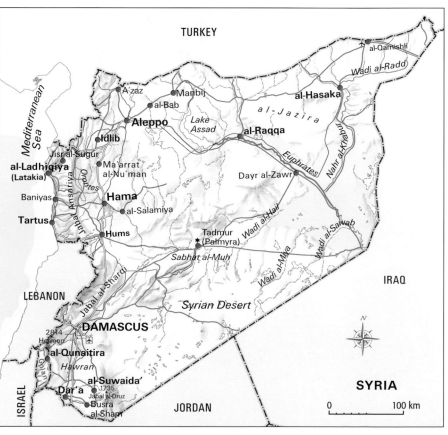

HISTORY

from 539 BCE
Under Persian rule

c.300 BCE
The beginning of Seleucid rule

64 BCE
Syria becomes part of the Roman Empire

From 395 CE
Under Byzantine rule

7th century
Islamization of Syria

616–750
Under the Omayyad, Damascus is the capital of the Islamic Empire

12th century
Christian Empire of the Crusaders

1516
Syria becomes part of the Ottoman Empire

1920
League of Nations places Syria under French mandate

1946
Syria becomes independent

1958–61
Union with Egypt as the United Arab Republic

1967
In the Six Day War with Israel, Syria loses the Golan Heights

1970
After a military coup, H. al-Assad becomes president

1973–74
War with Israel

1976
Syrian troops intervene in the civil war in Lebanon

1991
Syria takes part in the first Gulf War on the side of the Allies

2000
Death of al-Assad. He is succeeded by his son B. al-Assad

History and Politics

"Every man has two homelands–the Syrian homeland and his own homeland." This saying reflects the fact that the region of present-day Syria also forms part of the area regarded as the cradle of civilization. Because of its location, Syria was the meeting point of many great powers and a place of cultural exchange. The Syrian cities of Aleppo and Damascus vie for the status of the oldest continuously inhabited city in the world.

As early as the 3rd millennium BCE, Syria stood in the field of conflict of mighty empires and the sphere of influence of great cultures such as those of the Sumerians, Akkadians, Egyptians, Hittites, Babylonians, and Assyrians. The country was conquered many times.

From 539 BCE Syria was under Persian rule. After conquest by the Macedonians under Alexander the Great (356–23 BCE), Greek language and culture blossomed in Syria, particularly under the Seleucids. It was also during the Greek period that many cities, including Apamea and Duro Europos, on the Euphrates, were established in Syria. Pompey the Great incorporated Syria into the Roman Empire in 64 BCE. This golden age was continued under the Christian influence of the Byzantines, who conquered Syria in 395. Tremendous earthquakes and wars of attrition between Byzantium and the Persians ultimately weakened Syria, so that it was easily taken by Muslim Arabs, who conquered the country between 635 and 637.

Under Islamic rule

Under the rule of the Omayyads (661–750), Damascus became the capital of the Islamic Empire, although this status was later conferred on Baghdad. When the first Crusaders arrived in 1099, establishing a Christian empire shortly afterward, Syria, along with Palestine, took center stage in the political sphere. However, Damascus, Homs, and Aleppo, all three of which were centers of trade, escaped the consequences of the Christian conquest. After the Mongols, who swept through Syria driving out the Mamluks and destroying its cities, came the Ottoman Turks.

The Ottoman Empire

From 1516 to 1918, Syria was part of the Ottoman Empire. However the governors, who were appointed by Istanbul, were more interested in collecting taxes than in developing the region. After the collapse of the Ottoman Empire, France and Britain intervened in Syria to further their own interests. By the terms of the Sykes–Picot Treaty of 1916, Syria was given to France and French troops occupied the country.

Under the French mandate

Contrary to the promises of the colonial powers, the territory that makes up present-day Syria, Palestine, and Iraq was divided into small states, with the League of Nations transferring responsibility for Lebanon and Syria to France. In March 1920 King Faisal I (1885–1933) proclaimed the kingdom of Syria, but the League of Nations mandate was implemented in April, and Faisal was forced to abdicate.

Through the 1920s the numerous uprisings that occurred were put down by the French. During World War Two, British troops occupied the country. Although Syria's independence (which was formally declared in 1941) was confirmed in 1944, it was not until 1946 that British and French troops finally withdrew.

Chaos in domestic politics

Constant coups marked the first decades of Syria's independence. In 1958, Syria and Egypt joined to form the United Arab Republic (UAR), but Syria withdrew in 1961.

In 1963, the Ba'ath Party staged a coup and seized power. The ensuing years were characterized by clashes between right and left factions within the party. After further upheaval, the Ba'ath Party's leftist faction finally seized power in 1966. This led to a rift between Syria and Iraq, but to closer ties with the Soviet Union.

In 1970, General Hafez al-Assad (1930–2000) came to power after a bloodless coup and, supported by the military and the Alawites, an Islamic sect, he governed the country until his death.

Eternal conflict with Israel and influence in Lebanon

Together with other Arab states, Syria participated in the armed conflict with Israel. In 1967, after the Six Day War, the third major episode of Arab-Israel hostilities, Syria lost the Golan Heights. In the civil war that raged in Lebanon from 1975 to 1990, Syria intervened repeatedly as alliances changed, and from 1976 to 1980 Syrian troops were stationed in Lebanon. President Assad also exerted influence on the political situation in Lebanon. In 1989, by the terms of the Treaty of Ta'if, Syria was made the protector of Lebanon.

Since 1990, the Syrian government has been intensely engaged in Middle Eastern politics. Talks with Israel on the question of the return of the Golan Heights as a precondition for long-term peace in the Middle East have repeatedly broken down, and a successful conclusion is still out of sight.

Hafez al-Assad was President of Syria from 1970 until his death in 2000.

The city of Hama is famous for its norias. These giant waterwheels lift water into aqueducts and were part of the historic irrigation system that dates back to 1100 BCE

POLITICS

Government:
Socialist presidential republic

Head of state:
President

Legislature:
*National Assembly with
250 delegates elected for a
4-year term*

Administrative divisions:
*13 provinces (muhafazat),
capital district*

ECONOMY

*1 Syrian pound (SYP)
= 100 piastres*

Gross domestic product:
$33.4 billion US

Gross per capita income:
$1,560 US

Overseas trade:
*Imports $11.5 billion US
Exports $10.9 billion US*

Foreign debt:
$8.4 billion US

Economy, Traffic, and Communication

The legal foundations for promoting a free market economy in Syria were laid in the mid-1980s. The enthusiasm expressed by those in favor of a privatized economy at the beginning of the 1990s has given way to cautious reserve, and government bureaucracy is still keeping many national and foreign investors away.

Syria has its own modest oil reserves in the northeastern part of the country, and these account for a large part of its revenue. The country is also making efforts to increase its use of natural gas reserves, which are needed mostly for domestic energy production. The country's most important industries are petro-chemicals, foods, and textiles woven from home-grown cotton.

Agriculture in the Fertile Crescent

More than a quarter of Syria's population is engaged in agriculture. Accounting for 25 percent of the gross national product, agriculture is still the mainstay of Syria's economy. After the agricultural reforms of 1958 and 1980, most land is now in private or communal ownership.

Syria's most important exports are cotton, followed by wheat and barley, fruit (mainly apricots and figs), vegetables (mainly tomatoes), olives, and sugar beet. Stockbreeding is confined mainly to the country's population of semi-nomads: almost half of Syrian territory is pastureland.

Irrigation by ancient and modern methods

Arable land makes up about 25 percent of Syrian territory, and of this almost 30 percent is irrigated. In the region between the Euphrates and Khabur rivers, agricultural production was massively expanded thanks to major irrigation projects. Traditional irrigation systems are still used in the Hama region: norias, 20-m (66-ft)-high wooden wheels fitted with scoops, drone away as they lift precious water from the Orontes up to the level of the surrounding fruit orchards and vegetable fields.

Good transportation networks

As a transit area, Syria is an important link in the trading activities of neighboring Arab countries. Of the three ports on Syria's Mediterranean coast, Latakia is the major transit point for containerized cargo. Bulk goods are handled at Tartus, and Baniyas is the nation's oil port. About 20 percent of Syria's 95,000-km (51,300-mile)-long road network is now surfaced. Buses are the most important means of public transportation.

The railroad network, which now covers some 2,700 km (1,460 miles) and which is to be expanded, is still a less important means of transportation. There is an international airport at Damascus.

State-controlled media

Mobile telephones are a matter of course among the younger generation of Syrians, and Internet cafes are well-attended in the large towns and cities.

Syria has ten daily newspapers. Those with the largest circulation and broadest national coverage are *Tishreen*, *al-Ba'ath*, and *al-Thawra*.

JORDAN

THE COUNTRY

Official name:
Hashemite Kingdom of Jordan

Geographic coordinates:
*Western Asia; between 29° 10'
and 33° 20' north, and 35° and
39° 18' east*

Area:
*88,778 km²
(34,277 square miles)*

Capital:
Amman

Climate:
*Continental desert climate in the
south and east; Mediterranean
climate in mountain regions;
Amman 17.5°C (63.5°F)/401 mm
(15.8 in)*

Time zone:
Greenwich Mean Time + 2 hours

POPULATION

Number of inhabitants:
6.1 million

Population density:
*69 inhabitants/km2
(178 inhabitants/square mile)*

Population distribution:
*82% urban
18% rural*

Annual population growth:
2.4%

Life expectancy:
*Women 72 years
Men 71 years*

Religions:
Sunni Islam, Christianity

Languages:
*Arabic (official language),
English*

Literacy rate:
90%

In the heart of the Middle East, the Hashemite Kingdom of Jordan is a melting pot of history, religion, and culture. The country's climate and environment are influenced by its location in the region between the Mediterranean Basin and the northern Arabian Desert. Its population also reflects this transitional location.

Geography

Desert or desert-like steppe covers almost all the eastern part of the country, equivalent to three-quarters of Jordan's territory. Rainfall, which is very light, occurs only in winter, and sparse vegetation grows on low hills. In these arid conditions, agriculture is impossible without costly irrigation.

Jordan's fertile rift valleys

The Jordan Valley, which forms part of the Great Rift Valley and marks the border with Israel, makes up the western part of the country. The Jordan Valley is 410 km (255 miles) long, and 6–20 km (4–12.5 miles) wide. In the part of the valley that contains the Dead Sea, it descends to 400 m (1,312 ft) below sea level, forming the deepest depression on earth. Along the banks of the River Jordan lies the most fertile land in the country: it is irrigated by water pumped from the Jordan and the Yarmouk rivers. Bananas, citrus fruits, and tobacco are the most important crops: date palms are also grown in the southern part of the country.

In springtime the mountainous edge of the Jordan Valley is covered with an astonishingly rich vegetation comparable to that in Mediterranean coastal areas. Of the forest that once covered the country, nothing but a few patches of trees remain.

Plateau east of the Jordan Valley

On its eastern side, the Jordan Valley rises to a plateau that lies at altitudes of 600–1,700 m (1,969–5,577 ft), and that stretches from the border with Syria in the north to Ra's al-Naqb, beyond Petra, in the south. The plateau is deeply cut from east to west with wadis, seasonal water courses.

*In the desert, Jordan's police rely
on camels rather than cars.*

The ancient city of Petra was founded in the 6th century BCE. A narrow passage called the Siq leads to the city.

precipitation falls between November and March. While maximum temperatures may exceed 40°C (104°F) across the country, in desert regions daytime temperatures vary markedly.

Desert wildlife

Most of Jordan's wildlife consists of species that have adapted to life in desert conditions, where food and water are in short supply. Most characteristic are golden jackals, foxes, cape hares, and jerboas. The 300 species of birds found in Jordan are mainly migratory birds, and arrive in the country's oases in huge flocks in spring and autumn. Jordan also has a population of reptiles, most of which are harmless, and some extraordinarily colorful marine life on the Gulf of Aqaba. The coral reefs and the variety of tropical fish are well-known here, and they attract many divers.

Population

Jordan has one of the highest birth rates in the world, and more than one third of the population is under 15. About 98 percent of the population is made up of ethnic Arabs, including over 1.9 million Palestinians. Ethnic minorities include Circassians, Armenians, Kurds, and Turks.

Circassians and other minorities

Circassians make up 1 percent of Jordan's population. This reflects the fact that Jordan has received many political refugees, and continues to do so today. The Circassians, who are Sunni Muslims, are descended from immigrants who fled the Caucasus in 1878 to escape Russian oppression, and who were settled by the Ottomans in what was then Transjordan. Today this group is fully integrated into Jordanian society, and some of its members hold high office in the country's government.

Turks from Central Asia and Baha'is, members of a religious sect from Iran, also found refuge in Jordan, where they settled to escape religious persecution in their native countries. Small communities of Druze, a religious sect that has certain characteristics in common with Muslims, live on the border with Syria.

Over 90 percent of the population are Sunni Muslims. About six percent of Jordan's population is Christian: most are Armenians and because of their loyalty to the Jordanian royal family and the latter's religious tolerance, they enjoy high status in politics and business. Jordan's population of Christians is concentrated mainly in the northwest of the country.

The road that winds along the Wadi al-Mujib is referred to as the King's Highway in the Fourth Book of Moses. From this wadi, there are breathtaking views of the deeply cut landscape all around.

The mild climate of the plateau allows the cultivation of olives and grain. Vines, fruits, and vegetables are grown on terraced land in the l-Balqa governorate, in the center of the plateau. Uncultivated areas of the plateau are mostly covered by grassy steppe in the north, and wormwood steppe in the south.

This part of the country is inhabited by Bedouin, most of whom have a traditional nomadic or semi-nomadic lifestyle, and who live mainly by breeding goats, sheep, and camels. In the recent past a semi-nomadic existence became more common, with pastoralist Bedouin spending the winter in the country's eastern desert regions and in summer taking their herds up to the plateau where they live in permanent or semi-permanent settlements.

Transition zone from Mediterranean to desert climate

Jordan lies in a transitional zone where a Mediterranean climate merges into a continental desert climate, with rainfall becoming lighter toward the east. Summers are typically hot and dry, although evenings are cool and nights in the desert are frequently cold. The plateau around Amman sometimes receives heavy snowfall. Most

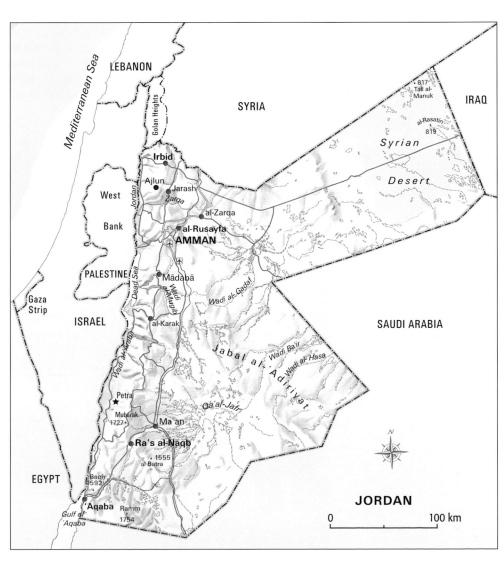

HISTORY

1516
The country becomes part of the Ottoman Empire

1920
As the mandate for Palestine and Transjordan, the League of Nations places the country under British administration

1921
The Emirate of Transjordan is created

1946
Jordan becomes independent

1948
Jordan annexes the West Bank

1953
Coronation of King Hussein II

1967
After the Six Day War, Israel occupies the West Bank

1988
In favor of a Palestinian state, Jordan relinquishes claim to the West Bank

1994
An end to hostilities is agreed with Israel

1999
Abdullah II succeeds Hussein II

History and Politics

In 1516 eastern Jordan became part of the Ottoman Empire. The early history of the country that was to become known as Transjordan and finally as the Hashemite Kingdom of Jordan began 400 years later, with an Arab revolt against the Ottomans in Mecca.

As a political entity, Jordan was established in the aftermath of World War One, when the region was under British administration. It was made an emirate in 1922, and became an independent kingdom in 1946; since 1948 it has been closely involved with assisting Palestinian refugees. Today Jordan looks to tourism to strengthen its economy.

The nation and its historical roots

After negotiation with the British High Commissioner for Egypt, Hussain I (1853–1931), who became Sharif of Mecca in 1908, was promised an Arab empire, provided that the Ottomans could be overcome. Hussain led a revolt against the Ottomans, and Arab revolts against them soon spread to Mecca and Jeddah. However, under the terms of the Sykes-Picot Treaty signed in 1916, Britain and France divided the territory promised to Hussain. In 1917 the port city of Aqaba was occupied by Arab troops led by T.E. Lawrence (1888–1935), known as Lawrence of Arabia.

When the Ottoman Empire ended, an Arab empire, which included east Jordan, was established in 1918. It was ruled by Faisal I (1885–1933), a member of the Hashemite dynasty. In 1921 his brother Abd Allah ibn Hussain I (1882–1951) became Emir of Transjordan, ruling under British control. Faisal I then became King of Iraq. Palestine remained under British administration, but, following a later British proposal, Transjordan was separated from Palestine in 1922, becoming an independent emirate. Jordan was finally granted independence in 1946, when it became officially known as the Hashemite Kingdom of Jordan.

A place of refuge for Palestinians

When the state of Israel was established in 1948, the Palestinians who already inhabited this territory were expelled or forced to flee. Hundreds of thousands flooded into the West Bank, on the River Jordan, and into Jordan itself. During the Six Day War in 1967, when Israel occupied the West Bank, many of these refugees were forced to flee once again: this resulted in a further 300,000 Palestinians moving to the East Bank. During the First Gulf War against Iraq (1990–91) Jordan accepted another 300,000 displaced Palestinians, most of whom had been living in Kuwait.

Many Palestinian refugees and their descendants live in camps around al-Zarqa, Irbid, and Ajlun, in northeastern Jordan. Over time, some of these camps have become extensive temporary settlements, such as al-Baqaa near Amman, where 78,000 refugees live. Social services, healthcare, and schooling for children are provided by the United Nations, with the help of religious organizations, and water, electricity, telephones, and sewage systems are provided by the Jordanian authorities. Jordan readily allows refugees to acquire Jordanian citizenship. International labor organizations and Jordanian companies are assisting in the efforts to create jobs for the refugees.

The Palestinian refugees still regard Palestine as their homeland, and are reluctant to relinquish their right to return. Given the political climate in the Middle East, with Jordan moving closer to Israel and wishing to remain on good terms with its other neighbors, proposals have been made for Jordan to take over running the refugee camps in perpetuity, and for the United Nations to withdraw.

A stable monarchy?

Under the constitution passed in 1952, Jordan is a constitutional hereditary monarchy. The government was shaped by King Hussein II, who ruled from 1952 until his death

The King Abdullah I Mosque was built between 1982 and 1989 and offers room for up to 3000 believers.

View of the town of Aqaba from the Gulf. Aqaba is of strategic importance to Jordan since it is the country's only seaport.

POLITICS

Government:
Constitutional hereditary monarchy

Head of State:
King

Legislature:
Chamber of Deputies with 110 members elected for a 4-year term, and Senate with 55 members appointed by the king

Administrative divisions:
12 governorates

ECONOMY

Currency:
1 Jordanian dinar (JOD) = 1,000 fils

Gross domestic product:
$14.1 billion US

Gross per capita income:
$2,650 US

Overseas trade:
*Imports $13.5 billion US
Exports $4.5 billion US*

Foreign debt:
$7.5 billion US

in 1999. He was succeeded by his eldest son Abd Allah ibn Hussein II (b. 1962), who became officially known as King Abdullah II. The constitution guarantees the monarch's extensive authority, and the cabinet and prime minister have little influence. The king can also dissolve the cabinet at any time.

From 1989 there have been some incipient attempts to move toward democracy, but at the beginning of his rule King Abdullah II made it clear that the kingdom would continue to be governed by royal authority. The first independent elections took place in 2003, during which independent royalist candidates won an overwhelming majority of seats.

Economy, Traffic, and Communication
Jordan is an agricultural country whose industrial infrastructure is only just developing. However, agriculture still accounts for just 2 percent of the country's gross domestic product. The focal point of Jordan's economy is the Jordan Valley and the neighboring mountains around Amman, but with a developing economic infrastructure the southwest of the country is becoming increasingly important. Here, iron, cement, potash, and fertilizer are the major industries. The largest processing factories are a cement plant near Amman, an oil refinery at al-Zarqa, and a fertilizer complex near Aqaba, where rich deposits of phosphate are processed. There are factories for food processing and textile production. Fertilizer production and the pharmaceutical industry are also important contributors to Jordan's economic output.

Vital service sector
While agriculture and industry, which is barely developed, account for about 15 percent of the country's gross national product, the service sector is much larger, accounting for over 80 percent. About half of all Jordanians work in state administration or government institutions,

or are employed by the army, the security services, and the police.

Since the 1990s the country's health and education sectors have been developing rapidly. Because standards of healthcare in Jordan are considerably higher than those of other Arab countries, many foreign patients come to Jordan for medical treatment.

Important roads and the media
Most transportation in Jordan is by road. Surfaced roads connect all important cities, and the major highway through the country is the north–south road from Irbid, on the northern border, through Amman, and on southward to Aqaba. This axial road runs almost parallel to the country's only railroad, which forms part of the once-famous Hejaz Railway and which is used only for transporting phosphate to Aqaba.

The leading Arab newspapers in Jordan include *al-Rai* and *al-Dustour*, and the English-language *Jordan Times*. Radio and television are state-controlled. The international Arabic satellite channels are very popular. Mobile telephones and the internet are gaining in popularity.

Tourism
As an important source of foreign revenue for Jordan, tourism is being developed into a major aspect of its economy. However, the success of the country's tourist industry depends largely on the political situation in the Middle East. The main attractions include the ancient city of Petra, and Roman town of Jarash, and Madaba, with its splendid mosaics.

From Petra to al-Karak, Jordan has a wealth of impressive sites that stand as monuments to its distant and eventful history. Amman, the country's capital, traces its history back to Biblical times, but here history melds with modernity. The King's Highway is an ancient route that connects many important sites and historic towns in the region.

IRAQ

THE COUNTRY

Official name:
Republic of Iraq

Geographic coordinates:
*Western Asia; between 29°
and 37° north, and 39° and
48° 30' east*

Area:
*438,317 km²
(169,240 square miles)*

Capital:
Baghdad

Climate:
*Subtropical, predominantly desert
climate; Baghdad 22.4°C (72°F)/
83 mm (3.2 in); Basra 25.7°C
(78°F)/106 mm (4.2 in); Mosul
21.1°C (70°F)/ 59 mm (2.3 in)*

Time zone:
Greenwich Mean Time + 3 hours

POPULATION

Number of inhabitants:
29.5 million

Population density:
*67 inhabitants/km²
(174 inhabitants/square mile)*

Population distribution:
*67% urban
33% rural*

Annual population growth:
2.6%

Life expectancy:
*Women 71 years
Men 68 years*

Religions:
*Shia Islam, Sunni Islam,
Christianity*

Languages:
Arabic, Kurdish

Literacy rate:
65%

The Euphrates and Tigris rivers cut through the predominantly sparse deserts of Iraq, and their fertile banks run like green bands between desert, coast, and mountains. In common with the land, contrasts are also characteristic of the country's different cultures. In past decades Iraq has not only been the target of international condemnation and attack, but has also suffered internal strife, with the country's seemingly unbridgeable domestic conflicts shaping the lives of the Iraqi people. In the past, Iraqi regimes, notably that of Saddam Hussein, have repeatedly carried out brutal repressions of Shiites and Kurds, as well as other minorities.

Geography

The dominating landscapes are high mountains, rivers, desert, and a narrow coastal strip. The country's coastline is about 60 km (37 miles) long.

Euphrates and Tigris—Iraq's lifelines

From its neighboring states of Turkey and Iran the foothills of the Taurus and Zagros mountains extend into

*Baghdad's al-Kadhimain Mosque was built in the
16th century CE and boasts elaborate colorful tiles.*

northeastern and eastern Iraq. These mountains are predominantly rugged and reach altitudes of over 3,000 m (9,843 ft). Further inland, the high mountains drop down to the land between two rivers, the Euphrates and Tigris.

This region, which is also known as Mesopotamia (literally 'land between the rivers'), is one of the oldest inhabited regions on earth and even considered as the cradle of civilization. It remains the heartland and granary of this Middle Eastern state. Both major rivers criss-cross the country from northwest to southeast. In their middle reaches, the water is used for irrigation agriculture, with vast citrus and date palm groves which have replaced the original vegetation of oak, sycamore, willow, and poplar trees. Extensive swamps with vast reed beds have developed around their lower reaches, offering a resting place for flocks of various species of migratory birds.

About 150 km (63 miles) north of the estuary to the Gulf, the Euphrates and Tigris combine in the Shatt al-Arab. West of the Euphrates, the landscape slowly rises up to the Syrian Desert, which stretches to the borders with Syria, Jordan, and Saudi Arabia. This region is dominated by desert vegetation interspersed with tussock grass and briars.

A subtropical climate with extreme contrasts

The country's climate is characterized by a subtropical climate with winter rains. The hot, dry summers are followed by wetter winters. While an entire year without rain is possible in the Syrian Desert, the high mountains of the northeast often get snow in the winter. The annual rainfall in these mountain areas can reach more than 1,000 mm (39 in), while the land of the two rivers often receives less than 30 mm (1 in) of precipitation a year.

In the capital Baghdad, which is situated roughly in the geographic center of the country, the average monthly temperatures from January to July range between 9°C and 33°C (between 48°F and 91°F). Some summers, however, have even seen extreme temperatures of more than 50°C (122°F).

Population

Iraq's population varies greatly from region to region. Densely populated conurbations such as Baghdad are in stark contrast to the largely unpopulated regions of the southwest. Inevitably, the banks of the Euphrates and Tigris have long been the preferred settlement areas.

However, nomadic and semi-nomadic lifestyles are still common in rural areas.

Weakened by three Gulf wars

Many parts of the population live in extreme poverty. The Gulf wars cost not only many lives, but have also caused countless families to lose all their worldly possessions. The supply situation in some parts of the country is catastrophic and many citizens do not have sufficient access to food and medical supplies. Even after the end of the Third Gulf War (2003) and the fall of the regime under Saddam Hussein, it will be years until the supply situation for the entire Iraqi population improves enough to satisfy all their needs.

Peoples and languages

More than three-quarters of Iraqis are Arabs. The Kurds, who predominantly live in the north of the country, make up the largest minority (15 percent). The population also consists of Turkmen, Iranian, Armenian, and Syrian people. The official language is Arabic, while the Kurds speak Kurdish, and other ethnic minorities often speak their own languages.

Shiites and Sunnis

Almost all Iraqis are devout Muslims, but there are also small Christian and Jewish communities. The Shiites are by far the largest religious group, followed by the Sunnis. The Shiites predominantly live in the southern parts and in the center

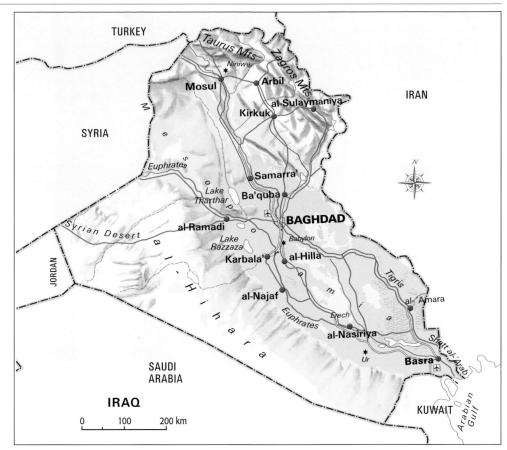

of the country. Iraq is home to some of the holiest Shiite sites, such as Karbala and al-Najaf. The shrine of the third imam Hussain (626–80 CE) in Karbala is an especially important place of pilgrimage.

However, the differences between the various religious communities are more apparent and deep-rooted in Iraq than in most other predominantly Muslim countries. The Shiite majority was severely suppressed by the Sunni minority under Saddam Hussein, and problems persist. Systematic discrimination led to numerous Shiite uprisings, which were defeated violently by the Sunni state power. Several hundreds of thousands of Shiites have been killed in past decades.

Kurdish tragedy

The fate of the Kurds, a proud, independent nation of farmers and cattle drovers, who mainly live in northern Iraq, is similar to that of the Shiites. After the Arabs, Turks, and Persians, they make up the fourth-largest population group in the Middle East. They are famous for their artistic tapestries and high levels of education. Kurdish women enjoy more freedom in society than women in other Middle Eastern communities.

The minaret of the Great Mosque of Samarra. Built from 848 to 851 CE, this mosque was once the largest in the world. The spiral minaret is 52 meters high and 33 meters wide at the bottom.

They are not veiled and can hold high tribal and political positions.

After several years of civil war, the government in Baghdad granted the Kurds the right of autonomy in 1970. However, these promises were not kept and renewed fighting erupted. After a border agreement with Iraq, Iran stopped its support of the Kurdish people in 1975. Following the First Gulf War (1980–88), which saw many Kurds fight for Iran, Iraqi troops destroyed hundreds of Kurdish villages. Many Kurds fled to Turkey and Iran. In the wake of the Second Gulf War (1991), during which the Kurds were subjected to poison gas attacks, their area of settlement was put under UN protection. During the Third Gulf War (2003), the Kurdish territory was of great strategic importance.

Between Orient and Occident

Despite the significance of Islamic traditions, Western influences are apparent in the streets of the big cities. This is reflected, among other things, in the bazaars, where veiled women shop with their daughters, who are often dressed in jeans and t-shirts and wear make-up. While modern clothes were until recently frowned upon, they now feature strongly in day-to-day life in Baghdad. However, the cultural differences with North America and Western Europe are still huge, although there are a few nightclubs with cabaret and dancing in the capital, frequented by the rich Iraqi elite. Nevertheless, such luxury cannot hide the fact that poverty is widespread in Iraq.

HISTORY

539 BCE
After the conquest of Babylon by Cyrus II, the country becomes part of the Persian Empire

750–1258 CE
Central province of the Islamic Empire under the Abbasid Caliphs

1534
The Turks conquer Baghdad

1638
The whole of Iraq is annexed to the Ottoman Empire

1920
Iraq becomes British mandated territory

1932
The country gains independence

1961
The Kurds try to assert their claim for autonomy through an uprising

1980
The Iraqi army attacks Iran; start of the First Gulf War

1987–88
Poison gas attacks against the Kurds

1988
Armistice treaty with Iran

1990
Iraq annexes Kuwait

1991
The Second Gulf War ends in the defeat of Iraq

1993
Despite international isolation and a disastrous economic situation, S. Hussein manages to consolidate his power

1998
Conflicts surrounding UN weapons inspections lead to US air strikes against Iraq

2003
US and British coalition attacks Iraq and overthrows S. Hussein's regime

2005
During the first free parliamentary elections for 50 years, the Shiite party, the United Iraqi Alliance, under Ayatollah A. Sistani, wins 48.1% of votes

2006
Saddam Hussein sentenced to death and executed on December 30.

2007–08
Turkish attack on PKK positions in northern Iraq

Babylon's famous Ishtar Gate was contructed around 575 BCE on the north side of the city. German architect and archaeologist Robert Koldewey reconstructed the gate in Berlin's Pergamon Museum in the 1920s CE.

History and Politics

The area of today's Iraq has seen a changeable history. For thousands of years, the region between the Euphrates and Tigris was home to some of the earliest civilizations in the Middle East, and has attracted people from the surrounding regions. Irrigation agriculture, divided labor, and the first writing shaped the advanced civilizations of the Sumerians, Babylonians, and Assyrians. Over the years, after frequent power switches, the area became a target for European colonial powers, and the 20th century was characterized by great upheaval and conflict. Ten years after the demise of the monarchy, the Baath Party came to power in 1968 and established itself as the dominating political force. The end of the Third Gulf War has meant that Iraq has entered a new and, it is hoped, democratic era.

Mesopotamia—advanced civilization of the Sumerians

The earliest settlements have been dated to some time around 6000 BCE. Then, the people lived in huts made from reeds, which were found in abundance along the riverbanks and the estuary opening onto the Gulf. More stable were the later pile dwellings. In the 4th millennium BCE, the Sumerians founded the first cities. Complex irrigation systems with dense canal networks allowed year-round supply of staple foods to the population.

Economic and social life was based on the division of labor. The use of the potter's wheel enabled the people to make various objects, and the clay-brick residential dwellings and temples in the cities were adorned with sculptures. One of the greatest cultural achievements of the Sumerians was the invention of cuneiform writing, made by impressing wedge-shaped, tapering wooden styluses into soft clay tablets.

Around 3000 BCE most of the approximately 500,000 Sumerians lived in cities such as Ur, a powerful city state. The fall of the Sumerian civilization began around 2350 BCE with the advance of the Akkadians, whose royal dynasty ruled the region for several centuries.

Babylon and Assyria

In the 18th century BCE, the kingdom of Babylonia developed on the lower reaches of the Euphrates and Tigris and lasted for about 1,200 years. Metal-processing and the production of fabrics, dyes, and jewelry dominated the flourishing economy. The Babylonians had close trade connections to Egypt and Asia Minor. Akkadian, the language of the Babylonians, was of great significance for a long time as the language of science and diplomacy in ancient times.

During the 8th century BCE, Babylon was influenced by Assyria, a center of power in the north of Mesopotamia, which was expanding southward. In 689 BCE, Babylon was destroyed by the Assyrians. In the aftermath, the Assyrian Empire ruled over the entire region between the Gulf and Egypt. Only under Nebuchadnezzar II (606–562 BCE) did Babylon regain its old splendor. The 'Hanging Gardens of Babylon,' one of the Seven Wonders of the Ancient World, are widely attributed to him.

From Persian to Ottoman rule

In the second half of the 6th century BCE, the region was conquered by the Persians, then in 331 BCE by Alexander the Great (356–323 BCE). During the rule of the Seleucids and the Parthians, which followed Alexander's time, the Greek and Persian cultures became intermingled. In the 2nd century CE, Mesopotamia came under Roman rule, and in the following century it was integrated into the empire of the Persian Sassanids. In 634, the area was conquered by Muslim Arabs. Under the Abbasid Caliphate, Baghdad became the capital of Islamic culture from 750 onward, until it was ransacked and destroyed by the Mongols in 1258. For several centuries, Ottoman and Persian rulers fought for influence in the region, until the Ottomans finally prevailed in 1534.

The focus of European powers

In 1903, the Germans financed and supervised the construction of the Baghdad railroad. The Germans' ambition for expansion of their influence by means of this railroad, which would connect with Berlin, displeased Great Britain whose troops occupied Baghdad during World War One in 1917. A year later, the entire area between the Euphrates and Tigris was under British control. During the further course of the war, the British supported uprisings by the population against the existing Ottoman rule. In 1920 Great Britain was awarded the mandate over Iraq by the United Nations, and Faisal I (1885–1933) was

Government:
Federal parliamentary Republic

Head of state:
President

Legislature:
National Congress with 275 members for a 4-year term, with 25% women; Presidency Council consisting of three members

Administrative divisions:
18 provinces; three of them constitute Iraqi Kurdistan Autonomous Region with its own government

Members of Syria's Druze community protest US policy in the Middle East in 1998. They display posters of Iraq's president Sadam Hussein and Syrian President Assad showing their solidarity with Iraq's president.

crowned king of the kingdom of Iraq in 1921. Even after the abolition of the British mandate, the Iraqi rulers followed a benevolent policy toward the British empire and took part in World War Two on the side of the Allies.

From kingdom to republic

On July 14, 1958, Iraq was declared a republic after the collapse of the monarchy. This was preceded by a coup, in which King Faisal II (1935–58) was killed. The new rulers abandoned the pro-Western course of their predecessors. However, the new political structure did not bring Iraq stability, and after the overthrow of the government on July 17, 1968, the Baath Party seized power. Thanks to a rise in crude oil prices, the revenue of this OPEC member rose significantly. After the resignation of President Hassan al-Bakr, Saddam Hussein (1937-2006) became head of the Iraqi government on July 16, 1979.

Immediately after taking office, Saddam Hussein started building his totalitarian regime. Influential positions were filled by members of his family and clan, and any opposition was violently suppressed. Nevertheless, he could rely on great support from the population. Three Gulf Wars, however, brought the country devastation and misery, and the Third Gulf War led to the fall of Saddam in 2003. The victorious coalition forces consequently declared the Iraqi Baath Party to be dissolved.

Reconstructing Iraq

The coalition forces did not succeed in bringing stability to the country. This led to frequent shootings and attacks on the US Army by insurgents. Many parts of the Iraqi population asked for troops to be pulled out of the country quickly. In July 2003 the US administration introduced a Ruling Council, which mainly consisted of

Shiites and took over the running of day-to-day government affairs. However, the situation did not change for the better as was hoped with the arrest of Saddam Hussein in December 2003.

After the successful formation of an interim government on June 1, 2004, which consisted of all relevant ethnic groups as well as women, the Iraqis were granted sovereignty by the US administration on June 28, 2004. In order to guarantee safety, the coalition remained in the country. Until the parliamentary election at the end of January 2005, a National Council was established as an interim government, in which all the significant religious groups, peoples, and interest groups were represented. Even though there is not a day without a suicide bombing or assassination, the Iraqis have pursued their democratic path and at the end of January 2005 went to the ballot boxes for the first time in 50 years in order to elect a new parliament.

Provincial elections followed in January 2009 and in March 2010 Iraqis were called to elect the Council of Representatives of Iraq who will elect the Prime Minister and President.

Three wars within two decades have inevitably had devastating effects on the country. The Iraqi population has suffered immensely under both the attacks and the economic embargoes. Supplies of all kinds, but particularly of medical supplies, have been non-existent at times in many areas of the country and there are still many problems to this day.

Although Saddam Hussein's regime survived the first two Gulf Wars, it fell as a result of the third in 2003. Since then, Iraq is being rebuilt—politically as well as economically—a process that is proving harder than expected and will take many years to complete.

Saddam Hussein was Iraq's president from 1979 until the coalition invasion of the country in 2003.

ECONOMY

Currency:
*1 Iraqi dinar (IQD)
= 1,000 fils*

Gross domestic product:
$50.4 billion US

Gross per capita income:
$ 1,708 US

Overseas trade:
*Imports $29.7 billion US
Exports $30.1 billion US*

Debt:
$55.5 billion US

Economy, Traffic, and Communication

Iraq's economy is traditionally geared toward the agricultural sector, and from early in its history the construction of irrigation systems has reaped great rewards. The 20th century brought with it exploitation of the country's huge crude oil reserves, but the economic growth experienced during the 1970s ended with the First Gulf War against Iran. The effects of two further wars led to economic collapse. The country is currently undergoing a painful and complex phase of reconstruction and complete restructuring.

Nothing is like it used to be since the Third Gulf War and the collapse of Saddam Hussein's regime. The United Nations and coalition forces are trying to ensure and oversee the swiftest possible reconstruction of the country's infrastructure.

Agriculture with a long tradition of irrigation

The rise of early advanced civilizations in the area of present-day Iraq was based on complex irrigation systems. Thanks to elaborate canal networks, water from remote rivers was transported to regions away from the river courses, which could consequently be cultivated. Over the centuries some techniques have been preserved, others further refined. Despite the dry climate in many parts of the country, Iraq achieves remarkable harvests, although only one-tenth of its territory can be used for agriculture. Pluvial agriculture (watered by rain) is possible only in the mountain regions of northern Iraq.

The most successful agricultural regions are still the areas surrounding the great Euphrates and Tigris rivers. The most important crop is the date palm, which grows in vast groves. Other important cultivated products are grain (mainly barley, wheat, and rice), fruit (citrus fruit, pomegranates, and figs), vegetables, cotton, and tobacco.

The past decades have seen a greater investment in irrigation projects, which have opened up new, dry areas for the cultivation of foodstuffs, and this has led to increased productivity.

Regional problems are the salinization of land through evaporation and—more importantly—the dependence on the water level of the Euphrates and Tigris. The neighboring states of Turkey and Syria have constructed several dams and therefore have greater control over the outflow level.

Crude oil—the basis of the economy

Iraq has one of the largest crude oil deposits in the world. This OPEC member state has—after Saudi Arabia, Iran, and Canada—the biggest resources of crude oil worldwide. The largest refineries can be found along the Gulf near the city of Basra, in the east near the border with Iran, and in the north between Kirkuk and Mosul. Numerous pipelines run through the country.

Crude oil was first discovered in 1927 near Mosul. Following the nationalization of the crude oil sector in 1972 and numerous price increases for this 'black gold,' the country's revenues have grown considerably.

UN embargo and its effects

Thanks to the high rewards from the export of crude oil, Iraq enjoyed sustained economic growth. This prosperity came to an end, however, with the First Gulf War (1980–88) against Iran. Industrial development was neglected in favor of massive armament and foreign debts rose dramatically. However, the country's economic situation was to become even worse. Following the occupation of Kuwait by Iraqi troops in 1990, the United Nations imposed stringent economic sanctions against Iraq.

Kurds celebrate the first free election in Iraq in January 2005.

Iraqi workers performing routine maintenance at al-Dura oil refinery in Baghdad in 2004.

As a consequence, the country was isolated from the world economy and the supply situation of many vital goods and products to its population deteriorated drastically. The Iraqi economy was at breaking point. In view of this situation, the United Nations allowed the country the resumption of crude oil exports as part of the 'oil for food' program. A considerable proportion of the proceeds from these exports went into a compensation fund, to pay for damage caused by the war. The relaxation of the embargo brought some relief, and allowed the country to supply its population with the food and medicines it so sorely needed. In addition, Iraq managed to raise the maximum limit imposed on the export of crude oil in 1999.

After the end of the Third Gulf War (March/April 2003), all UN sanctions with the exception of the weapons embargo were lifted by a UN resolution in May 2003. The 'oil for food' program was consequently brought to an end and a development fund for Iraq set up. The proceeds from the export of crude oil now go into this fund, which supports humanitarian projects and the reconstruction of the country's infrastructure.

Infrastructure and media

The country is currently in a phase of huge reconstruction. Its infrastructure suffered further damage in the Third Gulf War. Traffic networks and communication installations have been put out of action or destroyed—for example, Baghdad's international airport, which is situated 18 km (11 miles) south of the capital. Civil aviation in the country has been abandoned, while rail connections to the neighboring states have been cut and all ports closed. Road traffic is therefore of utmost importance.

The network, which has remained largely intact in many parts of the country, comprises about 38,000 km (23,600 miles) of sealed roads.

With a great deal of vital international support, the country is also trying to improve and modernize its communications sectors as quickly as possible. Under the rule of the Baath Party, the media was subject to state censorship. The US civil administration, CPA, funds the Iraqi Media Network channel, several radio stations, and the *al-Sabah* newspaper. The most important independent paper is *al-Zaman*.

Basra, March 2003: a family of refugees leaves the city under siege as the situation deteriorates.

SAUDI ARABIA

THE COUNTRY

Official name:
Kingdom of Saudi Arabia

Geographic coordinates:
*Arabian Peninsula: between 16°
and 32° north, and 34° 30' and
56° east*

Area:
*2,240,000 km²
(868,730 square miles)*

Capital:
Riyadh

Climate:
*Dry, hot, desert climate; Riyadh
24.6°C (76.3°F)/81 mm (3.2 in);
Jeddah 28.3°C (82.9°F)/64 mm
(2.52 in)*

Time zone:
Greenwich Mean Time + 3 hours

POPULATION

Number of inhabitants:
25.3 million

Population density:
*11 inhabitants/km²
(29 inhabitants/square mile)*

Population distribution:
*88% urban
12% rural*

Annual population growth:
2.1%

Life expectancy:
*Women 78 years
Men 74 years*

Religion:
*Sunni (Wahhabi) Islam, Shia
Islam*

Languages:
*Arabic (official language),
English*

Literacy rate:
86%

With its monarchy and power structure closely linked to Islam, the Kingdom of Saudi Arabia is in one sense still rooted in the past. But in a country where religious police enforce Islamic conduct yet where modern consumerism beckons, influential Saudis are seeking to reorientate the population toward the modern world. The fact that Saudi Arabia has the world's largest reserves of oil and natural gas is, simultaneously, a progressive driving force and a barrier to development.

Geography

More than half of Saudi Arabia consists of sandy desert, with great expanses of undulating dunes that stretch out to infinity like a yellow sea. With other rocky deserts, salt deserts, and steppes, these arid regions account for 99 percent of Saudi Arabia's territory. The Romans knew this area as *Arabia deserta*, or 'barren Arabia,' and from time immemorial nomads have journeyed across it with their camel caravans.

The country has two natural borders: the Red Sea on its western side, and the Arabian Gulf on its eastern side.

al-Rub' al-Khali—the Empty Quarter

The largest desert on the Arabian Peninsula is al-Rub' al-Khali, the notorious Empty Quarter. Stretching from

Wild camels graze the barren desert.

Yemen in the south, this great desert occupies a huge area of southeastern Saudi Arabia, and continues northeastward into the United Arab Emirates and Oman. The driest and most inhospitable desert on earth, al-Rub' al-Khali is uninhabited: it is feared by most, and even the Bedouin dare not penetrate its interior. But its unique beauty is revealed from the air: consisting of seemingly endless dunes, it is the largest homogenous area of sand in the world.

The Najd, a stony, rocky desert in the center of the country, has a stratified, terraced surface. The terraces are bordered by ravine-like river valleys that are filled with debris washed down when the rivers are full: however, the river beds here may be completely dry for several years in succession. The Najd Plateau is bordered by al-Dahna, a desert that lies like a narrow crescent on its eastern side.

Farther north is al-Nafud, a red sand desert that extends northward into Syria. The Arabian Mountains are dotted with craters and *harras*, patches of solidified lava.

The western mountains

Two almost contiguous mountain ranges border the Red Sea. To the north is Hijaz, which has a rocky volcanic landscape, and to the south is the Asir range: thanks to the monsoon, annual rainfall here reaches 1,000 mm (40 in), making this the only fertile region in the country. On their western side, both mountain ranges slope steeply down toward the Red Sea. In the southwest lies Jabal Sawda, which, at 3,133 m (10,279 ft), is Saudi Arabia's highest mountain, and the Tihama, alluvial plains that border the Red Sea.

Saudi Arabia has only a few rivers and other bodies of water, and these are insignificant. The wadis, or seasonal water courses, are full only after rare periods of rainfall, and it is only along the wadis and at the foot of mountains that groundwater or springs can be tapped for the maintenance of plantations in the oases.

The country without rain

The climate of Saudi Arabia is hot and extremely dry. In the interior, rain may not fall for periods of up to ten years. The climate on the coastal lowlands is hot and humid, but even here rainfall is low. In Riyadh, the capital, the average January temperature is 14°C (57°F), and in July it is 42°C (108°F).

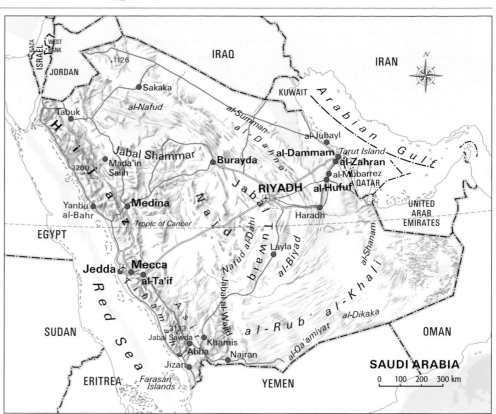

Population

In Saudi society, identity is traditionally strongly oriented toward one's tribe or clan. In the towns and villages of Asir or Najd, for example, anyone who cannot prove their descent from a certain tribe is considered to be socially inferior. Established links to a clan in which all members have a common ancestor result in the fact that an individual cannot make decisions in favor or against his clan, but must submit to the wishes and loyalties of all other clan members.

Democracy

More than 50 percent of the population of Saudi Arabia is made up of sedentary Bedouin, whose culture is nevertheless closely based on nomadism. Despite the trend toward urbanization in Saudi Arabia, Bedouin life is still the basis of Saudi cultural identity. This is why there is a wide divergence of opinion in debates on the Saudi version of democracy, which is based on Bedouin mores. The central question is whether the tribe, which is supposed to give an individual his identity, is more important than individual autonomy and freedom of independent thought and action.

Islam and the modern world

The history and destiny of Saudi Arabia and of its ruling family are directly linked to the interpretation of Islam known as Wahhabism. Wahhabi Sunnis constitute the majority of the population of Saudi Arabia. The Shiite minority, who in business and society are often treated as inferior, inhabit the eastern part of the country.

Unlike Shiites, Sunnis recognize the first four caliphs as the legitimate successors of the Prophet Muhammad (c. 570–632). Wahhabism, a reform that aimed to simplify adherence to Islam, evolved in the 18th century. It is ascetic, spiritual, and non-materialistic, a basic tenet being that money destroys the connection to God.

For Saudi Arabians this also means that, in public, men and women are still segregated. Women must be almost completely veiled, and they are forbidden to drive. Alcohol and public amusements are prohibited. The Mutaween, or religious police, also known as the Committee for the Promotion of Virtue and the Prevention of Vice, enforces adherence to the Islamic moral code.

Consumerism

In Saudi Arabia there is a growing conflict between Islam and tribal customs on the one hand, and the modern Western world and the appetite for consumerism that it embodies on the other.

The most sacred site in Islam, the Kaaba is located in Mecca. While performing the Hajj millions of pilgrims visit the site every year.

When its oil reserves suddenly made Saudi Arabia fantastically wealthy, some Bedouin made the transition from their desert tents to the modern consumerist world within a single generation. Long-standing trade relations between Saudi Arabia and the USA are reflected in consumerism: in the evenings during the month of Ramadan, when fasting is observed from sunrise to sunset, many Saudis get into luxury limousines and jeeps and drive to shopping malls, where CDs, videos, and satellite televisions await buyers. However, during prayer times, to which Muslims are called five times a day, businesses are closed.

The ruling house of Saud and an influential elite are considering introducing a new openness so as to remove the contradiction between the Mutaween and the modern westernized world that many Saudis embrace. However, many Saudis still wish to preserve a genuine Islamic way of life free from foreign influences.

HISTORY

1932
The kingdom of Saudi Arabia is proclaimed under Abd al-Aziz Al Saud III

1953–64
Reign of King Saud bin Abd al-Aziz

1964–75
Reign of King Faisal ibn Abd al-Aziz ibn Saud

1973
Saudi Arabia cuts off oil supplies to countries supporting Israel

1982
Death of King Khalid ibn Abd al-Aziz, who is succeeded by King Fahd ibn Abd al-Aziz

1991
Saudi Arabia fights against Iraq in the First Gulf War

1992
National Consultative Council is set up and new constitution adopted

2000
A border agreement with Yemen is signed

2005
Death of King Fahd ibn Abd al-Aziz, who is succeeded by King Abdullah ibn Abd al-Aziz

POLITICS

Government:
Islamic absolute monarchy

Head of State:
King

Legislature:
National Consultative Council with 150 members appointed by the king

Administrative divisions:
13 regions

ECONOMY

Currency:
1 Saudi riyal (SAR) = 100 halalas

Gross domestic product:
$349.1 billion US

Gross per capita income:
$13,980 US

Overseas trade:
*Imports $81.2 billion US
Exports $230.0 billion US*

Debt:
$52.9 billion US

King Abd al-Aziz Al Saud proclaimed the kingdom of Saudi Arabia in 1932.

History and Politics

The House of Saud is so prominent that it would be hard to imagine recent world history without it. This is the dynasty that founded and gave its name to the Kingdom of Saudi Arabia, and that has ruled it ever since. While remaining faithful to the canons of Islam, this forward-looking dynasty has also striven to lead the country out of the past and into the modern world.

In the 15th century the ancestors of the Saud family established a small kingdom near Riyadh. In about 1750, Emir Muhammad ibn Saud (1726–66) and the Islamic reformer Sheikh Muhammad ibn Abd al-Wahhab (1720 –92) united the kingdom's fragmented tribes in the new kingdom of Najd and, calling for a return to Islam in its original form, they created a theocratic state.

The flag of Saudi Arabia shows the green banner of Islam with the inscription "There is no god but God, and Muhammad is his Messenger," and a pair of scimitars, which symbolize the military successes in the history of Islam.

The road to exile

In the early 19th century, the Saudi Wahhabi empire extended from the Red Sea to the Syrian Desert in the north and to the borders of present-day Oman in the south, but it was effectively part of the Ottoman Empire, which had claimed the whole region. In 1891, differences within the dynasty led to the division of the country between individual clans. The House of Saud then went into exile in Kuwait.

The double kingdom

In 1902, Abd al-Aziz ibn Saud III (1880–1953) reconquered the desert fortress of Riyadh with the help of the Emir of Kuwait. He won over most of the tribes of the old empire and breathed new life into the Wahhabi movement for Islamic reform. In 1915, during World War One, Britain recognized the emir as an independent ruler of Najd. Ibn Saud declared himself King of Mecca and Medina in 1926, and in 1927 became King of Najd. In 1932 he united both kingdoms to form the double kingdom of Saudi Arabia.

Arabia of the Sauds

The House of Saud comprises some 5,000 princes and 40,000 other family members. Politically, it is guided by the need to retain its power. Under this regime, religion and politics are one: the absolute rulers of the House of Saud call their monarchy 'God's stewardship.' There is no constitution and, in spite of a Basic Law, they are fundamentally guided by the Qur'an and the Sunna (a corpus of traditional Islamic laws). As such, the Saudi monarch is both the secular head of state and spiritual leader: he heads the legislature, the executive, and the judiciary, and controls public life through the precepts of Islam, the state religion. There are no recognized political parties in Saudi Arabia, although some are emerging. The government consists of a Council of Ministers responsible to the king.

King Fahd ibn Abd al-Aziz (1982–2005), who succeeded his brother Khalid ibn Abd al-Aziz (1975–82) in 1982, initially upheld an archaic theocracy, which governed on the basis of Sharia (or Islamic) law.

King Fahd—the eleventh of Ibn Saud's sons, who number at least 43—was assisted in his career by his mother, who belonged to the Sudairis, one of the most prominent clans in the Arab world. Since 1995, when King Fahd's health began to fail, Crown Prince Abdullah ibn Abd al-Aziz (b. 1924) governed the country, and became king on Fahd's death in 2005. The ministers of state, of defense, and of foreign affairs are also members of the royal family.

Breaking away from the past

In the days before Saudi Arabia was a major oil producer, and before this status had brought the trappings of the modern world in its wake, the way of the life of the Saudi royal family was rooted in the past. King Faisal ibn Abd al-Aziz Ibn Saud (1964–75), who came to power after the dethronement of his brother Saud (1953–64), distributed wealth so skillfully that the majority of Saudis are proud patriots. Saudi Arabia also survived the war with Yemen, as well as Arab defeats in conflicts with Israel. But when the power of the Saud family became underpinned by revenue from oil, poor regions and tribes considered to be socially inferior became breeding grounds for extremists.

Withdrawal of US protection

The house of Saud imposed a strict religious code, making Saudi Arabia the most conservative country in the Islamic world, and the influence of Islam on political decisions is increasing. To calm anti-Western sentiment in the Islamic world, the royal dynasty broke its 'oil for security' alliance with the USA. Since 2003 American troops that were brought in to protect the king's family have almost completely left the country in order to fight the war in Iraq.

Oil pipelines in Ras Tanura connect to a tanker.

Thanks to its oil reserves, and the creation of OPEC in 1960, Saudi Arabia gained great political leverage. In 1973 it imposed an oil embargo on those Western countries that supported Israel after the latter had occupied Palestinian territory. When the embargo was lifted the price of crude oil increased exponentially. This escalation led to a situation where about 2 percent of the world's gross national product was flowing into the OPEC countries. As a result, Saudi Arabia also became an important player on the international political stage. The country's oil revenues rose from $4.3 billion US in 1973 to $101 billion US in 1980.

Controversial aid organizations

As the ruler of Mecca, the royal dynasty is also the ruler of the spiritual center of the Islamic and Arab worlds. It claims religious leadership in the Islamic *umma*, the community of believers. The Organization of Islamic Conference of heads of states, founded under King Faisal, was established to promote Islamic policy according to Saudi demands in the surrounding Islamic states of the Middle East.

However, because of international pressure, the country's political leadership now aims to monitor Islamic missionary activities more closely, because through Saudi aid organizations money was allegedly being pumped into al-Qaeda.

The prince's peace plan

Since the beginning of the 1940s, oil wealth has increased Saudi Arabia's influence on the international stage. In 2002, Crown Prince Abdullah's peace initiative for the Middle East—a 'land for peace' deal between Israel and Palestine—met with support from the Arab League. With regard to the Palestinian issue, the royal dynasty is concerned about its personal legitimacy and credibility in the Arab world, in the West, and in its own country.

Economy, Traffic, and Communication

An American corporation once paid $50,000 US in gold to Saudi Arabia in exchange for the right to drill for oil. This set in motion a revolution that was to propel Saudi Arabia into the modern age. The country has the planet's largest oil deposits, and so supplies most of the world's oil needs. Since the end of World War Two, this has given Saudi Arabia considerable influence in the Western world.

Oil has given Saudi Arabia the largest national revenue of any country in the Arab world. At the beginning of the 1950s, the Arabian-American Oil Company (ARAMCO) pledged to the kingdom 50 percent of its net income from oil drilled in Saudi Arabia.

Today Saudi ARAMCO is the world's largest oil corporation and is now fully owned by Saudi Arabia. About 25 percent of all the country's oil wells are controlled by the company.

Funding for ambitious projects

Over the past 35 years, revenue from oil has been pumped into wide-ranging modernization projects. These have included irrigation and domestic water supplies, agricultural processing, and health as well as the justice, social, and educational systems. As part of the rapid urbanization of Saudi Arabia that took place in the 1970s, futuristic cities were built. Foreign contractors, particularly from South Korea, were brought in to build roads, install telephone systems, and lay gas and petrol pipes. Desalination plants and electricity stations, universities and hospitals, radio and television stations, and high-rise buildings for administration and business purposes were also built. Working as representatives, partners, and intermediaries for European, American, and Far Eastern companies, the Bedouin became successful businessmen.

Increase in power of oil-producing nations

During the oil revolution in the 1970s, the multinational corporations lost their hold over the oil fields of the Middle East, the most important source of energy. Until then, the oil-producing countries had been paid only a third of the price at which crude oil was sold on the world market. Because the multinational companies had kept oil prices artificially low for over half a century, oil had been an undervalued resource: production at that time was an enormously wasteful process, and global consumption was extravagant.

When the multinational corporations reduced the price of crude oil still further, Saudi Arabia and other countries whose national economies depended on the export of crude oil formed the Organization of Petroleum Exporting Countries (OPEC). Their aim was to create a coordinated oil policy and stabilize oil prices.

Pressure to diversify and reform

The Second Gulf War which began in 2003 forced oil prices upward and brought billions of petro-dollars into the kingdom's treasury. However, pressure to broaden the country's economic base is a challenge that remains to be tackled. High unemployment among the male population and a huge national debt call for rapid action. For some time the government has been trying to increase the percentage of jobs occupied by Saudis: through 'Saudization,' plans are in place for young Saudis in particular to take a larger share of the more than six million jobs held by foreign workers, mostly in low-paid sectors.

King Abdullah ibn Abd al-Aziz (b. 1924) has been particularly instrumental in introducing wide-ranging reforms and opening the economy to Western markets. Under him, Saudi Arabia's manufacturing industries and private sector have received a boost, and foreign investment has been allowed in. The service sector is now growing rapidly. The development of the country's infrastructure and of its oil-refining industry has contributed to improvements in the standard of living. Thanks to new irrigation systems, the country is now self-sufficient in wheat, poultry, and dairy products.

Transportation and communication

Although camels, the time-honored ships of the desert, are still essential for the deployment of goods in desert regions, Saudi Arabia has an excellent transportation infrastructure. Almost every family has a car, but the easiest way to travel over longer distances between cities is by air. Jeddah and Yanbu al-Bahr, on the Red Sea, as well as al-Jubayl and al-Dammam, on the Arabian Gulf, have modern international ports. A high-speed train service runs between al-Dammam and Riyadh.

Saudi Arabia has eleven daily newspapers. National newspapers with the highest circulations are *al-Riyadh*, *Arab News*, *Okaz*, and *al-Jazirah*, but they are controlled by strict censorship.

KUWAIT

Kuwait is a small piece of infertile desert that gained immense wealth thanks to its possession of gigantic petroleum reserves. A blossoming national economy and a generous welfare system were the results, until Saddam Hussein decided to invade and annex the country; so began the Second Gulf War. The immense cost of reconstruction following this war made the Kuwaiti government think hard about cutting back on its social services.

Geography

Kuwait is bordered in the south by Saudi Arabia and to the north by Iraq. It is located at the northwestern tip of the Arabian Gulf. The inhabited islands Faylaka, Bubiyan, and Warba are also part of the state. Midway along the coast is Kuwait Bay. The landscape is covered for the most part by undulating desert with only a few oases, and in the interior there are wide areas of sand dunes. In the west a sandstone plateau has an elevation of up to 290 m (951 ft). In the northeast are isolated salt marshes. Water for drinking in Kuwait is available only through the desalination of seawater.

Frost does occur at times in the interior on winter nights, and almost all of the rainfall occurs in the cooler winter, typically up to 100 mm (4 in). In summer it is hot and the air is dry except along the coast, where it is often very humid.

Population

Kuwait's crude oil reserves, which it started to pump and export in 1946, have made it one of the richest countries in the world, yet it has only a small population. This situation created an enormous demand for manpower to

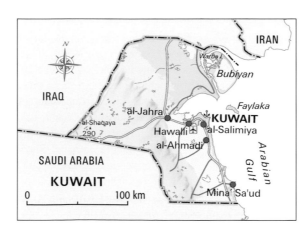

assist in the construction of its modern infrastructure. Consequently, the Kuwaitis themselves, who often wear the Dishdasha, a white garment that goes all the way down to the feet, and the Kuffiyah, headgear held in place with a cord, now represent the minority in comparison to the numerous immigrants who have come to work in the country. Non-Kuwaitis (now approximately 60 percent of the population) came mainly from Egypt, India, Bangladesh, Sri Lanka, Pakistan, and Syria. Kuwaiti citizens are, on the whole, skeptical about their foreign fellow citizens, because the occupation by Iraq (1990–91) received some positive reactions among certain immigrant groups. With the help of the new reform of 'Kuwaitization' the government wants to reduce the country's dependence on foreign workers.

The inhabitants of Kuwait belong predominantly to the Sunni branch of Islam. There is also a Shiite minority, who live mainly in the capital of Kuwait and the oil centers. The few Christians are mostly Roman Catholic.

History and Politics

The shock and devastation of the Second Gulf War was a reminder to the Kuwaiti people about the dangers of being economically dependent on oil reserves. As a result, less state control and a more flexible economy are on the agenda. Social services and subsidies for native people, such as tax-free and free medical services, are to be reduced to help pay for the high costs of the country's reconstruction.

History

Water shortages forced members of the Arabian Anizza people from Najd (Saudi Arabia) to move into the area of Kuwait in the 18th century, on the coast of which the Portuguese had established a fort (Arabic *kuwait* means 'small fort'). In 1756 the Kuwait settlement became a sheikhdom when a sheikh from the al-Sabah family was appointed emir, a position that is hereditary under the current dynasty. In the 19th century the emir was appointed a provincial governor of the Ottoman Empire. Since Great Britain granted independence to Kuwait in 1961, Kuwait has been a monarchy with a single-chamber parliament, although the parliament—when not dissolved outright—has found it difficult to influence the ruler's policies.

Iraq tried several times to claim sovereignty over Kuwait as part of the former Ottoman province of Basra, as well as occupying its border regions. In August 1990, Iraqi forces attacked Kuwait and proclaimed it the 19th Iraqi province. The emir had to flee and ruled from exile, while any Kuwaiti citizens who did not hide themselves were taken with other foreigners to be used as human shields by Iraq. In parallel with a UN trade embargo, the USA began Operation Desert Shield, which was expanded to a huge military offensive (Operation Desert Storm), in the course of which a multi-national alliance of armed forces liberated Kuwait. By the end of the Gulf War, the economy and infrastructure of the emirate had been badly damaged.

Since the Iraqi invasion, billions of US dollars have been invested in Kuwaiti reconstruction. Due to the massive damage, the port city now looks completely different. Houses, streets, and the airport have been even more minutely planned and perfectly constructed. As a sign of democratization, the National Assembly was the first building to be rebuilt.

Economy, Traffic, and Communication

The economic boom came with the oil industry, with Kuwait ranking fifth in the world in terms of oil reserves. It also became the state with the world's fifth-highest gross per capita income. Oil is the main export commodity of the country and increases the public revenue up to 80 percent. Hundreds of thousands of jobs have been created due to the rapid progress of modernization and industrialization within the country, and modern training and welfare systems have been established.

The emirate has the oil and natural gas business largely under its own control. It was one of the founders of the Organization of Petroleum Exporting Countries (OPEC), which aimed to ensure that the oil producers profited from the 'black gold' themselves rather than the big oil companies. In the middle of the 1970s Kuwait nationalized the whole of its oil industry, and the government pays 10 percent of oil income into "funds for the protection of future generations."

Tourism

Since 1994 tourism has been promoted by the state as a future market, and about 79,000 tourists visit the country annually. Kuwait is worth seeing, especially as a stopover on the way to more distant holiday destinations.

Kuwait Towers

The 'Kuwait Towers,' two water towers and a television tower in the style of minarets, have been a symbol of the modern Kuwait and its capital since 1979. In the dome of each of the towers sits a revolving restaurant and a panorama deck with a view over the city. Yet between the skyscrapers and five-star hotels are found the older houses of the traders' families as well as the old historical fishing harbor, all of which are protected as national historical monuments.

Other architectural places of interest are Sadu House, built from coral and gypsum, and the remains of the old city gates. The Sief Palace, with the emir's and ministers' offices, is built on the site where the independent state of Kuwait was proclaimed.

HISTORY

1899
Emir Mubarak al-Kabir signs protectorate treaty with Britain

1938
Oil discovered

1961
Independence from Britain

1990
Invasion of Kuwait by Iraq leads to Second Gulf War in early 1991

1994
Iraq officially recognizes Kuwait's sovereignty, territorial integrity and political independence within the borders determined by the UN

2005
Parliament grants female suffrage

2006
Sheikh Sabah al-Ahmad al-Jabir al-Sabah nominated by the government and confirmed as new Emir by parliament

POLITICS

Government:
Constitutional hereditary monarchy

Head of state:
Emir

Legislature:
National Assembly with 50 elected members

Administrative divisions:
6 governorates

ECONOMY

Currency:
1 Kuwaiti dinar (KWD) = 1,000 fils

Gross domestic product:
$80.8 billion US

Gross per capita income:
$30,630 US

Overseas trade:
Imports $24 billion US
Exports $64.3 billion US

Debt:
$17.7 billion US

Kuwait's impressive skyline has been changing significantly within the last few years because of many construction projects.

BAHRAIN

THE COUNTRY

Official name:
Kingdom of Bahrain

Geographic coordinates:
*Arabian Peninsula; between
26° 28' and 25° 37' north,
and 50° 33' east*

Area:
712 km2 (275 square miles)

Capital:
Manama

Climate:
*Desert climate with significant
atmospheric humidity; Bahrain
26.4°C (76.2°F)/76 mm (3 in)*

Time zone:
Greenwich Mean Time + 3 hours

POPULATION

Number of inhabitants:
766,000

Population density:
*1,076 inhabitants/km²
(2,785 inhabitants/square mile)*

Population distribution:
*90% urban
10% rural*

Annual population growth:
1.4%

Life expectancy:
*Women 77 years
Men 72 years*

Religions:
Sunni Islam, Shia Islam

Languages:
*Arabic (official language),
English*

Literacy rate:
89%

According to certain myths, the Garden of Eden was situated in Bahrain, and this small country is indeed a paradise for tourists from the much stricter kingdom of Saudi Arabia. It is also a haven for the offshore banks that have a free hand in the world's most liberal economy after the USA and Luxembourg, and for the citizens who fought for the democratization of what is now a constitutional monarchy.

Geography

Bahrain, the only island state and the smallest country on the Arabian Peninsula, consists of 33 islands, only six of which are inhabited. The country, which is 3.5 times the size of Washington D.C., is situated in the Gulf of Bahrain off the east coast of Saudi Arabia. Bahrain Island (Bahrayn), the largest island, is connected to the islands of Muharraq and Sitra by causeways. Saudi Arabia can be reached from Bahrain Island via a 25-km (15-mile)-long causeway extending across Umm Na'san.

A land of palms

The islands are characterized by desert-like plains, especially in the south. Karst springs make the 6-km (4-

Al-Fateh Mosque on Bahrain Island provides room for up to 7,000 worshippers.

mile)-broad plain in the north of the main island fertile, but are not enough to create lakes or streams. Irrigated agriculture is carried on in large oases. Thanks to this fresh water, Bahrain was able to become the 'Land of the Million Palms,' for it is here that dates were cultivated. However, due to land clearing and the scarcity of water little remains of the once-abundant palms. At 134 m (439 ft), Jabal al-Dukhan, located in the center of the main island, is the country's highest elevation and is at the same time the reservoir for most of Bahrain's oil wells.

The summer months (May to September) are unpleasantly sultry due to Bahrain's subtropical climate, with temperatures reaching up to 45°C (113°F). There are small amounts of rainfall in winter. Autumn is pleasant from October onward, with temperatures ranging from 20°C (68°F) to 25°C (77°F).

Population

The Bahraini population is a mix of Arabians and Persians. A good 90 percent of the people live in the towns and cities. More than 80 percent of Bahrainis are Muslim: 65 percent Shiite, 35 percent Sunni. Foreigners make up more than one-third of the population of 700,000. Indian, Pakistani, and Iranian minorities who have lived in the country for generations are also recognized as citizens.

The official language is Arabic, while English is usually used in business and trading circles. The languages of the minorities, such as Hindi, Urdu, and Persian, are also commonly used.

Manners and customs

Although traditions are still upheld, especially integration into tribes and large families, very few women wear the veil. Here they are able to live, study, and work in a far more liberated manner than in other Gulf states.

Politeness decrees that guests drink two small cups of coffee or tea when invited. The soles of the feet may not be shown when one is sitting cross–legged on a cushion or sofa, and under no circumstances should something be given or received using the left hand.

History and Politics

Traces of settlements more than 8,000 years old have been found in Bahrain. In the third millennium BCE, Bahrain was known as Dilmun by the Sumerians, for whom, as well as the Babylonians, it was an important center for trade with the Indus Valley. Dilmun achieved wealth and

An old fishing boat sits on the beach of Manama.

HISTORY

1783
Al Khalifa dynasty rules Bahrain

1820
Protectorate treaty with Britain

1971
Independence

2002
Constitutional reform: Bahrain becomes constitutional monarchy; Parliamentary and local elections

POLITICS

Government:
Constitutional monarchy

Head of state:
King

Legislature:
Parliament with 40 elected members and Consultative Council with 40 appointed members

Administrative divisions:
5 districts

ECONOMY

Currency:
1 Bahraini dinar (BHD) = 1,000 fils

Gross domestic product:
$15.4 billion US

Gross per capita income:
$14,370 US

Overseas trade:
*Imports $9.4 billion US
Exports $12.4 billion US*

Foreign debt:
$7.3 billion US

prosperity, and from the 14th to the 16th centuries pearl fishing brought about the economic heyday of Bahrain. However, its wealth and convenient location were also disadvantageous because the islands were regularly attacked and conquered by Assyrians, Persians, and Arabians, and, later on, by the Portuguese and Turks. In 1783, the Al Khalifa family from Kuwait took over from the Persian rulers; the family is still in power today. From 1820 to 1971, when independence was achieved, Bahrain was a British protectorate.

The people fight to have their say

In 1975 the constitution of 1973 was repealed and parliament was dissolved. The system of absolute monarchy remained until February 2002, when Sheikh Hamad Ibn Isa Al Khalifa (b. 1950), the head of state and king, introduced constitutional reforms. Bahrain's transformation into a constitutional monarchy, the introduction of the right to vote for women and their enablement to stand as candidates in elections, as well as limited democratization, were the consequences of protests that began in the 1990s among the rural Shiite population. An opposition movement based in London had also denounced human rights abuses, and following the reforms, the human rights situation has improved significantly. Trade unions have been authorized, and free parliamentary elections took place in 2002 and 2006. For the first time moderate Islamists and independent candidates were elected to the first house of the legislature, despite a boycott by the Shiite opposition. However, half of the members of the first house and the members of the advisory second house are appointed by the king.

Economy

The extraction and processing of mineral oil are of great importance for the economy. Extraction of the crude oil deposits began in 1934, and for decades, the 'black gold' produced up to 80 percent of public revenue. In addition, natural gas is a significant source of income. Bahrain also refines imported mineral oil for its neighbor, Saudi Arabia, among others, with whom it also cooperates very closely on various economic levels. Some of Bahrain's Saudi Arabian partners, for example, are involved in a large project aimed at attracting luxury tourism to the south of the main island.

Oil and beyond

Because the deposits of crude oil will be exhausted in the future, Bahrain has, since 1975, been promoting the establishment of offshore banks; it has thus developed into the largest banking and trading center in the Arabian Gulf. In order to be able to work without any tax liability, the banks pay high license fees to the Bahraini government. The government has also been implementing a broad program of industrialization for when the deposits of crude oil dry up. Aluminum production is still very important: the world's second-largest aluminum works are located in Bahrain.

Traditional crafts (especially gold work) and pearl fishing, which used to be so profitable, play only a secondary role today. Small amounts of fruit and vegetables are cultivated, and poultry is also bred. Fishing is important locally. Bahrain has a relatively free economy. Compared to other countries in the Middle East it is even considered to be the freest.

Tourism

Some five million visitors, mostly from the neighboring Gulf states, come to Bahrain every year, making tourism one of the fastest-growing sectors. Weekend travelers, particularly those from the neighboring Arabian states, are attracted by Bahrain's liberal attitude toward alcohol and the fun to be had in the various amusement parks located here. Visitors can, for example, dive for pearls or take a cruise in an Arabian two-masted sambuk. Direct flights are also offered from Europe.

QATAR

THE COUNTRY

Official name:
State of Qatar

Geographic coordinates:
*Arabian Peninsula; between
24° 30' and 26° 15' north, and
50° 40' and 52° 30' east*

Area:
11,525 km² (4,449 square miles)

Capital:
Doha

Climate:
*Desert climate with significant
atmospheric humidity on the
coasts; Doha, 26°C (79°F)/
75 mm (3 in)*

Time zone:
Greenwich Mean Time + 3 hours

POPULATION

Number of inhabitants:
856,000

Population density:
*74 people/km²
(192 people/square mile)*

Population distribution:
*92% urban
8% rural*

Annual population growth:
3.5%

Life expectancy:
*Women 77 years
Men 71 years*

Religion:
Sunni Islam

Language:
Arabic

Literacy rate:
89%

Caravan routes have become multi-lane highways, along which cars instead of camels travel on their way to the palaces, modern multi-story buildings, and luxury hotels. Modern buildings with glass facades have replaced the tents and windowless huts made from palm leaves and mud. Qatar has once been one of the poorest countries in the world, but is now one of the richest thanks to its crude oil and natural gas reserves.

Geography

The Qatar Peninsula, on the southern coast of the Arabian Gulf into which it juts like a thumb, is surrounded by coral reefs. This Middle Eastern state is located in the northeast of the Arabian Peninsula and borders Saudi Arabia in the south. The slightly wavy limestone plain where it is situated has hardly any drinking water and is to a large extent infertile. Indeed, Qatar is one of the driest and most arid countries in the world. Apart from a few oases, it is characterized by rocky and gravelly desert. Crude oil pipelines laid on the desert sand finance seawater desalination plants. The south has stunning sand dunes, some of which rise to heights of 40 m (131 ft) and salt marshes that glitter in the sunshine.

A desert climate, with significant atmospheric humidity on the coasts, predominates in Qatar. Due to the high temperatures and the extreme aridity (less than 100 mm/ 4 in of rain per year), the vegetation is sparse. In the summer months (May to September), it is unbearably hot—daytime temperatures of 40°–50°C (104°–122°F) are not uncommon in Doha, the capital city.

Population

Qatar's population has tripled since it began to export crude oil. Emigrants returned home and were followed by immigrants: Asians from the Indian subcontinent, Arabs from North Africa and Iran, as well as North American and European experts. The resultant one-to-five ratio of citizens to foreigners has the potential to cause conflicts. Only every 50th person employed in private enterprise is a Qatari.

Their name is their fortune

Native Qataris are the descendants of the Bedouins who have been living on the peninsula for centuries. Tribal loyalties mean that the leading positions in politics, administration, and society are reserved for the descendants of the founders of the state. In accordance with Bedouin tradition, the ruling Al Thani family ensures the well-being of the people. Through ownership of land, immunity from taxation, free primary and secondary school education, free water, electricity, and health insurance, the people have a share in the government budget. Qataris mainly work for the state and earn additional income by means of the sponsorship principle, whereby foreign companies are opened and run under their names.

*A donkey owner dressed in Arab finery offers
rides for children at the old Souq*

Dazzling jewelry and yachts

Although Qataris profess a belief in a particularly puritan strain of Islam, known as Sunni Wahhabism, many of them lead a life of ease. They enjoy showing off status symbols, and often demonstrate their wealth through the acquisition of yachts and jewelry. However, traditional habits are maintained within the family behind tinted glass windows and high walls. Although Qatari women are well-educated, few of them use the opportunity to practice a profession because of their family bonds and wealth.

History and Politics

Some fifty thousand years ago, when it was inhabited by people for the first time, the peninsula was green and fertile. Then the aridity increased. Very few people continued to live here, and foreign powers found it uninteresting because of this lack of water. However, the presence of pearls and its position near shipping routes did act as a stimulus, initially for the Romans and Greeks, and later for other colonial powers. Until 1971, when it achieved independence, Qatar was at various times ruled by the Ottoman Empire, Great Britain, and, in particular, by Bahrain (which is located to the northwest of Qatar) and the Al Khalifa tribe, which still rules Bahrain.

Qatar became an independent sheikhdom for the first time in 1868. It was able to step out from the shadow of rich Bahrain when it began to extract its own oil reserves and thrived as a result of the subsequent economic boom under the Al Thani dynasty, which has been living in Qatar since the 18th century.

Sheikh Hamad bin Khalifa Al Thani (b. 1952) has been head of state since 1995. He deposed his father in a bloodless coup and began to implement reforms. In April 2003, 96 percent of the electorate voted in favor of the new constitution which provides for the setting-up of a parliament. However, the monarchy remains hereditary and the emir retains the supreme decision-making powers. Islamic law, known as Sharia, continues to form the basis of all laws. Nevertheless, the freedom to express one's

opinion as well as freedom of the press and religious freedom have been established in the new constitution. Since 2002, the USA has been overseeing its military presence in the Middle East, North Africa, and central and south Asia from its military airbase in Qatar.

Economy

After the collapse of the pearl trade at the beginning of the 1930s, Qatar's economic recovery started when it began to export crude oil in 1949. The boom that followed changed Qatar from a desert country into a rich, industrialized state.

Today, Qatar is among the ten richest countries on the planet thanks to its oil reserves. The country, which has the third-largest deposits of natural gas in the world, does not need to worry about its prosperity in the future. Currently all of its wealth is based on crude oil and natural gas, but gas liquefaction plants, the iron and steel industry, cement production, the fertilizer sector, and the manufacture of synthetic materials are set to broaden the base of the economy.

Tourism

Qatar is striving to develop tourism and one aim is to make the Qatari capital, Doha, into a metropolis for sport in Asia. Tourists are attracted by shopping centers, magnificent boulevards, a golfing paradise, the gold bazaar, and desert tours. In recent years, luxury hotels with artificial sandy beaches have shot up out of the ground like mushrooms. Doha's many mosques, including the Grand Mosque and the Abu Bakir al-Siddiq Mosque, are also impressive. Treasures from the past are kept in the old Feriq al-Salata Fort, which is now the national museum. Most of the interesting sites are located in the north of the country, in particular, at the medieval maritime trading metropolis of al-Zubara, where the massive Qalit Marir Fortress is to be found.

Doha boasts an impressive skyline with a wealth of new buildings

HISTORY

1638
Qatar comes under Ottoman rule

1868
Qatar becomes an independent sheikdom

1916–71
British protectorate

1971
Qatar gains independence

2005
Constitutional reform

2008
Agreement with Saudi Arabia regarding the frontier

POLITICS

Government:
Absolute monarchy

Head of state:
Emir

Legislature:
Parliament with 30 elected and 15 appointed members

Administrative divisions:
10 districts

ECONOMY

Currency:
1 Qatari riyal (QAR) = 100 dirham

Gross domestic product:
$91 billion US

Gross per capita income:
$59,000 US

Overseas trade:
*Imports $12.4 billion US
Exports $30.6 billion US*

Foreign debt:
$25.7 billion US

UNITED ARAB EMIRATES

THE COUNTRY
....

Official name:
United Arab Emirates

Geographic coordinates:
Arabian Peninsula; between 23° and 26° north, and 51° and 56° 30' east

Area:
*77,700 km²
(30,000 square miles)*

Capital:
Abu Dhabi

Climate:
*Desert climate;
Abu Dhabi 24.1°C (75.3°F)/
47 mm (2 in), Dubai 26.7°C
(80°F)/75 mm (3 in)*

Time zone:
Greenwich Mean Time + 4 hours

Spurting oil wells have allowed fairytale dreams to come true in this federation of seven largely autonomous Arab emirates, founded in 1971. The result has been a Manhattan in Abu Dhabi, heavenly luxury in Dubai, absolute tax exemption in Sharjah, and new sources of income for the four smaller emirates, which missed out on the oil billions.

Geography

The United Arab Emirates (UAE) extend along the Persian Gulf from west to east: Abu Dhabi, which makes up 86 percent of the area of the United Arab Emirates; Dubai, which is 90 percent desert; Sharjah Ajman Umm al-Qaiwain, and Ras al-Khaimah, which were once legendary for their pirates; and Fujairah, which is located on the east coast, on the Gulf of Oman, and thus provides the Emirates with access to the Indian Ocean.

The Burj al-Arab in Jumeira, Dubai is among the most luxurious hotels in the world.

A desert land between a pirate coast and the Gulf of Oman

The United Arab Emirates (UAE) are located in the southeast of the Arabian Peninsula. In the south and west, they consist largely of flat desert land with sand dunes and salt pans along the coast. Flat plains and desert regions join together in the interior of the country, while typical desert oases are found in the desert itself. The biggest of these are al-Ayn, located 160 km (99 miles) to the east of Abu Dhabi, and the Liwa oases in the south of the country. Toward the south, the desert landscape merges into the vast Rub' al-Khali sand desert.

The northern part of the country is characterized by stony plains and the al-Hajar mountain range, which adjoins the chains of sand dunes. The precipitous chains of the Oman mountain range, which reaches 3,000 m (9,842 ft) in places and extends along the peninsula in a northerly direction to Cape Musandam on the northern tip, fall away steeply to the narrow, fertile coastal plain. Fujairah, whose boundary is formed by the huge al-Hajar mountains, surprises visitors with its lakes, waterfalls, and wadis. Due to the construction of reservoirs, it now boasts fertile valleys full of date palms and a growing agricultural sector.

Strong tides along the pirate coast

The country's coastline, which is often referred to as the 'Pirate Coast', is 750 km (466 miles) in length. A land ridge up to 200 m (656 ft) high in places adjoins the coast, which is 50 km (31 miles) at its widest point; off of this lie many islands. Sandbanks, coral reefs, shallows, and areas containing mud flats are characteristic of this flat section of coastline, where the ebb and flow of the tides have such a powerful influence that the landscape is continuously changing. Further inland, flat salt deserts broken by salt marshes border each other.

A desert in bloom

Mangroves can be seen growing on the shores of the Arabian Gulf and the Gulf of Oman, and green oases, found even in the interior of the country, often surprise visitors to the desert regions. Close to Abu Dhabi, vegetation sprouts in the desert: bougainvilleas, palm trees, oleander, acacias, tamarisks, and camel trees are all winning out over the sand and stone. It is easy to forget that the United Arab Emirates is located in the subtropical belt. However, good irrigation, mainly in the form of desalinated seawater and rainwater, guarantees an astonishing range of magnificent plants in the towns and cities, and even along the highways.

Sand carried along by the Shamal

The climate is hot and dry the whole year round. On the coast, temperatures in August reach extremes of up to 45°C (113°F), and the atmospheric humidity can reach maximum levels as high as 99 percent. The daily temperature rises significantly as one travels into the interior of the country, while at the same time the atmospheric humidity decreases. At night, it can become bitterly cold.

In winter, which lasts from October until May, and until February on the coast, temperatures range from 20°C (68°F) to 35°C (95°F), although the atmospheric humidity is lower. Rain falls mainly in the mountains in January and February. The annual level of precipitation reaches 100 mm (4 in). Sandstorms frequently cross the land, accompanied by the Shamal, a strong wind that blows from the north and the west, and the hot Khamsin wind, which blows from a southerly direction in the summer.

Population

Since the oil boom in the United Arab Emirates turned the world on its head in the 1960s, its inhabitants have entered the modern age via the fast lane.

Tradition and progress here lead a parallel existence. In some places, the high-tech modernity of Western skyscrapers rubs shoulders with historic Arabian baroque to form a new type of cityscape. Palaces with swimming pools are expanding in the desert like rococo architecture. At the same time, modest huts and tents have not yet completely disappeared from view.

In remote stretches of the desert, you may meet Bedouins with refurbished Mercedes limousines fitted with special bodywork and placed on truck wheels. As in the past, camels, albeit sometimes loaded onto trucks, still move along the roadways which are well-developed and extensive. In Dubai, older nomads still roam the desert with their animals and tents, while sandboarders practice dune skiing by gliding down the dunes.

A state maintained by gifts

Marriage is a family matter, remaining mainly within the one tribe. Tribes consist of related clans, each of which determines a family's position within society. Although comprising only one-quarter of the population, the native inhabitants' life and customs are shaped by Bedouin tribal law. Ten percent still live a nomadic lifestyle.

Property conditions remain unchanged. The land belongs to the sheikh dynasties, so they also own the oil. However, there has been no rebellion because the general standard of living for those with a local passport is very high.

Education, healthcare, social assistance, and pensions are largely (still) paid for by the state. Young married couples receive water, electricity, a home, and land as gifts. The per capita income of the inhabitants remains one of the highest in the world. Inhabitants are exempt from paying tax.

Foreigners building the modern state

Only 15 percent of the 1.2 million inhabitants of Dubai are indigenous. The top positions in politics and business are held by Emirates citizens with degrees, mostly from Western universities. Expatriates come from some 120 different countries and may remain here only until retirement age: British, French, Americans, Germans, and Swiss bring know-how into the country, while Indians, Pakistanis, and Filipinos do the less well-paid work. As in the other sheikhdoms the change to a modern oil state was only possible with the assistance of foreign workers. It is significant that Islam, the state religion in all the emirates and adhered to by the native inhabitants, has not led to a confrontation with the different beliefs and cultures of the immigrant workers.

Each section of the population leads its own life here in the Emirates. There are few restrictions on the lifestyles of Westerners. The native inhabitants, who are known as 'the locals' by foreigners, choose to live according to Arab traditions in private, sometimes withdrawing to the desert for the occasional weekend of traditional living and eating. Traditional clothing is still worn: a wool shirt and a flowing robe with headgear held in place by a circular piece of fabric. Men usually wear light colors and women dark colors together with jewelry adorning ears, arms and fingers.

The traditional way of life prevails. The dignity of the elder is inherited and persists within the social structures. Families and clans are ruled by a chief. As is the case in the Bedouins' tents, home life is marked by separate sections for men and women. Although increasing numbers of the more well-to-do women are educated, and some even practice a profession, most of the body is covered by a veil when they are in public.

POPULATION

Number of inhabitants:
4.5 million

Population density:
58 inhabitants/km²
(150 inhabitants/square mile)

Population distribution:
77% urban
23% rural

Annual population growth:
4%

Life expectancy:
Women 78 years
Men 73 years

Religion:
Sunni Islam

Languages:
Arabic (official language),English

Literacy rate:
91%

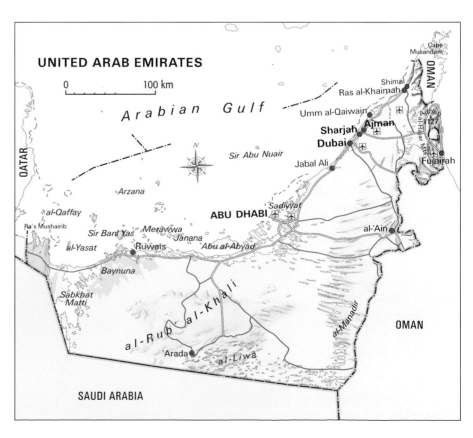

HISTORY

1853
Great Britain acquires supremacy in the Arabian Gulf

1892
Sheikhdoms obliged to recognize Great Britain as sole protectorate

1952
Formation of 'Council of Rulers'

1971
Proclamation of the 'Federation of the United Arab Emirates' by six of the treaty states. The emir of Abu Dhabi, Sheik Zayed bin Sultan Al Nahyan, becomes head of state

1972
Ras al-Khaimah joins the federation

1996
Adoption of the provisional constitution of 1971

1999–2002
Border treaty with Oman

2004
Sheikh Khalifa bin Zayed Al Nahyan becomes president following the death of his father

History and Politics

There is evidence that nomadic Bedouin tribes and fishermen were already living in the area around 2500 BCE. Many of the present-day tribes can trace their history all the way back to immigrants who came from Marib (Yemen) in the 2nd century.

In the Middle Ages the region was part of the Kingdom of Hormuz, which controlled access to and trade in the Gulf of Oman. Arab Bedouins from the Qawasim tribe, who were also seafarers, settled along the north of the Gulf coast. Their descendants still rule the northern emirates today. From the 15th century onward, the Portuguese, Dutch, and British in succession had bases in the Arabian Gulf.

In 1820 the first treaties were signed between the local rulers and Great Britain, which wanted to secure its maritime routes for trade with India and also to move against the pirates. As Trucial States, or treaty states, the Gulf sheikhdoms signed many treaties in the following hundred years, in which the British were granted far-reaching powers and rights.

In 1892 the sheikhdoms were obliged to recognize Great Britain as sole protector, and in 1902 they became a British protectorate. However, internally, the sheikhdoms remained autonomous.

Change of power from the Qawasim tribe to the Bani Yas tribe

The emirates have existed in their present form since the middle of the 19th century. At their head are tribal confederations, such as the Qawasims or the Bani Yas, which are made up of fifteen to twenty factions led by the ruling Al Nahyan clan.

One side effect of the 1853 peace treaty with the British was that the Qawasim tribe lost power, which switched

The oldest building in Dubai is the Fahidi Fort.

to the Bani Yas dynasty. The latter was the most powerful of all of the Bedouin tribes domestically and was composed of forebears of the present-day ruling families of Abu Dhabi and Dubai. The Bani Yas originally settled in the region around the Liwa oases, on the edge of al-Rub' al-Khali, but moved to Abu Dhabi in 1739.

Ready to form a federation

Tribal feuds, boundary disputes, and discord within the ruling families did not facilitate the creation of the United Arab Emirates, although all of the sheikhs were convinced of the necessity of doing so. A council of emirs, which began to vote on matters in individual states, was created in 1952 in the form of the 'Trucial Council.' Great Britain's withdrawal in the 1960s led to uncertainty in the area of foreign affairs. The unevenly distributed deposits of mineral oil and the covetousness of the emirates' larger neighbors led to the founding of the United Arab Emirates (UAE) in 1971 and, at the same time, to state independence. In 1972 Ras al-Khaimah was the last emirate to join the UAE.

Political system: the Majlis principle

The political systems in the emirates have traditionally been based on the Majlis principle. The Majlis is actually the tent in which the sheikh, as leader of the tribe, meets with the heads of the clans, who are subordinate to him. The Majlis is both parliament and government: it lays down the political guidelines and pronounces judgments.

A federation with tribal lobbyists

The UAE, with its tribal structures, is a national federation made up of seven autonomous emirates without any clear internal borders, each with its own administrative bodies and budgets, and each governed by an emir or a sheikh. The emirates are therefore autonomous in an economic sense. The head of state is the president, who is elected for five years, and who, together with the vice president, governs the Supreme Council, the highest organ of the federation. The Supreme Council consists of the rulers of the seven emirates and is, in fact, both the legislature and the executive. Abu Dhabi and Dubai have a right of veto. The federation government is in theory chosen by the Supreme Council to deal with matters of legislation, but actually fulfills only administrative tasks.

Economy

Trading, pearl fishing, and piracy ensured that the coffers were filled long before the oil boom began. Between the 17th and 19th centuries, Sharjah, Ajman, Umm al-Qaiwain, and Ras al-Khaimah were notorious and their location was known as the 'pirate coast.' Dubai, with its tradition of free trade, was different from the other emirates. It levied customs duties in its ports and established itself as a trading center in the 19th century.

Just when fishing and pearl fishing were becoming less valuable to the inhabitants of the Arab emirates, who at that time numbered 200,000, the 'black gold' was discovered in Abu Dhabi and Dubai in 1958. The boom followed, and since 1962, crude oil has been exported from the UAE.

Dubai Marina project is located some 25 km southwest of Dubai City.

POLITICS

Government:
Federation of autonomous emirates

Head of state:
President

Legislature:
Supreme Council, formed by the rulers of the seven emirates; federal national council with 40 appointed members

Administrative divisions:
7 emirates

ECONOMY

Currency:
1 United Arab Emirates dirham (AED) = 100 fils

Gross domestic product:
$192 billion US

Gross per capita income:
$26,210 US

Overseas trade:
*Imports $102 billion US
Exports $157 billion US*

Foreign debt:
$39.8 billion US

All of the sheikhdoms benefited from the rich deposits of crude oil in Abu Dhabi and Dubai. Furthermore, the infrastructure created thanks to this great prosperity is turning the Emirates into an attractive new tourist destination.

A number of free trade zones made Dubai the axis for trade in the southeast of the Arabian Gulf. Dubai is also the largest trading center for gold in the Middle East and an international banking center. Industrial and economic developments are proceeding at a rapid pace, especially in Abu Dhabi and Dubai.

Tourism

The cosmopolitan Dubai leads Abu Dhabi in the tourism stakes. With desert safaris, fishing on the high seas, diving, luxury hotels, clear water, sun, sand, duty-free shopping, camel races, and late-night discos, it attracts many well-off travelers. Another unique feature is the Burj al-Arab, which, at 321 m (1,053 ft), is the world's tallest hotel and, at the same time, the only one on the planet awarded seven stars. With twenty-eight double-height stories and 202 suites surrounding the largest hotel atrium in the world, it is the destination of choice for many who wish to live in the lap of luxury. Shaped like a boat's billowing sail, it rises up into the sky on an artificial island.

Sharjah also invested large amounts of money in tourism, but lost its position in the race due to a ban on alcohol. Since 2001 Fujairah has been trying to attract tourists using the al-Hajar mountain range in the hinterland and its superb underwater attractions. Most of the fine sandy beaches in the remaining emirates, which have also built hotel complexes, are still largely empty. They offer diving opportunities and are as worthy of a trip as the picturesque ruins of Shimal and the dhow shipyards, where traditional working methods are still used.

Al-Tawila Power and Desalination Complex, Abu Dhabi provides up to 230 million liters (95 million gallons) of water per day.

OMAN

THE COUNTRY

Official name:
Sultanate of Oman

Geographic coordinates:
*Arabian Peninsula; between
16° 30' and 26° 30' north, and
53° and 60° east*

Area:
*309,500 km²
(119,498 square miles)*

Capital:
Muscat

Climate:
*Borderline tropical, arid, dry
climate; Muscat 28.4°C (83.1°F)/
106 mm (4 in)*

Time zone:
Greenwich Mean Time + 4 hours

Oman extends along the eastern tip of the Arabian Peninsula and borders the Arabian Sea in the south and west. Most people live in the coastal regions, since much of the interior consists of uninhabitable desert. The incense trade and ship-building have a long history in the country. Indeed, the Omanis have a reputation as an old trading people, who were carrying on overseas trade with countries in the Far East and East Africa from early times.

Geography
The national territory also includes some small islands located in the Arabian Sea, such as the Kuria Muria Islands and, to the northeast of the United Arab Emirates, the small, but strategically important, exclave of Musandam, located at the tip of the Ru'us al-Jibal Peninsula ('mountain heads') in the Strait of Hormuz.

Mountainous landscapes
The north of the country is taken up by the geologically varied al-Hajar mountain ranges, whose highest peak, the Jabal al-Akhdar, rises up to about 3,000 m (9,850 ft). These mountains separate the extensive deserts in the interior of the country from the Batina coastal plain, which constitutes the economic core of the country. Streams from the al-Hajar mountain range supply the plain with sufficient water for irrigational agriculture. However, the streams flowing from the mountain range

to the desert interior of the country dry up before they can join up to form lakes. Desert extends across large areas of the interior, while in the southwest the land rises to the mountains of the Qara range. Due to its abundant aromatic bushes, this region is also known as the 'land of incense.'

Tropical to subtropical heat
Almost all of the country is located in the tropics; only the extreme northern end juts out across the Tropic of Cancer and into the subtropics. In accordance with its location, the climate in Oman is hot all year round.

There are significant variations in atmospheric humidity between the dry desert regions and the more humid coastal regions. The only rain worth mentioning falls there between June and September under the influence of the monsoon, but levels seldom reach more than 100 mm (4 in) a year in the lowlands, although they can exceed 400 mm (15 in) in the al-Hajar mountain ranges. The average annual temperatures throughout the country are between 25°C (77°F) and 30°C (86°F). However, extreme levels of up to 50°C (122°F) have been reached in the hottest regions.

Date palms predominate
Statistically, there are four date palms to every inhabitant of the country. These trees find ideal conditions in which to grow in the extremely dry regions in the interior of the country. Thorn bushes thrive in parts of the otherwise barren desert regions, while the more humid mountainsides are covered in acacias, cedars, and olive trees. Incense trees are the predominant plant species in Dhofar. The resin that issues from the bush-like incense trees was coveted so much in ancient times that it was weighed with gold. It is gathered before the monsoon in March and April, then dried and sold as a much sought-after scent ingredient.

Population
All Omani nationals are Arabs, but there is a large resident Asian population, most of whom come from India, Pakistan, and Bangladesh, and live mainly in the coastal regions.

The official language of the country is Arabic, while English is important as a trading language. The state religion is Islam, in which more than 80 percent of the inhabitants profess a belief. Although the Ibadite strain of

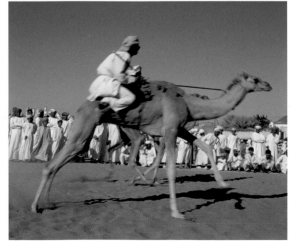

*Camel races are very popular
in many Arab countries.*

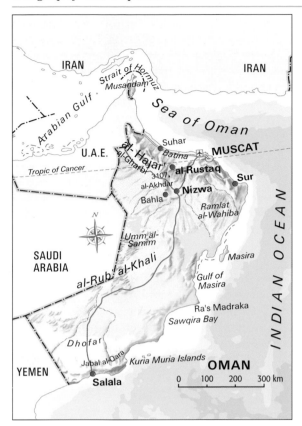

POPULATION

Number of inhabitants:
2.7 million

Population density:
9 inhabitants/km²
(23 inhabitants/square mile)

Population distribution:
72% urban
28% rural

Annual population growth:
3.2%

Life expectancy:
Women 76 years
Men 71 years

Religion:
Islam

Languages:
Arabic

Literacy rate:
81%

Islam predominates in the interior of the country, most of the people living along the coast are either Sunnis or Shiites.

The country's education and healthcare systems are well-developed, and the literacy rate has been systematically raised. Average life expectancy has risen due to an improvement in the supply of medicines and a continuing large drop in infant mortality.

Arts and crafts

Oman's craft industry has greatly enriched Arabic culture. Great success has been achieved in the area of boat-building in particular, while woodcarving is an accomplished art form in the country. Particularly beautiful carvings can be found on the heavy doors of fortresses and on the windows of many merchants' houses and premises. These stylish forms of work have introduced striking new motifs and design cues into the clay architectural forms, which tend to be otherwise rather plain.

The art of silver workmanship also has a long tradition in Oman. For millennia, silversmiths have produced beautiful works, for example, exquisite teapots, coffeepots, and, especially, incense-holders. And although the famous curved, silver daggers are today no longer used as a weapon, they have lost nothing of their importance as a symbol of masculinity. They are often worn over the stomach on festive occasions.

Students at Sultan Qabus University in Muscat. The University was founded in 1986 and is Oman's only public university.

Men wearing traditional garments playing dominoes in Muscat.

HISTORY

1741
The Al Bu Said dynasty gains power; it is still ruling the country

1891
Great Britain becomes protector

1959
The sultan of Muscat and Oman ousts the imam of the Ibadites

1970
Sultan Qabus bin Said forces his father to abdicate

1975
Left–wing rebellion ended

1982
Oman signs Memorandum of Understanding with Great Britain

1996
Oman passes a constitution

1997
Female suffrage introduced

2002
National border treaty with United Arab Emirates

2003
Elections for the advisory council: all citizens over the age of 21 permitted to vote for the first time

2006
Free trade agreement with the USA

History and Politics

In ancient times, incense from Oman reached Europe and Mesopotamia via the Incense Trail, although in around 400 CE the incense trade lost much of its value. In the 6th century, Oman became a Persian dependency. The people adopted Islam in the 7th century. After the Persians were driven out of the country, Oman acquired a monopoly in the Arab trade with the Far East, and Muscat and Suhar grew to be important ports. By using the seasonally changing monsoon winds, traders sailed as far as East Asia and along the African coast. In this way, valuable goods—silk, gold, ivory, and spices—reached the Arab world.

Under the influence of European powers

This prosperity, however, led to tribal battles and attracted invaders in their droves. European powers also vied with each other to rule the economically thriving region. The Portuguese conquered Muscat in 1507, but subsequently had to defend the city against the British and Persians. To this end, the Portuguese built several fortresses along the coast until they were driven out in 1650. In 1741 the Persians were repelled by Ahmed bin Said, the first imam in the Said dynasty, which still rules today. At the beginning of the 19th century Oman experienced its greatest period of expansion. But with the decline in maritime trade and the loss of Zanzibar in 1856, the heyday of the kingdom, which was now ruled as a sultanate, ended. Toward the end of the 19th century Great Britain acquired an influence in the region and, in 1891, founded the protectorate of Muscat and Oman.

Sultan Said bin Taimur, who governed from 1932 onward, pursued a deliberately nationalistic course which led to the country becoming isolated in terms of its foreign policy. Due to the lack of export revenue, expenditure in the area of social services was neglected. The bitter battles fought between rebellious mountain tribes and the sultan from 1963 onward led to Great Britain leaving the country.

A new regime

A form of renaissance began in July 1970 when the sultan was removed from power by his son, Qabus bin Said (b. 1940). The infrastructure developments he had promised were speedily implemented, with the costs covered by revenue from crude oil exports. As the standard of living increased, there was a further significant decrease in the age-old tribal conflicts, and Sultan Qabus bin Said continues to reign over this re-emerging nation.

Resin from the frankincense tree (Boswellia sacra) is used to produce frankincense of various qualities.

POLITICS

Government:
*Absolute monarchy
(Sultanate)*

Head of state:
Sultan

Legislature:
*Consultative Council with 83
elected members and Council of
State with 70 appointed members*

Administrative divisions:
5 regions, 3 governorates

ECONOMY

Currency:
*1 Omani rial(OMR)
= 1,000 baizas*

Gross domestic product:
$35.7 billion US

Gross per capita income:
$11,120 US

Overseas trade:
*Imports $9.9 billion US
Exports $21.2 billion US*

Foreign debt:
$4.3 billion US

*Omani Schoolboys in Sidab wearing the traditional embroidered
Omani cap, the kumma, and traditional robe, the dishdasha.*

Economy

Oman was an important trading power from the Middle
Ages until the 19th century. Today, it lives on the proceeds
of its crude oil exports, although these deposits are being
depleted, and the government is endeavoring to put the
economy onto a broader basis.

Oman has developed rapidly because of its crude oil,
which forms the economic backbone of the sultanate. The
most productive beds are located in the south of the al-
Hajar mountain ranges and in the Governorate of Dhofar,
although the reserves are expected to be exhausted by
the middle of this century. This is the reason why the
sultanate is increasingly investing in the mining of other
raw materials, such as natural gas, copper ore, and marble.
Generous subsidies are also being offered to induce foreign
investors to set up businesses and manufacturing companies in Oman.

Agriculture is limited to the thin strip of coast and
some oases in the interior of the country. The main products grown are dates, citrus fruits, coconuts, bananas,
vegetables, cereals, and tobacco.

Oman has two important international ports. In addition to the commercial port of Mina Sultan Qabus near
Muscat, the port of Mina Raysut near Salala was expanded
to become a major container terminal.

*Qabus Mosque in Nizwa. Nizwa
was Oman's capital in the 6th
and 7th centuries CE.*

YEMEN

THE COUNTRY

Official name:
Republic of Yemen

Geographic coordinates:
*Arabian Peninsula; between
12° and 19° north, and
42° 25' and 53° east*

Area:
*527,970 km²
(203,850 square miles)*

Capital:
Sanaa

Climate:
*Desert climate; Sanaa 24.6°C
(76.3°F)/250 mm (10 in); Aden
32.3°C (90.1°F)/39 mm (1.5 in)*

Time zone:
Greenwich Mean Time + 3 hours

POPULATION

Number of inhabitants:
22.2 million

Population density:
*42 inhabitants/km²
(109 inhabitants/square mile)*

Population distribution:
*29% urban
71% rural*

Annual population growth:
3.4%

Life expectancy:
*Women 65 years
Men 61 years*

Religion:
Sunni Islam

Languages:
*Arabic (official language),
English*

Literacy rate:
55 %

Diverse terrain, terraced fields, and ancient Arab architecture are the hallmarks of Yemen, the country at the southern tip of the Arabian Peninsula where the people are known for their great pride and magnificent hospitality. Although one can still find signs of the fabled orient here, Yemen is also very much a developing country, struggling with all the associated political, social, and economic problems that come with that status.

Geography

Yemen is a country of stark contrasts, consisting of coastal areas, volcanic mountain chains, and highland plains separated by broad stretches of desert. Owing to its comparatively frequent rainfall, it is the most fertile country on the Arabian Peninsula. Yemen is bordered to the west by the Red Sea, and to the south by the Gulf of Aden.

The terrain: a question of contrasts

The Tihama is a semi-desert stretch of coastline along the Red Sea, which quickly rises to become a high mountain massif, dropping off toward the northeast in the direction of the Great Arabian Desert, also known as al-Rub' al-Khali (the 'Empty Quarter'). The highest peak in this mountain range, and in all of Yemen itself, is the Jabal al-Nabi Shu'ayb at 3,666 m (12,030 ft), located to the west of the capital city Sanaa.

The southern coastal plain on the Indian Ocean, by way of a complete contrast, merges into the Arabian plateau in the north (reaching an altitude of up to 2,000 m/ 6,562 ft). In this region, more than any other in the country, are found fertile, deeply cut intermittent stream beds, or wadis, in the valleys. In the southeast of Yemen, in the region of the same name, the 400-km (248-mile)-long Wadi Hadramaut is the largest valley in the country.

Sanaa is famous for its elaborate architecture. The old fortified city was added to the UNESCO world cultural heritage list in 1986.

Also part of Yemen's national territory are the islands of Kamaran and Perim in the Red Sea and the Socotra Archipelago, which lies off the African Cape of Guardafui (Ras Asir) at the eastern tip of the Somali peninsula.

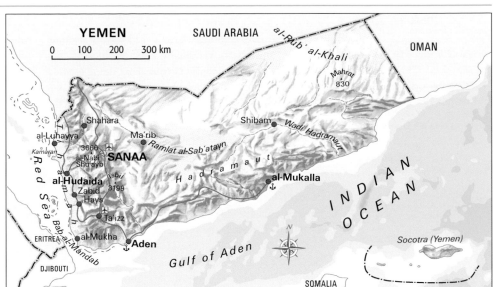

The flora and fauna of the mountain and desert regions

The country's flora is quite surprising in its diversity, despite the barren and seemingly inhospitable appearance of the mountain and desert regions. The broad spectrum of plant life ranges from desert plants to subtropical aquatic plants. In the river valleys are found tamarisks, and the coastal area of the Red Sea is filled with mangroves. Figs, styrax, sweet gum trees, and acacias thrive in the valleys and high plains. Sweet-sop trees, which can reach a height of 3 m (10 ft) and have pink flowers in the spring, thrive in various regions throughout the country. Owing to the differing elevations, the range of agricultural crops grown is also very diverse, from millet and incense trees, to date palms and coffee. In the Tihama region, special preference is given to undemanding crops such as cob millet and cotton; otherwise the flora and fauna resemble those of an African savannah. Fruit, vegetables, coffee, dates, maize, and potatoes are grown in those areas with adequate precipitation. Many parts of the valleys serve as oases for irrigation, and resemble fertile gardens with extensive groves of palm trees.

Work and farm animals include cattle, asses, camels, goats, and sheep. Vultures inhabit the mountains, while flamingoes and pelicans can be found on the coast of the Tihama region.

The life-giving rainy season

Yemen's climate corresponds to the ever-changing nature of the terrain; the country is divided into three very different climatic zones. In the Tihama, conditions are very hot and humid. The average temperature is around 28°C (82.4°F), but temperatures occasionally climb to above 40°C (104°F). The humidity is extremely high. Climatic conditions are the most favorable in the central highlands (1,000–2,000 m/ 3,281–6,562 ft), where the average temperature is 25°C

(77°F) and precipitation is quite abundant, particularly on the western face of the mountains. In the upper highlands (2,000–3,000 m/ 6,562–9,843 ft), the precipitation is less again and in the winter it can be quite cold.

There are two rainy seasons, in the spring and late autumn. These are of the utmost importance to the country's agriculture, although the rainfall is not very evenly distributed. While there is hardly any precipitation to speak of on the coasts, the amount of rainfall increases as you approach the mountains and decreases again in the highlands.

Population

Tribal affiliations, Islam, and Arabic culture form the central pillars of society in the southern Arabian Peninsula. Although Yemen is democratically governed today, an individual's allegiance to his tribe is still a factor, though not as important as it once was. The tribes are mainly composed of sedentary farmers in the hilly parts of Yemen and the Tihama, as well as nomads or semi-nomads. The population density is greatest in the highlands.

African and Asian influences

The population is made up almost exclusively of Yemeni Arabs, though there are also small minorities of Indians and Somalis living here. The proximity of the African continent is clearly felt in the coastal plain of the Tihama, where the close, traditional ties with Africa are not only evidenced by the negroid element among the local inhabitants, but can also be seen in the traditional hut painting. In many respects, the villages of this region are organized in a similar way to tribal African societies.

In the Wadi Hadramaut area, an Asian element is evident among the offspring of Yemeni merchants who returned to their homeland from Indonesia. Both the architectural style of the houses and the colorful clothing worn by the men are clear evidence of the close ties that exist to Southeast Asia.

Languages and religion

The country's official language is Arabic, but English is an important language for commerce. Although there is religious freedom in Yemen, 99 percent of the population practices Islam. The Muslim population further divides into the Shiite denomination of the Saidites and the Sunni denomination of the Shafiites, with the latter making up the majority.

As late as 1970, 90 percent of the Yemeni populace was illiterate, but after a large effort on the part of the government the illiteracy rate has dropped to 45 percent. Of course, the Yemeni people's love for the spoken word has very deep roots, with the tradition of storytelling developing as a result of the caravan trade. The stories of the merchants, who brought goods from all over the world—silk from China, cinnamon, sapphires, and diamonds from India, and incense, myrrh, gold, and ivory from Africa—were themselves a valuable commodity, helping to pass the time during their long treks through the desert.

The houses of Shibam are all made of mud bricks. Shibam is often referred to as the Manhattan of the desert.

YEMEN

HISTORY

1517–1635
Yemen occupied by Ottoman troops

1839
Aden taken by Great Britain, followed by expanded British influence over all of South Yemen

1918
North Yemen gains its independence

1967
South Yemen gains its independence

1971–72 and 1978–79
War between North and South Yemen

1990
North and South Yemen are united to become the Republic of Yemen

1994
Southern moves for secession are put down by force

1998–99
Tribal feuds in the north threaten internal security

2000
Yemen and Saudi Arabia resolve border issues

2007
Clashes between security forces and Shiite rebels in the northern province of Sadah

History and Politics

For a long time, North and South Yemen were separate states. Reunification was finally achieved in 1990, but not without various conflicts caused by the alienation of certain elements of its people. After its impressive and long history as a crossroads for the caravans and as the land of incense, today, sadly, Yemen is a poor country. It is, however, trying to stabilize and develop its economy through a range of reforms.

Several ancient kingdoms existed on the territory that makes up present-day Yemen. These include the kingdoms of Minaean, Homeritae, and Sheba, of which the latter is probably the best known. The most famous ruler of ancient Yemen is the fabled Queen of Sheba, whose visit to Solomon is mentioned in both the Bible and the Qur'an. Her actual origins remain a mystery to this day. Despite her fame, we can only speculate as to whether she really was a historical figure, but it does seem highly likely that a female ruler of her description did exist. Nevertheless, her legend is still quite popular among the Yemeni people, who know her as Bilqis.

Arabia Felix: the land of incense

The Romans called the country Arabia Felix or 'Happy Arabia,' since it was not only a fertile region, but was also considered the original source of much sought-after incense. The so-called 'Incense Trail,' one of the most important trade routes of the ancient world, led through Yemen and ushered in a golden era in the region that lasted from the 5th century BCE to the 1st century CE. Thereafter, the incense trade route waned in importance and the kingdom entered a steady period of decline.

Independence after foreign rule

Islam spread throughout the southern part of the Arabian Peninsula around 630 CE. From the 7th century on, the people were the subjects of the Caliphate of Damascus, and southern Arabia was later ruled by the Abbasids of Baghdad.

From 1517 to 1635, large parts of present-day Yemen belonged to the Ottoman Empire. In 1839, the British took Aden and, little by little, they were able to expand their rule to include South Yemen.

During the mid-19th century, the Turks again attempted to conquer Yemen. After occupying Sanaa in 1872, they soon ruled all of North Yemen. In the period that followed there were many uprisings against the Turks and the cry for national sovereignty grew louder. North Yemen finally gained its independence in 1918 as the Kingdom of Yemen, which was officially recognized by Saudi Arabia in 1934.

Civil wars and a united Yemen

After the downfall of the monarchy in 1962, North Yemen was proclaimed the Arab Republic of Yemen. Following this, however, a bitter civil war broke out in North Yemen between royalist and republican factions that lasted until 1970. Ali Abdullah Saleh (b. 1942) seized control of the government four years after the 1974 military coup.

After the British left South Yemen in 1967, the National Liberation Front (NLF) seized power after civil unrest that bordered on outright civil war. They proclaimed the People's Republic of Yemen, which was renamed the Democratic People's Republic of Yemen after 1970. In this socialist country with Marxist overtones the 1970s and 1980s were marked by several internal political clashes and upheavals.

By 1972, both Yemeni states had agreed in principle to a political union, but this failed to become a reality due to their insurmountable political and ideological differences. Repeated border conflicts sprang up in the period that followed. After a military conflict in 1979, both Yemeni states agreed to a plan for reunification that same year. However, union as a republic only finally took place in 1990. Unresolved negotiations concerning the distribution of power between the north and the south once again led to a civil war and the secession of South Yemen in 1994. After only two months, the victorious North declared the civil war to be over.

Yemen's capital Sanaa has a population of roughly 1.7 million inhabitants. The city is constantly growing due to migration and population growth in general.

POLITICS

Government:
Islamic presidential republic

Head of state:
President

Legislature:
Parliament with 301 delegates elected for six years, Schure Council with 111 nominated members

Administrative divisions:
20 governorates; capital district

ECONOMY

Currency:
1 Yemeni rial (YER) = 100 fils

Gross domestic product:
$19.1 billion US

Gross per capita income:
$760 US

Overseas trade:
*Imports $6.6 billion US
Exports $7.2 billion US*

Foreign debt:
$5.5 billion US

For many years the transfer of funds from Yemenis who lived in the oil-producing countries of the Arabian Gulf was of great economic importance. However, owing to the country's pro-Iraqi attitude during the Gulf War in 1991, almost a million Yemeni guest workers were expelled from Saudi Arabia and the other Gulf states. Unemployment increased dramatically and the economic situation worsened.

Transportation in the desert
Only a small portion of the road network is paved with asphalt (approximately 6,200 km/3,853 miles of the 71,000 km/44,117 miles or so). The remaining roads are mainly desert tracks. Bus routes link the cities. Yemen does not have a railroad system, so airlines and water transport are very important.

Information on world events
Newspapers are available in both Arabic and English. Examples are *al-Jumhuriyya, al-Thawra* (both in Arabic), and the *Yemen Observer* and *Yemen Times* (both in English). Radio and television are state-controlled. The telecommunications sector has developed rapidly over the last few years.

Tourism
Exotic cities, colorful bazaars, and winding alleys—of all the Arab countries, Yemen comes closest to embodying the preconceived notion of the orient. The beauty of ancient Arab architecture, which is the expression of a centuries-old and highly developed culture, is in harmony with the dramatic landscapes. The many surviving structures from the country's golden age alone make the trip worthwhile.

An old bridge near Shahara, built in 1539 CE.

Economy, Traffic, and Communication
Owing to the terrain, only a small part of the country is suitable for arable farming. For thousands of years the Yemenis have been using ingenious irrigation systems for their intensive terraced farming. In the dry regions of the country animal husbandry predominates, with the herdsmen keeping goats, sheep, cattle, asses, and camels. On the coast, fishing for tuna, mackerel, and sardines is common.

The land of the coffee bush
Along with Ethiopia, Yemen is considered to be the birthplace of coffee. The coffee bush was once cultivated in the mountain areas of Yemen at elevations of between 1,000 and 2,000 m (3,281 and 6,562 ft) and transported to al-Mukha (the city that gave mocha its name) and al-Hudaida. Yemen held the monopoly on coffee between the 17th and 18th centuries.

The cultivation of coffee in Central American and South American countries brought the decline of Yemen's coffee exports and the country was no longer able to compete. Today, coffee is cultivated in only a few areas. The coffee crop has been largely replaced by the qat bush, the leaves of which contain a mild narcotic. This drug is very popular in Yemen and men can often be seen chewing qat leaves in the afternoons.

Little industry and high unemployment
The industrial sector is still minuscule, and with the exception of the oil refineries of Aden and Ma'rib, there are no notable industrial areas. Traditional handicrafts such as the production of silver and leather goods continue to play an important role in the economy.

Children in the town of Hababah, in Yemen's mountainous western part.

Index of Map Names

Aadan Yabaal   O   **SP**   25   Jb 44
① ② ③ ④ ⑤
Search concept   Icon   Nation   Page   Search grid designation

② Icons

◻ ...... Country	⬠ ...... Island	≈ ...... Ocean, Sea	⬡ ...... Landscape
◩ ...... Capital city	⏶ ...... Mountain range	∼ ...... Lake, River	
⊙ ...... Administrative unit	△ ...... Mountain	⚲ ...... National park	
O ...... Place	⌓ ...... Cape	★ ...... Point of major interest	

③ Sovereign States and Territories

Algeria	A	Iraq	I	Mauritania	MA	Saudi Arabia	SA
Bahrain	B	Jordan	J	Morocco	MO	Somalia	SO
Comoros	C	Kuwait	K	Oman	O	Sudan	SU
Djibouti	D	Lebanon	LE	Palestine	P	Syria	SY
Egypt	E	Libya	LI	Qatar	Q	Tunisia	T

United Arab Emirates   UAE
Yemen   Y

1-9

1st Cataract ∼ **E** 15 Hj 33
3rd Cataract ∼ **SU** 20 Hg 36
4th Cataract ∼ **SU** 20 Hj 36
5th Cataract ∼ **SU** 21 Hj 36
6th Cataract ∼ **SU** 20 Hj 37

A

Aadan Yabaal O **SO** 25 Jb 44
Abadla O **A** 11 Ge 30
Aba al-Dud O **SA** 84 Hp 32
Abaida △ **D** 24 Hp 40
Abalessa △ **A** 18 Gj 34
Abar al-Mashi O **SA** 84 Hm 33
Aba al-Rukham O **SA** 86 Ja 36
al-'Abbasiya O **SU** 20 Hh 39
Abdelcader O **SO** 24 Hp 40
'Abd al-Kuri ⬠ **Y** 87 Je 39
Abd al-Magid O **SU** 20 Hj 38
Ab-e Sirvan ∼ **I** 83 Ja 28
Abha O **SA** 86 Hp 36
Abhe Bad ∼ **D** 24 Hp 40
Abidiya O **SU** 21 Hj 36
al-Abiodh Sidi Cheikh O **A** 11 Gg 29
Abjelil O **MO** 10 Gd 28
Abnub O **E** 14 Hh 32
al-'Abr O **Y** 86 Jb 37
'Abri O **SU** 20 Hh 35
'Abs O **Y** 86 Hp 37
Abu al-Abyad ⬠ **UAE** 88 Je 33
Abu 'Ali ∼ **LE** 82 Hk 28
Abu 'Ali ⬠ **SA** 85 Jc 32
Abu 'Ammar O **SA** 21 Hk 37
Abu 'Arish O **SA** 86 Hp 37
Abu Ballas O **E** 14 Hf 33
Abu Darba O **E** 15 Hj 31
Abu Darikha O **SY** 82 Hl 28
Abu Dawn O **SU** 20 Hj 37
Abu Dis O **SU** 21 Hj 36
Abu Dom O **SU** 20 Hh 37
Abu Dulayq O **SU** 21 Hj 38
Abu Faruh O **I** 83 Hp 29
Abu Gabra O **SU** 22 Hf 40
Abu Ghirban O **SU** 20 Hh 36
Abugrin O **LI** 12 Gp 30
Abu Gubayba O **SU** 20 Hh 40
Abu Hamad O **SU** 21 Hj 36
Abu Hashim O **SU** 20 Hh 40
Abu Hugar O **SU** 21 Hj 39
Abu Jisra O **I** 83 Ja 30
Abu Kabir O **E** 15 Hh 30
Abu Kabisa O **SU** 20 Hf 39
Abu Kamal O **SY** 82 Hn 28
Abu Maztariq O **SU** 22 Hf 40
Abu Mina ★ **E** 14 Hg 30
Abu Oir O **E** 14 Hg 30
Abu Ourqas O **E** 14 Hh 32
Abu Rudeis O **E** 15 Hj 31
Abu Rukba O **SU** 20 Hh 39
Abu Saffar O **SU** 21 Hj 37
Abu Shuwayyir O **I** 83 Jb 30
Abu Simbel ★ **E** 15 Hh 34
Abu Suhair O **I** 83 Ja 30
Abu Tig O **E** 15 Hh 32
Abu Tunaytin O **SU** 20 Hh 38
Abu 'Uruq O **SU** 20 Hh 38

Abu 'Uwaijila O **E** 15 Hj 30
Abu Zabad O **SU** 20 Hg 39
Abu Zanima O **E** 15 Hj 31
Abu Zayyan O **LI** 12 Gn 29
Abwong O **SU** 22 Hj 41
Abyad O **SU** 20 Hf 39
Abyar Ali O **SA** 84 Hm 33
Abyar al-Shuwayrif O **LI** 12 Gn 31
Abyei O **SU** 22 Hg 41
Achaacha O **A** 11 Gg 27
Acheb O **A** 12 Gl 31
Achegtim O **MA** 16 Ga 36
Achguig al-Adam O **MA** 16 Ga 36
Adaim al-Hulay O **SA** 86 Hn 35
al-'Adam O **LI** 19 Hd 30
Adam O O 89 Jg 34
Adan al-Sugra O **Y** 86 Ja 39
Adaouda △ **A** 18 Gj 34
Adarama O **SU** 21 Hk 37
Adarot O **SU** 21 Hk 37
Adda ∼ **SU** 22 He 41
Ad Darsia O **LI** 13 Hc 29
al-Adeb Larache O **A** 12 Gl 32
Adel Bagrou O **MA** 17 Gc 38
Adelei O **SO** 25 Ja 44
Aden O **Y** 86 Ja 39
'Adfa O **SA** 84 Hn 31
Adinsoone O **SO** 24 Jc 41
Adiri O **LI** 12 Gn 32
Adok O **SU** 22 Hh 41
Adrar O **A** 11 Gf 32
Adrar ⏶ **A** 12 Gk 33
Adrar Ouarâne ⏶ **MA** 16 Fp 35
Adrar Adjeloho ⏶ **A** 12 Gl 33
Adrar Ahellakane ⏶ **A** 11 Gj 32
Adrar Ikohahoène △ **A** 12 Gl 33
Adrar In Hihaou △ **A** 18 Gh 34
Adrar Mariaou △ **A** 12 Gl 34
Adrar-n-Ahnet ⏶ **A** 11 Gh 33
Adrar-n-Aklim △ **MO** 10 Gb 30
Adrar Tedjorar △ **A** 18 Gj 34
Adrar Tidderidjaouine ⏶ **A** 17 Gg 34
Adrar Tintejert △ **A** 11 Gh 33
'Afak O **I** 83 Ja 29
Af Barwaarqo O **SO** 24 Jc 42
Affollé ⏶ **MA** 16 Ga 38
Afgooye O **SO** 25 Ja 44
'Afif O **SA** 84 Hp 34
Aflou O **A** 11 Gg 28
Afmadow O **SO** 25 Hp 45
Afrin O **SY** 82 Hl 28
Aftoût ech Chergui ⬡ **MA** 16 Fn 37
Agadir O **MO** 10 Ga 30
Agargar O **MO** 16 Fn 34
Agaru O **SU** 23 Hk 40
Agdz O **MO** 10 Gb 30
Aghir O **T** 12 Gm 29
Aghouinit O **MO** 16 Fp 34
Aghreïjit O **MA** 16 Fp 35
Agiert O **MA** 16 Gb 37
Agmar O **MA** 16 Ga 33
Agouenirt O **MA** 17 Gc 37
Aguelt ez Zerga O **MA** 16 Fp 36
Aguemour ⬡ **A** 11 Gj 32
al-Âguer ⏶ **MA** 16 Ga 37
Aguilâl Fai O **MA** 16 Fn 36
Agwampt ∼ **SU** 21 Hk 36
Agwei ∼ **SU** 23 Hj 40
Agwok O **SU** 22 Hj 42
Ahad al-Masara O **SA** 86 Hp 37
Ahad Rafida O **SA** 86 Hp 36

al-Ahdar O **SA** 84 Hl 31
Ahfir O **MO** 11 Ge 28
al-Ahmadi O **K** 85 Jb 31
Ahwar O **Y** 86 Jb 39
al-'Ain O **SU** 20 Hg 37
al-'Ain O **UAE** 88 Jf 33
Ain al-'Arab O **SA** 82 Hm 27
'Ain al-Bakra O **SA** 85 Jb 34
Aïn al-Béli O **A** 11 Gj 29
Ain Benian O **A** 11 Gh 27
Âïn-Benimathar O **MO** 11 Ge 29
Aïn Ben Tili O **MA** 16 Gb 33
Aïn Bessem O **A** 11 Gh 27
Âin al-Chair O **MO** 11 Ge 29
Ain Dar O **SA** 85 Jc 33
Ain Defla O **A** 11 Gg 27
Aïn Deheb O **A** 11 Gg 28
Aïn Draham O **T** 12 Gl 27
Aïn Fakrour O **A** 12 Gk 27
Ain Fekan O **A** 11 Gf 28
Aïn al-Hadiel O **A** 11 Gh 28
Ain al-Hadjadj O **A** 11 Gh 32
Aïn al-Hadjar O **A** 11 Gg 28
Ain al-Hamara O **A** 11 Gh 28
'Ain Hamud O **I** 83 Ja 30
'Ain Ibn Fuhaid O **SA** 84 Ja 32
'Ain 'Isa O **SY** 82 Hm 27
Aïn Kercha O **A** 12 Gk 28
Aïn Kermes O **A** 11 Gg 28
Ain-Leuho O **MO** 10 Gd 29
Aïn Madhi O **A** 11 Gh 29
Aïn al-Melh O **A** 11 Gj 28
Aïn M'Lila O **A** 12 Gk 27
'Ain al-Naft O **I** 83 Hp 29
Ain al-Orak O **A** 11 Gg 29
Aïn Oulmene O **A** 11 Gj 28
Ain Oussera O **A** 11 Gh 28
Âin Saadane O **MO** 10 Gd 30
Ain Sefra O **A** 11 Gf 29
Aïn Skhouna O **A** 11 Gg 28
'Ain Sukhna O **E** 14 Hh 31
'Ain Tabagbug O **E** 14 Hf 31
Aïn Tamr O **T** 12 Gl 29
Aïn Taya O **A** 11 Gh 27
Aïn-Tédelès O **A** 11 Gg 28
Ain Temouchent O **A** 11 Gf 28
al-Aïoun O **MO** 11 Ge 28
Âit-Baba O **MO** 10 Gb 30
Aït-Benhaddou ★ **MO** 10 Gc 30
Âit-Mellou O **MO** 10 Gb 30
Âit-Youssef-ou-Ali O **MO** 10 Gd 28
al-Aja'iz O O 89 Jg 36
Ajdabiya O **LI** 13 Hb 30
Ajman O **UAE** 88 Jf 33
al-'Ajrud O **E** 15 Hk 30
Akaba Pass △ **SU** 21 Hl 36
Akabli O **A** 11 Gg 32
Akasha O **SU** 20 Hh 35
Akashat O **I** 82 Hn 29
Akbou O **A** 11 Gj 27
Akchâr ⬡ **MA** 16 Fn 36
Akhmim O **E** 15 Hh 32
Akjoujt O **MA** 16 Fn 36
Akka O **MO** 10 Gb 31
Aknoul O **MO** 10 Ge 28
Akoke O **SU** 22 Hj 41
Akop O **SU** 22 Hg 41
Akot O **SU** 22 Hh 42
Akubo O **SU** 23 Hj 42
Akubu ∼ **SU** 23 Hj 42
Akwot ∼ **SU** 22 Hh 42
Alaïli Dadda O **D** 24 Hp 39

al-'Alamayn O **E** 14 Hg 30
Alamo O **SO** 25 Hp 43
al-Angaf ⊙ **I** 83 Hp 30
'Alaqan O **SA** 84 Hk 31
Aleg O **MA** 16 Fp 37
Aleppo O **SY** 82 Hl 27
Alexandria O **E** 14 Hg 30
Algeria ◻ **A** 11 Gj 31
Algiers ◩ **A** 11 Gh 27
al-Alia O **A** 11 Gj 29
Ali Hasan O O 89 Jh 34
Ali Sabiet O **D** 24 Hp 40
Allal-bou-Fenzi O **MO** 10 Gb 30
Allal-Tazi O **MO** 10 Gc 28
Alnif O **MO** 10 Gd 30
al-Qasr O **E** 14 Hg 33
Altar-Est O **A** 12 Gl 31
Altun Kupru O **I** 83 Ja 28
Aluakluak O **SU** 22 Hh 42
Amadi O **SU** 22 Hh 43
al-'Amadiya O **I** 83 Hp 27
Amadror ⬡ **A** 12 Gk 33
al-Amain Bin Sana'a O **SA** 84 Hm 32
al-'Amar O **SA** 84 Ja 33
al-'Amara O **I** 83 Jb 30
Amellougui O **MO** 10 Gc 30
Amentego O **SU** 20 Hh 36
Amguid O **A** 11 Gj 32
al-'Amiriya O **E** 14 Hg 30
Amizmiz O **MO** 10 Gb 30
Amman ◩ **J** 82 Hk 30
Amon O **MO** 10 Ga 31
Amouguèr O **MO** 10 Gd 29
Amourj O **MA** 17 Gc 37
Amphithéâtre ★ **T** 12 Gm 28
Amran O **Y** 86 Hp 38
'Amrit O **SY** 82 Hk 28
al-'Amuda O **I** 83 Ja 30
'Ana O **I** 82 Hn 28
Anakch O **MO** 16 Fp 32
Anaza Ruwala ⏶ **SA** 84 Hl 30
al-Anbar ⊙ **I** 83 Hp 29
Anesbaraka O **A** 18 Gj 36
'Angara ∼ **SU** 22 He 40
Anjar ★ **LE** 82 Hk 29
Annaba O **A** 12 Gk 27
Annofliyah O **LI** 13 Ha 30
Annoual O **MO** 10 Ge 28
Anou-n-Bidek O **A** 18 Gj 36
Anti-Atlas ⬠ **MO** 10 Gb 31
Anti-Lebanon ⏶ **LE** 82 Hk 29
Antlat O **LI** 13 Hc 30
Antufash ⬠ **Y** 86 Hp 38
Aouînât al-Zbil O **MA** 16 Gb 37
al-Aouinet O **A** 12 Gk 28
Aoukâr ⬡ **MA** 16 Ga 36
Aoulef O **A** 11 Gg 32
Aoulouz O **MO** 10 Gb 30
Aousard O **MO** 16 Fn 34
Aqaba O **J** 82 Hk 31
al-'Aqaba al-Sagira O **E** 15 Hj 33
'Aqiq O **SU** 21 Hm 36
al-'Aqiq O **SA** 86 Hn 35
Aqra O **I** 83 Hp 27
Arab O **SU** 21 Hk 37
Arabian Desert ⬡ **E** 14 Hh 31
Arabian Gulf ≈ 85 Jc 31
Arabian Sea ≈ 89 Jj 36
'Arada O **UAE** 88 Je 34
Arak O **A** 11 Gh 33
Ar'ar O **SA** 84 Hn 30

Aratâne O **MA** 16 Gb 36
'Arbat O **I** 83 Ja 28
Arbil ⊙ **I** 83 Hp 27
Arbil O **I** 83 Ja 27
Ardit O O 88 Je 36
Ard Miri △ **SO** 24 Jb 40
al-Argoub O **MO** 16 Fm 34
al-Aricha O **A** 11 Gf 28
al-Arida O **SA** 86 Hp 37
al-'Arish O **E** 15 Hj 30
'Arja O **SA** 84 Ja 33
Armant O **E** 15 Hj 33
Aroma O **SU** 21 Hk 38
Arqu O **SU** 20 Hh 36
al-Arrouch O **A** 12 Gk 27
Arta O **D** 24 Hp 40
al-Artawi O **SA** 85 Ja 33
Artemou O **MA** 16 Fp 38
Arzana ⬠ **UAE** 88 Je 33
Arzew O **A** 11 Gf 28
Asedirad ⏶ **A** 11 Gg 33
'As 'Êla O **D** 24 Hp 40
al-Ashhara O O 89 Jh 35
Ashkida O **LI** 12 Gp 32
al-'Ashuriya O **I** 83 Hp 30
Asilah O **MO** 10 Gc 28
Asla O **A** 11 Gf 29
Ásni O **MO** 10 Gc 30
Assa O **MO** 10 Gb 31
al-Assaba ⏶ **MA** 16 Fp 37
Assadjene △ **A** 18 Gk 34
al-'Assafiya O **SA** 84 Hm 31
Assa Gaïla O **D** 24 Hp 39
Assaka O **MO** 10 Gb 31
al-Sa'laniya O **SA** 84 Hp 32
Aswan O **E** 15 Hj 33
Asyut O **E** 14 Hh 32
Atakor ⏶ **A** 18 Gj 34
Atâr O **MA** 16 Fp 35
al-Atawala O **SA** 86 Hn 35
Atbara O **SU** 21 Hj 37
'Atbara ∼ **SU** 21 Hk 37
Ateppi ∼ **SU** 22 Hj 44
Atonyia O **MO** 10 Gb 32
al-Atshan O **SU** 21 Hk 39
al-Atwa O **SA** 84 Hp 31
Auliya Dam ∼ **SU** 20 Hj 38
Awabi O O 89 Jg 34
'Awali O **B** 85 Jd 32
Awbari O **LI** 12 Gn 32
Awbari Sand Sea ⬡ **LI** 12 Gm 31
Aw Dheegle O **SO** 25 Ja 45
Awdiinle O **SO** 25 Hp 44
Aweil O **SU** 22 Hf 41
Awjila O **LI** 13 Hc 31
al-'Ayn O O 89 Jg 34
Ayn al-Ghazala O **LI** 19 Hd 29
Ayod O **SU** 22 Hj 41
Ayoni O **SU** 22 Hf 41
'Ayoûn al-'Atroûs O **MA** 16 Gb 37
Azaz △ **A** 11 Gh 32
A'zaz O **SY** 82 Hl 27
Azazga O **A** 11 Gj 27
Azeffâl ⬡ **MA** 16 Fn 36
Azemmour O **MO** 10 Gb 29
Azilal O **MO** 10 Gc 30
Azirir ∼ **A** 11 Gh 32
al-'Aziziya O **I** 83 Ja 29
al-'Aziziyah O **LI** 12 Gn 29
Azrou O **MO** 10 Gc 29
Azzaba O **A** 12 Gk 27

B

al-Ba'a'it ○ SA 84 Hn 32
Baajun Islands ♁ SO 25 Hp 46
Baalbek ★ LE 82 Hl 28
Baalbek ○ LE 82 Hl 29
Baardheere ○ SO 25 Hp 44
al-Bab ○ SY 82 Hl 27
Bababé ○ MA 16 Fp 37
Baba Gurgur ○ I 83 Ja 28
Babanusa ○ SU 20 Hf 40
Bab-Besen △ MO 10 Gd 28
Babil ⊙ I 83 Ja 29
Bab al-Mandab ～ 24 Hp 39
Bab-Taza ○ MO 10 Gd 28
Babylon ★ I 83 Ja 29
Bacaadweyn ○ SO 24 Jb 42
Bactili ○ SO 25 Hn 45
al-Bad' ○ SA 84 Hk 31
Bada ○ SA 84 Hl 32
al-Bada'i' ○ SA 84 Hp 33
al-Badari ○ E 15 Hh 32
Badena ～ SO 25 Hn 46
al-Badi ○ I 82 Hn 28
al-Badi' ○ SA 85 Jb 35
al-Badi'a ○ SA 86 Hp 37
Badra ○ I 83 Ja 29
Badr wa-Hunain ○ SA 84 Hm 34
Baédiam ○ MA 16 Fp 38
Bagaia ○ SU 20 Hh 40
Bagdad ⊙ I 83 Ja 29
Baghdad ▣ I 83 Ja 29
Bagoosaar ○ SO 25 Ja 43
al-Baha ○ SA 86 Hn 35
Bahariya Oasis ▱ E 14 Hg 31
Bahla ○ O 89 Jg 34
al-Bahra ○ K 85 Jb 31
Bahra ○ SA 86 Hm 35
Bahrain ◘ B 85 Jd 33
Bahr al-'Arab ～ SU 22 He 40
Bahr al-Ghazal ～ SU 22 Hg 41
Bahr al-Jabel White Nile ～ SU 22 Hh 41
Bahr Yusuf ～ E 14 Hh 31
Bahr al-Zaraf ～ SU 22 Hh 41
al-Baida' ○ Y 86 Ja 39
Baida' Natil ○ SA 84 Hn 32
Baihan al-Qasab ○ Y 86 Ja 38
Ba'iji ○ I 83 Hp 28
Ba'ir ○ J 82 Hl 30
Baish ○ SA 86 Hp 37
Bait al-Faqih ○ Y 86 Hp 38
Bajil ○ Y 86 Hp 38
Bakhma ○ I 83 Hp 27
Balad al-Mala ○ I 83 Ja 28
Balad Ruz ○ I 83 Ja 29
Bal Asmar ○ SA 86 Hp 36
Balat ○ E 14 Hg 33
Balcad ○ SO 25 Ja 44
Balho ○ D 24 Hp 39
Baljurashi ○ SA 86 Hn 36
Balloul ○ A 11 Gg 28
Balos ○ SU 21 Hk 39
Baltim ○ E 14 Hh 30
al-Balyana ○ E 15 Hh 32
Bandarbeyla ○ SO 24 Jd 41
Bandar Murcaayo ○ SO 24 Jc 40
Bandar Wanaag ○ SO 24 Ja 41
Banha ○ E 14 Hh 30
Bani 'Atiyah ▱ SA 84 Hl 31
Bani 'Amir ○ SA 86 Hp 36
Bani Mazar ○ E 14 Hh 31
Baninah ○ LI 13 Hc 29
Bani Walid ○ LI 12 Gn 30
Baniyas ○ SY 82 Hk 28
Bannaanka Saraar ▱ SO 24 Ja 41
Banta ○ SO 25 Hp 45
Baq'a' ○ SA 84 Hp 32
Ba'quba ○ I 83 Ja 29
Bara ○ SU 20 Hh 39
Baraawe ○ SO 25 Ja 45
Baraka ○ SU 22 Hf 40
Barakat ○ SU 21 Hj 38
Barbar ○ SU 21 Hk 36
Bardaale ○ SO 24 Jb 42
Bardaras ○ I 83 Hp 27
al-Bardi ○ LI 13 He 30
Bargaal ○ SO 24 Jd 40
Barika ○ A 11 Gj 28
Baris ○ E 14 Hh 33
Bari Si Mohamed ～ MO 10 Gc 29
Bariya ○ I 82 Hp 28
Barka' ○ O 89 Jg 34
Barkéwol al-Abiod ○ MA 16 Fp 37
Barqah al-Bayda ▱ LI 13 Hb 30
Barqin ○ LI 12 Gn 32
Barrage Djorf-Torba ～ A 11 Ge 30
Barrage Idriss ～ MO 10 Gd 28
Barrage al-Mansour Eddahbi ～ MO 10 Gc 30
Barrage al-Massira ～ MO 10 Gc 29
Barrage Mohamed 5 ～ MO 11 Ge 28
Barrage Youssef Ben Tachfine ～ MO 10 Gb 31
Barramiya ○ E 15 Hj 33
Barriyat al-Bayyuda ▱ SU 20/21 Hj 37
al-Barun ○ SU 21 Hj 40
al-Basiri ○ SY 82 Hl 28
al-Basra ⊙ I 83 Jb 30
Basra ○ I 83 Jb 30
Bassikounou ○ MA 17 Gd 38
Basunda ○ SU 21 Hk 39
Bat ○ O 89 Jg 34
al-Batina ♁ SA 85 Jc 32
Batina ▱ O 89 Jg 33
Batina ▱ O 89 Jg 34
Batna ○ A 11 Gk 28
Batn al-Jul ○ J 82 Hk 31
al-Bauga ○ SU 21 Hj 36
al-Bawiti ○ E 14 Hg 31
al-Bayadh ○ A 11 Gg 29
al-Bayda ○ LI 13 Hc 29
Baydhabo ○ SO 25 Hp 44
Baynuna ▱ UAE 88 Je 34
Bèchar ○ A 11 Ge 30
al-Begeir ○ SU 21 Hj 36
Beirut ▣ LE 82 Hk 29
Beja ○ T 12 Gl 27
Bejaja ○ A 11 Gj 27
Beledweyne ○ SO 25 Ja 43
Belesc Cogani ○ SO 25 Hn 45
Belgo ○ SU 22 Hj 40
Belhirane ○ A 11 Gk 30
Benahmed ○ MO 10 Gc 29
Ben Badis ○ A 11 Gf 28
Benghazi ○ LI 13 Hb 29
Ben Guerdane ○ T 12 Gm 29
Benguerir ○ MO 10 Gc 29
Beni-Abbès ○ A 11 Ge 30
Beni Boufran ○ MO 10 Gd 28
Beni Hammad ★ A 11 Gj 28
Beni Haoua ○ A 11 Gg 27
Beni Hassan ○ T 12 Gm 28
Beni Ikhlef ○ A 11 Gf 31
Beni Kheddache ○ T 12 Gm 29
Beni-Mellal ○ MO 10 Gc 29
Beni Ounif ○ A 11 Gf 29
Beni Saf ○ A 11 Gf 28
Beni Slimane ○ A 11 Gh 27
Beni Smir △ MO 11 Gf 29
Beni Suef ○ E 14 Hh 31
Beni Tajjite ○ MO 10 Ge 29
Beni-Val ○ MO 10 Ge 29
Ben Mehidi ○ A 12 Gk 27
Bennichchâb ○ MA 16 Fn 36
Benoud ○ A 11 Gg 29
Ben-Slimane ○ MO 10 Gc 29
Ben S'Rour ○ A 11 Gj 28
Bentiu ○ SU 22 Hg 41
Ben Zireg ○ A 11 Gf 30
Berbera ○ SO 24 Ja 40
Bereeda ○ SO 24 Jd 40
Berenice ○ E 15 Hk 34
Berkane ○ MO 11 Ge 28
Berrahal ○ A 12 Gk 27
Berrechid ○ MO 10 Gc 29
Berriane ○ A 11 Gh 29
al-Beru Hagai ○ SO 25 Hn 44
Bet She'an ○ J 82 Hk 29
Bettioua ○ A 11 Gf 28
Beyra ○ SO 24 Jb 42
al-Beyyed ○ MA 16 Ga 35
al-Bi'ar ○ SA 84 Hm 34
Biba ○ E 14 Hh 31
Bidbid ○ O 89 Jh 34
Bigori ○ SU 21 Hk 40
al-Bijadiya ○ SA 84 Hp 33
Bikubiti △ LI 19 Hd 34
Bilbais ○ E 15 Hh 30
Biloo ○ SO 25 Hp 45
Bilqas ○ E 15 Hh 30
Bin Ghashir ○ LI 12 Gn 29
Bin Jawwad ○ LI 13 Hb 30
Bin-al-Ouidane ○ MO 10 Gc 29
Bint Jubail ○ LE 82 Hk 29
Bio Addo ○ SO 25 Ja 44
Biougra ○ MO 10 Gb 30
Bi'r Abraq ○ E 15 Hk 34
Bi'r Abu Garadiq ○ E 14 Hg 30
Bi'r Abu Hashim ○ E 15 Hk 34
Bi'r Abu al-Husain ○ E 14 Hg 34
Bi'r Abu Minqar ○ E 14 Hf 32
Bi'r Abu Zaïma ○ SU 20 Hg 38
Birak ○ LI 12 Gp 32
Bi'r al-'Alaqah ○ LI 12 Gp 31
Bir Ali Ben Khelifa ○ T 12 Gm 28
Bi'r Allaq ○ LI 12 Gm 30
Bir al-Amdar ○ A 11 Gk 29
Bir' Amrâne ○ MA 16 Gb 34
Bir-Anzarane ○ MO 16 Fn 34
Bir al-Ater ○ A 12 Gk 28
Bi'r al-'Atrun ○ SU 20 Hf 36
Bi'r A'yad ○ LI 12 Gn 29
Bi'r Baili ○ E 14 He 30
Bîr Bel Guerdâne ○ MA 16 Ga 33
Bi'r Bin 'Isa ○ LI 12 Gp 30
Bi'r Dhu'fan ○ LI 12 Gp 29
Bir Djedid ○ A 12 Gk 29
Bi'r Durb ○ SA 84 Hn 33
Bi'r al-Fakama ○ SU 21 Hj 37
Bi'r Fatima ○ I 82 Hp 28
Bi'r al-Fatiyah ○ LI 12 Gn 31
Bi'r Fuad ○ E 14 Hf 30
Bir' Furawiya ○ SU 20 Hd 38
Bir-Gandouz ○ MO 16 Fm 35
Bir al-Gâreb ○ MA 16 Fm 35
Bi'r al-Ghanam ○ LI 12 Gn 29
Bi'r al-Gidami ○ E 15 Hj 32
Bi'r al-Guzayyil ○ LI 12 Gm 31
Bi'r al-Hasa ○ E 15 Hk 34
Bi'r Hasana ○ E 15 Hj 30
Bi'r Hasmat 'Umar ○ SU 21 Hk 35
Bi'r Hatab ○ SU 20 Hj 35
Biri ○ SU 22 Hf 42
Biri ～ SU 22 Hf 42
Bi'r Ibn Hirmas ○ SA 84 Hl 31
Bi'r Jifghafa ○ E 15 Hj 30
Bi'r Jubni ○ LI 13 He 30
Bi'r Juraibi'at ○ I 83 Ja 31
al-Birk ○ SA 86 Hn 36
Bi'r al-Kammuniya ○ LI 12 Gp 31
Birkat al-'Amya' ○ SA 84 Hp 31
Birkat Qarun ～ E 14 Hh 31
Birkat Saira ○ SU 20 Hd 39
Bi'r Khalaf Allah ○ LI 12 Gn 32
Bi'r Khalida ○ E 14 Hf 30
Bi'r Kiau ○ SU 21 Hk 35
Bi'r al-Mastutah ○ LI 12 Gn 33
Bi'r Misaha ○ E 14 Hf 34
Bîr Mogrein ○ MA 16 Ga 33
Bi'r Müdakim ○ LI 12 Gn 29
Bi'r Nahid ○ E 14 Hg 30
Bi'r Nauarai ○ SU 21 Hk 35
Bi'r Nazsira ○ LI 12 Gm 30
Bi'r al-Nugaym ○ SU 21 Hk 36
Bir Qar'at ad Dibah ○ LI 12 Gl 31
Bi'r Qaryas ○ LI 13 Ha 31
Bi'r al-Qat ○ LI 12 Gp 31
Bi'r al-Qatif ○ LI 13 He 30
Birrim ♁ SA 84 Hl 33
Bir Senia ○ A 11 Gf 29
Bi'r Shalatain ○ E 15 Hk 34
Bir Soltane ○ T 12 Gl 29
Birtam-Tam ○ MO 10 Gd 29
Bi'r Tarfawi ○ E 14 Hg 34
Bi'r Taziet ○ LI 12 Gn 33
Bi'r Tin Abundą ○ LI 12 Gn 32
Bir Touila ○ T 12 Gl 29
Bi'r Umm Hibal ○ E 15 Hj 34
Bi'r al-'Utaylah ○ LI 12 Ha 30
Bi'r Zaltan ○ LI 13 Hb 31
Bir Zar ○ T 12 Gl 30
Bisellia ○ SU 22 Hf 42
Bisha ○ SA 86 Hp 35
Biskra ○ A 11 Gj 28
al-Biyad ▱ SA 85 Jb 35
Bizerte ○ T 12 Gl 27
Bled Tisseras ～ A 12 Gk 32
Blida ○ A 11 Gh 27
Blue Nile ～ SU 20 Hj 39
Bobuk ○ SU 21 Hk 40
Bogué ○ MA 16 Fn 37
Boli ○ SU 22 Hg 42
Boorama ○ SO 24 Hp 41
Boosaaso ○ SO 24 Jc 40
Bor ○ SU 22 Hh 42
al-Bordj ○ A 11 Gg 28
Bordj Bou Arreridj ○ A 11 Gj 27
Bordj Bounaama ○ A 11 Gg 28
Bordj Bourguiba ○ T 12 Gl 29
Bordj Jenein ○ T 12 Gl 30
Bordj Machened Salah ○ T 12 Gm 29
Bordj Messouda ○ A 12 Gl 30
Bordj Mokhtar ○ A 17 Gg 35
Bordj Omar Driss ○ A 12 Gk 31
Borne ○ A 12 Gk 33
al-Borouj ○ MO 10 Gc 29
Bou Akba ○ A 10 Gc 31
Boualem ○ A 11 Gg 29
Bou Ali ○ A 11 Gf 32
Bouânane ○ MO 11 Ge 29
Bouârfa ○ MO 11 Gf 29
Bouchouaymiy ○ MO 16 Fm 34
Boû Ctaila ○ MA 16 Gb 38
Boû Dib ○ MA 16 Gb 36
Boudnib ○ MO 10 Ge 30
Bougaa ○ A 11 Gj 27
Boû Gâdoûm ○ MA 17 Gc 38
Bougtob ○ A 11 Gf 28
Bouira ○ A 11 Gh 27
Bou-Ismaïl ○ A 11 Gh 27
Bou-Izakarn ○ MO 10 Gb 31
Boujad ○ MO 10 Gc 29
Boujdour ○ MO 16 Fn 32
Bou Kadir ○ A 11 Gg 28
Bou Keltoum △ MO 11 Ge 28
Boukra ○ MO 16 Fp 32
Bouli ○ MA 16 Ga 38
Boumalne-du-Dadès ○ MO 10 Gd 30
Boûmdeïd ○ MA 16 Ga 37
Boumerdes ○ A 11 Gh 27
Bou Mertala ○ MA 16 Gb 35
Bou Mréga ○ MA 16 Ga 37
Boû Nâga ○ MA 16 Fp 36
Boû Rjeimât ○ MA 16 Fn 36
Bou-Saada ○ A 11 Gj 28
Bou Sfer ○ A 11 Gf 28
Boussemghoun △ A 11 Gf 29
Boutilimit ○ MA 16 Fn 37
Bouzghaia ○ A 11 Gg 27
Brezina ○ A 11 Gg 29
Bshirri ○ LE 82 Hk 28
Bu Athla ○ LI 13 Hc 31
Bu'ayrat al-Hsun ○ LI 12 Gp 30
Bublyan ♁ K 85 Jc 31
Bud Bud ○ SO 25 Jb 43
Buggayq ○ SA 85 Jc 33
Buhairat al-Burullus ～ E 14 Hh 30
Buhairat al-Manzila ～ E 14 Hh 30
Buhairat Nuba ～ SU 20 Hh 35
Buhairat Shari ～ I 83 Ja 28
Buhairat al-Timsah al-Murra ～ E 15 Hj 30
al-Bukairiya Riyad ○ SA 84 Hp 32
Bu Kammash ○ LI 12 Gm 29
Bulaq ○ E 14 Hh 33
Bu Lifiyat ○ UAE 88 Je 33
Bullaxaar ○ SO 24 Ja 40
Bumba ○ LI 19 Hd 29
Bunduqiya ○ SU 22 Hh 43
Buqda Caqable ○ SO 25 Ja 43
Buraan ○ SO 24 Jc 40
al-Buraika ○ SA 86 Hm 35
Buraika △ Y 87 Jc 38
al-Buraimi ○ O 88 Jf 33
Buram ○ SU 22 He 40
Buraq ○ SY 82 Hl 29
Burayda ○ SA 84 Hp 32
Burco ○ SO 24 Ja 41
Burg al-'Arab ○ E 14 Hg 30
Burj ○ O 88 Je 37
Bur Tinle ○ SO 24 Jb 42
Burum ○ Y 87 Jc 38
Busaira ○ SY 82 Hn 28
al-Busaita' ▱ SA 84 Hm 30
Busra al-Sham ○ SY 82 Hl 29
Busseri ～ SU 22 Hf 42
Butat Raya ～ SU 22 He 40
Buulo Burte ○ SO 25 Ja 44
Buulo Xaawo ○ SO 25 Hn 44
Buurdhuubo ○ SO 25 Hn 44
Buur Gaabo ○ SO 25 Hk 45
Buur Hakkaba ○ SO 25 Ja 44
Buur Heybe △ SO 25 Ja 44
Byblos ★ LE 82 Hk 28

C

Cadaado ○ SO 24 Jb 42
Cadadley ○ SO 24 Ja 41
Cadale ○ SO 25 Jb 44
Cairo ▣ E 15 Hh 31
Calansclo Sand Sea ▱ LI 13 Hc 32
Calie Corar △ SO 25 Ja 44
Cal Madow ⛰ SO 24 Jc 40
Cal Miskaat ⛰ SO 24 Jc 40
Caluula ○ SO 24 Jd 40
Cangrâfa ○ MA 16 Fp 37
Cap Beddouza ⌓ MO 10 Gb 29
Cap Bougaroun ⌓ A 12 Gk 27
Cap des Trois Fourches ⌓ MO 11 Ge 28
Cape Bon ⌓ T 12 Gm 27
Cape Guardafui ⌓ SO 24 Jd 40
Cap Garbon ⌓ A 11 Gf 28
Cap Juby ♁ MO 10 Fp 32
Cap Rhir ⌓ MO 10 Ga 30
Cap Serrat ⌓ T 12 Gl 27
Cap Sim ⌓ MO 10 Ga 30
Cap Spartel ⌓ MO 10 Gc 28
Cap Takouch ⌓ A 12 Gk 27
Carthage ★ T 12 Gm 27
Casablanca ○ MO 10 Gc 29
Catama ○ SO 25 Hn 44
Caynabo ○ SO 24 Jb 41
Ceel Afweyn ○ SO 24 Jb 41
Ceelayo ○ SO 24 Jc 40
Ceel Buur ○ SO 25 Jb 43
Ceel Dheer ○ SO 25 Jb 44
Ceel Dheere ○ SO 25 Ja 43
Ceel Duubo ○ SO 25 Ja 44
Ceel Gaal ○ SO 24 Jd 40
Ceel Huur ○ SO 25 Jc 43
Ceel Maxamed Cali ○ SO 25 Jb 44
Ceerigaabo ○ SO 24 Jb 40
Chaanba ▱ A 11 Gh 31
Chabet al-Akra ★ A 11 Gj 27
Chahbounia ○ A 11 Gh 28
Chaîne des Bibans ⛰ A 11 Gj 27
Châr ○ MA 16 Fp 35
Charouïne ○ A 11 Gf 31
Chebba ○ T 12 Gm 28
Chefchaouen ○ MO 10 Gd 28
Chegga ○ A 11 Gj 28
Chegga ○ MA 17 Gd 33
Cheïrik ○ MA 16 Fp 35
Chelghoum al-Aïd ○ A 11 Gj 27
Chellal ○ A 11 Gj 28
Chemaia ○ MO 10 Gb 29
Chenachane ○ A 10 Gd 32
Chenacharte ～ A 10 Gd 33
Chenini ○ T 12 Gm 29
Cherchell ○ A 11 Gh 27
Cheria ○ A 12 Gk 28
Chetaibi ○ A 12 Gk 27
Chiamboni ○ SO 25 Hn 46
Chichaoua ○ MO 10 Gb 30
Chidu ○ SU 23 Hj 41
Chinguetti ○ MA 16 Fp 35
al-Chlef ○ A 11 Gg 27
Choûm ○ MA 16 Fp 35
Cilat ○ I 83 Jb 29
Cir Kud ○ SO 25 Hp 44
Col du Zad △ MO 10 Gd 29
Collo ○ A 12 Gk 27
Comoros ◘ C 25 Hp 51
Comoros Archipelago ♁ C 25 Hp 51
Constantine ○ A 12 Gk 27
Corniche des Dahra ▱ A 11 Gg 27
Cumar ○ SO 25 Ja 44
Cyrenaica ▱ LI 13 Hc 30
Cyrene ★ LI 13 Hc 29

D

al-Dab'a ○ E 14 Hg 30
al-Dabba ○ SU 20 Hh 36
Daga ～ SU 23 Hj 41
Dagaari ○ SO 24 Jb 42
Daga Post ○ SU 23 Hj 41
Dagash ○ SU 21 Hj 36
Dagmar ○ O 89 Jh 34
Dahab ○ E 15 Hk 31
Dahaban ○ SU 86 Hm 35
al-Dahawa ○ LI 13 Hc 33
al-Dahna' ▱ SA 84/85 Ja 32
Dahra ▱ LI 13 Ha 31
Dahr Qualâta ▱ MA 17 Gc 36
Dahr Tîchît ▱ MA 16 Gb 36
Dahshur ○ E 15 Hh 31
Dahuk ○ I 83 Hp 27
Dahuk ⊙ I 83 Hp 27
al-Daid ○ UAE 88 Jf 33
Daïet Akhicha ～ A 11 Gg 31
al-Dair ○ E 15 Hj 33
Dair Mawas ○ E 14 Hh 32
al-Dakhla ○ MO 16 Fm 34
Dakhla Oasis ▱ E 14 Hg 33
Dalami ○ SU 22 Hh 40
al-Dali' ○ Y 86 Ja 39
Dalja ○ E 14 Hh 32
Damad ○ SA 86 Hp 37
Damanhur ○ E 14 Hh 30
Damar ○ Y 86 Ja 38
Damascus ▣ SY 82 Hl 29

Damazine ○ **SU** 21 Hk 40
al-Damer ○ **SU** 21 Hj 37
Dam Gamad ○ **SU** 20 Hf 39
Damietta ○ **E** 15 Hh 30
al-Damman ○ **SA** 88 Jd 32
Damrur ○ **SA** 86 Hm 35
Damt ○ **Y** 86 Ja 38
Dandara ★ **E** 15 Hj 32
Dank ○ **O** 88 Jg 34
Daoud ○ **A** 11 Gf 28
Dara ∼ **SO** 25 Hp 45
Dar'a ○ **SY** 82 Hl 29
Darafisa ○ **SU** 20 Hj 39
Daraw ○ **E** 15 Hj 33
al-Darb ○ **SA** 86 Hp 37
Darband-e Khan ○ **I** 83 Ja 28
Dar al-Barka ○ **MA** 16 Fn 37
Dar Chioukh ○ **A** 11 Gh 28
Darfur ⌓ **SU** 20 Hd 39
al-Dar al-Hamra' ○ **SA** 86 Hn 35
Darin ○ **SA** 88 Jd 32
Darj ○ **LI** 12 Gm 30
Dar Mujahhar ○ **Y** 86 Ja 39
Darna ○ **LI** 19 Hd 29
Darsa ♣ **Y** 87 Je 39
Das ♣ **UAE** 88 Je 33
Dauka ○ **O** 88 Je 36
Daus ○ **SA** 86 Hn 35
al-Dawadimi ○ **SA** 84 Hp 33
Dawir ○ **SU** 22 Hj 41
Dayrut ○ **E** 14 Hh 32
Dayr al-Zawr ○ **SY** 82 Hm 28
Dchira ○ **MO** 16 Fp 32
Dead Sea ∼ **J** 82 Hk 30
Debalo ○ **SU** 22 Hh 41
Debdou ○ **MO** 11 Ge 29
Degache ○ **T** 12 Gl 28
Dehiba ○ **T** 12 Gm 29
Deim Bukhit ○ **SU** 22 Hf 42
Deira ○ **UAE** 88 Jf 33
Dekhlet Nouâdhibou ∼ **MA** 16 Fm 35
Delgo ○ **SU** 20 Hh 35
Dellys ○ **A** 11 Gh 27
Demnate ○ **MO** 10 Gc 30
Dendāra ○ **MA** 17 Gc 37
Dera ∼ **SO** 25 Hn 45
Derri ○ **SO** 25 Jb 43
Derudeb ○ **SU** 21 Hl 37
Dham-al-Khayl ○ **MO** 16 Fp 33
Dhaya ○ **A** 11 Gf 28
Dhiinsoor ○ **SO** 25 Hp 44
Dhofar ⌓ **O** 88 Je 37
Dhooble ○ **SO** 25 Hn 45
Dhurbo ○ **SO** 24 Jd 40
Dhuudo ○ **SO** 24 Jd 41
Dhuusa Mareeb ○ **SO** 25 Jb 43
Diat al-Tulul ⌓ **SY** 82 Hl 29
Diba ○ **UAE** 88 Jg 33
Dibage ○ **I** 83 Hp 28
Diban ○ **J** 82 Hk 30
al-Dibdiba ⛰ **SA** 85 Jb 31
Di Bin ○ **Y** 86 Ja 38
al-Dibin ○ **Y** 87 Jd 37
Dibis ○ **E** 14 Hg 34
Dibs ○ **SU** 20 He 39
al-Diffa ⌓ **LI** 13 He 30
Dijha ∼ **I** 83 Jb 30
Dijla ∼ **I** 83 Jb 29
al-Dikaka ⌓ **SA** 88 Jd 36
Dikhil ○ **D** 24 Hp 40
Dikirnis ○ **E** 15 Hh 30
al-Dilam ○ **SA** 85 Jb 34
Dilling ○ **SU** 20 Hg 39
Dindar ♀ **SU** 21 Hk 39
Dinder ∼ **SU** 21 Hj 39
Di Qar ⊙ **I** 83 Jb 30
Diqdaqa ○ **UAE** 88 Jf 33
Dir Di ○ **SU** 22 Hg 42
al-Dir'iya ○ **SA** 84 Hp 33
al-Dir'iya ○ **SA** 85 Jb 33
Dirrah ○ **SU** 20 Hf 39
Dishna ○ **E** 15 Hj 32
Dissain ♣ **SA** 86 Hn 37
Disuq ○ **E** 14 Hh 30
al-Diwaniya ○ **I** 83 Ja 30
Diyala ⊙ **I** 83 Ja 29
Djamàa ○ **A** 11 Gk 29
Djanet ○ **A** 12 Gl 33
Djebel Adrar Soula △ **A** 12 Gk 33
Djebel Aïssa △ **A** 11 Gf 29
Djebel Amour ⛰ **A** 11 Gg 29
Djebel Antar △ **A** 11 Gf 29
Djebel Atafaitafa △ **A** 12 Gk 33
Djebel Babor △ **A** 11 Gj 27
Djebel Ben Amar ○ **A** 11 Gg 28
Djebel Ben Tadjine ⛰ **A** 10 Gd 31
Djebel Bou Kahil ⛰ **A** 11 Gh 28
Djebel Fernane △ **A** 11 Gj 28
Djebel Goûfi △ **A** 12 Gk 27
Djebel in Azzene ⛰ **A** 11 Gg 32
Djebel Ksel △ **A** 11 Gg 29
Djebel Ounane △ **A** 12 Gk 33
Djebel Oust △ **MO** 11 Gf 29
Djebel Serkout △ **A** 18 Gk 34
Djebel Settaf △ **A** 11 Gh 32
Djebel Tebaga ⛰ **T** 12 Gl 29
Djebel Telerhteba △ **A** 12 Gk 33
Djebel Tenouchfi △ **A** 11 Gf 28
Djebel Touaris △ **A** 11 Ge 31
Djebel Toucha △ **A** 11 Gf 30
al-Djelfa ○ **A** 11 Gh 28
Djemila ○ **A** 11 Gj 27
Djeniene Bou Rzeg ○ **A** 11 Gf 29
Djibouti ◘ **D** 24 Hp 40
Djibouti ▣ **D** 24 Hp 40
Djiguéni ○ **MA** 16 Gb 38
Djonâba ○ **MA** 16 Fp 37
Djorf Torba ○ **A** 11 Ge 30
al-Djouf ⌓ **MA** 16 Gb 36
Dogoba ○ **SU** 22 Hh 42
Doha ▣ **Q** 85 Jd 33
Doka ○ **SU** 21 Hk 39
Doleib Hill ○ **SU** 22 Hh 41
Domoni ○ **C** 25 Ja 52
Dongola Donqula ○ **SU** 20 Hh 36
Dongotona Mountains ⛰ **SU** 23 Hj 43
Donqula Dongola ○ **SU** 20 Hh 36
Dorale ○ **D** 24 Hp 40
Dorra ○ **D** 24 Hp 39
Dougga ★ **T** 12 Gl 27
Douz ○ **T** 12 Gl 29
Dra Afratir ⌓ **MO** 16 Fp 33
Drar Souttouf ⌓ **MO** 16 Fn 35
Drean ○ **A** 12 Gk 27
al-Du'ayn ○ **SU** 20 Hf 40
Duba ○ **SA** 84 Hk 32
Dubai ○ **UAE** 88 Jf 33
al-Dubai'a ○ **SA** 85 Jb 33
al-Dubai'a ○ **UAE** 88 Je 33
Dubeibat ○ **SU** 20 Hg 39
Dudduumo ○ **SO** 25 Hp 45
Dugaimiya ○ **SA** 85 Jc 33
Dugdug ○ **SU** 22 Hg 41
Dugwaya ○ **SU** 21 Hk 37
al-Dujail ○ **I** 83 Hp 29
Du Jibla ○ **Y** 86 Hp 39
Dukan ○ **I** 83 Ja 28
Dukan Buhairat ∼ **I** 83 Ja 27
Duk Fadiat ○ **SU** 22 Hh 42
Duk Falwil ○ **SU** 22 Hh 42
Dukhan ○ **Q** 85 Jd 33
Dukhna ○ **SA** 84 Hp 33
Dulaihan ○ **SA** 84 Hn 32
al-Dulaimiya ○ **SA** 84 Hp 33
Dulai' Rasid ○ **SA** 84 Hp 33
Duma ○ **SY** 82 Hl 29
Dumat al-Jandal ○ **SA** 84 Hm 31
Dunes de Dokhara ⌓ **A** 11 Gj 29
Dungunab ○ **SU** 21 Hl 35
Dungunab ♣ **SU** 21 Hl 35
Dunqul ○ **E** 15 Hh 34
Duqaila ♣ **Y** 86 Hp 37
Duqm ○ **O** 89 Jg 36
Durdur ∼ **SO** 24 Hp 40
Durma ○ **SA** 85 Jb 33
Durukhsi ○ **SO** 24 Ja 41
Dush ○ **E** 14 Hh 33
Du Sheikh ○ **I** 83 Ja 29
al-Duwaym ○ **SU** 20 Hh 39
Duwwa ○ **O** 89 Jh 35
Dzioua ○ **A** 11 Gj 29

E

Edjeleh ○ **A** 12 Gl 32
Egypt ◘ **E** 14 Hf 32
Eidukal ∼ **SU** 21 Hk 36
Eilai ○ **SU** 20 Hh 37
Ein Mansur ○ **SU** 20 Hf 38
Ekamour ○ **MA** 16 Ga 37
Elephantine Island ★ **E** 15 Hj 33
Elma Laboid ○ **A** 12 Gk 28
Enfida ○ **T** 12 Gm 27
Enjil ○ **MO** 10 Gd 29
En Tmadé ○ **MA** 16 Ga 36
Erfoud ○ **MO** 10 Gd 30
Erg al-Atchane ⌓ **A** 11 Gf 31
Erg Bourarhet ⌓ **A** 12 Gl 32
Erg Chech ⌓ **DZ/RIM** 10/11 Gc 34
Erg d'Admer ⌓ **A** 12 Gl 33
Erg Iguidi ⌓ **MA** 17 Gc 33
Erg Issaouane ⌓ **A** 12 Gk 32
Erg n' Ataram ⌓ **A** 17 Gg 34
Erg al-Raoui ⌓ **A** 10/11 Ge 31
Erg Tifernine ⌓ **A** 12 Gk 32
Eriba ○ **SU** 21 Hl 37
Erkowit ○ **SU** 21 Hl 36
Ermil Post ○ **SU** 20 Hf 39
Essaouira ○ **MO** 10 Ga 30
al-Eulma ○ **A** 11 Gj 27
Euphrates ∼ **I** 82 Hn 28
Eyl ○ **SO** 24 Jc 42
Ezo ○ **SU** 22 Hf 43

F

Faddoi ○ **SU** 22 Hj 41
Fafadun ○ **SO** 25 Hn 44
Faghmah ⊙ **Y** 87 Jc 37
Fagrinkotti ○ **SU** 20 Hh 36
Fagwir ○ **SU** 22 Hh 41
al-Fahs ○ **T** 12 Gl 27
Fa'id ○ **E** 15 Hj 30
al-Faidami ○ **Y** 87 Je 37
al-Faid Majir ○ **LI** 12 Gp 29
Fairan ○ **E** 15 Hj 31
al-Faisaliya ○ **SA** 86 Hn 35
Faiyiba ○ **SU** 20 Hh 38
al-Falluga ○ **I** 83 Hp 29
Fangak ○ **SU** 22 Hh 41
al-Faouar ○ **T** 12 Gl 29
al-Faq' ○ **UAE** 88 Jf 33
Faqus ○ **E** 15 Hh 30
Farafra Oasis ⌓ **E** 14 Hg 32
Far'aoun ○ **MA** 16 Fp 36
Farasan ♣ **SA** 86 Hn 37
Farasan Islands ♣ **SA** 86 Hn 37
al-Farcya ○ **MO** 10 Ga 32
al-Farda ○ **Y** 87 Jc 38
Fargha ∼ **SU** 21 Hk 39
al-Farsha ○ **SA** 86 Hp 37
Fasad ○ **O** 88 Je 36
al-Fasher ○ **SU** 20 He 39
al-Fashn ○ **E** 14 Hh 31
Fask ○ **MO** 10 Gb 31
Fassala Néré ○ **MA** 17 Gd 38
Fassanu ○ **LI** 12 Gn 30
al-Fath ○ **O** 88 Jg 34
Fatitet ○ **SU** 23 Hj 42
Fattasha ○ **SU** 20 Hh 38
al-Faw ○ **I** 83 Jc 31
al-Fawwara ○ **SA** 84 Hp 32
Faylaka ⌂ **K** 85 Jc 31
al-Fayyum ○ **E** 14 Hh 31
Fdérik ○ **MA** 16 Fp 34
Feidh Botma ○ **A** 11 Gh 28
Felaou ○ **A** 18 Gj 36
Ferdjioua ○ **A** 11 Gj 27
Feriana ○ **T** 12 Gl 28
Fèz ○ **MO** 10 Gd 28
Fezzan ⌓ **LI** 12 Gm 33
al-Fifi ○ **SU** 22 He 40
Figuig ○ **MO** 11 Gf 29
Filim ○ **O** 89 Jh 35
Fkih-Ben-Salah ○ **MO** 10 Gc 29
Foggaret al-'Arab ○ **A** 11 Gh 32
Foggaret ez Zouba ○ **A** 11 Gh 32
Fomboni ○ **C** 25 Hp 52
Foro Burunga ○ **SU** 19 Hd 39
Forthassa Gharbia ○ **A** 11 Gf 29
Foul Bay ∼ **E** 15 Hk 34
Foumbouni ○ **C** 25 Hp 51
Foum-Zguid ○ **MO** 10 Gc 30
Frenda ○ **A** 11 Gg 28
al-Fuhaihil ○ **K** 85 Jc 31
Fujairah ○ **UAE** 89 Jg 33
Fuka ○ **E** 14 Hf 30
al-Fula ○ **SU** 20 Hg 40
al-Fuqaha' ○ **LI** 13 Ha 32
al-Furaishi ○ **SA** 84 Hm 33
Furqlus ○ **SY** 82 Hl 28

G

Gaalkacyo ○ **SO** 24 Jb 42
al-Gaa Taatzebar ⌓ **A** 11 Gh 33
al-Gabalayn ○ **SU** 20 Hj 39
Gabès ○ **T** 12 Gm 29
Gabir ○ **SU** 22 He 41
Gabras ○ **SU** 22 Hf 40
Gacanka Xaafuun ∼ **SO** 24 Jd 40
Gadein ○ **SU** 22 Hg 41
Gafsa ○ **T** 12 Gl 28
al-Gail ○ **Y** 87 Jd 38
Galegu ○ **SU** 21 Hk 39
Galegu ∼ **SU** 21 Hk 39
Gallabat ○ **SU** 21 Hk 39
al-Gallâouîya ○ **MA** 16 Ga 35
Galool ○ **SO** 25 Hp 44
Gal Shiikh ○ **SO** 24 Jb 40
Gal Tardo ○ **SO** 25 Ja 44
Galtat-Zemmour ○ **MO** 16 Fp 33
al-Gambole ○ **SO** 25 Ja 44
Gamid az-Zinad ○ **SA** 86 Hn 36
Gamra ○ **MA** 16 Fp 37
Gamsa ○ **E** 15 Hj 32
al-Ganamiya ○ **SA** 85 Jb 33
Gananita ○ **SU** 21 Hj 36
Ganat as-Suwais ∼ **E** 15 Hj 30
Gâneb ○ **MA** 16 Ga 36
al-Garabulli ○ **LI** 12 Gn 29
Garacad ○ **SO** 24 Jc 42
Garada ○ **SU** 20 Hh 36
Garadag ○ **SO** 24 Jb 41
Gara-Ekar △ **A** 18 Gj 36
Gara Khannfoussa △ **A** 12 Gk 32
Garbahaarrey ○ **SO** 25 Hn 44
Gardaba ⌓ **LI** 19 Hd 31
al-Garef ○ **SU** 21 Hk 40
Garet al-Djenoun △ **A** 11 Gj 33
Gar et Tarf ∼ **A** 12 Gk 28
al-Gargarat ○ **MO** 16 Fm 35
Garmabe ○ **SU** 22 Hh 43
Garoowe ○ **SO** 24 Jc 41
Garsala ○ **SO** 25 Ja 44
Garsila ○ **SU** 20 Hd 39
Garub ○ **Y** 87 Je 37
Gassi Touil ⌓ **A** 12 Gk 31
al-Gat ○ **SA** 85 Ja 33
Gatanga ○ **SU** 22 Hf 42
Gatti ○ **SA** 84 Hl 30
al-Gaura ○ **SU** 21 Hk 37
Gawwar ♣ **SA** 84 Hl 33
al-Gayli ○ **SU** 20 Hj 37
Gaza ○ **P** 82 Hk 30
al-Gazala ○ **SA** 84 Hn 32
Gaza strip ⊙ **P** 82 Hj 30
Gdyel ○ **A** 11 Gf 28
Gebeit ○ **SU** 21 Hl 36
Gebel ,Elba △ **E** 15 Hl 34
al-Gedaref ○ **SU** 21 Hk 38
Geesaley ○ **SO** 24 Jd 40
Gel ∼ **SU** 22 Hg 42
Gellab ○ **SU** 22 He 41
Gellinsoor ○ **SO** 24 Jb 42
Gemmeiza ○ **SU** 21 Hk 37
Gemmeiza ○ **SU** 22 Hg 42
Gemmeiza ○ **SU** 22 Hh 43
al-Ghaba ○ **SU** 20 Hh 36
Ghaba ○ **O** 89 Jg 35
al-Ghabsha ○ **SU** 20 Hh 39
Ghadamis ○ **LI** 12 Gl 30
Ghadduwa ○ **LI** 12 Gp 32
Ghallamane ⌓ **MA** 16 Ga 34
Gharb Binna ○ **SU** 20 Hg 36
Ghard Abu Muharrik ⌓ **E** 14 Hg 31
Ghardaïa ○ **A** 11 Gh 29
al-Ghardaqa Hurghada ○ **E** 15 Hj 32
Ghardimaou ○ **T** 12 Gl 27
al-Gharif ○ **SA** 84 Hm 34
Gharig ○ **SU** 22 Hf 40
Gharyan ○ **LI** 12 Gn 29
Ghat ○ **LI** 12 Gm 33
Ghazaouet ○ **A** 11 Gf 28
al-Gheddiya ○ **MA** 16 Ga 37
al-Ghomode ○ **LI** 12 Gm 33
Ghomrassen ○ **T** 12 Gl 29
Ghoraffa ○ **A** 12 Gk 29
al-Ghrayfa ○ **LI** 12 Gn 32
Ghriss ○ **A** 11 Gg 28
Ghubaysh ○ **SU** 20 Hf 39
Ghubbat al-Qamar ∼ **Y** 87 Je 37
Gialalassi ○ **SO** 25 Ja 44
al-Giara ○ **SO** 25 Hn 46
Gilf Kabir Plateau ⛰ **E** 14 He 34
Girau ○ **I** 83 Hp 28
Girban ○ **SU** 22 Hh 40
Girza ○ **E** 14 Hh 31
Giza ○ **E** 14 Hh 30
Gleibat Boukénni ○ **MA** 16 Gb 38
Gobur ○ **SU** 22 Hh 43
Godatair ○ **SU** 22 Hf 41
Godhyogol ○ **SO** 24 Hp 41
Godinlabe ○ **SO** 24 Jb 43
Gogrial ○ **SU** 22 Hg 41
Golan ⛰ **SY** 82 Hk 29
Gole ○ **I** 83 Ja 28
al-Goléa ○ **A** 11 Gh 30
Golfe de Cintra ∼ **MO** 16 Fm 34
Golweyn ○ **SO** 25 Ja 45
Goranlega ∼ **SO** 25 Hn 46
Gorges ★ **A** 11 Gh 27
Gorgol ∼ **MA** 16 Fp 37
Gorgol Blanc ∼ **MA** 16 Fp 37
Gorgol Noire ∼ **MA** 16 Fp 37
Gouiret Moussa ○ **A** 11 Gh 30
Goulmima ○ **MO** 10 Gd 30
Gouray ○ **MA** 16 Fp 38
Gouraya ○ **A** 11 Gg 27
Gourrama ○ **MO** 10 Gd 29
Grande Kabylie ⌓ **A** 11 Gh 27
Great Eastern Erg ⌓ **A** 11 Gj 31
Great Sand Sea ⌓ **LI** 19 Hd 31
Great Western Erg ⌓ **A** 11 Gf 30
Grizim ∼ **A** 10 Ge 33
Gromballa ○ **T** 12 Gm 27
Guban ⌓ **SO** 24 Hp 40
Guelb er Rîchât △ **MA** 16 Ga 35
Guelltat Sidi Saad ○ **A** 11 Gg 28
Guelma ○ **A** 12 Gk 27
Guelmine ○ **MO** 10 Ga 31
al-Guérara ○ **A** 11 Gf 31
Guerara ○ **A** 11 Gj 29
Guercif ○ **MO** 10 Ge 28
Guérou ○ **MA** 16 Fp 37
al-Guetar ○ **T** 12 Gl 28
Guissèr Mechra-Benâbbou ○ **MO** 10 Gc 29
Gulf of Aden ≈ 24 Ja 40
Gulf of Aqaba ≈ 82 Hk 31
Gulf of Gabès ∼ **T** 12 Gm 28
Gulf of Hallaniyat ∼ **O** 88 Jf 37
Gulf of Hammamet ∼ **T** 12 Gm 27
Gulf of Masira ∼ **O** 89 Jh 35
Gulf of Sirte ≈ 13 Ha 29
Gulf of Suez ∼ **E** 15 Hj 31
Gulf of Tadjoura ∼ **D** 24 Hp 40
Gulf of Tunis ∼ **T** 12 Gm 27
Gunna ○ **SU** 22 Hf 42
Gurri ○ **SU** 19 Hd 39
Guwaifat ○ **UAE** 88 Jd 33
Guwayr ○ **SU** 21 Hj 37

H

Haaway ○ **SO** 25 Hp 45
al-Haba ○ **UAE** 88 Jf 33
Habar Cirir ○ **SO** 25 Ja 43
Habarut ○ **O** 88 Je 37
al-Habbaniya ○ **I** 83 Hp 29
al-Habbariya ○ **I** 82 Hn 29
Habob ∼ **SU** 21 Hk 36
Habshan ○ **UAE** 88 Je 34
al-Had ○ **MO** 10 Gc 30
Hada ○ **SA** 84 Hn 34
Hadaliya ○ **SU** 21 Hl 37
al-Hadar ○ **I** 82 Hp 28
Hadbaram ○ **O** 88 Jf 37
al-Hadd ○ **O** 89 Jh 34
Hadda' ○ **SA** 86 Hm 35
Haddad Bani Malik ○ **SA** 86 Hn 35
al-Haddar ○ **SA** 86 Ja 34
Hadibu ○ **Y** 87 Je 39
al-Hadita ○ **SA** 84 Hl 30
al-Hadjar ○ **A** 12 Gk 27
Hadramaut ⌓ **Y** 86 Jb 38
Hadraniya ○ **I** 83 Hp 28
Hafar al-Batin ○ **SA** 85 Jb 31
Haffouz ○ **T** 12 Gl 28
Hafirat al-'Aida ○ **SA** 84 Hm 32
Hafirat Nisah ○ **SA** 85 Jb 33
Hagar Banga ○ **SU** 20 Hd 40
Hagg 'Abd Allah ○ **SU** 21 Hj 38
al-Haggounia ○ **MO** 10 Fp 32
Hahaya ○ **C** 25 Hp 51
Ha'il ○ **SA** 84 Hn 32
Haima' ○ **O** 88 Jg 36
Hainin ○ **Y** 87 Jc 38
al-Ha'it ○ **SA** 84 Hn 33
al-Haiz ○ **E** 14 Hg 31
al-Hajar ⛰ **O** 89 Jg 34
al-Hajara ⛰ **SA** 84 Hn 30
al-Hajarain ○ **Y** 87 Jc 38
Hajar al-Sharqi ⛰ **O** 89 Jh 34
Hajda ○ **Y** 86 Hp 39
al-Hajeb ○ **MO** 10 Gd 29
Hajeb al-Ayoun ○ **T** 12 Gl 28
Hajja ○ **Y** 86 Hp 38
al-Hajr ○ **SA** 85 Jb 33

Halabja O **I** 83 Ja 28
Hala'ib O **E** 15 Hl 34
Halat 'Ammar O **SA** 84 Hk 31
Halgen O **SO** 25 Ja 43
Haliban O **SA** 84 Ja 34
al-Hallaniyat ⚓ O 88 Jf 37
Halwan al-Khunfa △ **SA** 84 Hm 31
Hama O **SY** 82 Hl 28
al-Hamad ⌒ **SA** 84 Hm 30
Hamada de la Daoura ⌒ **A** 10 Gd 31
Hamada de Tindouf ⌒ **A** 10 Gb 32
Hamada du Drâa ⌒ **A** 10 Gc 31
Hamada du Guir ⌒ **MO** 10 Ge 30
Hamada ed Douakel ⌒ **A** 10 Gc 32
al-Hamada al-Hamra' ⌒ **LI** 12 Gm 31
Hamada Tounassine ⌒ **A** 10 Gc 31
Hamaguir O **A** 11 Ge 30
Hamamah O **LI** 13 Hc 29
Hamamed al-Nasla ⌒ **LI** 12 Gm 30
al-Hamar O **SA** 85 Jb 34
al-Hamasin O **SA** 86 Ja 35
al-Hamel O **A** 11 Gh 28
al-Hami O **Y** 87 Jc 38
Hamid O **SU** 20 Hh 35
Hamidiya O **SY** 82 Hk 28
Hamim O **UAE** 88 Jf 34
Hamir O **Y** 86 Hp 38
al-Hamja O **SA** 84 Hp 33
al-Hamma O **T** 12 Gl 29
al-Hammam O **E** 14 Hg 30
al-Hammam O **I** 83 Hp 30
Hammamet O **T** 12 Gm 27
al-Hammami ⌒ **MA** 16 Fp 34
Hammam-Lif O **T** 12 Gm 27
Hamra O **SU** 22 Hg 40
al-Hamra △ **O** 89 Jg 34
Hamrat al-Shaykh O **SU** 20 Hf 38
Hamrat al-Wuzz O **SU** 20 Hh 38
Hanadet Bet Touadjine ⌒ **A** 11 Gf 30
al-Hanakiya O **SA** 84 Hn 33
Hanaqin O **I** 83 Ja 28
Han ar-Rahba O **I** 83 Hp 30
Hanid O **SA** 85 Jc 32
al-Haniya O **LI** 13 Hc 29
Han Mugida O **SU** 20 Hj 36
Hannik O **SU** 20 Hj 36
al-Haouaria O **T** 12 Gm 27
Haoud al-Hamra O **A** 11 Gk 30
al-Haouita O **A** 11 Gh 29
Haouza O **MO** 10 Ga 32
al-Haql O **SA** 84 Hk 31
al-Haqw O **SA** 86 Hp 37
al-Haraba O **LI** 12 Gm 30
Harad O **Y** 86 Hp 37
Haradh O **SA** 85 Jc 33
Haraja O **SA** 86 Hp 37
al-Harf O **Y** 86 Ja 37
Hargeysa O **SO** 24 Hp 41
Harib O **Y** 86 Ja 38
Haro ~ **SO** 25 Hn 45
Harrat al-Buqum ⌒ **SA** 86 Hn 35
Harrat Hadan ⌒ **SA** 86 Hn 35
Harrat Haibar ⌒ **SA** 84 Hm 33
Harrat Rahat ⌒ **SA** 84 Hm 34
Harrat al-'Uwairid ⌒ **SA** 84 Hl 32
al-Haruj al-Aswad ⌒ **LI** 13 Ha 32
al-Hasa' ⌒ **SA** 85 Jc 32
al-Hasaka O **SY** 82 Hn 27
al-Hasani ⚓ **SA** 84 Hl 33
Hashab O **SU** 20 He 39
al-Hasi O **Y** 87 Jc 38
Haskanit O **SU** 20 Hf 40
Hâssei Mbârek O **MA** 16 Ga 37
Hassi-al-Ahmar O **MO** 10 Ge 29
Hassi al-Alimar O **A** 11 Gg 28
Hassi Bahbah O **A** 11 Gg 28
Hassi Barouda O **A** 11 Gg 31
Hassi Bedjedjene O **A** 12 Gl 32
Hassi Bedoud O **MO** 10 Ge 29
Hassi Bel Guebbour O **A** 11 Gk 31
Hassi al-Belrem O **A** 11 Gh 32
Hassi Berrekhem O **A** 11 Gj 29
Hassi-Bou-Allala O **A** 11 Ge 30
Hassi bou Bernous O **A** 11 Ge 32
Hassi Brahim O **MO** 10 Gb 31
Hassi Daoula O **A** 11 Gj 29

Hassi-Delaa O **A** 11 Gh 29
Hassi el-Kerma O **MO** 10 Gb 31
Hassi Fahl O **A** 11 Gh 30
Hassi Fougani O **A** 10 Gd 30
Hâssi Foûini O **MA** 17 Gc 37
Hassi Habadra O **A** 11 Gj 32
Hassi Hadour O **A** 11 Gf 30
Hassi Himana O **A** 11 Ge 31
Hassi Ifertas O **LI** 12 Gm 31
Hassi Imoulaye O **A** 12 Gl 31
Hassi in Akeouet O **A** 12 Gl 32
Hassi Inifel O **A** 11 Gh 31
Hassi-Khannfous O **A** 11 Gh 31
Hassi al-Khebi O **A** 10 Gd 31
Hassi Kord Meriem O **A** 11 Ge 31
Hassi al-Krenig O **A** 11 Gh 32
Hassi Mahzez O **A** 10 Gd 31
Hassi Maraket O **A** 11 Gh 30
Hassi Messaoud O **A** 11 Gj 30
Hassi al-Mounir O **A** 10 Gc 31
Hassi Moussa O **A** 11 Gg 31
Hassi Ntsel O **A** 12 Gk 32
Hassi-Onuz O **MO** 10 Ga 31
Hassi Ras al-Erg O **A** 11 Gh 31
Hassi R'Mel O **A** 11 Gh 29
Hassi Safiet Iniguel O **A** 11 Gh 30
Hassi Settala O **A** 11 Gh 29
Hassi Tabankort O **A** 12 Gk 31
Hassi Tabelbalet O **A** 12 Gk 32
Hassi Tartrat O **A** 10 Gc 32
Hasy Hague O **LI** 12 Gm 32
Hasy in Agiuel O **LI** 12 Gm 32
Hatra ★ **I** 82 Hp 28
al-'Haura O **Y** 86 Jb 39
Haur-Abdallah ~ **I** 85 Jc 31
Haur Dalmg ~ **I** 83 Ja 29
Haur Dayat ~ **I** 83 Hl 29
Haur al-Habbaniya ~ **I** 83 Hp 29
Haur al-Hammar ~ **I** 83 Jb 30
Haur al-Hawiza ~ **I** 83 Jb 30
Haur al-Sa'diya ~ **I** 83 Jb 29
Haur al-Shubaika ~ **I** 83 Ja 29
Hautat Bani Tamin O **SA** 85 Jb 34
Hawalli O **K** 85 Jb 31
Hawar ⚓ **B** 85 Jd 33
al-Hawatah O **SU** 21 Hk 39
Hawijat Arban O **I** 82 Hn 28
al-Hawwari O **LI** 19 Hd 33
Haya O **SU** 21 Hl 36
Hayban O **SU** 22 Hh 40
Hays O **Y** 86 Hp 39
Hayy al-Mahatta O **SA** 85 Jb 33
al-Hazm O **Y** 86 Ja 37
Hazoua O **T** 12 Gk 29
Hebron O **P** 82 Hk 30
Heirane O **A** 11 Gf 32
Hejaz ⌒ **SA** 84 Hm 33
Hennaya O **A** 11 Gf 28
Herbagat O **SU** 21 Hl 36
Hermon △ **LE** 82 Hk 29
al-Hibak ⌒ **SA** 88 Je 35
al-Hibak ⌒ **SA** 88 Je 36
High Atlas ⌒ **MO** 10 Gb 30
High Dam ★ **E** 15 Hj 34
High Plateaus ⌒ **A** 11 Gf 29
al-Hijaz ⌒ **SA** 84 Hl 33
Hili O **UAE** 88 Jf 33
al-Hilla O **SU** 20 Hf 39
al-Hilla O **I** 83 Ja 29
al-Hindiya O **I** 83 Hp 29
Hirafok O **A** 11 Gj 34
al-Hisana O **SA** 86 Hn 35
Hisn al-Sahabi O **LI** 13 Hc 30
al-Hisw O **SA** 84 Hn 33
Hit O **I** 83 Hp 29
Hiw O **E** 15 Hj 33
Hobyo O **SO** 25 Jc 43
al-Hoceima O **MO** 10 Ge 28
Hodh ⌒ **MA** 16 Gb 37
Hodmo ~ **SO** 24 Jb 40
Hoggar ⌒ **A** 18 Gj 34
Hoja Wajeer O **SO** 25 Hn 46
Holhol O **D** 24 Hp 40
al-Homr O **A** 11 Gj 34
Hooda △ **SO** 24 Jd 40
Hoshib ~ **SU** 21 Hk 36
Houeiriye O **MA** 17 Gc 37
Houmt Souk Jerba O **T** 12 Gm 29
al-Huari O **LI** 19 Hd 33
al-Hudaida O **Y** 86 Hp 38
al-Hufayyira O **SA** 85 Ja 33
al-Hufrah al-Sharqiya ⌒ **LI** 12 Gp 32
al-Hufuf O **SA** 85 Jc 33
Hulaiba O **K** 85 Jb 30

al-Hulaifa al-Sufla O **SA** 84 Hn 33
al-Hulwa O **SA** 85 Jb 34
Hulwan O **E** 15 Hh 31
Humari O **SU** 21 Hk 37
al-Humeida O **SA** 84 Hk 31
Hums O **SY** 82 Hl 28
Hun O **LI** 12 Gp 31
al-Huqf O **O** 89 Jg 35
Huraimila O **SA** 85 Jb 33
Hurdiyo O **SO** 24 Jd 40
Husain al-Gafus O **I** 83 Ja 29
al-Husayhisa O **SU** 21 Hj 38
al-Hushaibi O **SA** 84 Hp 33
Husheib O **SU** 21 Hk 38
Hut O **Y** 86 Hp 37
al-Huwaymi O **Y** 86 Jb 38
al-Huwaysah O **O** 89 Jg 34

I

Ibb O **Y** 86 Ja 39
Ibba ~ **SU** 22 Hg 42
Ibba O **SU** 22 Hg 43
Ibra O **O** 89 Jh 34
Ibri O **O** 89 Jg 34
Ibshaway O **E** 14 Hh 31
Iche O **MO** 11 Gf 29
Ida-Oumarkt O **MO** 10 Gb 31
'Idd al-Ghanam O **SU** 20 He 40
Ideles O **A** 18 Gj 34
Idfu O **E** 15 Hj 33
Idiriya O **MO** 10 Ga 32
Idlib O **SY** 82 Hl 28
al-Idrissa O **A** 11 Gh 28
al-Idwa O **SA** 84 Hp 32
Ifetesene △ **A** 11 Gj 33
Ifrane O **MO** 10 Gd 29
Igherm O **MO** 10 Gb 30
Ighil Tzane O **A** 11 Gg 28
Igli O **A** 11 Ge 30
Iguetti O **MA** 16 Gb 33
Iguídi Ouan Kasa ⌒ **LI** 12 Gm 33
Iherir O **A** 12 Gl 33
Ihitsa O **LI** 12 Gn 33
Iidaan O **SO** 24 Jc 42
Ijkharra O **LI** 13 Hc 31
Ijoukak O **MO** 10 Gb 30
Ikoto O **SU** 23 Hj 43
Île Kiji ⚓ **MA** 16 Fm 36
Île Tidra ⚓ **MA** 16 Fm 36
Illizi O **A** 12 Gl 32
Imatong Mountains ⌒ **SU** 22 Hj 43
Imi-n-Tanoute O **MO** 10 Gb 30
Imlily O **MO** 16 Fn 34
Immouzzer-des-Ida-Outanane O **MO** 10 Gb 30
Imouzèr-du-Kandar O **MO** 10 Gd 29
Imtan O **SY** 82 Hl 29
In Afellahlah △ **A** 12 Gl 34
In Amenas O **A** 12 Gl 31
In Amguel O **A** 11 Gj 34
In Atteï O **A** 18 Gk 35
In Belbel O **A** 11 Gg 32
In Ecker O **A** 11 Gj 33
Inezgane O **MO** 10 Gb 30
In Ezzane O **A** 12 Gm 34
In Ghar O **A** 11 Gg 32
In Herene O **LI** 12 Gm 32
Injana O **I** 83 Ja 28
Innahas Chebbi ~ **A** 11 Gh 32
I-n-Quezzam O **A** 18 Gj 36
In Salah O **A** 11 Gh 32
In Ziza O **A** 18 Gh 34
Iouigharacène △ **MO** 10 Gc 29
iouïk O **MA** 16 Fm 36
Iraq O **I** 83 Hp 29
Irarraren ~ **A** 11 Gj 32
Irbid O **J** 82 Hk 29
Irhil M'Goun △ **MO** 10 Gc 30
Iriki ~ **MO** 10 Gc 31
al-'Irqa O **Y** 86 Jb 39
'Irsal O **LE** 82 Hl 28
al-'Is O **SA** 84 Hm 33
Isaaq Jilible ~ **SO** 25 Hn 45
al-'Isawiya O **SA** 84 Hl 30
Ishan Salib O **I** 83 Ja 30
al-'Ishash O **SA** 84 Hm 32
Iskushuban O **SO** 24 Jd 40
al-Isma'iliya O **E** 15 Hj 30
Isna O **E** 15 Hj 33
Issoro O **SU** 22 Hj 44
Itquiy O **MO** 16 Fp 32
'Iyal Bakhit O **SU** 20 Hg 39
Izki O **O** 89 Jg 34

Izra' O **SY** 82 Hl 29

J

Jabal Abadad △ **SU** 21 Hk 36
Jabal Abu Di'ab △ **E** 15 Hk 33
Jabal Adar Gwagwa △ **E** 15 Hk 34
Jabal al-'Adiriyat ⌒ **J** 82 Hl 30
Jabal al-Aja ⌒ **SA** 84 Hn 32
Jabal Akakus ⌒ **LI** 12 Gm 33
Jabal al-Akhdar ⌒ **LI** 13 Hc 29
Jabal al-Akhdar ⌒ **O** 89 Jg 34
Jabal Ali O **UAE** 88 Jf 33
Jabal Arkenu △ **LI** 14 He 34
Jabal Asoteriba △ **E** 15 Hk 37
Jabal Asoteriba △ **SU** 21 Hl 35
Jabal Ataqa △ **E** 15 Hj 31
Jabal Auliya O **SU** 20 Hj 38
Jabal Baqir △ **J** 82 Hk 31
Jabal Barkal ★ **SU** 20 Hh 36
Jabal al-Barqa △ **E** 15 Hj 33
Jabal al-Batra △ **J** 82 Hk 31
Jabal Bin Ghanima ⌒ **LI** 12 Gp 33
Jabal Bozi △ **SU** 21 Hj 39
Jabal-Dair △ **SU** 20 Hh 39
Jabal Dauran △ **Y** 86 Ja 38
Jabal Erba △ **SU** 21 Hl 35
Jabal al-Garda ⌒ **LI** 19 Hd 33
Jabal Garf △ **E** 15 Hk 34
Jabal Gharib △ **E** 15 Hj 31
Jabal Gumbiri △ **SU** 22 Hh 43
Jabal Gurabi △ **E** 14 Hg 31
Jabal Gurad △ **SU** 21 Hk 36
Jabal Gurgei △ **SU** 20 He 39
Jabal Hamala △ **E** 15 Hk 33
Jabal Hamoyet △ **SU** 21 Hl 37
Jabal Hamrin △ **I** 83 Hp 28
Jabal al-Hasawina ⌒ **LI** 12 Gn 31
Jabal al-Hasha △ **Y** 86 Ja 39
Jabal al-Hawa'ish ⌒ **LI** 19 Hd 33
Jabal Hayban △ **SU** 20 Hh 40
Jabal Hilal △ **E** 15 Hj 30
Jabal Homot Tohadar △ **SU** 21 Hl 36
Jabal Isbil △ **Y** 86 Ja 38
Jabal al-Jalala al-Bahriya △ **E** 15 Hh 31
Jabal al-Jhir △ **Y** 87 Je 39
Jabal Kaiai △ **SU** 21 Hl 36
Jabal Kasangor △ **SU** 23 Hk 43
Jabal Katrina △ **E** 15 Hj 31
Jabal Kuror △ **SU** 20 Hh 35
Jabal al-Lauz △ **SA** 84 Hk 31
Jabal Magara △ **E** 15 Hj 30
Jabal Mahrat ⌒ **Y** 87 Jd 37
Jabal Manar △ **Y** 86 Ja 38
Jabal Marra △ **SU** 20 He 39
Jabal al-Maruf ⌒ **LI** 13 Hb 33
Jabal Mazmum △ **SU** 21 Hj 39
Jabal Mismar △ **SU** 21 Hk 36
Jabal Mubarak △ **J** 82 Hk 30
Jabal Muqsim △ **SU** 21 Hj 36
Jabal Musa Mount Sinai △ **E** 15 Hj 31
Jabal al-Nabi Shu'ayb △ **Y** 86 Hp 38
Jabal Nafusa ⌒ **LI** 12 Gm 30
Jabal Nuqayy ⌒ **LI** 19 Hb 34
Jabal Nuqrus △ **E** 15 Hk 33
Jabal Nuqum △ **Y** 86 Ja 38
Jabal Ofreik △ **SU** 21 Hk 37
Jabal al-Qahb △ **SA** 84 Ja 33
Jabal al-Qamar ⌒ **Y** 87 Je 37
Jabal al-Qara △ **O** 88 Je 37
Jabal Qatrani △ **E** 14 Hh 31
Jabal Qattar △ **E** 15 Hj 32
Jabal Radwa △ **SA** 84 Hm 33
Jabal Rafit △ **SU** 20 Hj 35
Jabal Rashid ⌒ **SY** 82 Hl 28
Jabal Ra's Madhar △ **SA** 84 Hl 33
Jabal al-Ruwaq ⌒ **SY** 82 Hl 29
Jabal Sabbag △ **Y** 86 Hj 31
Jabal Sabidana △ **SU** 21 Hl 36
Jabal Sabir △ **Y** 86 Ja 39
Jabal al-Sawda' ⌒ **LI** 12 Gp 31
Jabal Sha'ib △ **Y** 86 Hj 32
Jabal Shammar ⌒ **SA** 84 Hm 32
Jabal Shimhan ⌒ **O** 88 Jf 37
Jabal al-Siba' △ **E** 15 Hk 33
Jabal Tadrart ⌒ **A** 12 Gm 33
Jabal Tallasa △ **SU** 21 Hj 36
Jabal Tarhuni △ **LI** 19 Hd 34
Jabal Teljo △ **SU** 20 He 38

Jabal Thamer △ **Y** 86 Ja 39
Jabal al-Tih ⌒ **E** 15 Hj 31
Jabal al-Tubaiq ⌒ **SA** 84 Hl 31
Jabal Tuwaiq ⌒ **SA** 85 Ja 33
Jabal Uda △ **SU** 21 Hl 35
Jabal Umm Ba'anib △ **E** 15 Hj 32
Jabal al-'Urf △ **E** 15 Hj 32
Jabal Uweinat △ **LI** 14 He 35
Jabal Waddan △ **LI** 12 Ha 31
Jabal al-Wajid ⌒ **SA** 86 Ja 36
Jabal Yu'alliq △ **E** 15 Hj 30
Jabal al-Zalma' △ **SA** 84 Hm 32
Jabal Zaltan ⌒ **LI** 13 Hb 31
Jabal al-Zanna O **UAE** 88 Je 33
Jabarona O **SU** 20 Hf 37
Jabla O **SY** 82 Hl 28
Jacal O **SO** 25 Jb 43
Jaceel ~ **SO** 24 Jd 40
Jadib O **Y** 87 Je 37
al-Jadida O **MO** 10 Gb 29
al-Jadida O **E** 14 Hg 31
Jadu O **LI** 12 Gm 30
al-Jafara O **SA** 86 Ja 34
al-Jafat O **O** 89 Jg 34
al-Jafr O **J** 82 Hl 30
al-Jafr ~ **J** 82 Hl 30
al-Jafura ⌒ **SA** 88 Jd 33
al-Jaghbub O **LI** 13 He 31
Jaharah O **SA** 84 Hm 32
Jahnin O **O** 88 Je 37
al-Jahra O **K** 85 Jb 31
al-Jaida O **Y** 87 Jc 38
al-Jaida O **Y** 87 Jd 37
Jalajil O **SA** 85 Ja 33
Jalala O **I** 83 Ja 28
al-Jalamid O **SA** 84 Hn 30
Jaliba O **I** 83 Jb 30
Jalu O **LI** 13 Hc 31
Jalu Oasis ⌒ **LI** 13 Hc 31
Jamaame O **SO** 25 Hp 45
al-Jamaliya O **E** 15 Hh 30
Jamjamal O **I** 83 Ja 28
al-Jamliya O **Q** 85 Jd 33
Jamum O **SA** 86 Hm 35
al-Janad O **Y** 86 Ja 39
Janana O **UAE** 88 Je 33
Jarablus O **SY** 82 Hl 27
Jarandal O **J** 82 Hk 30
Jarara O **SA** 85 Jb 32
Jarash O **J** 82 Hk 29
Jasiira O **SO** 25 Ja 45
Jassan O **I** 83 Ja 29
al-Jawar ⌒ **SA** 85 Jc 33
al-Jawf O **LI** 19 Hd 33
al-Jaws al-Kabïr O **LI** 12 Gm 29
al-Jazira ~ **SY** 82 Hm 27
Jbel Grouz ⌒ **A** 11 Gf 29
Jebala ⌒ **MO** 10 Gd 28
Jebel Aqachi △ **MO** 10 Gd 29
Jebel Azourki △ **MO** 10 Gc 30
Jebel Bani ⌒ **MO** 10 Gc 31
Jebel Bou Iblane ⌒ **MO** 10 Gd 29
Jebel Bou Ladiab △ **T** 12 Gl 29
Jebel Bou Naceur △ **MO** 10 Gd 29
Jebel Ouarkziz ⌒ **MO** 10 Ga 31
Jebel Tazzeka △ **MO** 10 Gd 28
Jebel Toubkal △ **MO** 10 Gc 30
Jebiniana O **T** 12 Gm 28
Jedda O **SA** 86 Hm 35
Jefawa O **SU** 20 Hd 40
al-Jem O **T** 12 Gm 28
al-Jemâa O **MO** 10 Gb 30
Jemâa-Ida-Oussemlal O **MO** 10 Gb 31
Jendouba O **T** 12 Gl 27
al-Jeneina O **SU** 19 Hd 39
Jenin O **P** 82 Hk 29
Jerada O **MO** 11 Ge 28
Jerba Island ⚓ **T** 12 Gm 29
Jericho O **P** 82 Hk 30
Jeruf O **J** 82 Hk 30
al-Jezira ⌒ **SU** 21 Hj 38
Jiddat al-Harasis ~ **O** 88 Jf 36
Jidhi O **SO** 24 Hp 40
Jihana O **Y** 86 Ja 38
Jiiqley O **SO** 25 Ja 43
Jijel O **A** 11 Gj 27
Jilib O **SO** 25 Hp 45
Jinah O **E** 14 Hh 33
Jirja O **E** 15 Hh 32
Jirriban O **SO** 24 Jc 42
al-Jisha O **SA** 85 Jc 33
Jisr al-Sugar O **SY** 82 Hl 28
Jiyati O **UAE** 88 Je 34
Jizan O **SA** 86 Hp 37
Jizzin O **LE** 82 Hk 29
Jof O **T** 12 Gm 29
Jonglei Canal ~ **SU** 22 Hh 42

Jordan ⌇ **J** 82 Hk 29
Jordan ❑ **J** 82 Hk 30
Jorf O **MO** 10 Gd 30
Jowhar O **SO** 25 Ja 44
Jreida O **MA** 16 Fm 36
Jreïf O **MA** 16 Fp 37
Juba O **SU** 22 Hh 43
Jubail O **LE** 82 Hk 28
al-Jubayl O **SA** 85 Jc 32
Jubba O **SA** 84 Hn 31
Juda O **SA** 85 Jc 33
Judayyidat O **SA** 84 Hn 30
Judayyidat Hamir O **I** 84 Hn 30
Jufra Oasis ⌒ **LI** 12 Ha 31
Jumaira O **UAE** 88 Jf 33
Juniya O **LE** 82 Hk 29
Junqoley O **SU** 22 Hh 42
Jur ⌇ **SU** 22 Hg 41
Jurin O **I** 83 Hp 27
Juwaiza O **UAE** 88 Jf 33

K

Kabkabiya O **SU** 20 He 39
Kabna O **SU** 20 Hj 36
Kabshan O **SA** 84 Hp 33
Kabushiya O **SU** 21 Hj 37
al-Kadada O **SU** 21 Hj 37
Kadugli O **SU** 22 Hg 40
Kaédi O **MA** 16 Fp 37
Kafia Kingi O **SU** 22 He 41
Kafr O **E** 14 Hg 30
Kafr al-Sheikh O **E** 14 Hh 30
Kagmar O **SU** 20 Hh 38
al-Kahfa O **SA** 84 Hp 32
Kaiemothia O **SU** 23 Hk 43
Kairouan O **T** 12 Gm 28
Kajo Kaji O **SU** 22 Hh 44
Kaka O **SU** 22 Hj 40
al-Kala O **A** 12 Gl 27
Kalaat Khasba O **T** 12 Gl 28
Kalabsha ★ **E** 15 Hj 34
Kalba O **UAE** 89 Jg 33
al-Kalban O **O** 89 Jh 35
Kalis O **SO** 24 Jc 41
Kallar O **I** 83 Ja 28
Kalokitting O **SU** 20 He 39
al-Kamak Thebes ★ **E** 15 Hj 33
Kamaran O **Y** 86 Hp 38
Kamaran �}{ **Y** 86 Hp 38
Kambut O **LI** 13 He 30
al-Kamil O **SA** 84 Hm 34
al-Kamil O **O** 89 Jh 34
al-Kamilin O **SU** 21 Hj 38
Kampala O **SU** 22 He 41
Kamsuuma O **SO** 25 Hp 45
Kangen ⌇ **SU** 23 Hj 42
Kangi O **SU** 22 Hf 41
Kankossa O **MA** 16 Ga 38
al-Kantara O **A** 11 Gj 28
Kapoeta O **SU** 23 Hj 43
al-Karak O **J** 82 Hk 30
al-Kararim O **LI** 12 Gp 29
Karbala O **I** 83 Hp 29
Karbala ⊙ **I** 84 Hn 30
Karima O **SU** 20 Hh 36
Karin O **SO** 24 Ja 40
Karin O **SO** 24 Jc 40
Karling O **SU** 20 Hh 39
Karma O **SU** 20 Hh 36
Karora O **SU** 21 Hm 37
Karthala △ **C** 25 Hp 51
Kas O **SU** 20 He 39
Kasangor O **SU** 23 Hj 43
Kasaro O **SU** 22 Hj 39
Kasba-Tadla O **MO** 10 Gc 29
Kasdir O **A** 11 Gf 29
Kassala O **SU** 21 Hl 38
Kasserine O **T** 12 Gl 28
Kataouâne O **MA** 17 Gc 37
al-Kathiri ⌒ **E** 17 Jc 37
Katla O **SU** 20 Hg 40
al-Katouat O **MO** 10 Gc 29
al-Kawa O **SU** 20 Hj 39
Kawajena O **SU** 22 Hg 42
Kayli O **SU** 23 Hk 40
Kebili O **T** 12 Gl 29
al-Kef O **T** 12 Gl 27
al-Kelaa-des-Srarhna O **MO** 10 Gc 29
Kelibia O **T** 12 Gm 27
Kenadsa O **A** 11 Ge 30
Kenamuke Swamp ⌇ **SU** 23 Hj 42
Kénitra O **MO** 10 Gc 28
Keri Kera O **SU** 20 Hj 39
Kerkenah ⌂ **T** 12 Gm 28
Kerkouane ★ **T** 12 Gm 27
Kersinyané O **MA** 16 Ga 38

Kerzaz O **A** 11 Gf 31
Ketama O **MO** 10 Gd 28
Keur Massène O **MA** 16 Fm 37
Keyala O **SU** 22 Hj 43
al-Khabba O **SA** 84 Hn 32
Khabou O **MA** 16 Fp 38
Khabrat al-Dawish O **K** 85 Jb 31
al-Khabura O **O** 89 Jg 34
Khadnan O **I** 83 Hp 27
Khaibar O **SA** 84 Hm 33
Khaibar al-Ganub O **SA** 86 Hp 36
Khalfallah O **A** 11 Gg 28
Khalid O **I** 83 Ja 29
Khalij Abu Khashha'ifa ⌇ **E** 14 Hf 30
Khalij al-'Arab ⌇ **et** 14 Hg 30
Khalij at-Tina ⌇ **E** 15 Hj 30
Khalij al-Bumba ⌇ **LI** 19 Hd 29
Khalij al-Kuwait ⌇ **K** 85 Jb 31
Khalij al-Sallum ⌇ **E** 14 He 30
al-Khalil O **O** 89 Jg 36
al-Khalis O **I** 83 Ja 29
Khamis O **SA** 86 Hp 36
Khamis al-Bahr O **SA** 86 Hn 36
Khanasir O **SY** 82 Hl 28
Khan al-Baghdadi O **I** 82 Hp 29
al-Khandaq O **SU** 20 Hh 36
Khangar Sidi Nadji O **A** 12 Gk 28
Khan al-Mahawil O **I** 83 Ja 29
Khan Yunis O **P** 82 Hj 30
Khan Zur O **I** 83 Ja 28
al-Khaoula O **MO** 10 Ga 31
Kharga al-Kharija O **E** 14 Hh 33
Kharga Oasis ⌒ **E** 14 Hh 33
al-Kharj O **SA** 85 Jb 33
Khartoum ⊡ **SU** 20 Hj 38
Khartoum North O **SU** 20 Hj 38
al-Khasab O **O** 88 Jg 32
Khashm al-Qirba O **SU** 21 Hk 38
Khashm al-Qirba Dam ⌇ **SU** 21 Hk 38
al-Khatim O **UAE** 88 Jf 33
al-Khatt ⌒ **MA** 16 Ga 34
Khatt et Toueïrja ⌇ **MA** 16 Fn 36
al-Khaukha O **Y** 86 Hp 39
al-Khawr O **Q** 85 Jd 33
Khaz'aliya al-Nashwa O **I** 83 Jb 30
Khazzan al-Rusayris ⌇ **SU** 21 Hk 40
Khemis-des-Zemamra O **MO** 10 Gb 29
Khemis Miliana O **A** 11 Gh 27
Khemisset O **MO** 10 Gc 29
Khenchela O **A** 12 Gk 28
Khenifra O **MO** 10 Gd 29
Kherba O **A** 11 Gg 27
Kherrata O **A** 11 Gj 27
Khatt Atoui ⌇ **MA** 16 Fn 35
al-Khiran O **K** 85 Jc 31
Khirbat Isriya O **SY** 82 Hl 28
Khor Abu Sunt ⌇ **SU** 20 Hh 35
Khor Adar ⌇ **SU** 22 Hj 41
Khor' Angar O **D** 24 Hp 39
Khor Baraka ⌇ **SU** 21 Hl 37
Khor Duleyb ⌇ **SU** 23 Hj 40
Khor Fakkan O **UAE** 89 Jg 33
Khor Nyanding ⌇ **SU** 22 Hj 41
Khor Tumat ⌇ **SU** 23 Hk 40
Khor Veveno ⌇ **SU** 22 Hj 42
Khosrovio O **I** 83 Ja 28
Khouribga O **MO** 10 Gc 29
al-Khroub O **A** 12 Gk 27
al-Khubar O **SA** 88 Jd 32
Khulais O **SA** 84 Hm 34
al-Khums O **LI** 12 Gp 29
Khurais O **SA** 85 Jb 33
Khurayt O **SU** 20 Hf 39
al-Khurma O **SA** 86 Hp 35
al-Khuwair O **SA** 84 Hp 32
al-Khuwayr O **Q** 85 Jd 33
al-Khuwayr O **O** 88 Jf 34
Khuwei O **SU** 20 Hg 40
Kibish O **SU** 23 Hk 43
al-Kidan ⌒ **SA** 88 Je 34
Kidepo O **SU** 23 Hj 43
Kiffa O **MA** 16 Ga 37
Kifri O **I** 83 Ja 28
Kigille O **SU** 23 Hj 41
Kigille O **SU** 23 Hk 41
Kimun al-Mata'ina O **E** 15 Hh 33
Kinyeti △ **SU** 22 Hj 44
Kirané O **MA** 16 Ga 38
al-Kirbekan O **SU** 20 Hj 36
Kirit O **SO** 24 Jb 41
Kirkuk O **I** 83 Ja 28
Kismaayo O **SO** 25 Hp 46
Kitaf O **Y** 86 Ja 37

Kiyat O **SA** 86 Hn 36
Kobenni O **MA** 16 Gb 38
Kodok O **SU** 22 Hj 41
Kokwo O **SU** 23 Hk 43
Kom Ombo O **E** 15 Hj 33
Kongor O **SU** 22 Hh 42
Kordofan ⌒ **SU** 20 Hg 39
Kortala O **SU** 20 Hh 39
Kosha O **SU** 20 Hh 35
Kouinine O **A** 12 Gk 29
Koulbous O **SU** 19 Hd 38
Koûroudjél O **MA** 16 Ga 37
Ksar-al-Boukhari O **A** 11 Gh 28
Ksar Chellala O **A** 11 Gh 28
Ksar Ghilane O **T** 12 Gl 29
al-Ksar-al-Kbir O **MO** 10 Gc 28
al-Kseur O **A** 11 Gj 27
al-Ksiba O **MO** 10 Gd 29
al-Ksour O **T** 12 Gl 28
Ksour Essaf O **T** 12 Gm 28
Kubara O **O** 89 Jg 34
Kubbum O **SU** 20 Hd 40
al-Kufa O **I** 83 Ja 29
Kufra Oasis ⌒ **LI** 19 Hd 33
Kuhayli O **SU** 20 Hj 36
Kukur O **SU** 21 Hj 40
Kulaykil O **SU** 19 Hd 38
Kulaykili O **SU** 20 He 40
Kulshabi O **SU** 22 Hg 40
al-Kumait O **I** 83 Jb 29
Kumzar O **O** 89 Jg 32
Kungila O **SU** 23 Hj 40
al-Kuntilla O **E** 15 Hk 31
Kuri O **SU** 20 Hh 36
Kuria Maria Islands ⌂ O 88 Jf 37
Kurkur O **E** 15 Hj 34
Kurmuk O **SU** 23 Hk 40
Kurti O **SU** 20 Hh 36
Kuru ⌇ **SU** 22 Hf 42
Kusti O **SU** 20 Hj 39
al-Kut O **I** 83 Ja 29
Kut al-Hayy O **I** 83 Ja 29
Kutum O **SU** 20 He 38
Kuwait O **I** 83 Jb 29
Kuwait ❑ **K** 85 Jb 31
Kuwait ⊡ **K** 85 Jc 31
Kuwara O **SU** 20 Hg 40
Kuysanjaq O **I** 83 Ja 27

L

Laas Caano O **SO** 24 Jc 42
Laascaanood O **SO** 24 Jb 41
Laaso Dawaco O **SO** 24 Jc 40
Laasqoray O **SO** 24 Jc 40
Laâyoune O **MO** 10 Fp 32
al-Labbal O **SA** 84 Hn 31
Labda Leptis Magna ★ **LI** 12 Gp 29
Labkha O **SA** 85 Ja 33
Lac d'Aleg ⌇ **MA** 16 Fn 37
Lac Rkîz ⌇ **MA** 16 Fn 37
al-Ladhiqiya Latakia O **SY** 82 Hk 28
La Galite ⌂ **T** 12 Gl 27
Laghonat O **A** 11 Gh 29
La Gouera O **MO** 16 Fm 35
al-Lagowa O **SU** 20 Hg 40
Lahij O **Y** 86 Ja 39
Laila Outka △ **MO** 10 Gd 28
La Jaram O **MA** 10 Ga 32
Lake Assad ⌇ **SY** 82 Hm 28
Lake Assal ⌇ **D** 24 Hp 40
Lake Nasser ⌇ **E** 15 Hj 34
Lake Razzaza ⌇ **I** 83 Hp 29
Lake Tharthar ⌇ **I** 83 Hp 29
Lakhcheb O **MA** 16 Ga 36
Lakhdaria O **A** 11 Gh 27
Lalyo O **SU** 22 Hh 43
Lamalaga ⌒ **MO** 16 Fm 34
La Marsa O **T** 12 Gm 27
Lamindo O **SU** 22 Hh 43
La'oueïssi O **MA** 16 Fp 37
Laqiyat Arba'in O **SU** 20 Hf 35
Laqiyat 'Umran O **SU** 20 Hg 36
Larache O **MO** 10 Gc 28
Larba O **A** 11 Gh 27
Latakia al-Ladhiqiya O **SY** 82 Hk 28
al-Latifiya O **I** 83 Hp 29
Laudar O **Y** 86 Ja 39
Lauqa O **SA** 84 Hp 31
Layla O **SA** 85 Jb 34
Lebanon ❑ **LE** 82 Hk 28
Lebanon Mountains ⌒ **LE** 82 Hk 29
Leego O **SO** 25 Ja 44

Lemluia O **MO** 16 Fp 32
Lemsid O **MO** 16 Fn 32
Leptis Magna ★ **LI** 12 Gp 29
Leqceiba O **MA** 16 Fp 37
Ler Zerai O **SU** 22 Hf 40
Lesportes de Fer ★ **A** 11 Gj 27
Letfata O **MA** 16 Fp 37
Libya ❑ **LI** 13 Hb 33
Libyan Desert ⌒ **LI** 19 Hd 32
al-Lihin O **SA** 84 Hm 33
Lima O **O** 89 Jg 33
Lina O **SA** 84 Hp 31
al-Lit O **SA** 86 Hn 35
Litani ⌇ **LE** 82 Hk 29
al-Liwa O **UAE** 88 Je 34
al-Liwa' O **O** 89 Jg 33
Li Yubu O **SU** 22 Hf 43
Lobira O **SU** 23 Hj 43
Loga O **SU** 22 Hh 43
Lol ⌇ **SU** 22 Hf 41
Loming O **SU** 23 Hj 43
Loronyo O **SU** 22 Hj 43
Lorzot O **T** 12 Gm 30
Lotukel ⌂ **SU** 23 Hj 43
Lousserie O **MA** 16 Ga 37
Lowelli O **SU** 23 Hj 43
Loyada O **D** 24 Hp 40
Lughaye O **SO** 24 Hp 40
al-Luhayya O **Y** 86 Hp 38
Luth O **SU** 22 Hh 42
Luuq O **SO** 25 Hp 44
Luxor O **E** 15 Hj 33

M

al-Maad O **A** 11 Gj 27
Ma'an O **J** 82 Hk 30
Ma'aniya O **I** 83 Hp 30
Ma'arrat al-Nu'man O **SY** 82 Hl 28
Ma'bar O **Y** 86 Ja 38
Mabruk O **LI** 13 Ha 30
Madagoi ⌇ **SO** 25 Hp 45
al-Madaniqa O **SA** 86 Hp 37
Madbar O **SU** 22 Hh 42
Madeir O **SU** 22 Hg 42
Madero O **SO** 25 Hn 46
Ma'din O **SY** 82 Hm 28
Madinat-al-Abyar O **LI** 13 Hc 29
Madinat al-Shirq O **Y** 86 Hp 38
Madinat Nasir O **E** 15 Hj 33
Madinat-al-Sadat O **E** 14 Hh 30
Madol O **SU** 22 Hf 41
Madraka O **SA** 84 Hm 34
Madu O **SU** 20 Hf 38
al-Mafaza O **SU** 21 Hk 39
Mafrak O **SA** 84 Hm 34
al-Mafraq O **J** 82 Hl 29
Mafruq O **Y** 86 Hp 39
al-Magarim O **Y** 86 Jb 38
Maghagha O **E** 14 Hh 31
Maghama O **MA** 16 Fp 38
Maghnia O **A** 11 Gf 28
Magoura O **A** 11 Gf 28
Magra O **A** 11 Gj 28
Magrur O **SU** 20 Hh 38
Magtá Lahjar O **MA** 16 Fp 37
Magwe O **SU** 22 Hj 43
al-Mahabisha O **Y** 86 Hp 37
Mahadday Weeyne O **SO** 25 Ja 44
al-Mahakik ⌒ **SA** 88 Jd 35
al-Mahalani O **SA** 84 Hp 32
al-Mahalla al-Kubra O **E** 14 Hh 30
al-Mahariq O **E** 14 Hh 33
Mahattat 10 O **SU** 21 Hj 36
Mahattat 2 O **SU** 20 Hh 35
Mahattat 5 O **SU** 20 Hj 35
Mahattat 6 O **SU** 20 Hj 35
Mahattat 8 O **SU** 20 Hj 35
Mahattat Dab'a O **J** 82 Hl 30
Mahattat Talata O **E** 15 Hj 30
al-Mahbas O **MO** 10 Gb 32
Mahbub O **SU** 20 Hg 39
Mahda O **O** 88 Jf 33
Mahd al-Dahab O **SA** 84 Hn 34
Mahdia O **T** 12 Gm 28
al-Mahjil O **Y** 86 Ja 37
Mahmiya O **SU** 21 Hj 37
al-Mahmudiya O **I** 83 Ja 29
al-Mahra O **Y** 87 Jd 38
Mahres O **T** 12 Gm 28
al-Mahwit O **Y** 86 Hp 38
Maidi O **Y** 86 Hp 37
Maif'a O **Y** 86 Jb 38
Maiqu' O **SA** 84 Hm 31
Maisan ⊙ **I** 83 Jb 30
Maiurno O **SU** 21 Hj 39

al-Majardal O **SA** 86 Hn 36
al-Majma'a O **SA** 85 Ja 33
Majz O **Y** 86 Hp 37
Makha'il O **SA** 86 Hn 36
Makhfar al-Busayya O **I** 83
Makhfar al-Hammam ⌇ **SY** 82 Hm 28
Makhmur O **I** 83 Hp 28
Makinat Shihan O **O** 88 Je 37
al-Makmin O **I** 82 Hp 30
Maks al-Qibli O **E** 14 Hh 33
Makthar O **T** 12 Gl 28
Mâl O **MA** 16 Fp 37
al-Malah O **A** 11 Gf 28
Malakal O **SU** 22 Hh 41
al-Malamm O **SU** 22 Hg 41
Maleit ⌇ **SU** 22 Hg 42
Malek O **SU** 22 Hh 42
Malha O **SU** 20 He 38
Mallawi O **E** 14 Hh 32
Mallawiya O **SU** 21 Hk 38
Malut O **SU** 22 Hj 40
al-Manadir ⌒ **UAE** 88 Jf 34
Manaha O **Y** 86 Hp 38
Manama ⊡ **B** 85 Jd 32
Manama O **UAE** 88 Jf 33
al-Manaqil O **SU** 21 Hj 38
Manas O **SO** 25 Hp 44
Manbij O **SY** 82 Hm 27
Mandali O **I** 83 Ja 29
Mandheera O **SO** 24 Ja 41
Manfalut O **E** 14 Hh 32
al-Mannsour O **A** 11 Gf 32
Mansoura O **A** 11 Gj 27
al-Mansura O **E** 15 Hh 30
al-Mansura O **E** 15 Hh 32
al-Mansuriya O **Y** 86 Hp 38
Maqrat O **Y** 87 Ja 38
al-Maqrun O **LI** 13 Hb 30
Maqteïr ⌒ **MA** 16 Ga 35
Marada O **LI** 13 Hb 31
Marakhayy O **Y** 87 Jc 38
al-Maramiya O **SA** 84 Hl 33
al-Marashi O **Y** 86 Ja 37
Marawah O **LI** 13 Hc 29
Marawi Merowe O **SU** 20 Hh 36
al-Marawi'a O **Y** 86 Hp 38
al-Mard O **I** 83 Hp 29
Mareeq O **SO** 25 Jb 44
Mareth O **T** 12 Gm 29
al-Marfa' O **UAE** 88 Je 33
Marhoum O **A** 11 Gf 28
Ma'rib O **Y** 86 Ja 38
Maridi O **SU** 22 Hg 43
Maridi ⌇ **SU** 22 Hg 43
al-Marj O **LI** 13 Hc 29
Marmul O **O** 88 Jf 36
Marquq O **SU** 22 Hh 41
Marrakech O **MO** 10 Gc 30
Marrat O **SA** 85 Ja 33
al-Marsa O **A** 11 Gj 27
Marsa 'Alam O **E** 15 Hk 33
Marsa al-Burayqa O **LI** 13 Hb 30
Marsa Matruh O **E** 14 Hf 30
Marsa Mubarak O **E** 15 Hk 33
Martil O **MO** 10 Gd 28
Martuba O **LI** 19 Hd 29
al-Maruqa O **LI** 12 Gn 32
Maryal Bai O **SU** 22 Hf 41
Marzuq O **LI** 12 Gn 33
Masabb Rashid ⌇ **E** 14 Hh 30
Masagaweyn O **SO** 25 Jb 44
al-Masaiqa O **O** 89 Jg 34
Ma'sal O **SA** 85 Ja 33
Mascara O **A** 11 Gf 28
Mashra' al-Raqq O **SU** 22 Hg 41
Masira ⌂ **O** 89 Jh 35
Masira Channel ⌇ **O** 89 Jh 35
Maskane O **SY** 82 Hm 27
al-Masna'a O **O** 89 Jg 34
al-Masqa O **SA** 86 Hp 37
Massarole O **SO** 25 Ja 44
Massif de Dahra ⌒⌒ **A** 11 Gg 27
Massif de l'Aurès ⌒⌒ **A** 11 Gj 28
Massif de l'Ouarsenis ⌒⌒ **A** 11 Gg 28
Mastura O **SA** 84 Hm 34
Masyaf O **SY** 82 Hl 28
al-Matama O **Y** 86 Ja 37
al-Matamma O **SU** 21 Hj 39
Ma'tan O **LI** 19 Hd 34
Ma'tan al-Sahra O **LI** 19 Hc 35
al-Matariya O **E** 14 Hh 30
Mateur O **T** 12 Gl 27
al-Matmarfaq O **MO** 16 Fp 32
Matmata O **T** 12 Gm 29
al-Matna O **SU** 21 Hk 39
Matrouha O **T** 12 Gk 29
Ma'tuq O **SU** 20 Hj 38

Maugris O **MA** 16 Fn 36
Mauqaq O **SA** 84 Hn 32
Mauritania ◘ **MA** 16 Ga 35
Mawat O **I** 83 Ja 28
Maxaas O **SO** 25 Ja 43
al-Maya O **A** 11 Gh 29
Maya O **SU** 21 Hj 39
al-Mayadin O **SY** 82 Hm 28
Maydh O **SO** 24 Jb 40
Mazoula O **A** 12 Gk 31
al-Mazraʾa O **J** 82 Hk 30
Mazrub O **SU** 20 Hg 39
M'Beni O **C** 25 Hp 51
Mbout O **MA** 16 Fp 37
Mcherrah ⌐ **A** 10 Gd 32
M'Chouneche O **A** 12 Gk 28
M'Doukal O **A** 11 Gj 28
Mecca O **SA** 86 Hm 35
Mecheria O **A** 11 Gf 29
Mechra Bel-Ksiri O **MO** 10 Gd 28
Mechroha O **A** 12 Gk 27
Medd Allah O **MA** 17 Gd 38
Médéa O **A** 11 Gh 27
Medenine O **T** 12 Gm 29
Méderdra O **MA** 16 Fn 37
Medi O **SU** 22 Hh 43
Medina O **SA** 84 Hm 35
Mediouna O **MO** 10 Gc 29
Medjedel O **A** 11 Gh 28
Medrissa O **A** 11 Gf 29
Meeladeen O **SO** 24 Jc 40
Megeitia O **SU** 20 Hh 38
al-Meghaier O **A** 12 Gj 29
Meguidene ⌐ **A** 11 Gg 31
Mehdia O **A** 11 Gg 28
Mekmene Ben Amar O **A** 11 Gf 29
Meknassy O **T** 12 Gl 28
Meknès O **MO** 10 Gd 29
Mellam O **SU** 20 He 39
Mellit O **SU** 20 He 38
Memphis ★ **E** 15 Hh 31
Menaa O **A** 11 Gj 28
Menawashei O **SU** 20 He 39
Menchia O **T** 12 Gl 29
Mendes O **A** 11 Gg 28
Mendiya-Plage O **MO** 10 Gc 28
Mendopolo O **SU** 22 Hh 43
al-Menzel O **MO** 10 Gd 29
Menzel Bourguiba O **T** 12 Gl 27
Menzel Chaker O **T** 12 Gm 28
Menzel Temime O **T** 12 Gm 27
Meredoua O **A** 11 Gg 33
Merekeen O **A** 12 Gl 31
Merga O **SU** 20 Hf 36
Meridja O **A** 11 Ge 30
Merka O **SO** 25 Ja 45
Meroe Royal City ★ **SU** 21 Hj 37
Merouana O **A** 11 Gj 28
Merowe O **SU** 20 Hh 36
Merrawwa ⌓ **UAE** 88 Je 33
Mertoutek O **A** 11 Gj 33
Meschetti O **SO** 25 Hn 45
Mesopotamia ⌐ **SY** 82 Hn 28
Messaad O **A** 11 Gh 28
Messeied O **MO** 10 Ga 32
Mètlaoui O **T** 12 Gl 28
Metlili Chaamba O **A** 11 Gh 29
al-Mhaïjrât O **MA** 16 Fm 36
Mhamid O **MO** 10 Gd 31
Midar O **MO** 10 Ge 28
Middle Atlas ⌂ **MO** 10 Gc 29
Midelt O **MO** 10 Gd 29
al-Midnab O **SA** 84 Hp 33
Migre O **SU** 21 Hk 38
al-Mihrad ⌐ **SA** 88 Je 35
Mijek O **MO** 16 Fp 34
Mila O **A** 12 Gk 27
Milhat O **I** 83 Hp 28
al-Milia O **A** 12 Gk 27
Miliana O **A** 11 Gh 27
Mimoun O **A** 11 Gf 28
Mina' ʿAbdallah O **K** 85 Jc 31
Mina' Saʿud O **K** 85 Jc 31
al-Mintirib O **O** 89 Jh 34
al-Minya O **E** 14 Hh 31
al-Miqdadiya O **I** 83 Ja 28
Mirbat O **O** 88 Jf 37
Mirhleft O **MO** 10 Ga 31
Miringoni O **C** 25 Hp 52
Mirsaale O **SO** 24 Jc 43
Mirsale O **SO** 24 Jb 43
Mishwara O **Y** 86 Ja 38
Miski O **SU** 20 He 38
Mismar O **SU** 21 Hk 36
Misrata O **LI** 12 Gp 29
Missour O **MO** 10 Ge 29
Misterei O **SU** 19 Hd 39
Mitatib O **SU** 21 Hk 38
Mit Ghamr O **E** 15 Hh 30

Mitsamiouli O **C** 25 Hp 51
Mizdah O **LI** 12 Gn 30
Mobdoua O **MA** 17 Gc 38
Mogadishu ◙ **SO** 25 Ja 45
Moghrar O **A** 11 Gf 29
Mohammadia O **A** 11 Gg 28
Mohammedia O **MO** 10 Gc 29
Moili ⌓ **C** 25 Hp 52
Moknine O **T** 12 Gm 28
Monastery of Saint Caterine ★ **E** 15 Hk 31
Monastir O **T** 12 Gm 28
Mongalla O **SU** 22 Hh 43
Mônguel O **MA** 16 Fp 37
Mont du Metal △ **A** 18 Gl 35
Monts de Daïa ⌂ **A** 11 Gf 28
Monts de Oulad Naïl ⌂ **A** 11 Gh 28
Monts des Ksour ⌂ **A** 11 Gf 29
Monts des Nementcha ⌂ **A** 12 Gk 28
Monts de Tlemcen ⌂ **A** 11 Gf 28
Monts du Mouydir ⌂ **A** 11 Gj 33
Monts du Zab ⌂ **A** 11 Gj 28
Monts Gautier ⌂ **A** 18 Gl 34
Morobo O **SU** 22 Hh 44
Morocco ◘ **MO** 10 Gc 29
Moroni ◙ **C** 25 Hp 51
Mortesoro O **SU** 23 Hj 40
Mortesoro O **SU** 23 Hk 40
Mosteghanem O **A** 11 Gf 28
Mosul O **I** 83 Hp 27
Moucha Islands ⌓ **D** 24 Hp 40
Moudjéria O **MA** 16 Fp 37
Moulares O **T** 12 Gl 28
Moulay Bouâzza O **MO** 10 Gc 29
Moulay Bousselhame O **MO** 10 Gc 28
Moulay Idriss O **MO** 10 Gd 29
Moulhoule O **D** 24 Hp 40
Mouloud O **MO** 24 Hp 40
Mount Sinai △ **E** 15 Hj 31
Mrara O **A** 11 Gj 29
al-Mreiti O **MA** 16 Gc 34
M'saken O **T** 12 Gm 28
Msak Mallat ⌂ **LI** 12 Gm 33
Msak Mustafit ⌐ **LI** 12 Gm 33
M'Sila O **A** 11 Gj 28
al-Mubarrez O **SA** 85 Jc 33
Mudaibi O **O** 89 Jh 34
al-Mudailif O **SA** 86 Hn 36
al-Mudairib O **O** 89 Jh 34
Mudaisis O **O** 88 Jf 34
Mudarraq O **SA** 84 Hp 32
Mudawwa O **J** 82 Hk 31
Muday O **O** 88 Je 37
Mugaira O **SA** 84 Hm 32
Mughsail O **O** 88 Je 37
al-Muglad O **SU** 22 Hf 40
Muhagiria O **SU** 20 He 40
Muhaiwir O **I** 82 Hn 29
Muhammadiya O **I** 83 Hp 29
al-Muhammadiyah O **MO** 10 Gc 29
Muhammed Qol O **SU** 21 Hl 35
al-Muharraq O **B** 85 Jd 32
al-Mukalla O **Y** 87 Jc 38
Mukawwaʾ ⌓ **SU** 21 Hl 35
al-Mukha O **Y** 86 Hp 39
al-Mulailih O **SA** 84 Hm 33
Mundri O **SU** 22 Hh 43
al-Munqatiʿ O **Y** 86 Ja 38
Muqakoori O **SO** 25 Ja 43
Muqshin O **O** 88 Jf 36
Murizidié Pass ⌂ **LI** 12 Gp 34
Musaimïr O **Y** 86 Ja 39
al-Musalla O **O** 89 Jg 34
al-Musallamiya O **SU** 21 Hj 38
Musallim O **O** 89 Jg 35
al-Musayyib O **I** 83 Hp 29
al-Musharifa O **SY** 82 Hm 27
Mushayfat O **SU** 20 Hh 40
Mut O **E** 14 Hg 33
al-Mutanna O **I** 83 Ja 30
al-Mutiʾa O **E** 14 Hh 32
Mutsamudu O **C** 25 Ja 52
al-Muwailih O **SA** 84 Hk 32
Muwassam O **SA** 86 Hp 37
Muwassam O **Y** 86 Hp 37
al-Muzahimiya O **SA** 85 Jb 33
Mvolo O **SU** 22 Hg 42

N

Naʿam O **SU** 22 Hg 41

Naʿam ⌐ **SU** 22 Hg 43
Naama O **A** 11 Gf 29
Naʿama O **E** 15 Hk 32
al-Naʾan O **SA** 85 Jb 34
Nabadeed O **SO** 24 Hp 41
Nabalat O **SU** 20 Hh 38
Nabatiya t-Takhta O **LE** 82 Hk 29
Nabeul O **T** 12 Gm 27
Nabga O **UAE** 88 Jf 33
al-Nabhaniya O **SA** 84 Hp 33
al-Nabk O **SY** 82 Hl 28
al-Nabk O **SA** 84 Hm 30
Nablus O **P** 82 Hk 29
Nabq O **E** 15 Hk 31
Nador O **MO** 16 Ge 28
al-Nafud ⌐ **SA** 84 Hm 31
Nafud al-Dahi ⌐ **SA** 86 Ja 35
Nafud al-Sirr ⌐ **SA** 85 Ja 33
Nafud al-ʿUraik ⌐ **SA** 84 Hp 33
Nagichot O **SU** 23 Hj 43
al-Nahl O **E** 15 Hj 31
Nahr Baru ⌐ **SU** 23 Hj 41
Nahr al-Qash ⌐ **SU** 21 Hl 38
Nahr al-Zab ⌐ **I** 83 Hp 27
Nahr al-Zabas ⌐ **I** 83 Hp 28
al-Nahud O **SU** 20 Hg 39
al-Naʾi O **SA** 84 Hp 32
Naʿid Abar O **SA** 86 Hp 37
Naʾif al-Ajil O **I** 83 Ja 30
Naima O **SU** 20 Hj 38
al-Najaf O **I** 83 Hp 30
Najd O **SA** 84 Hp 33
Naj ʿHammadi O **E** 14 Hh 33
Najran O **SA** 86 Ja 37
Nalut O **LI** 12 Gm 30
Nangolet O **SU** 23 Hj 43
Naqada O **E** 15 Hj 33
Naqil al-Farda ⌐ **Y** 86 Ja 38
Nasir O **SU** 23 Hj 41
al-Nasiriya O **I** 83 Jb 30
Nasmah O **LI** 12 Gn 30
Natih O **O** 89 Jg 34
Nbâk O **MA** 16 Fn 37
Nbeiket al-Ahouâch O **MA** 17 Gd 37
Ndzouani ⌓ **C** 25 Ja 52
Nebelat al-Hagana O **SU** 20 Hg 39
Neffatia O **T** 12 Gm 29
Nefta O **T** 12 Gk 29
Nefza O **T** 12 Gl 27
Negrine O **A** 12 Gk 28
Nekob O **MO** 10 Gd 30
Néma O **MA** 17 Gc 37
New Halfa O **SU** 21 Hk 38
Ngangala O **SU** 22 Hh 43
Ngazidja ⌓ **C** 25 Hp 51
Ngoussa O **A** 11 Gj 29
Niaro O **SU** 22 Hh 40
Niemelane O **MA** 16 Fp 36
Nile ⌐ **E** 14 Hh 31
Nimjat O **MA** 16 Fn 37
Nimrud ★ **I** 83 Hp 27
Nimule O **SU** 22 Hj 44
Nimule National Park ♀ **SU** 22 Hj 44
Ninawi ⊙ **I** 82 Hn 28
Niniwe ⌐ **I** 83 Hp 27
Nioût O **MA** 17 Gc 37
Nisab O **SA** 83 Ja 31
Nisab O **Y** 86 Jb 38
Nishtun O **Y** 87 Je 38
Nizwa O **O** 89 Jg 34
Nizzana O **E** 15 Hk 30
Nooleeye O **SO** 25 Jb 43
Nouâdhibou O **MA** 16 Fm 35
Nouakchott ◙ **MA** 16 Fm 36
Nouâmghâr O **MA** 16 Fm 36
Ntatrat O **MA** 16 Fn 37
Nterguent O **MA** 16 Fp 36
al-Nuʾairiya O **SA** 85 Jc 32
Nuba O **SU** 20 Hh 36
Nuba Mountains ⌂ **SU** 20 Hh 39
Nubian Desert ⌂ **SU** 20 Hh 35
Nuhaida O **O** 89 Jg 34
Nukhaib O **I** 82 Hn 29
Nukhayla Merga O **SU** 20 Hf 36
al-Nuʿman ⌐ **SA** 84 Hk 32
al-Nuʾmaniya O **I** 83 Ja 29
Numatinna ⌐ **SU** 22 Hf 42
Nuqab O **Y** 86 Ja 38
al-Nuqra O **SA** 84 Hn 33
Nurei O **SU** 19 Hd 38
Nuri ★ **SU** 20 Hh 36
Nuwaibiʾ al-Muzayyina O **E** 15 Hk 31
al-Nuwaisib O **K** 85 Jc 31
Nyala O **SU** 20 He 39
Nyamlell O **SU** 22 Hf 41

Nyiel O **SU** 22 Hh 42
Nzara O **SU** 22 Hg 43

O

al-Obeid O **SU** 20 Hg 39
Obock O **D** 24 Hp 40
Odrus ⌐ **SU** 21 Hl 36
al-Ogla O **A** 12 Gk 29
al-Ogla Gasses O **A** 12 Gk 28
Oglat Beraber O **A** 10 Ge 30
Oglat al-Faci O **A** 10 Gd 32
Oglat al-Faci O **A** 12 Gl 31
Oglat Marhboura O **A** 11 Gf 29
Ohanet O **A** 12 Gl 31
Old Dongola ★ **SU** 20 Hh 36
Oman ◘ **O** 88 Jf 36
Omdurman O **SU** 20 Hh 38
Oodweyne O **SO** 24 Ja 41
Opari O **SU** 22 Hj 44
Oran O **A** 11 Gf 28
Ouadâne O **MA** 16 Ga 35
Ouad Nâga O **MA** 16 Fn 36
Ouadou ⌐ **MA** 16 Ga 38
Oualâta O **MA** 17 Gc 37
Ouallen O **A** 11 Gg 33
Ouârâne ⌂ **MA** 16 Ga 35
Ouargla O **A** 11 Gj 30
Ouarzazate O **MO** 10 Gc 30
al-Ouatia O **MO** 10 Ga 31
Ouèʾa O **D** 24 Hp 40
al-Oued O **A** 12 Gk 29
Oued al-Abiod O **MA** 16 Fp 37
Oued Aguemour ⌐ **A** 11 Gj 32
Oued Amadror ⌐ **A** 12 Gk 33
Oued al-Arab ⌐ **A** 12 Gk 28
Oued Assaq ⌐ **MO** 16 Fn 33
Oued al-Asyuti ⌐ **E** 14 Hh 32
Oued al-Attar ⌐ **A** 11 Gj 29
Oued Barika ⌐ **A** 11 Gj 28
Oued Besbes ⌐ **A** 11 Gj 28
Oued Bou Ali ⌐ **A** 11 Gh 30
Oued Chebaba ⌐ **A** 11 Gh 31
Oued Chlef ⌐ **A** 11 Gg 27
Oued Daoura ⌐ **A** 10 Gd 30
Oued Djedi ⌐ **A** 11 Gh 28
Oued Dra ⌐ **MO** 10 Gb 31
Oued Drâa ⌐ **MO** 10 Gc 30
Oued al-Fahl ⌐ **A** 11 Gj 30
Oued Fessi ⌐ **T** 12 Gm 29
Oued Garfa ⌐ **MA** 16 Fp 38
Oued al-Gharbi ⌐ **A** 11 Gg 29
Oued Grou ⌐ **MO** 10 Gc 29
Oued Guélaour ⌐ **MA** 16 Fp 37
Oued Guir ⌐ **A** 11 Ge 30
Oued al-Hadjadj ⌐ **A** 11 Gj 31
Oued al-Hallaïl ⌐ **A** 12 Gk 28
Oued al-Ham ⌐ **A** 11 Gh 28
Oued al-Hamra ⌐ **MA** 16 Gb 32
Oued Ilafergh ⌐ **A** 17 Gg 35
Oued in Sokki ⌐ **A** 11 Gh 31
Oued Irharhar ⌐ **A** 11 Gj 32
Oued Isly ⌐ **MO** 11 Gf 28
Oued Ittel ⌐ **A** 11 Gj 28
Oued Jenein ⌐ **T** 12 Gl 30
Oued al-Kebir ⌐ **T** 12 Gl 28
Oued Khârroûb ⌐ **MA** 16 Gb 34
Oued al-Khatt ⌐ **MO** 16 Fp 33
Oued al-Korima ⌐ **A** 11 Gf 29
Oued Laouni ⌐ **A** 18 Gj 35
Oued al-Ma ⌐ **MA** 16 Gb 33
Oued Massine ⌐ **A** 11 Gh 32
Oued Mehaiguene ⌐ **A** 11 Gh 29
Oued Meirir ⌐ **A** 11 Gf 28
Oued Mejerda ⌐ **T** 12 Gl 27
Oued al-Mela ⌐ **A** 11 Gj 31
Oued Mellal ⌐ **MO** 10 Gc 29
Oued Mellegue ⌐ **A** 12 Gl 27
Oued Melloulou ⌐ **MO** 10 Ge 29
Oued Meskiana ⌐ **A** 12 Gk 28
Oued Messaoud ⌐ **A** 11 Gf 31
Oued Metlili ⌐ **A** 11 Gh 29
Oued Mial ⌐ **A** 11 Gh 31
Oued Mina ⌐ **A** 11 Gg 28
Oued Moulouya ⌐ **MO** 10 Ge 29
Oued Mya ⌐ **A** 11 Gj 30
Oued Namous ⌐ **A** 11 Gh 28
Oued al-Nsa ⌐ **A** 11 Gh 29
Oued Ouerrha ⌐ **MO** 10 Gd 28
Oued Oumer-Rbia ⌐ **MO** 10 Gb 29
Oued Ouret ⌐ **A** 12 Gl 33
Oued Retem ⌐ **A** 11 Gj 29
Oued Rhiou O **A** 11 Gg 28

Oued Rhir ⌐ **A** 11 Gk 29
Oued Rhumel ⌐ **A** 12 Gk 27
Oued Saoura ⌐ **A** 11 Gf 31
Oued Sebou ⌐ **MO** 10 Gc 28
Oued Sefioum ⌐ **A** 11 Gf 28
Oued al-Seggeur ⌐ **A** 11 Gg 29
Oued Sidi Hasseur ⌐ **A** 11 Gg 28
Oued Siliana ⌐ **T** 12 Gl 27
Oued Soummam ⌐ **A** 11 Gj 27
Oued Sud ⌐ **MO** 10 Gb 30
Oued Tadant ⌐ **A** 18 Gk 34
Oued Tadjataret ⌐ **A** 18 Gk 34
Oued Tafassasset ⌐ **A** 18 Gl 34
Oued Tagrina ⌐ **A** 18 Gk 35
Oued Takalo ⌐ **A** 18 Gk 34
Oued Takisset ⌐ **A** 12 Gm 33
Oued Tamanrasset ⌐ **A** 17 Gg 34
Oued Tarfa ⌐ **E** 15 Hh 31
Oued Tari ⌐ **A** 11 Gh 33
Oued Tekhammat ⌐ **A** 12 Gl 32
Oued Tekouiat ⌐ **A** 18 Gh 34
Oued Tenuchchad ⌐ **MO** 10 Gb 32
Oued Tichkatine ⌐ **A** 18 Gj 35
Oued Tigzerte ⌐ **MO** 10 Gb 31
Oued Tilia ⌐ **A** 11 Gg 32
Oued Timeldjame ⌐ **A** 11 Gh 31
Oued Timissit ⌐ **A** 12 Gl 33
Oued Tin Amzi ⌐ **A** 18 Gj 35
Oued Tin Hadjène ⌐ **A** 12 Gk 33
Oued Tin Tarabine ⌐ **A** 18 Gk 35
Oued Tirahart ⌐ **A** 17 Gh 34
Oued Tirhemar ⌐ **A** 12 Gk 32
Oued Tirine ⌐ **A** 18 Gk 34
Oued Tisnale ⌐ **A** 11 Gj 31
Oued Tlelat O **A** 11 Gf 28
Oued Torset ⌐ **A** 12 Gl 33
Oued Touil ⌐ **A** 11 Gh 28
Oued Tournde ⌐ **A** 18 Gm 34
Oued Zazir ⌐ **A** 18 Gj 35
Oued Zegrir ⌐ **A** 11 Gh 29
Oued-Zem O **MO** 10 Gc 29
Oued Zenati O **A** 12 Gk 27
Oued Zeroud ⌐ **T** 12 Gl 28
Oued Ziz ⌐ **MO** 10 Gd 30
Oued Zmertène ⌐ **T** 12 Gl 29
Oued Zousfana ⌐ **A** 11 Gf 30
Ouenza O **A** 12 Gl 28
Ouezzane O **MO** 10 Gd 28
Oufrane O **A** 11 Gg 31
Oujâf O **MA** 16 Gc 37
Oujda O **MO** 11 Ge 28
Oujeft O **MA** 16 Fp 35
Oukaimeden O **MO** 10 Gc 30
Oukré O **MA** 16 Ga 37
Oulad-Teïma O **MO** 10 Gb 30
Ouled Allenda O **A** 11 Gk 29
Ouled Djellal O **A** 11 Gj 28
Oulmes O **MO** 10 Gc 29
Oum al-Achar O **A** 10 Gb 31
Oumache O **A** 11 Gj 28
Oum al-Bouaghi O **A** 12 Gk 27
Oumcheggag O **MO** 16 Fp 32
Oum Djerane O **A** 11 Gg 28
Oumm al-Khezz O **MA** 16 Ga 37
Ounara O **MO** 10 Gb 30
Ourlal O **A** 11 Gj 28
Outat-Oulad-al-Haj O **MO** 10 Ge 29
Outoul O **A** 18 Gj 34

P

Pachala O **SU** 23 Hk 42
Palestine ◘ **P** 82 Hk 29
Palmyra O **SY** 82 Hm 28
Paloich O **SU** 22 Hj 40
Paqiu O **SU** 22 Hh 42
Parc National de Cédres ♀ **A** 11 Gg 28
Parc National de l'Ichkeul ♀ **T** 12 Gl 27
Parc National des Oiseaux du Djoudi ♀ **MA** 16 Fm 37
Parc National du Banc d'Arguin ♀ **MA** 16 Fm 35
Passe d'Amogjâr △ **MA** 16 Fp 35
Passe de Djoûk △ **MA** 16 Fp 37
Passe de Soufa △ **MA** 16 Ga 38

Peili ○ **SU** 22 Hf 42
Perim ⛬ **Y** 86 Hp 39
Petite Kabylie ▭ **A** 11 Gj 27
Petra ★ **J** 82 Hk 30
Philae ★ **E** 15 Hj 34
Pibor ∼ **SU** 23 Hj 42
Pibor Post ○ **SU** 23 Hj 42
Pic Tiska △ **A** 18 Gl 34
Plateau du Fadnoun ⛰ **A** 12 Gk 32
Plateau du Rekkam ⛰ **MO** 11 Ge 29
Pongo ∼ **SU** 22 Hf 41
Port Safaga ○ **E** 15 Hj 32
Port Said ○ **E** 15 Hj 30
Port Sudan ○ **SU** 21 Hl 36
Port Tewfik ○ **E** 15 Hj 31
Puig ○ **SU** 22 Hg 41
Pyramids of Abu Sir ★ **E** 14 Hh 31
Pyramids of Dahshur ★ **E** 14 Hh 31
Pyramids of Giza ★ **E** 14 Hh 31
Pyramids of Saqqara ★ **E** 14 Hh 31

Q

al-Qa'amiyat ▭ **KSA/YE** 87 Jc 37
Qadam ○ **SU** 22 Hg 40
al-Qadisiya ⊙ **I** 83 Ja 30
Qadub ○ **Y** 87 Je 39
Qafa ○ **O** 88 Je 37
al-Qaffay ⛬ **UAE** 88 Jd 33
al-Qahmah ○ **SA** 86 Hn 36
al-Qa'iya ○ **SA** 84 Hp 33
al-Qala'a ○ **LI** 12 Gp 30
Qala'an-Nahl ○ **SU** 21 Hk 39
Qalansiya ○ **Y** 87 Je 39
Qal'at Hamidi ○ **I** 83 Hp 29
Qal'at al-Mu'azzam ○ **SA** 84 Hl 32
Qal'at Salih ○ **I** 83 Jb 30
Qal at Sukkar ○ **I** 83 Jb 30
Qal'e Dize ○ **I** 83 Ja 27
Qalhat ○ **O** 89 Jh 34
al-Qaliba ○ **SA** 84 Hl 31
Qalti al-Adusa ○ **SU** 20 Hf 37
Qalti Immaseri ○ **SU** 20 He 38
Qalti al-Khudeira ○ **SU** 20 Hf 37
Qalyub ○ **E** 14 Hh 30
Qaminis ○ **LI** 13 Hb 30
Qana ○ **SA** 84 Hn 32
Qandala ○ **SO** 24 Jc 40
al-Qantara ○ **E** 15 Hj 30
Qara ○ **E** 14 Hf 31
Qara ○ **SA** 84 Hn 31
Qara Dag ⛰ **I** 83 Ja 28
Qarah Dag ⛰ **I** 83 Hp 27
Qararat al-Hayyirah ∼ **LI** 12 Gp 32
Qararat al-Kalb ∼ **LI** 12 Gp 32
Qarat as Sab'a △ **LI** 13 Ha 32
Qarat al-Harah ⛰ **LI** 12 Gp 32
Qarat Khalaf Allah △ **LI** 13 Ha 32
al-Qardaba ○ **LI** 19 Hd 29
Qardho ○ **SO** 24 Jc 41
al-Qarya al-Sharqiya ○ **LI** 12 Gn 30
Qaryat Abu Nujaym ○ **LI** 12 Gp 30
al-Qaryatain ○ **SY** 82 Hl 28
Qaryat al-Fa'idiya ○ **LI** 13 Hc 29
Qaryat Shumaykh ○ **LI** 12 Gn 30
Qaryat al-'Ulya ○ **SA** 85 Jb 32
al-Qasabat ○ **LI** 12 Gp 29
Qasar bu Hadi ○ **LI** 13 Ha 30
Qasir al-Kharrubah ○ **LI** 13 Hc 29
Qasr Ahmad ○ **LI** 12 Gp 29
Qasr 'Amiq ○ **I** 82 Hn 29
Qasr al-Farafra ○ **E** 14 Hf 32
Qasr al-Jady ○ **LI** 13 He 30
Qasr Khulayf ○ **LI** 12 Gn 32
Qasr Larocu ○ **O** 88 Je 37
Qasr al-Qarn ○ **LI** 13 He 30
Qasr al-Shaqqa ○ **LI** 13 He 30
Qa'taba ○ **Y** 86 Ja 39
Qatana ○ **SY** 82 Hl 29
Qatar □ **Q** 85 Jd 33
al-Qatif ○ **SA** 85 Jc 32
al-Qatn ○ **Y** 87 Jc 38
al-Qatrana ○ **J** 82 Hl 30
al-Qatrum ○ **LI** 12 Gp 33
Qattara Depression ▭ **E** 14 Hf 31
Qawam al-Hamza ○ **I** 83 Ja 30
al-Qawz ○ **SU** 21 Hj 37
Qawz Ragab ○ **SU** 21 Hk 37
Qaysan ○ **SU** 23 Hk 40
Qerri ○ **SU** 20 Hj 37
al-Qibliya △ **E** 15 Hj 31
Qift ○ **E** 15 Hj 33
Qilwa ○ **SA** 86 Hn 36
Qina ○ **E** 15 Hj 32
Qiryat Shemona ○ **LE** 82 Hk 29
al-Qishla ○ **I** 85 Jc 31
Qishn ○ **Y** 87 Jd 38
Qooriga Neegro ∼ **SO** 24 Jc 42
Qoryooley ○ **SO** 25 Ja 45
al-Qrtawiya ○ **SA** 85 Ja 32
Quadi Qadisha ★ **LE** 82 Hl 28
al-Quaiti ▭ **Y** 87 Jc 38
al-Qualayd Bahri ○ **SU** 20 Hh 36
al-Qualidia ○ **MO** 10 Gb 29
Quasair 'Amra ★ **J** 82 Hl 30
Quayvara ○ **I** 83 Hp 28
al-Qubba ○ **LI** 19 Hd 29
Qudaih ○ **SA** 85 Jc 32
Qued M'Zab ∼ **A** 11 Gj 29
al-Qunaitira ○ **SY** 82 Hk 29
al-Qunfuda ○ **SA** 86 Hn 36
Qurayd ○ **SU** 22 Hh 40
al-Qurayyat ○ **SA** 84 Hl 30
Qurayyat ○ **O** 89 Jh 34
Qurdud ○ **SU** 22 Hg 40
Qureida ○ **SU** 20 He 40
al-Qurna ○ **I** 83 Jb 30
Qurnat al-Sauda' △ **LE** 82 Hk 28
Qus ○ **E** 15 Hj 33
Qusaiba ○ **I** 82 Hn 28
al-Qusair ○ **SY** 82 Hl 28
al-Qusair ○ **I** 83 Ja 30
Qusayr ○ **E** 15 Hk 32
al-Qus Taima ○ **E** 15 Hk 30
al-Qutaifa ○ **SY** 82 Hl 29
al-Qutayna ○ **SU** 20 Hj 38
Qutuf ○ **UAE** 88 Je 34
al-Quwair ○ **I** 83 Hp 27
al-Quwaisi ○ **SU** 21 Hk 39
al-Quwara ○ **SA** 84 Hp 32
al-Quz ○ **SA** 86 Hn 36
al-Quza ○ **Y** 87 Jc 38

R

Raas Binna ⌓ **SO** 24 Jd 40
Raas Caluula ⌓ **SO** 24 Jd 40
Raas Gabbac ⌓ **SO** 24 Jd 41
Raas Khansir ⌓ **SO** 24 Ja 40
Raas Macbar ⌓ **SO** 24 Jd 41
Raas Xaafuun ⌓ **SO** 24 Jd 40
Rabaa ○ **A** 12 Gl 30
Rabaable ○ **SO** 24 Jc 41
Rabak ○ **SU** 20 Hj 39
Rabat ▣ **MO** 10 Gc 29
Rabig ○ **SA** 84 Hm 34
Rabyana ○ **LI** 19 Hd 33
Rachid ○ **MA** 16 Ga 36
al-Rachidia ○ **MO** 10 Gd 30
Rada' ○ **Y** 86 Ja 38
al-Radisiya Bahri ○ **E** 15 Hj 33
Radom ○ **SU** 22 He 41
Rafah ○ **E** 15 Hj 30
al-Rafid ○ **SY** 82 Hk 29
Rafkha' ○ **SA** 84 Hp 31
Rafsai ○ **MO** 10 Gd 28
Raga ○ **SU** 22 He 41
Raghwan ○ **SA** 86 Hm 35
al-Rahad ○ **SU** 20 Hh 39
al-Rahad ∼ **SU** 20 Hj 38
Rahad al-Bardi ○ **SU** 22 Hd 40
al-Rahhaliya ○ **I** 83 Hp 29
Rahib ○ **SU** 20 Hf 37
al-Rahibat ○ **LI** 12 Gm 30
al-Rahida ○ **Y** 86 Ja 39
Rahouia ○ **A** 11 Gg 28
Raida ○ **Y** 86 Hp 38
al-Rain ○ **SA** 86 Ja 34
Ra'is ○ **SA** 84 Hm 34
Raisut ○ **O** 88 Je 37
Rako ○ **SO** 24 Jc 41
al-Ramadi ○ **I** 83 Hp 29
Ramallah ▣ **P** 82 Hk 30
Raml ○ **I** 83 Ja 28
Ramlat al-Jafa ▭ **SA** 88 Jf 35
Ramlat al-Sab'atayn ▭ **Y** 86 Ja 38
Ramlat al-Wahiba ▭ **O** 89 Jh 34
Ramlat Zallaf ▭ **LI** 12 Gn 32
Rams ○ **UAE** 88 Jf 33
al-Ramta ○ **J** 82 Hk 29
Randa ○ **D** 24 Hp 40
Randale ∼ **D** 24 Hp 39
Rangnom ○ **SU** 22 Hh 41
Raniya ○ **I** 83 Ja 27
al-Rank ○ **SU** 20 Hj 40
Ranya ar-Rawdah ○ **SA** 86 Hp 35
Raqdalin ○ **LI** 12 Gm 29
al-Raqqa ○ **SY** 82 Hm 28
al-Raquba ○ **LI** 13 Hb 31
Ra's Abu Dara ⌓ **E** 15 Hl 34
Ra's Abu Madd ⌓ **SA** 84 Hl 33
Ra's Abu Rasas ⌓ **O** 89 Jh 35
Ra's Abu Shajara ⌓ **SU** 21 Hl 35
Ra's al-Abyad ⌓ **SA** 84 Hm 34
Ra's 'Asis ⌓ **SU** 21 Hm 36
al-Rasatin △ **J** 82 Hm 29
Ra's Banas ⌓ **E** 15 Hk 34
Ra's Baridi ⌓ **SA** 84 Hl 33
Ra's al-Barr ○ **E** 15 Hh 30
Ra's al-Bayad ⌓ **Y** 86 Hp 38
Ra's Bir ⌓ **D** 24 Hp 40
Ra's Fartak ⌓ **Y** 87 Je 38
Ra's Gharib ○ **E** 15 Hj 31
Rashad ○ **SU** 20 Hh 40
Ra's Hatiba ⌓ **SA** 84 Hm 34
Rashid Rosetta ○ **E** 14 Hh 30
Rashidiya ○ **SY** 82 Hn 27
Ra's al-Hilal ○ **LI** 19 Hd 29
Rashsha ○ **Y** 86 Jb 38
Ra's al-Kabsh ⌓ **O** 89 Jh 35
Ra's al-Kalb ⌓ **Y** 87 Jc 39
Ra's Karaba ⌓ **SA** 84 Hl 33
Ra's Kasr ⌓ **SU** 21 Hm 36
Ra's al-Khafji ○ **SA** 85 Jc 31
Ras al-Khaimah ○ **UAE** 88 Jf 33
Ras Lanuf ○ **LI** 13 Hb 30
Ras al-Ma ○ **A** 11 Gf 28
Ra's Madraka ⌓ **O** 89 Jg 36
Ra's Mami ⌓ **Y** 87 Jf 39
Ra's Muhammad ⌓ **E** 15 Hk 32
Ra's Muhammad National Park ⚲ **E** 15 Hk 32
Ra's Musadam ⌓ **O** 89 Jg 32
Ra's Mushairib ⌓ **UAE** 88 Jd 33
Ra's al-Naqb ○ **J** 82 Hk 30
Râs Nouâdhibou ⌓ **MA** 16 Fm 35
Ra's Rakan ○ **Q** 85 Jd 32
al-Rass ○ **SA** 84 Hp 33
Rass Ajdir ○ **T** 12 Gm 29
Ra's Sajir ⌓ **O** 88 Je 37
Ra's Sharbitat ⌓ **O** 89 Jg 37
Ra's Sharwain ⌓ **Y** 87 Jd 38
Ra's Shu'b ⌓ **Y** 87 Je 39
Râs Tafarît ⌓ **MA** 16 Fm 35
al-Rastan ○ **SY** 82 Hl 28
Ra's Tannura ○ **SA** 88 Jd 32
Ra's al-Tarfa ⌓ **SA** 86 Hp 37
Râs Timirist ⌓ **MA** 16 Fm 36
Ra's Warfalla ▭ **LI** 12 Gp 31
al-Rauda ○ **E** 14 Hh 32
al-Rauda ○ **SA** 85 Ja 33
al-Rauda ○ **Y** 86 Jb 38
al-Raudatain ○ **K** 85 Jb 31
Raudat Habbas ○ **SA** 84 Hp 31
Rawa ○ **I** 82 Hn 28
Rawanduz ○ **I** 83 Ja 27
al-Rawda ○ **SA** 86 Hp 35
Rayat ○ **I** 83 Ja 27
al-Rayyan ○ **Q** 85 Jd 33
Rebiana Sand Sea ▭ **LI** 13 Hb 33
Redeyef ○ **T** 12 Gk 28
Red Sea ≈ 86 Hm 35
Regaïa ○ **MO** 10 Gd 28
Reggane ○ **A** 11 Gf 32
Reggou ○ **MO** 10 Ge 29
Rejaf ○ **SU** 22 Hh 43
Remada ○ **T** 12 Gm 29
al-Remla ○ **T** 12 Gm 28
Rhemiles ○ **A** 10 Gd 31
Rhourd al-Baguel ○ **A** 12 Gk 30
al-Ribat ○ **SY** 82 Hn 28
Rich ○ **MO** 10 Gd 29
Rif ⛰ **MO** 10 Gd 28
al-Rifa'i ○ **I** 83 Jb 30
Rijal Alma ○ **SA** 86 Hp 36
Riyadh ▣ **SA** 85 Jb 33
Rkîz ○ **MA** 16 Fn 37
Rmel-al-Abiod ▭ **T** 12 Gl 30
Rokom ○ **SU** 22 Hh 43
Rommani ○ **MO** 10 Gc 29
Rosetta ○ **E** 14 Hh 30
Rosso ○ **MA** 16 Fn 37
Rouhia ○ **T** 12 Gl 28
Royal City ★ **SU** 21 Hj 37
al-Ru'at ○ **SU** 20 Hh 39
al-Rubai'iyah ○ **SA** 84 Ja 32
al-Rub' al-Khali ▭ **SA** 86 Ja 37
Rudhane ye Cangule ∼ **I** 83 Jb 29
Rufa'a ○ **SU** 21 Hj 38
Rugheiwa ○ **SU** 20 Hh 37
Rumah ○ **SA** 85 Jb 33
Rumaila ○ **I** 83 Jb 30
Rumbek ○ **SU** 22 Hg 42
Rumeila ○ **SU** 21 Hk 39
Rummana ○ **E** 15 Hj 30
al-Ruqai ○ **SA** 85 Jb 31
Ruqayba ○ **SU** 20 Hh 38
al-Rusafa ○ **SY** 82 Hm 28
al-Rusayfa ○ **J** 82 Hl 30
al-Rusayris ○ **SU** 21 Hk 40
Rusayris Dam ∼ **SU** 21 Hk 40
al-Rustaq ○ **O** 89 Jg 34
al-Rutaimi ∼ **SY** 82 Hm 28
al-Rutba ○ **I** 82 Hn 29
Ru'us al-Jibal ⛰ **O** 88 Jg 32
al-Ruwaida ○ **SA** 85 Ja 33
al-Ruways ○ **Q** 85 Jd 32
Ruweis ○ **UAE** 88 Je 33
Ruwi ○ **O** 89 Jh 34

S

Saakow ○ **SO** 25 Hp 45
Sab 'Abar ○ **SY** 82 Hl 29
al-Sabaya ⛬ **SA** 86 Hn 36
Sabha ○ **LI** 12 Gp 32
Sabhat al-Muh ∼ **SY** 82 Hm 28
Sabkhat Ghuzayyil ∼ **LI** 13 Hb 31
Sabkhat al-Haysha ∼ **LI** 12 Gp 30
Sabkhat Matti ∼ **UAE** 88 Je 34
Sabkhat Mujazzam ∼ **LI** 12 Gl 30
Sabkhat Shunayn ∼ **LI** 13 Hc 30
Sabkhat Umm al-'Izam ∼ **LI** 12 Gp 30
Sabrata ★ **LI** 12 Gn 29
Sabt al-'Ulya ○ **SA** 86 Hn 36
Sabya ○ **SA** 86 Hn 36
Sabya ○ **SA** 86 Hp 37
Sa'da ○ **Y** 86 Hp 37
Sadam ○ **O** 89 Jg 34
al-Sadara ○ **Y** 87 Jc 38
al-Sadawi ○ **SA** 85 Jb 31
Sadd al-Ali High Dam ★ **E** 15 Hj 34
Sadh ○ **O** 88 Jf 37
Sadiyyat ⛬ **UAE** 88 Jf 33
Sadwan ⛬ **E** 15 Hk 32
Safaga ⛬ **E** 15 Hk 32
Safaha ○ **SU** 22 Hf 41
Safaja ⛰ **SA** 84 Hm 32
al-Saff ○ **E** 15 Hh 31
Safi ○ **MO** 10 Gb 29
Safi ○ **J** 82 Hk 30
Safita ○ **SY** 82 Hl 28
Safra' ○ **I** 82 Hn 28
Sâgallou ○ **D** 24 Hp 40
Sagne ○ **MA** 16 Fp 38
Saguia al-Hamra ∼ **MO** 10 Ga 32
Saguia al-Hamra ∼ **MO** 16 Fp 32
Sah ○ **UAE** 88 Je 34
Sahaba ○ **SU** 20 Hh 36
Saharan Atlas ⛰ **A** 11 Gf 29
al-Sahba ○ **SA** 85 Jb 33
Saheib ○ **SU** 20 He 40
Sahm ○ **O** 89 Jg 33
Sahra Marzuq ▭ **LI** 12 Gn 33
Sahra' Surt ▭ **LI** 13 Ha 30
Sahra al-Tih ▭ **E** 15 Hj 30
Saïda ○ **A** 11 Gg 28
Saidia ○ **MO** 11 Ge 28
Saihut ○ **Y** 87 Jd 38
al-Sail al-Kabir ○ **SA** 86 Hn 35
Sai'un ○ **Y** 87 Jc 38
Sajd ⛬ **SA** 86 Hn 37
Sajir ○ **SA** 85 Ja 33
Saka ○ **MO** 10 Ge 28
Sakaka ○ **SA** 84 Hn 31
Sakiet Si Youssef ○ **T** 12 Gl 27
al-Salabikh ○ **UAE** 88 Jf 33
Salagle ○ **SO** 25 Hp 45
Salahleh ○ **SO** 24 Ja 41
Salakhaddin ⊙ **I** 83 Hp 28
Salala ○ **SU** 21 Hl 35
Salala ○ **O** 88 Jf 37
al-Salamiya ○ **SY** 82 Hl 28
al-Salamiya ○ **SA** 85 Jb 33
Salasil ○ **Y** 87 Jc 37
Salé ○ **MO** 10 Gc 28
Salée ○ **MA** 16 Gb 36
Sali ○ **A** 11 Gf 32
Salif al-Dahi ○ **Y** 86 Hp 38
Salima ○ **SU** 20 Hg 35
al-Salimiya ○ **K** 85 Jc 31
Salkhad ○ **SY** 82 Hl 29
Sallom ○ **SU** 21 Hl 36
al-Sallum ○ **E** 14 He 30
al-Salman ○ **I** 83 Ja 30
al-Salt ○ **J** 82 Hk 30
Salwa ○ **Q** 85 Jd 33
al-Salwa ○ **SA** 88 Jd 33
Salwa Bahri ○ **E** 15 Hj 33
Sama'il ○ **O** 89 Jh 34
Samalusi ○ **LI** 13 Hc 29
Samalut ○ **E** 14 Hh 31
Samarra' ○ **I** 83 Hp 28
al-Samawa ○ **I** 83 Ja 30
Samaysa Dheer ○ **SO** 24 Jc 40
Samha ⛬ **Y** 87 Je 39
al-Samha ○ **UAE** 88 Jf 33
Samira' ○ **SA** 84 Hn 32
Samita ○ **SA** 86 Hp 37
Samnu ○ **LI** 12 Gp 32
Samsam ○ **SU** 21 Hk 39
Sana ○ **Y** 87 Jc 37
Sanaa ▣ **Y** 86 Ja 38
Sanafir ⛬ **E** 15 Hk 32
al-Sanamain ○ **SY** 82 Hl 29
Sanaw ○ **Y** 87 Jd 37
Sangav ○ **I** 83 Ja 28
Sâni ○ **MA** 16 Ga 37
Sanyat al-Daffa ○ **LI** 13 He 30
Sapo ∼ **SU** 22 Hf 41
Saqadi ○ **SU** 21 Hj 39
Saqain ○ **Y** 86 Hp 37
Saqiya ○ **I** 83 Hp 28
Saqr ○ **Y** 87 Jd 38
Saqra' ○ **Y** 86 Ja 39
Sarafara ∼ **SU** 22 Hh 40
Saraqeb ○ **SY** 82 Hl 28
Sarar ○ **Y** 87 Jd 38
Sarif ○ **Y** 87 Jd 37
Sarinleey ○ **SO** 25 Hn 44
Sarir al-Qattusah ▭ **LI** 12 Gp 32
Sarir Tibesti ⛰ **LI** 13 Ha 33
Sarir Umm 'Illah ▭ **LI** 12 Gn 32
al-Sarrar ○ **SA** 85 Jc 32
al-Sauda' ⛬ **O** 88 Jf 37
Saudi Arabia □ **SA** 84 Hm 32
Sauquira ○ **O** 89 Jg 36
al-Sawadiya ○ **Y** 86 Ja 38
Sawari ○ **I** 82 Hp 28
Sawkanah ○ **LI** 12 Gp 31
Sawqira Bay ∼ **O** 89 Jg 36
Sayda Sidon ○ **LE** 82 Hk 29
Saylac ○ **SO** 24 Hp 40
Sbaa ○ **A** 11 Gf 31
Sbeitla ○ **T** 12 Gl 28
Sea of Oman ≈ **O** 89 Jh 33
Sebdou ○ **A** 11 Gf 28
Sebkha Ain Belbela ∼ **A** 10 Gd 32
Sebkha Azzel Matti ∼ **A** 17 Gg 33
Sebkha de Timimoun ∼ **A** 11 Gf 31
Sebkha de Tindouf ∼ **A** 10 Gc 32
Sebkha al-Kebira ∼ **A** 11 Gf 28
Sebkha Mekerrhane ∼ **A** 11 Gg 32
Sebkha Ndrhamcha ∼ **MA** 16 Fn 36
Sebkha Oumm Debua ∼ **MO** 10 Fp 32
Sebkha Tah ∼ **MO** 10 Fp 32
Sebkhet Afouidich ∼ **MO** 16 Fn 35
Sebkhet Aghzoumal ∼ **MO** 16 Fp 33
Sebkhet Audal ∼ **MO** 16 Fp 32
Sebkhet Chemchâm ∼ **MA** 16 Fp 35
Sebkhet En Noual ∼ **T** 12 Gl 28
Sebkhet Gallanmane ∼ **MA** 16 Gb 34
Sebkhet Iguetti ∼ **MA** 16 Gb 33
Sebkhet Oumm al-Drous Guebli ∼ **MA** 16 Ga 34
Sebkhet Oumm al-Drous Telli ∼ **MA** 16 Ga 33
Sebkhet Sidi al-Hani ∼ **T** 12 Gm 28
Sebkhet Tanouzkka ∼ **MO** 16 Fn 34
Sebkhet Tidsit ∼ **MO** 16 Fn 34
Sedrata ○ **A** 12 Gk 27
Sefrou ○ **MO** 10 Gd 29
Sejenane ○ **T** 12 Gl 27

Sélibabi O MA 16 Fp 38
Selouane O MO 11 Ge 28
al-Semara O MO 16 Fp 32
Semei O SU 20 Hh 39
Semna O SU 20 Hh 35
Sennar O SU 21 Hj 39
Sennar Dam ~ SU 21 Hj 39
Sept-des-Gzoula O MO 10 Gb 29
Serouenout O A 12 Gk 33
Sétif O A 11 Gj 27
Settat O MO 10 Gc 29
Sewdayah ⌂ LI 13 Ha 31
Sfax O T 12 Gm 28
al-Sfire O SY 82 Hl 27
Sfissifa O A 11 Gf 29
Sfizel O A 11 Gf 28
Shabasha O SU 20 Hj 38
al-Shabb O E 14 Hg 34
Shabkha O SA 86 Ja 34
al-Shabrum O I 83 Hp 30
Shabwa O Y 86 Jb 38
Shaddadi O SY 82 Hn 27
al-Shafa O SA 86 Hn 35
al-Shafallahiya O SA 85 Jc 32
al-Shafra O SA 86 Hn 35
Shahara O Y 86 Hp 37
Shahat Cyrene ★ LI 13 Hc 29
Shahba O SY 82 Hl 29
Shahda Bohotleh O SO 24 Jb 41
Shahiliya O I 82 Hp 29
Shahrazur O I 83 Ja 28
Shaibara ⌂ SA 84 Hl 33
Sha'ib al-Dat ~ SA 84 Hp 33
Sha'ib Hisb ~ I 83 Hp 30
Shalaanbood O SO 25 Ja 45
Shalï al-Fil O SU 23 Hk 40
Shalim O O 88 Jf 36
al-Sha'm O UAE 88 Jf 32
Shambe O SU 22 Hh 42
al-Shamili O SA 84 Hn 32
al-Shamiya ⌂ I 83 Jb 30
Shamman O SU 21 Hk 39
al-Shamsiya O SA 84 Ja 32
al-Shanam ⌂ SA 88 Jd 35
al-Shaqaya △ K 83 Jb 31
Shaqlawa O I 83 Ja 27
Shaqqat al-Kharita ⌂ SA 86 Jb 37
Shaqra O SA 85 Ja 33
al-Sha'ra' O SA 84 Ja 33
al-Sha'ra' O SA 86 Hn 35
Sharafa O SU 20 Hf 39
Sharaf al-Ba'l O SA 84 Hk 31
al-Sharafiya O SA 86 Hn 35
al-Shara'i' O SA 86 Hn 35
al-Sharaura O SA 86 Jb 37
Sharif Ya'qub O SU 21 Hj 38
Sharjah O UAE 88 Jf 33
Sharkh O O 89 Jh 35
Sharma O SA 84 Hk 31
Sharm al-Sheikh O E 15 Hj 32
Sharmukhiya O I 83 Jb 30
al-Sharqat O I 83 Hp 28
Shary O SA 84 Hp 32
Shatawi O SU 20 Hh 38
al-Shatra O I 83 Jb 30
Shatt al-Arab ~ I 83 Jb 30
Shaubak O J 82 Hk 30
al-Shawal O SU 20 Hj 39
Shawaq O SA 84 Hl 32
Shayhk Sadin O SU 20 Hh 38
Shaykh Gok O SU 22 Hj 40
Shebeli O SO 25 Ja 44
Sheikh O I 83 Hp 28
Sheikh 'Abid O I 83 Jb 29
Sheikh Ahmad O I 83 Ja 29
Sheikh Faris O I 83 Jb 29
al-Sheikh Humaid O SA 84 Hk 31
al-Sheikh 'Utman O Y 86 Ja 39
Sheikh Zayed Canal ~ E 15 Hh 34
Shemkhiya O SU 20 Hj 36
Shendi O SU 21 Hj 37
Shibam O Y 87 Jc 38
Shibin al-Kum O E 14 Hh 30
Shiham O Y 86 Hp 38
al-Shihr O Y 87 Jc 38
Shiikh O SO 24 Ja 41
Shimbiris △ SO 24 Jb 40
al-Shinafiya O I 83 Ja 30
Shinas O O 89 Jg 33
al-Shisar O O 88 Je 36
Shott al-Chergui ~ A 11 Gf 28
Shott al-Djerid ~ T 12 Gl 29
Shott al-Fedjaj ~ T 12 Gl 29
Shott al-Gharsa ~ T 12 Gk 28
Shott al-Hodna ~ A 11 Gj 28
Shott al-Malah ~ A 11 Gj 29
Shott Melrhir ~ A 11 Gk 28

Shott Merouane ~ A 11 Gk 29
Showil ~ SU 20 Hh 38
al-Shu'aiba O SA 84 Hp 32
Shu'aib Gayyada ~ I 82 Hn 29
al-Shu'ba O SA 84 Ja 31
al-Shubaikiya O SA 84 Hp 33
Shubra al-Khaima O E 14 Hh 30
al-Shuhair O Y 87 Jc 38
al-Shuheit ~ SU 21 Hk 39
al-Shuqaiq O SA 86 Hn 37
al-Shuqqan ⌂ SA 85 Jc 35
al-Shura O I 83 Hp 28
al-Shurayk O SU 21 Hj 36
al-Shuwaimiya O O 88 Jf 37
al-Siayyira O SA 84 Hp 32
al-Sib O O 89 Jg 34
Siba O I 83 Jb 30
al-Siba O I 84 Ja 31
Sibdu O SU 22 Hf 40
Sibr O O 88 Jf 37
al-Sibt O SA 86 Ja 37
Sidi 'Abd al-Rahman O E 14 Hg 30
Sidi Aïssa O A 11 Gh 28
Sidi Akhfennir O MO 10 Ga 31
Sidi Ali O A 11 Gj 27
Sidi-Allal-al-Babravi O MO 10 Gc 28
Sidi Amor Bou Hajla O T 12 Gl 28
Sidi as Sayd O LI 12 Gn 29
Sidi Barrani O E 14 He 30
Sidi Bel Abbes O A 11 Gf 28
Sidi-Bennour O MO 10 Gb 29
Sidi-Bettache O MO 10 Gc 29
Sidi Boubekeur O A 11 Gg 28
Sidi Bouzid O T 12 Gl 28
Sidi-Hajjaj O MO 10 Gc 29
Sidi Hamadouche O A 11 Gf 28
Sidi-Harazem O MO 10 Gd 29
Sidi Ifni O MO 10 Ga 31
Sidi-Kacem O MO 10 Gd 28
Sidi Khaled O A 11 Gj 28
Sidi Khalifah O LI 13 Hb 29
Sidi-Mokhtar O MO 10 Gb 30
Sidi Moussa ~ A 11 Gj 32
Sidi-Moussa O MO 10 Gb 29
Sidi-Slimane O MO 10 Gc 28
Sidi-Smail O MO 10 Gb 29
Sidi Youssef O T 12 Gm 28
Sidon O LE 82 Hk 29
al-Sidr O LI 13 Hb 30
al-Sidr O E 15 Hj 31
al-Sidr O SA 84 Hm 34
Sif O Y 87 Jc 38
Sif Fatima O A 12 Gl 30
Sig O A 11 Gf 28
Sigira O Y 87 Jf 39
al-Sikr O I 83 Hp 30
Sila O UAE 88 Jd 33
Silet O A 18 Gj 34
Siliana O T 12 Gl 27
Silil O SO 24 Hp 40
Siltar O LI 13 Ha 30
Sima O C 25 Ja 52
Sina Daqha O SO 25 Jb 43
Sinai ⌂ E 15 Hj 31
Sinawan O LI 12 Gm 30
Singa O SU 21 Hj 39
Sinkat O SU 21 Hl 36
Sinnuris O E 14 Hh 31
Sinujiif O SO 24 Jc 41
Sirab O O 89 Jg 35
Sir Abu Nu'air ⌂ UAE 88 Jf 33
Sir Bani Yas ⌂ UAE 88 Je 33
Sirbin O E 15 Hh 30
Sirsiri O SA 88 Hj 43
Sirte O LI 13 Ha 30
Sirwa O Y 86 Ja 38
Sivé O MA 16 Fp 38
Siwa O E 14 He 31
Siwa Oasis ⌂ E 14 He 31
Siyeteb O SU 21 Hk 36
Skaymat O MO 16 Fn 33
Skhira O T 12 Gm 28
Skhirat O MO 10 Gc 29
Skhour-des-Rahamna O MO 10 Gc 29
Skikda O A 12 Gk 27
Skoura O MO 10 Gc 30
Slim O A 11 Gh 28
Sobat ~ SU 22 Hj 41
Socotra ⌂ Y 87 Jf 39
Sodiri O SU 20 Hg 38
Sohag O E 15 Hh 32
Somalia ◻ SO 25 Hp 45
Songo O SU 22 He 41
Sooyac O SU 25 Hp 45
Souf ⌂ A 12 Gk 29
Sougueur O A 11 Gg 28
Souk Ahras O A 12 Gk 27

Souk-al-Arba-du-Rharb O MO 10 Gc 28
Souk-Jemmaâ-des-Oulad-Abbo O MO 10 Gc 29
Souk-al-Kella O MO 10 Gd 28
Souk-Tleta-des-Akhasass O MO 10 Gb 31
Sour-al-Ghozlane O A 11 Gh 27
Sousse O T 12 Gm 28
Southern National Park ♀ SU 22 Hg 42
Sphinx ★ E 14 Hh 31
St. John's Island ⌂ E 15 Hl 34
Stile O A 11 Gj 28
Strait of Gibraltar ~ 10 Gd 28
Strait of Hormuz ~ 88/89 Jg 32
Suakin O SU 21 Hl 36
Suakin Archipelago ⌂ SU 21 Hm 36
al-Subiya O K 85 Jc 31
Sudan ◻ SU 20 Hg 38
Sudd Dinka ⌂ SU 22 Hh 41
as-Sudeira O SA 86 Hn 35
Sue ~ SU 22 Hg 42
Sue ~ SU 22 Hg 43
Suez O E 15 Hj 30
Suez Canal ★ E 15 Hj 30
Sufetula ★ T 12 Gl 28
Sug al-Jarrahi O Y 86 Hp 38
Suhar O O 89 Jg 33
al-Suhna O Y 86 Hp 38
al-Sukhna O SY 82 Hm 28
al-Suki O SU 21 Hj 39
Sulaib al-Tarfa' ⌂ SA 84 Hn 31
al-Sulaymaniya O I 83 Ja 28
al-Sulaymaniya ⊙ I 83 Ja 28
al-Sulayyil O SA 86 Ja 35
al-Sulb ⌂ SA 85 Jc 32
Suluntah O LI 13 Hc 29
Suluq O LI 13 Hc 30
al-Sumay O SU 22 Hf 41
al-Summan ⌂ SA 85 Ja 32
Suna O Y 87 Jc 38
Sungikai O SU 20 Hg 39
Suni O SU 20 He 39
Suqa-al-Gamal O SU 20 Hf 39
Suq al-Shuyuh O I 83 Jb 30
Suq Suwaiq O SA 84 Hm 33
Sur O LE 82 Hk 29
Sur O O 89 Jh 34
al-Surra O Y 86 Jb 39
Surt Sirte O LI 13 Ha 30
Susa O LI 13 Hc 29
al-Suwaida' O SY 82 Hl 29
al-Suwaidira O SA 84 Hn 33
Suwaihan O UAE 88 Jf 33
Suwailih O J 82 Hk 29
al-Suwair O SA 84 Hn 30
al-Suwaira O I 83 Ja 29
al-Suwairiqiya O SA 84 Hn 34
al-Suwar O SY 82 Hn 28
Syria ◻ SY 82 Hl 28
Syrian Desert ⌂ SY 82 Hm 29

T

Taba O E 15 Hk 31
Taba O SA 84 Hp 32
Tabala O SA 86 Hp 35
Tabaq O SU 21 Hj 35
Tabarjal O SA 84 Hm 30
Tabarka O T 12 Gl 27
Tabelbala O A 10 Ge 31
Taberdga O A 12 Gk 28
Tablat O A 11 Gh 27
Tabuk O SA 84 Hl 31
Tabur O SU 22 Hd 40
Tachiumet O LI 12 Gm 32
Taddert O MO 10 Gc 30
Tademait Plateau ⌂ A 11 Gg 31
Tadjem O A 11 Gh 29
Tadjentourt △ A 12 Gl 32
Tadjmout O A 11 Gh 33
Tadjoura O D 24 Hp 40
Tadjrouna O A 11 Gg 29
Tadmur Palmyra O SY 82 Hm 28
Tadrart Akakus ★ LI 12 Gm 33
al-Tafila O J 82 Hk 30
Tafilalt ⌂ MO 10 Gd 30
Tafraoute O MO 10 Gb 31
Tagab O SU 20 Hh 36
Tagânt ⌂ MA 16 Fp 37
Taghit O A 11 Ge 30
Tagoûrâret O MA 17 Gc 37
Tahalra ⌂ A 18 Gj 34
Tahar-Souk O MO 10 Gd 28

Tahat △ A 18 Gj 34
Tahifet O A 18 Gk 34
Tahrami O LI 12 Gp 33
Tahta O E 15 Hh 32
Taibet O A 12 Gk 29
al-Ta'if O SA 86 Hn 35
Taima O SA 84 Hm 32
Ta'izz O Y 86 Hp 39
Tajura' O LI 12 Gn 29
Taknis O LI 13 Hc 29
Takrit O I 83 Hp 28
Talat al-Timiat O SA 84 Hp 31
Talawdi O SU 22 Hh 40
Taldalt O MO 10 Gb 31
Taleex O SO 24 Jc 41
Talguharai O SU 21 Hk 36
Taliouine O MO 10 Gc 30
Tali Post O SU 22 Hh 43
al-Tall O SY 82 Hl 29
Tall 'Afar O I 82 Hp 27
Tall Birak O SY 82 Hn 27
Tall Huqna O I 82 Hp 27
Tallkalah O SY 82 Hl 28
Tall Kushik O SY 82 Hn 27
Tall al-Lakhm O I 83 Jb 30
Tall al-Manuk △ SY 82 Hm 29
Talmest O MO 10 Gb 30
Talsinnt O MO 10 Gc 29
al-Tamad O E 15 Hk 31
al-Tamad O SA 84 Hm 33
Tamadanet O A 12 Gl 31
Tamanhint O LI 12 Gp 32
Tamanrasset O A 18 Gj 34
Tamarit O O 88 Jf 37
Tamaso O SU 20 Hj 39
Tamassoumit O MA 16 Fp 36
Tamegroute O MO 10 Gd 30
Tamelelt O MO 10 Gc 30
Tamelhat O A 12 Gk 29
Tamezret O T 12 Gl 29
al-Tamimi O LI 19 Hd 29
al-Ta'min ⊙ I 83 Ja 28
Tamnun O Y 87 Jd 38
Tamri O MO 10 Ga 30
Tamud O Y 87 Jc 37
Tandalti O SU 20 Hh 39
Tan Emellel O A 12 Gl 32
Tanezrouft ⌂ A 17 Gf 34
Tanezrouft-n-Ahenet ⌂ A 17 Gg 34
al-Tanf O SY 82 Hm 29
Tangier O MO 10 Gc 28
Tanta O E 14 Hh 30
Tan-Tan O MO 10 Ga 31
Tanumah O SA 86 Hp 36
Taounate O MO 10 Gd 28
Taourirt O MO 11 Ge 28
Taouz O MO 10 Gd 30
Taqa O O 88 Jf 37
Taqttaq O I 83 Ja 28
al-Tarafiya O SA 84 Ja 32
Taraghin O LI 12 Gp 33
Tarat O A 12 Gl 33
al-Tarf O A 12 Gl 27
Tarfaya O MO 10 Fp 32
Targuist O MO 10 Gd 28
Tarhuna O LI 12 Gn 29
Tarib O SA 86 Hp 36
Tarif O UAE 88 Je 33
Tarim O Y 87 Jc 37
Tarmida O SA 85 Ja 33
Taroudant O MO 10 Gb 30
Tartus O SY 82 Hk 28
Tarwaniya O UAE 88 Jf 34
Tassili du Hoggar ⌂ A 18 Gj 35
Tassili n'Ajjer ⌂ A 12 Gk 33
Tata O MO 10 Gc 31
Tataouine O T 12 Gm 29
Tatlit O SA 86 Hp 36
Taufikia O SU 22 Hh 41
Tauliya O I 82 Hp 29
al-Tawil ⌂ SA 84 Hm 31
Tawilah O SU 20 He 39
Tawuq O I 83 Ja 28
Tawuq Cay ~ I 83 Ja 28
Tawurgha' O LI 12 Gp 29
Tayeeglow O SO 25 Ja 43
Taykan O LI 13 Hb 30
Tayyana O SY 82 Hn 28
al-Tayyara O SU 20 Hh 39
Taza O MO 10 Gd 28
Tazenakht O MO 10 Gc 30
Tazirbu O LI 13 Hc 33
Tazrouk O A 18 Gk 34
Tazzarine O MO 10 Gd 30
Tébessa O A 12 Gk 28
Tébourba O T 12 Gl 27
Téboursouk O T 12 Gl 27
Ted O SO 25 Hp 43

Teffedest ⌂ A 11 Gj 33
Teiti O SU 20 Hh 36
Telagh O A 11 Gf 28
Telemzane O A 11 Gj 29
Telerghma O A 11 Gk 27
Tell Atlas ⌂ A 11 Gf 28
Tell Tamr O SY 82 Hn 27
Temacine O A 11 Gj 29
Temple Amara ★ SU 20 Hh 35
Temple of Abydos ★ E 15 Hh 32
Temple of Horus ★ E 15 Hj 33
Temple of Kawa ★ SU 20 Hh 36
Temples of Musawwarat ★ SU 21 Hj 37
Temples of Naga ★ SU 21 Hj 37
Tendrara O MO 11 Gf 29
Ténès O A 11 Gg 27
Te-n-Guembo O MA 16 Gb 37
Tenoûmer △ MA 16 Ga 34
Terakeka O SU 22 Hh 43
Testour O T 12 Gl 27
Tetouan O MO 10 Gd 28
Tfaritiy O MO 10 Ga 32
Thadiq O SA 85 Ja 33
Thala O T 12 Gl 28
Thamad Bu Hashisha O LI 13 Hb 32
Thebes ★ E 15 Hj 33
The Brothers ⌂ Y 87 Je 39
Thenia O A 11 Gh 27
Theniet al-Had O A 11 Gh 28
Thoufi O A 12 Gk 28
Tiaret O A 11 Gg 28
Tiaret O T 12 Gm 30
Tiberghamine O A 11 Gg 31
Tibni O SY 82 Hm 28
Tichît O MA 16 Gb 36
Tichla O MO 16 Fn 35
al-Tichlilt O MA 16 Fp 37
Tiddis ★ A 12 Gk 27
Tidikelt Plateau ⌂ A 11 Gg 32
Tidjikja O MA 16 Ga 36
Tieta-de-Sidi-Bouguedra O MO 10 Gb 29
Tiflét O MO 10 Gc 29
Tighenif O A 11 Gg 28
Tigris ~ I 83 Jb 29
Tiguent O MA 16 Fn 37
Tigzirt O A 11 Gj 27
Tihama ⌂ SA 86 Hn 36
Tihama ⌂ Y 86 Hp 38
Tiji O LI 12 Gm 29
Tilemsen O MO 10 Ga 31
Tilrhemt O A 11 Gh 29
Tima O E 15 Hh 32
Timahdite O MO 10 Gd 29
Timbedgha O MA 16 Gb 37
Timelluline O A 12 Gl 31
Timgad ★ A 12 Gk 28
Timiaouine O A 17 Gg 35
Timimoun O A 11 Gf 31
al-Ti-m-Missaou O A 18 Gh 34
Timoudi O A 11 Gf 31
Tin Alkoum O A 12 Gl 33
Ti-n-Bessais O MA 16 Gb 34
Tindalo O SU 22 Hh 43
Tindouf O A 10 Gb 32
Tinerhir O MO 10 Gd 30
Tinfouchy O A 10 Gb 31
Tin Fouye O A 12 Gk 31
Tingal △ SU 20 Hh 40
Tingya O SU 22 Hj 40
Tini O SU 20 Hd 38
Tin Merzouga ⌂ A 12 Gm 34
Tin Rerhoch O A 18 Gh 35
Tinrhert Plateau ⌂ A 11 Gj 32
Tin Tadjant ~ A 17 Gg 35
Tintâne O MA 16 Ga 37
Tiouilît O MA 16 Fm 36
Tipaza O A 11 Gh 27
Tiran ⌂ E 15 Hk 32
Tirhatimine O A 11 Gh 33
Tisgui-Remz O MO 10 Gb 33
Tissemsilt O A 11 Gg 28
Tit O A 11 Gg 32
Tit O A 18 Gj 34
al-Tiwal O Y 86 Hp 37
Tizi-n-Tairhemt △ MO 10 Gd 29
Tizi-n-Tarhatine △ MO 10 Gc 30
Tizi Ouzou O A 11 Gj 27
Tiznit O MO 10 Gb 31
Tlemcen O A 11 Gf 28
al-Tleta-de-Oued-Laou O MO 10 Gd 28
Tmassa O LI 12 Gp 32
al-Tnine O MO 10 Gb 30
Togba O MA 16 Ga 37
Togga Ceel Madoobe ~ SO 24 Jc 41
Togga Dhud ~ SO 24 Jc 40
Togga Dhuudo ~ SO 24 Jd 41

Togga Giael ∿ **SO** 24 Jd 40
Togga Gono ∿ **SO** 24 Jd 41
Togga Jidali ∿ **SO** 24 Jb 40
Togga Nugaal ∿ **SO** 24 Jc 41
Togga Silil ∿ **SO** 24 Hp 40
Togga Tog Dheet ∿ **SO** 24 Ja 41
Togga Weyne ∿ **SO** 24 Jd 40
Tohat ⌂ **A** 11 Gf 32
Tokar O **SU** 21 Hl 36
Tolga O **A** 11 Gj 28
Tomat O **SU** 20 Hf 40
Tomat O **SU** 21 Hk 38
Tong O **SU** 22 Hg 42
Tong ∿ **SU** 22 Hg 42
Tonga O **SU** 22 Hh 41
Torit O **SU** 22 Hj 43
Toshka Lakes ∿ **E** 14 Hh 34
Tosi O **SU** 22 Hh 40
Totias O **SO** 25 Ja 44
Touâjîl O **MA** 16 Fp 34
Touggourt O **A** 11 Gk 29
Toujl O **MA** 16 Ga 38
Tourassine O **MA** 16 Ga 33
Tourîne O **MA** 16 Ga 34
Touroug O **MO** 10 Gd 30
Towot O **SU** 23 Hk 42
Tozeur O **T** 12 Gl 29
Trârza ⌂ **MA** 16 Fn 37
Trinkitat O **SU** 21 Hl 36
Tripoli ▣ **LI** 12 Gn 30
Tripoli O **LE** 82 Hk 28
Tripolitania ⌂ **LI** 12 Gm 30
Tsawah O **LI** 12 Gn 33
Tubas O **P** 82 Hk 29
Tubruq O **LI** 13 He 29
Tukra O **LI** 13 Hc 29
al-Tullab O **LI** 19 Hd 33
Tullus O **SU** 22 He 40
Tulul al-Ashaqif ∿ **J** 82 Hl 29
Tumair O **SA** 85 Ja 33
Tunaida O **E** 14 Hg 33
Tungaru O **SU** 22 Hh 40
Tunis ▣ **T** 12 Gm 27
Tunisia ▢ **T** 12 Gl 29
al-Tur O **E** 15 Hj 31
Turaba O **SA** 84 Hp 31
Turaba O **SA** 86 Hn 35
Turaif O **SA** 84 Hm 30
al-Turba O **Y** 86 Hp 39
al-Turba O **Y** 86 Ja 39
Turda O **SU** 22 Hg 40
Tursaq O **I** 83 Ja 29
Tuwal O **SA** 84 Hm 34
al-Tuwaysha O **SU** 20 Hf 39
Tuz Khurmatu O **I** 83 Ja 28
Tyre ★ **LE** 82 Hk 29

U

Ubaila O **I** 82 Hm 29
al-'Ubaila O **SA** 88 Jd 35
al-'Udaib O **SA** 84 Hl 32
al-Udaid O **SA** 88 Jd 33
Udayd O **SU** 21 Hk 38
al-Udayya O **SU** 20 Hg 39
Ufeyn O **SO** 24 Jc 40
al-'Ula O **SA** 84 Hl 32
Ulaim al-Zama △ **SA** 84 Hn 31
Ulu O **SU** 23 Hj 40
Umbelasha ∿ **SU** 22 Hd 41
al-'Umda O **SU** 20 Hg 40
Umm al-Aranib O **LI** 12 Gp 32
Umm Ashar al-Sharqiya O **SA** 85 Ja 32
Umm al-Ashtan O **UAE** 88 Je 34
Umm Bab O **Q** 85 Jd 33
Umm Badr O **SU** 20 Hg 38
Umm Barbit O **SU** 22 Hj 40
Umm Bel O **SU** 20 Hg 39
Umm al-Birak O **SA** 84 Hm 34
Umm Buru O **SU** 20 Hd 38
Umm Dafag O **SU** 22 Hd 40
Umm Dam O **SU** 20 Hh 39
Umm Defeis O **SU** 20 Hg 39
Umm Dubban O **SU** 20 Hg 38
Umm Haraz O **SU** 20 Hg 38
Umm Hawsh O **SU** 20 Hf 39
Umm Hitan O **SU** 20 Hh 40
Umm Inderaba ∿ **SU** 22 Hd 41
Umm al-Jamajim O **SA** 85 Ja 32
Umm Keiredim O **SU** 20 Hg 39
Umm Lajj O **SA** 84 Hl 33
Umm Marahik O **SU** 20 He 39

Umm Mirdi O **SU** 21 Hj 36
Umm al-Nar O **UAE** 88 Jf 33
Umm al-Qaiwain O **UAE** 88 Jf 33
Umm Qasr O **I** 83 Jb 30
Umm Qozein O **SU** 20 Hf 38
Umm Qulaita O **Y** 86 Jb 39
Umm Qurein O **SU** 20 Hg 37
Umm Rumetia O **SU** 20 Hh 37
Umm Ruwaba O **SU** 20 Hh 39
Umm Sa'ad O **LI** 13 He 30
Umm Sagung O **SU** 22 Hg 41
Umm Sa'id O **Q** 85 Jd 33
Umm al-Samim ∿ **O** 88 Jf 35
Umm Sayyala O **SU** 20 Hh 38
Umm Shugeira O **SU** 20 Hg 39
Umran O **SA** 85 Jc 33
'Unaiza Unayzah O **SA** 84 Ja 32
Unayzah O **SA** 84 Ja 32
United Arab Emirates ▢ **UAE** 88 Je 34
al-'Uqair O **SA** 85 Jc 33
al-'Uqayla O **LI** 13 Hb 30
al-'Uqda O **SU** 20 Hg 38
'Uqlat Ibn Jabrain O **SA** 84 Hn 32
'Uqlat al-Suqur O **SA** 84 Hp 33
Ur ★ **I** 83 Jb 30
al-'Uraiq ∿ **SA** 84 Hm 31
Urtayyan O **SA** 84 Hn 31
'Uruq Hibaka O **SA** 88 Jd 35
al-'Uruq al-Mu'tarida ∿ **SA** 88 Je 36
'Uruq Subai O **SA** 84 Hp 34
'Uruq Subai ⌂ **SA** 86 Hp 35
'Usaila O **SA** 85 Ja 33
'Usfan O **SA** 86 Hm 35
'Ushaira O **SA** 85 Ja 33
al-'Ushara O **SU** 20 Hj 38
Utaitiya O **SA** 85 Ja 33
al-'Utayshan O **SU** 21 Hk 37
'Utayyiq O **SA** 85 Jc 32
al-'Uwaiqila O **SA** 84 Hn 30
al-'Uwaynat O **LI** 12 Gm 33
Uweinat O **LI** 14 He 35
al-'Uyaina O **SA** 85 Jb 33
'Uyun O **SA** 85 Jc 33
'Uyun al-Jiwa' O **SA** 84 Hp 32
al-'Uzaim O **SA** 84 Hp 32
al-'Uzair O **I** 83 Jb 30

V

Vallée du Dadès ⌂ **MO** 10 Gc 30
Vallée du Drâa ⌂ **MO** 10 Gc 30
Valley of the Kings ★ **E** 15 Hj 33
Volubilis ★ **MO** 10 Gd 28

W

Waajid O **SO** 25 Hp 44
Waat O **SU** 22 Hj 41
Wada'a O **SU** 20 He 39
Wad al-Abbas O **SU** 21 Hj 39
Wad an-Nail O **SU** 21 Hj 39
Wad Banda O **SU** 20 Hg 39
Wad Ban Naqa O **SU** 21 Hj 37
Waddan O **LI** 12 Ha 31
Wad-Haddad O **SU** 21 Hj 39
Wad Hamid O **SU** 21 Hj 39
Wad Hassib O **SU** 20 Hf 40
Wadi al-'Allaqi ∿ **E** 15 Hj 34
Wadi Abu Dam ∿ **SU** 20 Hj 36
Wadi Abu Khinzir ∿ **SU** 20 Hh 38
Wadi Adana ∿ **Y** 86 Ja 38
Wadi al-Awra ∿ **LI** 13 Ha 30
Wadi 'Amd ∿ **Y** 86 Jb 38
Wadi 'Amiq ∿ **I** 82 Hn 29
Wadi 'Amur ∿ **SU** 21 Hk 36
Wadi Andam ∿ **O** 89 Jh 34
Wadi an Nashu' ∿ **LI** 12 Gn 32
Wadi al-'Aqiq ∿ **SA** 84 Hn 33
Wadi 'Araba ∿ **E** 15 Hj 31
Wadi al-'Araba ∿ **J** 82 Hk 30
Wadi 'Ar'ar ∿ **SA** 84 Hn 30
Wadi al-'Arish ∿ **E** 15 Hj 30
Wadi al-'Arish ∿ **E** 15 Hj 31
Wadi Asmara ∿ **SA** 84 Hn 32

Wadi Aswad ∿ **O** 88 Jg 34
Wadi Atina ∿ **O** 88 Je 37
Wadi al-Awra ∿ **LI** 13 Ha 31
Wadi al-Ayn ∿ **O** 89 Jg 34
Wadi Azum ∿ **SU** 19 Hd 39
Wadi az Zimam ∿ **LI** 12 Gp 31
Wadi Ba'ir ∿ **J** 82 Hl 30
Wadi Baish ∿ **SA** 86 Hp 37
Wadi Bana ∿ **Y** 86 Ja 39
Wadi Bani Hashbal ∿ **SA** 86 Hp 36
Wadi Barjuj ∿ **LI** 12 Gn 33
Wadi Barkol ∿ **SU** 20 Hh 37
Wadi-Batha ∿ **O** 89 Jh 34
Wadi al-Batin ∿ **SA** 85 Ja 31
Wadi Bayy al-Kabir ∿ **LI** 12 Gp 30
Wadi Bisha ∿ **SA** 86 Hp 35
Wadi-Dahsa ∿ **E** 14 Hh 32
Wadi Dama ∿ **SA** 84 Hk 32
Wadi Daur'an ∿ **Y** 86 Je 38
Wadi Derbeikan ∿ **SU** 21 Hk 36
Wadi Faihan ∿ **SA** 84 Hp 31
Wadi Fajr ∿ **SA** 84 Hl 31
Wadi-Farigh ∿ **LI** 13 Hb 30
Wadi-Fat ∿ **LI** 12 Gp 31
Wadi Faysal ∿ **LI** 12 Gn 30
Wadi Fegoh ∿ **E** 15 Hk 34
Wadi-Gadaf ∿ **J** 82 Hl 30
Wadi al-Gadaf ∿ **I** 82 Hn 29
Wadi Gadun ∿ **O** 88 Je 37
Wadi Ghadun ∿ **O** 89 Jg 36
Wadi al-Ghalla ∿ **SU** 20 Hg 40
Wadi al-Gina ∿ **SA** 84 Hn 30
Wadi Habauna ∿ **SA** 86 Ja 37
Wadi Hadramaut ∿ **Y** 87 Jd 38
Wadi al-Hail ∿ **SY** 82 Hm 28
Wadi Halfa O **SU** 20 Hh 35
Wadi Halfain ∿ **O** 89 Jg 34
Wadi al-Hamd ∿ **SA** 84 Hl 33
Wadi al-Hamim ∿ **LI** 19 Hd 30
Wadi Hamir ∿ **I** 84 Hn 30
Wadi Hamir ∿ **Y** 87 Jc 38
Wadi al-Hanakiya ∿ **SA** 84 Hn 33
Wadi al-Hasa ∿ **J** 82 Hl 30
Wadi al-Hauran ∿ **I** 82 Hm 29
Wadi al-Hauran ∿ **I** 82 Hm 29
Wadi al-Hawad ∿ **SU** 21 Hj 37
Wadi Hudain ∿ **E** 15 Hk 34
Wadi Huwar ∿ **SU** 20 He 37
Wadi Huwayt ∿ **SU** 21 Hj 35
Wadi Ibib ∿ **E** 15 Hk 34
Wadi Ibra ∿ **SU** 22 He 40
Wadi Irawan ∿ **LI** 12 Gm 32
Wadi Jabgaba ∿ **E** 15 Hj 34
Wadi al-Jarir ∿ **SA** 84 Hp 33
Wadi al-Jauf ∿ **Y** 86 Ja 37
Wadi al-Jiz' ∿ **Y** 87 Jd 37
Wadi al-Jizl ∿ **SA** 84 Hl 32
Wadi Kbir ∿ **LI** 12 Gp 30
Wadi Khudra ∿ **Y** 87 Jc 38
Wadi al-Khurr ∿ **I** 83 Hp 30
Wadi Kirbikan ∿ **SU** 20 Hj 36
Wadi al-Ku ∿ **SU** 20 He 39
Wadi Kunayr ∿ **LI** 12 Gp 32
Wadi Langeb ∿ **SU** 21 Hl 36
Wadi Langeb ∿ **SU** 21 Hl 37
Wadi Majrur ∿ **SU** 20 Hf 37
Wadi Makhya ∿ **Y** 87 Jc 38
Wadi Mauba ∿ **Y** 87 Jd 37
Wadi Maur ∿ **Y** 86 Hp 38
Wadi Maymun ∿ **LI** 12 Gm 30
Wadi al-Milk ∿ **SU** 20 Hg 37
Wadi al-Miya ∿ **SY** 82 Hm 28
Wadi Mugal ∿ **SU** 21 Hk 36
Wadi al-Mugib ∿ **J** 82 Hk 30
Wadi Muheit ∿ **SU** 20 Hj 37
Wadi Muqaddam ∿ **SU** 20 Hh 37
Wadi Muqshin ∿ **O** 88 Jf 36
Wadi Musa ∿ **J** 82 Hk 30
Wadi Nabi ∿ **SU** 21 Hj 35
Wadi Najran ∿ **SA** 86 Ja 37
Wadi Natash ∿ **E** 15 Hj 33
Wadi al-Natrun ∿ **E** 14 Hg 30
Wadi Oko ∿ **SU** 21 Hk 35
Wadi Qarqaraut ∿ **Y** 87 Jd 38
Wadi Qarzah ∿ **LI** 12 Gm 30
Wadi Qina ∿ **E** 15 Hj 32
Wadi Qitbit ∿ **O** 88 Jf 36
Wadi al-Radd ∿ **SY** 82 Hn 27
Wadi Raima ∿ **Y** 86 Hp 38
Wadi al-Ratqa ∿ **I** 82 Hn 29
Wadi Reseida ∿ **SU** 21 Hj 35
Wadi Rikat ∿ **O** 88 Jg 36

Wadi al-Rima ∿ **SA** 84 Hn 33
Wadi al-Risha' ∿ **SA** 84 Hp 33
Wadi Sahuq ∿ **SA** 84 Hn 33
Wadi al-Sawab ∿ **SY** 82 Hn 28
Wadi Sawfajjin ∿ **LI** 12 Gp 30
Wadi Seidna O **SU** 20 Hj 38
Wadi al-Sha'ba ∿ **SA** 84 Hn 32
Wadi al-Shati ∿ **LI** 12 Gn 32
Wadi Shihan ∿ **O** 88 Je 37
Wadi al-Shu'ba ∿ **LI** 19 Hd 30
Wadi Shurshut ∿ **LI** 12 Gm 30
Wadi al-Sirhan ∿ **SA** 84 Hl 30
Wadi Surdud ∿ **Y** 86 Hp 38
Wadi Tamat ∿ **LI** 13 Ha 30
Wadi Tanezzruft ∿ **LI** 12 Gm 33
Wadi Targhalat ∿ **LI** 12 Gp 29
Wadi al-Tartar ∿ **I** 83 Hp 28
Wadi Tatit ∿ **SA** 86 Hp 35
Wadi al-Tawil ∿ **I** 82 Hn 29
Wadi Tayin ∿ **O** 89 Jh 34
Wadi Tayyal ∿ **SA** 84 Hm 31
Wadi Tinis ∿ **LI** 12 Gm 33
Wadi al-Tubal ∿ **I** 82 Hp 29
Wadi Tubja ∿ **SA** 84 Hn 33
Wadi-Ua'ili ★ **SA** 84 Hm 30
Wadi al-Ubayy ∿ **I** 83 Hp 29
Wadi al-'Ubayyid ∿ **I** 84 Hn 30
Wadi al-Ulya ∿ **O** 89 Jg 34
Wadi Yadat ∿ **SU** 21 Hk 37
Wadi Zabid ∿ **Y** 86 Hp 38
Wadi al-Zaidun ∿ **E** 15 Hj 33
Wadi Zamzam ∿ **LI** 12 Gp 30
Wadi Zazamt ∿ **LI** 12 Gp 30
Wadi al-Zuhur ∿ **O** 88 Jf 37
Wad Medani O **SU** 21 Hj 38
al-Wafra O **K** 85 Jb 31
al-Waha O **LI** 13 Hb 31
al-Wajh O **SA** 84 Hl 32
Wal Athiang O **SU** 22 Hg 42
Wamis O **LI** 12 Gm 30
Wanleweeyn O **SO** 25 Ja 44
Warba ⚓ **K** 83 Jb 32
War Dhugulle O **SO** 25 Ja 44
War Galoh O **SO** 24 Jb 42
Warshiikh O **SO** 25 Ja 44
al-Wasiqa O **SA** 86 Hn 35
Wasit ⊙ **I** 83 Ja 29
al-Wasita O **E** 14 Hh 31
al-Wata ⌂ **O** 89 Jg 35
Wau ∿ **SU** 22 Hf 42
Wau O **SU** 22 Hg 42
Waw al-Kabir O **LI** 13 Ha 33
Waw al-Namus O **LI** 13 Ha 33
Wazirr O **T** 12 Gm 30
Webi Jubba ∿ **SO** 25 Hp 43
Wed Weil O **SU** 22 Hf 41
West Bank ⊙ **P** 82 Hk 29
Western Desert ⌂ **E** 14 Hf 31
Western Sahara ⊙ **MO** 16 Fp 33
White Nile ∿ **SU** 20 Hj 38
White Nile ∿ **SU** 22 Hh 41
al-Widyan ⌂ **I** 84 Hn 30
al-Wigh O **LI** 12 Gp 33
Wisil O **SO** 25 Jc 43
Wisil Dabaro O **SO** 24 Jc 42
al-Wittya O **LI** 12 Gm 29
Wuday'ah O **SA** 86 Jb 37
Wunagak O **SU** 22 Hj 41
Wun Rog O **SU** 22 Hg 41
Wun Shwai O **SU** 22 Hg 41

X

Xaafuun O **SO** 24 Jd 40
Xalin O **SO** 24 Jc 41
Xanda O **SO** 24 Jd 40
Xarardheere O **SO** 25 Jb 43
Xiis O **SO** 24 Jb 40
Xingalool O **SO** 24 Jc 41
Xingod O **SO** 24 Jc 42
Xuddun O **SO** 24 Jb 41
Xuddur O **SO** 25 Hp 43

Y

Yaaq Braaway O **SO** 25 Hp 45
Yadma O **SA** 86 Ja 36
Yafran O **LI** 12 Gn 29
Yambio O **SU** 22 Hg 43
Yamin O **I** 83 Jb 30

Yanbu' al-Bahr O **SA** 84 Hl 33
Yanbu' al-Nakhl O **SA** 84 Hm 33
Yanbu' al-Sinaiyah O **SA** 84 Hl 34
Yanqul O **O** 89 Jg 34
Yarim O **Y** 86 Ja 38
al-Yasat ⚓ **UAE** 88 Je 33
Yei O **SU** 22 Hh 43
Yei ∿ **SU** 22 Hh 43
Yemen ▢ **Y** 86 Ja 38
Yirol O **SU** 22 Hh 42
Yity O **Y** 89 Jh 34
Yoboki O **D** 24 Hp 40
Yoonzoy O **SO** 25 Hp 46
Youssoufia O **MO** 10 Gb 29

Z

Zabid O **Y** 86 Hp 38
Zabut O **Y** 87 Je 38
Zaër Zaïane ⌂ **MO** 10 Gc 29
Zafarana O **E** 15 Hj 31
al-Zafra ⌂ **UAE** 88 Jf 34
Zag O **MO** 10 Gb 31
Zaghouan O **T** 12 Gm 27
Zagora O **MO** 10 Gd 30
Zahla O **LE** 82 Hk 29
al-Zahran O **SA** 85 Jc 32
Zahran O **SA** 86 Hp 37
Zahrat al-Batn ⌂ **I** 83 Hp 30
Zahrez Chergui ∿ **A** 11 Gh 28
Zahrez Gharbi ∿ **A** 11 Gh 28
al-Zaidiya O **Y** 86 Hp 38
Zaio O **MO** 11 Ge 28
Zakhu O **I** 82 Hp 27
al-Zalaf O **SY** 82 Hl 29
Zalingei O **SU** 20 Hd 39
Zaltan O **LI** 13 Hb 31
Zamak O **Y** 86 Jb 37
Zaouatanlaz O **A** 12 Gl 33
Zaouia Sidi Moussa O **A** 12 Gk 31
al-Zaqaziq O **E** 15 Hh 30
Zar O **MA** 16 Fn 37
Zarghat O **SA** 84 Hn 32
Zarqa O **SU** 20 Hd 39
Zarqa ∿ **J** 82 Hk 29
Zarqa O **J** 82 Hl 30
Zarzaitine O **A** 12 Gl 31
Zarzis O **T** 12 Gm 29
Zawilah O **LI** 12 Gp 32
al-Zawiyah O **LI** 12 Gn 29
Zawiyat Masus O **LI** 13 Hc 30
Zawiyat al-Mukhayla O **LI** 19 Hd 29
Zelfana O **A** 11 Gj 29
Zembra ⚓ **T** 12 Gm 27
Zemmora O **A** 11 Gg 29
Zemmour ⌂ **MO** 16 Fp 33
Zeralda O **A** 11 Gh 27
Zeribet al-Oued O **A** 12 Gk 28
Ziban ⌂ **A** 11 Gj 28
Zifta O **E** 14 Hh 30
Zighan O **LI** 13 Hc 33
Zighout Youcef O **A** 12 Gk 28
al-Zilfi O **SA** 85 Ja 32
Zillah O **LI** 13 Ha 31
Zinjibar O **Y** 86 Ja 39
Zitouna O **A** 12 Gk 27
Zlitan O **LI** 12 Gn 29
Z'Malet al-Emir O **A** 11 Gh 28
Zouérat O **MA** 16 Fp 34
Zoûgh O **MA** 17 Gc 37
Zouireg O **A** 11 Gg 29
Zubair ⚓ **Y** 86 Hp 38
al-Zuhra O **Y** 86 Hp 38
Zuluma O **Y** 87 Jc 38
al-Zuma O **SU** 20 Hh 36
Zuwara O **LI** 12 Gn 29